Critical Perspectives on Canadian Theatre in English

General Editor Ric Knowles

2005

volume one   *Aboriginal Drama and Theatre*, ed. Rob Appleford
978-0-88754-792-8

volume two   *African-Canadian Theatre*, ed. Maureen Moynagh
978-0-88754-794-2

volume three   *Judith Thompson*, ed. Ric Knowles
978-0-88754-796-6

2006

volume four   *Feminist Theatre and Performance*, ed. Susan Bennett
978-0-88754-798-0

volume five   *George F. Walker*, ed. Harry Lane
978-0-88754-800-0

volume six   *Theatre in British Columbia*, ed. Ginny Ratsoy
978-0-88754-802-4

2007

volume seven   *Queer Theatre*, ed. Rosalind Kerr
978-0-88754-804-8

volume eight   *Environmental and Site-Specific Theatre*, ed. Andrew Houston
978-0-88754-806-2

volume nine   *Space and the Geographies of Theatre*, ed. Michael McKinnie
978-0-88754-808-6

PLAYWRIGHTS CANADA PRESS

416-703-0013 • orders@playwrightscanada.com • www.playwrightscanada.com

Queer
Theatre
in Canada

Critical Perspectives on Canadian Theatre in English

volume seven

Critical Perspectives on Canadian Theatre in English
volume seven

Queer Theatre
in Canada

Edited by Rosalind Kerr

Playwrights Canada Press
Toronto • Canada

Playwrights Canada Press
215 Spadina Avenue, Suite 230, Toronto, Ontario CANADA M5T 2C7
416-703-0013   fax 416-408-3402
orders@playwrightscanada.com • www.playwrightscanada.com

Financial support provided by the taxpayers of Canada and Ontario through the Canada
Council for the Arts and the Department of Canadian Heritage through the Book Publishing
Industry Development Programme, and the Ontario Arts Council.

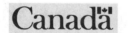 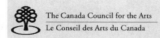

Cover image: Jin-me Yoon, between departure and arrival, 1996/1997. Partial installation
view, Art Gallery of Ontario. Video projection, video montage on monitor, photographic
mylar scroll, clocks with 3-D lettering, audio. Dimensions variable. Courtesy of the artist
and Catriona Jeffries Gallery, Vancouver.
Production Editor/Cover Design: JLArt

Library and Archives Canada Cataloguing in Publication

Queer theatre in Canada / edited by Rosalind Kerr.

(Critical perspectives on Canadian theatre in English ; v. 7)
Includes bibliographical references.
ISBN 978-0-88754-804-8

    1. Gay theater--Canada. 2. Homosexuality in the theater--Canada.
3. Canadian drama (English)--20th century--History and criticism.
I. Kerr, Rosalind, 1941- II. Series.

PS8169.H6Q84 2007   C812'.5409353   C2007-902789-X

First edition: May 2007
Printed and bound by Hignell Printing at Winnipeg, Canada.

I dedicate this volume

to all my queer students, colleagues, artists and friends

who have enriched my life

in the academy and the theatre over the years.

Table of Contents

General Editor's Preface

Critical Perspectives on Canadian Theatre in English sets out to make the best critical and scholarly work in the field readily available to teachers, students, and scholars of Canadian drama and theatre. In volumes organized by playwright, region, genre, theme, and cultural community, the series publishes the work of scholars and critics who have, since the so-called renaissance of Canadian theatre in the late 1960s and early 1970s, traced the coming-into-prominence of a vibrant theatrical community in English Canada.

Each volume in the series is edited and introduced by an expert in the field who has selected a representative sampling of the most important critical work on her or his subject since circa 1970, ordered chronologically according to the original dates of publication. Where appropriate, the volume editors have also commissioned new essays on their subjects. Each volume also provides a list of suggested further readings, and an introduction by the volume's editor.

It is my hope that this series, working together with complementary anthologies of plays published by Playwrights Canada Press, Talonbooks, and other Canadian drama publishers, will facilitate the teaching of Canadian drama and theatre in schools, colleges, and universities across the country for years to come. It is for this reason that the titles so far selected for the series—*Aboriginal Drama and Theatre, African-Canadian Theatre, Judith Thompson, Feminist Theatre and Performance, George F. Walker, Theatre in British Columbia, Queer Theatre, Environmental and Site Specific Theatre,* and *Space and the Geographies of Theatre*—are designed to work as companion volumes to a range of Canadian drama anthologies recently published or forthcoming from the country's major drama publishers that complement them: *Staging Coyote's Dream: An Anthology of First Nations Drama in English* (Playwrights Canada, 2003); the two volumes of *Testifyin': Contemporary African Canadian Drama* (Playwrights Canada, 2000, 2003); *Judith Thompson: Late 20th Century Plays* (Playwrights Canada, 2002); the various collections of plays by George F. Walker published by Talonbooks; *Playing the Pacific Province: An Anthology of British Columbia Plays, 1967-2000* (Playwrights Canada, 2001); and other projected volumes. I hope that with the combined availability of these anthologies and the volumes in this series, courses on a variety of aspects of Canadian drama and theatre will flourish in schools and universities within Canada and beyond its borders, and scholars new to the field will find accessible and comprehensive introductions to some of the field's most provocative and intriguing figures and issues.

Finally, the titles selected for *Critical Perspectives on Canadian Theatre in English* are designed to carve out both familiar and new areas of work. It is my intention that the series at once recognize the important critical heritage of scholarly work in the field and attempt to fill in its most significant gaps by highlighting important work from and about marginalized communities, work that has too often been neglected in courses on and criticism of Canadian drama and theatre. In its nationalist phase in the late 1960s and 70s, English-Canadian theatre criticism tended to neglect work by women, by First Nations peoples and people of colour, by Gay, Lesbian, Bi- or Trans-sexual artists, and by those working in politically, geographically, or aesthetically alternative spaces. While respecting, honouring, and representing important landmarks in Canadian postcolonial theatrical nationalism, *Critical Perspectives on Canadian Theatre in English* also sets out to serve as a corrective to its historical exclusions.

Ric Knowles

Acknowledgements

I would like to thank Playwrights Canada Press and Angela Rebeiro for supporting this important series, the general editor Ric Knowles for inviting me to put together this volume, and all the excellent contributors whose work is represented here. Ongoing conversations with several of them have made my task lively and interesting.

I also want to acknowledge the Department of Drama at the University of Alberta. Both the Chair Jan Selman and Associate Chair Kim McCaw have given their enthusiastic support. My graduate seminar in Canadian Queer Theatre (Winter 2006) and Jeffrey Gagnon helped to lay the research foundations. A grant from the President's Fund for the Creative and Performing Arts allowed me to engage the services of my editorial assistant Christopher Grignard who has made an outstanding contribution in many areas.

The first twelve articles in the volume are republished with the permission of the author and the publisher. Neil Carson's "Sexuality and Identity in *Fortune and Men's Eyes*" was first published in *Twentieth Century Literature* 18.3 (July 1972): 207–18; Robert Wallace's "Homo Creation: Towards a Poetics of Gay Male Theatre" first appeared (as "Homo Creation") in *jeu* in 1990; here it is reprinted with the permission of *Essays on Canadian Writing* 54 (1994); Reid Gilbert's "'That's Why I Go to the Gym': Sexual Identity and the Body of the Male Performer" first appeared in *Theatre Journal* 46 (1994): 477–88 and is reprinted with the permission from the Johns Hopkins University Press; Susan Bennett's "Only in Alberta?: Angels in America and Canada" was first published in *Theatre Research in Canada* 17.2 (Fall 1996): 160–74; Marcia Blumberg's "Queer(y)ing the Canadian Stage: Brad Fraser's *Poor Super Man*" was first published in *Theatre Research in Canada* 17.2 (Fall 1996): 175–87; a version of Darrin Hagen's "Wrestling with a Double Standard" first appeared in the June 1999 (Pride) issue of *Outlooks Newspaper* under the same title; a revised version of the article, "Why I Hate Wrestling (the Sport, Not the Foreplay!)", which appeared in *torquere* 1 (1999): 114–19, is reprinted here; an earlier version of Elaine Pigeon's "*Hosanna!* Michel Tremblay's Queering of National Identity" appeared in *Xcp: Cross-Cultural Poetics* 5 (1999): 23–40. The final version was published in the essay collection, *in a queer country: Gay and Lesbian Studies in the Canadian Context*. Ed. Terry Goldie (Vancouver, Arsenal Pulp Press, 2001); B.J. Wray's "The Elephant, the Mouse, and the Lesbian National Park Rangers" first appeared within the text, *in a queer country: Gay and Lesbian Studies in the Canadian Context*. Ed. Terry Goldie (Vancouver: Arsenal Press, 2001): 160–74; David Bateman's "'Performing Femininity' On Stage and Off: Confronting Effeminaphobia Through Drag Performance" was first published in *Canadian Theatre Review* 109 (Winter 2002): 38–41; Susan Billingham's "The Configurations of Gender in Tomson Highway's *Dry Lips Oughta Move to Kapuskasing*" was first published in *Modern Drama* 46.3 (Fall 2003): 358–80 and is reprinted by permission of University of Toronto Press Incorporated (www.utpjournals.com); Peter Dickinson's "Brothers' Keepers, or, The Performance of Mourning: Queer Rituals of Remembrance" was first published in *torquere* 6 (2004): 12–46; Bobby J. Noble's "Strange Sisters and Boy Kings: Post-Queer Tranz-Gendered Bodies in Performance" was first published in *Canadian Women's Studies* 24.2/3 (Winter/Spring 2005): 164–70. An extended version of this essay appears in TRiC/ RTaC Volume 27, issue 2. A version of J. Paul Halferty's "Queer and Now: The Queer Signifier at Buddies in Bad Times Theatre" is printed here with the permission of *Theatre Research in Canada/Recherches théâtrales au Canada*. The remaining articles are published here for the first time, with the permission of the authors.

Rosalind Kerr

Introduction. Queer Canadian Theatre

by Rosalind Kerr

In mapping the trajectory of queer theatre in English Canadian theatre, it is necessary to start with the foundational theatrical examples that represent the struggle to define gay and lesbian sexual identities that began back in the 1960s. Even more so than in the United States, Canadian gay and lesbian theatre has been concerned with articulating the problematic relationship between sexual and national identities and hence the 1960s were of crucial importance since that is the time period when many different liberation movements came together. Expo '67, held in Montreal, marked the emergence of a new phase of inquiry into what it meant to be Canadian. This question, always informed by the need to distinguish ourselves from the United States, was becoming further complicated by the Quiet Revolution that was taking place in Quebec as it emerged from centuries of economic depression and political and cultural oblivion. Not coincidentally, gay liberation movements were taking wing, soon to be validated by Prime Minister Pierre Trudeau's decriminalization of homosexuality in 1969. Up until that time, homosexual acts had been punishable by up to fourteen years in prison. The play which is usually considered to have introduced the taboo topic of homosexuality to Canadian Theatre is the late John Herbert's haunting prison drama *Fortune and Men's Eyes* (1967). It was considered so controversial at the time that it could not find a Canadian producer and had to premiere in New York. But within the next decade, the gay play arrived and in the half-century that has followed, as we shall see, Canadian theatre has been noticeably queered.

The twenty-one articles I have selected are intended to put together important pieces of the puzzle that add up to some kind of overview of where Canadian queer theatre is today and how we arrived here. At the moment we are lacking an up-to-date full-length study, although Robert Wallace's *Producing Marginality* (1990) and Peter Dickinson's *Here is Queer* (1999) continue to be important markers. However a great deal remains untold. My diverse selections were chosen to try to reflect the emergence of GLBT/queer theatre artists and the ways in which they have interacted with the academic, theatrical, local and national communities that were producing them. They are arranged in a somewhat misleading chronological order in that the last nine often reference time periods well before 2007.

It is important to alert readers to this unusual configuration of articles as it departs from the mandate of Critical Perspectives in significant ways. My research into articles between 1970 and the present uncovered a period of time from the 1970s to the early 1990s when most of the articles that were being written referenced gay/lesbian Quebec playwrights. It is really only in the mid-nineties that articles dealing with queer theatre pertaining to English Canadian scholars and theatre practitioners/spectators begin to appear. Hence, this volume has a heavy concentration on the last fifteen years in recognition that queer theatre really only begins during the 1990s. The need to balance out the representation of other forms of queer theatre than the established gay male playwrights led me to invite several scholars to share new work on lesbian, trans, queer contributions that had not been sufficiently documented. There remains a gap in my coverage of bi and non-white queer Canadian artists that I was not able to fill.

It is also necessary to explain why I have included three key articles on Quebec artists in a volume dedicated to Canadian theatre in English. My reasons for doing so reflect the enormous impact that Quebec queer theatre has had on English Canadian scholars and practitioners. Robert Wallace's "Homo Creation: Towards a Poetics of Gay Male Theatre" (1994) is a seminal work theorizing ways in which the group of gay male playwrights who followed Tremblay carved out a space for gay theatre; Elaine Pigeon's "*Hosanna!* Michel Tremblay's Queering of National Identity" (2001) brings together several decades of scholarship on *Hosanna* by looking at ways in which it changed from being a gay to a queer play. Since *Hosanna,* like many other gay Quebec plays that followed, has had a long and illustrious production history in its English version, it seems necessary to reference its importance in Canadian queer theatre studies. Louise H. Forsyth's "Passionate Performances: Pol Pelletier and Experimental Feminist Theatre beyond the Barriers of Language (1975–1985)" reminds English theatre scholars and practitioners that queer female voices were also being heard in translation outside of Quebec.

Before I introduce the articles it is necessary to lay out some definitions in order to understand the points of intersection between gay and lesbian theatre and queer theory. By the early 1990s the term queer replaced gay and lesbian in recognition of the need to move beyond the identity politics they implied. As Jacose sets it out:

> Queer, on the other hand ... exemplifies a more mediated relation to categories of identification. Access to the post-structuralist theorization of identity as provisional and contingent, coupled with a growing awareness of the limitations of identity categories in terms of political representation, enabled queer to emerge as a new form of personal identification and political organization. (77–78)

After Butler's expansion of Foucault, all gendered categories were exposed as constructions arising from "the stylized repetition of the body, as a set of repeated acts within a highly rigid regulatory frame" (1990:3). Butler's important notion of the performativity of gender, despite the ways in which it has been misunderstood, has also proven to be a tremendously useful concept for isolating the coercive practices that punish those who do not perform their genders correctly. Moreover, not even categories of sex are left intact since performativity applies just as much to the category of sexed bodies (1990:7). Once homosexuality is understood to be the effect of signifying practices, it becomes possible to rally against the normalizing categories that have attempted to other it. Thus, in "Critically Queer," Butler suggests ways in which queer theory can be transformed into a revolutionary praxis:

> Paradoxically, but also with great promise, the subject who is 'queered' into public discourse through homophobic interpellations of various kinds *takes up* or *cites* that very term as the discursive basis for an opposition. This kind of citation will emerge as *theatrical* to the extent that *it mimes and renders hyperbolic* the discursive convention that is also *reverses*. The hyperbolic gesture is crucial to the exposure of the homophobic law which can no longer control the terms of its own abjecting strategies. (18)

Queer theory has thus proved to be an immensely valuable tool for the study of gay and lesbian theatre practice, all the more so because, as American queer theatre theorist David Savran remarks, theatre is "the queerest art" (70), able to engage with Eve Sedgwick's polysemic referencing of queer as deriving from "the open mesh of possibilities, gaps, overlaps, dissonances and resonances, lapses and excesses of meaning when the constituent elements of anyone's gender, of anyone's sexuality aren't made (or *can't* be made) to signify monolithically" (8–9). What makes theatre the queerest art for Savran is its unique ability to "disarticulate and disrupt identity— whether the identity in question is that of the playwright, the performer, or the spectator" (70). As we turn now to look at the articles that make up this anthology, I will try to draw attention to different ways in which Canadian queer theatre engages with these theorizations and the evolving utopic possibilities they suggest.

The first article by Neil Carson, "Sexuality and Identity in *Fortune and Men's Eyes*," (1972) shows the preoccupation with questions of sexuality and identity that were of central concern in the 1970s. Carson's article is especially valuable because it not only engages with different versions of the text, it also uses them to propose that Herbert is not interested in sensationalizing violent homosexual prison sex but in raising important social and cultural issues about the ways in which sexual identities become criminalized. As he concludes, Herbert leaves us with the sense that the conditions inside the prison are mirror reflections of the oppressive relationships existing in the outside world.

The next article, Robert Wallace's "Homo Creation: Towards a Poetics of Gay Male Theatre" (1994), as he explains in his first note, is a translation from an earlier article written in French, representative of his thinking in 1988. Its groundbreaking importance to our understanding of the emergence of a Canadian gay theatre poetics derives from its detailing of the construction of a stage world in which homosexuality had become the central sexual and social construct. Referencing the host of gay playwrights who had emerged in Quebec after Tremblay, Wallace pays special attention to works by René-Daniel Dubois, Norman Chaurette and Michel Marc Bouchard, noting how they had succeeded in eroticizing the theatrical site through their inventive imagistic stagings. His elaboration on the ways in which specific gay Québécois theatre productions had succeeded in creating a self-referential site of difference stresses the fact that their rejection of normalizing naturalistic stage conventions works to expose the history of the oppressive conditions through which the family, church and state had punished homosexual behaviours. Praising them for producing theatre which could bring about both social reform and artistic transformation, Wallace suggests both here and elsewhere, that Quebec's example offers a model from which English Canadian gay theatre had much to learn.

The third article, Reid Gilbert's "'That's Why I Go To The Gym': Sexual Identity and the Body of the Male Performer" (1994), shows that the sex-gender identity debate was still front and centre as Gilbert references the way that the gay male body was staged in Robert Lepage's *Polygraph,* Terrence McNally's *Lips Together, Teeth Apart,* and David Drake's *The Night Larry Kramer Kissed Me.* To summarize, he posits that since the dominant culture regards the homosexual male body as an inferior feminized object to be scorned, even gay playwrights tend to follow suit by staging scenes in which heterosexual male characters are at least symbolically punished if they break the taboo of gazing upon a gay male body with desire. Gilbert's caution is that the kind of warning that gay male spectators are given of the sadomasochistic dangers that attend their open expressions of desire reinscribes the prohibitions that the dominant culture continues to enforce. As an interesting side note, when I discussed with Gilbert the appropriateness of including this article, he pointed to the treatment of the gay protagonists in the film "Brokeback Mountain" (2005). On the other hand, shortly after this article came out, Robert Wallace raised an interesting counter-argument in "Performance anxiety: "Identity," "Community," and Tim Miller's *My Queer Body,*" suggesting that perhaps Gilbert was placing too much emphasis on the spectator as the ultimate arbiter of meaning and not enough on the possibilities for ways in which the scenes could be staged to create a different kind of interaction between the gay performers and spectators.

The fourth article, Susan Bennett's "Only in Alberta?: *Angels in America* and Canada" (1996), contains vitally important information about the production and reception history of this quintessential American queer play across Canada as it problematizes the degree to which the play's American-ness cancelled out its intolerable homosexual content. Citing the kind of liberal tolerance expressed by the media all across major Canadian cities where the show was produced, Bennett also unearths the underlying homophobic panic it barely concealed. Thus when she sets up the harsh reactions that accompanied the Alberta Theatre Projects' staging of the epic in Calgary in 1996, she can make her case that the virulent attacks made by key Albertan institutions including government funding agencies and the media were just stating more openly the prejudices that the dominant culture everywhere shared. Indeed, she quotes the extreme right-wing *Alberta Report's* accurate observation that the play was more about politics than sex as a demonstration of the play's efficacy in exposing the intolerances of North American culture. Instead, Bennett makes the powerful point that Alberta simply used the opportunity to cut arts funding on the same grounds that Western societies have all been following: by treating it as undeserving and only of interest to a small minority. While Bennett leaves us with a sense that *Angels* confounds our intolerant-tolerance, her article memorializes the impact that this play has had on shaping our own sense of consumerist American queer.

The fifth article, Marcia Blumberg's "Queer(y)ing the Canadian Stage: Brad Fraser's *Poor Super Man*" (1996) brings into the foreground the question of what seems to be required to write a gay box-office success for English Canadian audiences. Blumberg wonders if Fraser is right when he claims that writing about Canadian identity issues is boring and out of touch. In any case, the commercial success that Fraser enjoyed from 1989 when *Unidentified Human Remains* premiered in Calgary up until the late 1990s as his biggest hit *Poor Super Man* (premiere Cincinnati 1994) was produced across Canada and beyond, attests to his winning formula. This formula, as Blumberg sets it out, embraces the diversity of the not-completely straight, gay, bi, lesbian and trans community and seeks to tell the sexually explicit stories of the erotic triangles that shape up between a range of characters as if they were of central concern to the dominant heterosexist audience. Playing with images and stylistic devices drawn from American popular culture, especially the comic book hero Superman myth, Fraser's frenetic destabilization of all facets of life in a big urban centre move us far away from any investigation of stable sexual identities. Blumberg's designation of this play as both queer and revolutionary in its call for social change derives mainly from her sense of the gay-artist-hero David's recognition at the end that he does not have to be Superman after all. Perhaps, *Poor Super Man*'s success can be understood if we regard David as a Canadian universal gay male subject, bearing similarities to his American counterpart in *Angels in America* (68).

The next article, Darrin Hagen's "Wrestling with a Double Standard" (1999), is included here to give a queer artist's views on the particular brand of hypocrisy that flourishes in an Alberta where, as Susan Bennett details it, a hue and cry was raised about the need to protect Alberta from the godless portrayal of diseased homosexuality in *Angels in America*. Hagen was struck by the wildly enthusiastic reception accorded to a very different show brought into Calgary and Edmonton by the WWF (the World Wrestling Federation) in 1996. Finding the displays of brute force, fake violence and bravado carried to criminal extremes, Hagen suggests that what really attracts the sold-out crowds is the glorification of straight white male power at the expense of everyone else. His graphic descriptions of the wild enthusiasm with which spectators reacted to scenarios such as the one which faked anal intercourse between men made it clear that such scenes were welcomed as long as it was made to appear that one partner was unwilling, or if they were followed up with mock punishments for any gay behaviour. What makes this uncensored brutality even harder to accept is Hagen's explanation of its popularity among not only adults but children who are part of the millions of viewers who tune in to WWF on a regular basis. Hagen leaves us with a very clear picture of the heavy homophobic price tag that comes with this so-called manly sport.

The seventh article, Elaine Pigeon's "*Hosanna!* Michel Tremblay's Queering of National Identity" (2001), marks the profound changes that have occurred in the production and reception of *Hosanna* since its 1973 Quebec premiere. Drawing on the important scholarship of Robert Schwartzwald, Pigeon discusses how Tremblay's presentation of the essentialized sexual identities of the transvestite Hosanna and the hyper-masculine Cuirette were originally read as a metaphor for the marginalized status of an oppressed Quebec. However, in a new Montreal production in 1991, endorsed by Tremblay, their sexual identities were made far more ambiguous and in the final moments when Hosanna strips down; since his drag has already been partly removed, it is already clear that he is a man. Thus when he calls himself a man, he is neither asserting an authentic sexual identity, nor letting Cuirette's (Queerete's) macho masquerade go unnoticed as any less constructed. As a result, the play could no longer be read as confirming Quebec's unique counterculture homosexual status vis-à-vis the normative heterosexual English Canadian and North American dominant one. Pigeon believes the 1991 production of *Hosanna* gives us the opportunity to extend the questioning of heterosexual gender categories to that of national identities beyond the boundaries of Quebec into the whole of Canada. Her thoughtful insight into the ways in which marginal identities keep asserting themselves and breaking up any exclusive definitions of what nationality is, finds that Hosanna and Cuirette's embracing of their queerness has a lesson for us all. A nice complement to Wallace's earlier article, Pigeon shows us a very positive queer trajectory for Quebec gay theatre.

The eighth article, B.J. Wray's "The Elephant, the Mouse and the Lesbian National Park Rangers" (2001), is the first to deal with lesbian artists and describes a site-specific event carried out by well-known Winnipeg-based video and performance artists, Shawna Dempsey and Lorri Millan. For three weeks, they patrolled the streets of Banff, Alberta in the guise of Lesbian National Park Rangers, handing out pamphlets, and among other things, running a recruitment day. They also roamed through other areas of the park, paddling canoes and hiking trails as part of their claiming of this very normative national space. What Wray draws our attention to is the ways in which they tried to disrupt both national and sexual identities by overwriting national symbols with their lesbian signature. She credits them with providing a critical commentary on the ways in which nation-making is constantly shaping who we are and, in noting that their whiteness may have been necessary to their successful impersonations, concludes that their performances reveal that the wilderness is a racialized as well as a heterosexualized space.

The next article, David Bateman's "'Performing Femininity' On Stage and Off: Confronting Effeminaphobia Through Drag Performance" (2002), uses incidents from Margaret Gibson's "Outrageous," which was turned into a drag musical by Brad Fraser and composer Joey Miller in 2001, to frame his investigations into ways to use drag performance to break down gender binaries. His goal in doing so is to offer us examples of his own aesthetic as a performer who wishes to refute the charge that drag is misogynist. Using his own performance piece, *A Particular Kind of Cross-Dresser*, he shows how his moving in and out of various costume and set pieces, embodying a variety of personae with diverse desires destabilizes any fixed gender categories. Bateman believes that it is in the power of drag performers of both sexes to offer a constant revisioning of a multi-gendered body whose on and off stage presence cannot then be denied. However, it may be important to note that he still demarcates bodies as discernably sexed and gendered.

The tenth article, Susan Billingham's "The Configurations of Gender in Tomson Highway's *Dry Lips Oughta Move to Kapuskasing*" (2003), looks at his treatment of masculinity and homosociality in the relationships in the play in order to show how precarious life on the Reserve has become for his people suffering from centuries of white oppression. The key incident she uses to reveal the internalized homophobia that has been layered over all the other complex layers of self-hatred and destructive behaviours occurs when Creature Nataways is physically restrained by Big Joey when he tries to stop Patsy/Nanabush's rape, since Big Joey wishes to see her suffer. We see the multiple layers of internalized abjection enacted on stage when Creature Nataways follows up with a confession of his love for Big Joey, even though Big Joey has viciously attacked him for his homosexuality. Billingham concludes by noticing that Highway never does overturn Joey's hateful attack, leaving homosexual love out of his final vision of a healthy heterosexual future on the Reserve. She sees his failure to even fantasize about the healing power that a two-spirited presence might have for Natives in reclaiming their past as something to be lamented.

The next article, Peter Dickinson's "Brothers' Keepers, or, The Performance of Mourning: Queer Rituals of Remembrance" (2004), offers a deeply poignant account of a range of different kinds of local memorials to multiple victims of hatred, violence, intolerance, discrimination, poverty and illness such as AIDS that he has either visited or witnessed in performances. Addressing his message to straight white men in particular as those who need to take responsibility for their inhumanity to the rest of the world, he uses his exploration of these ritual sites of mourning to remind us all of the need to recognize that this is the world we inhabit and are defined by. Describing first memorial sites to AIDS victims, the women killed by Marc Lepine, the Aborginal sex-trade workers, and finally, the impromptu squat at the cenotaph to protest home-lessness, Dickinson opens up a landscape that puts the gay-bashing that goes on in a neighbouring park into a new sombre light by its juxtaposition to the memorials. Stressing the importance of experiencing the performative and hence potentially transformative nature that comes from participating in queer rituals of remembrance and mourning, he then describes his reactions to the haunting beauty of Margie Gillis's dance for her brother who died from AIDS; Paula Vogel's celebration of her brother's life in *The Baltimore Waltz*; Terrence McNally's gay Jesus in *Corpus Christi*; and Moisés Kaufman and his Tectonic Theater Project's tribute to Matthew Shepard in *The Laramie Project*. He leaves us with a profound awareness that in our memorial vigils for our lost queer brothers we also need to mourn for our straight brothers whose violent acts we continue to condone. Once again, Dickinson's article, like many of those that precede it, draws attention to the ways in which the heteronormative world shapes and is shaped by the homosexual other it persecutes.

Article twelve, Bobby J. Noble's "Strange Sisters and Boy Kings: Post-Queer Tranz-Gendered Bodies in Performance" (2005) takes the anthology in a new direction in its foregrounding of tranz as a new and as yet unrepresentable body. He suggests that tranz-art and performance artists have made overdetermined binaristic gender categories unthinkable and in so doing have opened up a space for a post-queer practice of incoherence. To demonstrate ways in which artists have destabilized recognizable sex/gender categories, Noble offers examples from two Toronto-based performance artists: the drag king Deb Pearce (Man Murray) and the femme spoken-word artist Anna Camillieri. Pearce as Man Murray runs the gamut of failed hetero-normative femininity, disavowed female masculinity and queered gay masculinity, while Camillieri practices a viable political resistance through a post-queer fem(me)ininity, which exhibits a femininity that has gone awry. No longer discernably male or female as David Bateman's effeminate drag queens, Noble's performance artists exhibit what he calls a post-queer tranz desire that defies genital logic and promises a new day for feminism in that these artists control their knowability.

With the next article, Frances Latchford's "Get Your 'Boy' On!: The Politics of Parody and Embodiment in 'Drag' Performances in Toronto" (2007), we move into work that was commissioned for this volume to fill in certain historical and critical gaps. Latchford's mapping of the changes that drag king performance has undergone since its beginnings in the 1990s give us insights into the reasons why the focus has shifted away from gender parody to male/female sexual embodiment in the present. Working with her own experiences and the commentaries of such prominent drag kings as La Chica, and Suzy Richter, she locates The Greater Toronto Drag King Society (dk) in the social and political milieu that fostered its campy subversive impersonations critiquing iconic masculinity and femininity from an informed feminist-lesbian perspective. A list of the wide repertoire and the many events at which La Chica and her ensemble performed both at Buddies and at numerous Toronto bars makes it very clear that the group was in high demand with their many fans. It is interesting to note that Latchford believes that the key to the dks popularity lay in their emulation of the flamboyant style of Toronto's well-established drag queens and their shared targeting of a gay audience. In trying to determine what it is that has changed in the performance of today's drag kings such as King Flare, Gricel Severino and King's Ransom, she notes that the ironic critique is missing. However, whether or not present-day drag king performances are falling into reinscribing sex and gender roles by emphasizing embodiment, Latchford concedes that performers are grappling with new and exciting means of performing sexed bodies, especially now that the transgendered body has also to be factored in. Ultimately she wishes for a renewed balance between embodiment and parody in order to keep the resistance alive.

The fifteenth article, by Judith Anderson, "Making a Spectacle: The 'Danger' of Drag Performance in Two Canadian Pride Parades" (2007), uses footage and commentary from Pride parades in Winnipeg in 2005 and Toronto in 2003 and 2004 to argue that the spectacle of drag can destabilize any clear referent to discernable sexual/gendered identities. As such she proposes that Pride parades have a carniva-lesque potential to subvert normalizing conventions of the real. Her description of the footage at the Toronto Pride Parade in 2005 where "fashionably attired drag queens lead the way for a transsexual fairy princess whose stitch-marked breasts reveal her surgically-altered anatomy" creates a vivid picture of a scene where biology has become irrelevant to determining sex/gender differences. Describing the extravagant costumes and outlandish behaviour of both participants and spectators, she names

Pride parades "dangerous" in their temporary suspension of society's rules. Anderson's final argument, somewhat reminiscent of Bateman's, urges those who wish to perform a gender of their choice to take the spectacle off the stage and into the street.

Louise H. Forsyth's "Passionate Performances: Pol Pelletier and Experimental Feminist Theatre beyond the Barriers of Language (1975–1985)" (2007) returns us to the early years that Robert Wallace describes in the second article, and looks at the trajectory of Quebec performance artist Pelletier's career as it impacted on Quebec and English Canadian theatre over that decade. As co-founder of Théâtre Expérimental de Montréal in 1975, she brought a strong feminist-bisexual-lesbian voice to the all-female collective creations this company performed, demonstrating the profound cultural revolution that women in Quebec were experiencing as they broke free from the same oppressive institutions of family, church and state that the gay theatre artists were also detailing. A consummate multi-faceted artist, Pelletier's enormous contribution to the growth of feminist experimental theatre in Canada was fed by her hands-on knowledge that women had to claim their own space in yet another male-dominated institution. Involved in most of the ground-breaking experimental theatre that emerged from Quebec at this time, Pelletier acted explosive radical feminist roles in *La Nef des sorcières, À Ma Mère, à ma mère, à ma mère, à ma mère, à ma voisine,* and *Les Vaches de nuit.* The last, translated as *Night Cows,* a stunningly sensuous celebration of mother-daughter love, performed by Pelletier in a cow's mask, played all over Canada during the next decade. Between 1979 and 1985, Pelletier continued her feminist experiments as a cofounder of the Théâtre Expérimental des Femmes (TEF). Two notable productions, *La Lumière blanche* and *La Terre est trop courte, Violette Leduc,* were translated into English and remounted outside Quebec. The Toronto Nightwood production at the Theatre Centre in 1986 of *The Edge of Earth is Too Near* serves as an important milestone for Ontario audiences. While Pelletier includes lesbian characters in her oeuvre, Forsyth regards her as a quintessentially queer practitioner because of the way she challenges all received gender/sex norms through her erotically charged, experimental representations of women of all sexual orientations. Referencing Pelletier's stellar contribution to French and English-speaking theatre fills in some missing historical data on the role that radical feminist artists played in que(e)rying our sexual-national identities.

My article, "Staging Lesbian Sex and the City" (2007), surveys ways in which urban landscapes figure prominently in eight pieces taken from my recently published anthology, *Lesbian Plays: Coming of Age in Canada.* In recognizing that the work of lesbian artists has been consistently underrepresented in Canadian queer theatre, I argue that these plays have a lot to tell us about the changing constructions of the lesbian subject from the late 1980s to the present in urban Canada and, more specifically, in our largest urban centre, Toronto. Although my mapping of the ways in which the city has produced these artists is necessarily cursory, my intention is to reveal these pieces as representative of a substantial body of lesbian theatre that cannot be read apart from the site specific landscapes where these lesbian subjects find themselves empowered to explore their desires in productive ways. Alec Butler's *Black*

Friday; Shawna Dempsey and Lorri Millan's *Growing Up Suites I* and *II*; Lisa Lowe's *Dykes and Dolls*; Vivienne Laxdal's *Karla and Grif*; Susan G. Cole's *A Fertile Imagination*; Diane Flacks's *Random Acts*; Alex Bulmer's *Smudge*; and Corrina Hodgson's *Privilege* all reveal ways in which the city acts as a locus for the production and circulation of power through the kinds of social marginality it dictates. While it may be impossible to find a lesbian play with a universal queer subject, I argue that the city lesbian may have found a way to speak for the city-state.

Article seventeen, Ann Holloway's "Potluck Feminism—Where's the Meat?: Sonja Mills's Comedy of Resistance" (2007), introduces a different shade of lesbianism in the form of dyke monologist Sonja Mills whose career is tracked from the early 1990s to the present. Best known for her often bitingly sarcastic attacks on all forms of political correctness and especially that of conservative separatist lesbian feminists, Sonja developed her particular brand of stand-up in places like Buddies' Tallulah's Cabaret under the inspiration of Sky Gilbert who encouraged work that pushed at the sexual boundaries. Holloway offers vivid recreations of Mills's signature pieces: "WUWU" and "Dyke City" (1995) which parody the sexless 1980s "potluck feminism" that characterized women's studies feminism at the time; and "Dyke City Two: Secret of the Oooze" (1996), which inverted the convention of the traditional family sitcom. Starring the irrepressible, rude and crude, exuberant Frances, a self-parody of Mills, this dykecom not only satirizes the straight nuclear family but also sweeps away taboos relating to female sexuality—lesbian, straight, and in-between. For Holloway, Mills's closeness to her stage persona Frances increases her effect on audiences by doubling her iconoclastic impact and thus opening up a queer transformational theatre space where lesbian sexual desire can be reconfigured without the usual polite restraints.

The next article, Sky Gilbert's "Writing Gay: Is it Still Possible?" (2007), provides a retrospective rant on his own career as a gay-queer radical artist-playwright-theatre director and attempts to come up with some reasons why queer theatre has lost its edge. Citing his late 1980s drag queen plays as representing the height of his critical success, he blames the advent of AIDS for bringing the gay revolution to a crashing halt. Now that gays have sold out to consumerism and social conservatism, he believes that only the trans movement remains on the cutting edge. Fearful that gay, lesbian, queer and even transgendered artists will all find themselves co-opted, Gilbert presents himself as an increasingly isolated figure who will never abandon his gay vision even if he has to distribute his plays from his basement. His very ambivalence about the ability to stay on the outside in order to critique the new "normal" leaves the answer to his question hanging and open for the kind of discussion we find in the next two articles.

Article nineteen, Paul Halferty's "Queer and Now: the Queer Signifier at Buddies in Bad Times Theatre" (2007), goes in search of different shades of queer that can be discerned in Buddies' programming from 1979 to the present. Thus, the first "radically queer" period from 1979–1997 under Sky Gilbert's tenure abandoned gay and lesbian liberation politics and encouraged other marginalized identities from the sexual fringes to develop the kind of radical art that pushed at all the social and political boundaries. However, when the company moved to 12 Alexander Street in 1997, it entered into an "inclusively queer" stage for budgetary and other reasons. Halferty discerns that from 1997 to 2004, queer was reduced to a linguistic strategy as gay and lesbian theatrical expression came back to the fore without the radical critique. However from 2004 on, Halferty notes a new shift to "sexually/aesthetically queer," which re-defines and re-deploys queer to both interrogate the gamut of LGBT sexual identities, but also to include other artistic work that addresses non-mainstream issues of any kind. While Daniel MacIvor's *Cul-de-Sac* clearly belongs to the first, two other plays are definitely examples of the second. The first, Darren O'Donnell's *A Suicide-Site Guide to the City*," addresses the marginalized impoverished lives of most cultural workers; the second, Ann Holloway's *Kingstonia Dialect Perverso* breaks with mainstream art by featuring a female protagonist who offers graphic depictions of her sexual exploits. Halferty's tentative conclusion is to suggest that if queer is losing its potential to critique sexual subjectivities, it's not yet devoid of all subversive valence.

The next article, David Allan King's "Cultivating Queer: The Invisibility of the Canadian Gay Play" (2007), provides a retrospective look at the status of the gay play across Canada today. King sticks to the "gay play" in order to distinguish GLBT plays from other multicultural theatre groups who are now vying for the same pool of funding needed to sustain productions of their works. He fears for the future of GLBT theatre groups across Canada, noting the dozen existing companies in different Canadian cities that are struggling to maintain their GLBT mandates find themselves competing unsuccessfully with visible minorities. Echoing Halftery, he worries if the adoption of the term "queer" in the name of inclusivity will empty out the commitment to challenge conventions, and ends by urging "gay" theatre practitioners to remember what they stand for.

Mariko Tamaki's "Cheap Queers" (2007) closes the anthology on a somewhat lighter note with her personal account of participating in Cheap Queers, an annual cabaret that runs right before Toronto's Pride season in June. Describing her sheer delight in performing in such a crazy carnivalesque event, Tamaki revels in Moynan King's mandate that "anything goes." Whether this means that queer can now be stretched to cover any outrageous act with or without sexual content seems to be proven by Tamaki's performance in 2006 where she painted herself blue and ran around the stage slamming on a toilet seat with a bowling pin. Whether or not this performance makes a political statement, she loves the freedom it gives her to make queer whatever she chooses it to be. But if she is following her preferred definition of the moment from queer activist Matt Bernstein-Sycamore, a.k.a. Mattilda, she still wants queer to "have the radical potential to choose one's gender and one's sexual and social identities, to embrace a radical outsider's perspective, to create culture on our terms, and to challenge everything that's sickening about the dominant culture around us" (qtd. in Rasmussen 57).

While the material presented in these articles may appear to be too diverse to allow us to come to any conclusion as to where Canadian English queer theatre is today, I hope that I have at least set out a path to follow from those first gay liberation plays to the complex interrogations of the intersections of sexualities and nationalities which seem to inform so much of the work. Perhaps the strength of the oeuvre by gay/queer playwrights writing in both French and English owes something to our particularly Canadian quest for identity within the context of American culture. Perhaps the continuing imbalance between the representation of work by gay white men and all other sexual and racial minorities reveals that queer theatre was only a utopic fantasy. For Sue-Ellen Case the problem lies with the flawed mandate of Queer Nation and occurred very early on when they abandoned the anti-sexist, anti-homophobic, anti-racist, anti-poverty agendas of early activist coalition movements for an interrogation of "normal" that forgot all about the normalizing operations of patriarchy, capital and nation. As a result all queer activism did was

> reinstate the dominant social structures, lending its power to those who are already invested in the system, with the exception of their sexual identification. Not surprisingly, then, white middle-class men will form the constituency. Their culture, sub or not, will continue to be representative. (35)

If that is the case, then we need to be making queer theatre that takes responsibility for the ways in which our sexualities/nationalities continue to be produced inside the prevailing assimilationist discourses of consumer capitalism. Fighting to expand the definition of "queer" beyond its equation with "white, middle-class American homosexual" should give us all, white gay male artists included, new frontiers to queer.

(2007)

Works Cited

Butler, Judith. *Gender Trouble: Feminism and the Subversion of Identity.* London and New York: Routledge, 1990.

———. "Critically Queer." *Playing with Fire: Queer Politics, Queer Theories.* Ed. Shane Phelan. London and New York: Routledge, 1997. 11–29.

Case, Sue-Ellen. "Toward a Butch-Feminist Retro-Future." *Queer Frontiers: Millennial Geographies, Genders and Generations.* Ed. Joseph A. Boone et al. Madison, Wisconsin: U of Wisconsin P, 2000. 23–38.

Dickinson, Peter. *Here is Queer: Nationalisms, Sexualities and the Literature of Canada.* Toronto, Buffalo and London: U of Toronto P, 1999.

Herbert, John. *Fortune and Men's Eyes.* New York: Grove P, 1967.

Jacose, Anne Marie. *Queer Theory.* New York: New York UP, 1996.

Rasmussen, Debbie. "Running from the Altar." *Bitch Magazine.* Truth Issue 29 (2005): 52–57.

Savran, David. "The Queerest Art." *A Queer Sort of Materialism.* Ann Arbor: U of Michigan P, 2003. 56–81.

Sedgwick, Eve Kosofsky. *Tendencies.* Durham: Duke UP, 1993.

Wallace, Robert. *Producing Marginality. Theatre and Criticism in Canada.* Saskatoon, Saskatchewan: Fifth House Publishers, 1990.

———. "Performance anxiety: "Identity," "Community," and Tim Miller's *My Queer Body.*" *Modern Drama* 39.1 (Spring 1996): 97–114.

Sexuality and Identity in
Fortune and Men's Eyes

by Neil Carson

Fortune and Men's Eyes, a hard-hitting drama about prison life by John Herbert, is by all odds the most successful play to come out of Canada in recent years. Following a run off-Broadway in 1967, it has won a steadily growing audience in many parts of the world. It has been produced in the United States, Canada, Australia, England and Hawaii, and translated into six languages for productions in another nine European countries. It has been published by Grove Press and is the only play to be represented in the recent Penguin anthology, *Canadian Writing Today*. A film version distributed by MGM will introduce the play to many more spectators.

In spite of this very respectable international success (virtually unparalleled in the history of Canadian drama) Herbert continues to live in relative obscurity in his native Toronto ignored alike by the commercial theatre managers and by the literary critics. He has two plays under option to producers in New York and London but claims that no Canadian theatre has approached him for a new work. More surprising, perhaps, Herbert is not mentioned in any of the regular literary periodicals and it is impossible to find any serious comments about his play apart from theatre reviews in the daily newspapers.

This astonishing neglect is partly the result of the curious bias of Canadian criticism which is almost wholly literary and academic in orientation. But it is also due to the playwright's vision which in many ways undermines certain popular contemporary attitudes. One of the first critics to comment on this fact was the late Nathan Cohen of the *Toronto Star*. "What is unusual about *Fortune and Men's Eyes*," he wrote

> is the resistance of the entertainment departments of the press and other media to the play. It is not a case of indifference but active hostility. . . . *Fortune and Men's Eyes* poses a truly critical challenge. It asks deeply disturbing questions about long-established personal and social assumptions. (17 April 1967)

The personal and social assumptions to which Cohen refers are our conventional ideas about the relationship between sexuality and identity. For Herbert is challenging the popular post-Freudian notion that an individual is little more than the sum of his sexual behaviour. He is asserting that the significant human problems (Women's Lib and *Playboy* to the contrary) are not those related to glandular functions or even to social conventions. They are the problems which transcend sexual categories—the problems which arise in moments of crisis in war, in emergencies, in prison.

Much that is shocking about *Fortune and Men's Eyes* and much of its unusual power is the result of its grim authenticity. The drama is based on Herbert's own experiences in an Ontario reformatory and exhibits in a particularly emphatic way the violence and corruption of prison society. The protagonist is a young first-offender by the name of Smitty who is locked up with three other boys about his own age. His cell mates include Rocky, a vicious, unpredictable bully with a long prison record, Queenie, a flamboyant homosexual with a switchblade wit, and Jan, an introverted homosexual whose enigmatic manner has earned him the nickname Mona Lisa. Smitty's initiation into the homosexual politics of prison life comes shortly after his arrival. He learns that he has three alternatives: he can form a liaison with an "old man" in exchange for the protection his partner can give him; he can barter his favours more widely for influence and privileges; or he can risk asserting his independence and leave himself open to intimidation, beatings and gang rape. Smitty begins by submitting to the sexual demands of Rocky and ends up making a pass at Mona. At the end of the play a fight breaks out in the cell and Smitty protects himself by threatening the guard with blackmail. When Mona is punished in his place he turns on the other boys in the cell and vows to be revenged on society.

No aspect of the play has provoked more heated or more varied comment than its explicit treatment of homosexuality. In certain productions the emphasis on sexual sensationalism has been carried to grotesque extremes. For the Los Angeles revival of the play (which was subsequently taken to New York) director Sal Mineo felt it necessary to bring the offstage rape of Smitty into full view in case the audience might not be able to imagine "the horror of it." Furthermore, he seemed to think that he could convey

> the utter deterioration of the principal character by having him masturbate to an obbligato of the moans of his newly-discovered lover being flogged offstage. (qtd. in *Variety* 29 October 1969)

The London version of the play was marred in a similar way. Taking advantage of recently relaxed censorship laws, the director had the actors play one short scene in the nude.

If producers have sometimes shown a rather shallow understanding of the play, a surprising number of critics have failed to see much deeper. The *Variety* reviewer of the London production called it

> a meaty, frank look at homosexuality and corruption in a Canadian reformatory ... primarily a form of diversion which will have limited appeal ... its thin story line concerns a young heterosexual serving his first reformatory term, sharing a dormitory with three convicted homos and swiftly becoming depraved. (13 November 1968)

Clive Barnes in the *New York Times* wrote that the play was an indictment of the North American prison system which showed that

> prison's isolation of the sexes led, inevitably to homosexuality … The theme of the play was centered around the degradation of one young man who is brutalized to the point of complete insensitivity. (23 October 1969)

One of the few critics to see more in the play than a sensational exposé of our antiquated penal institutions was Nathan Cohen. Cohen felt that the play is critically important because it is a

> deeply felt account of how people in … degrading circumstances, however distorted, find themselves an accommodation. The play unpeels layer after layer of search for position, for love, for self-respect as well as survival. (20 October 1967)

Apart from Cohen's brief but penetrating comments there has been no serious attempt to probe very far beneath the naturalistic surface of the play to what Herbert once called (somewhat pretentiously perhaps) the "social connotations of the play and the … eternal, larger elements of the idea" (qtd. in *Variety* 8 October 1969).

I have suggested that this critical neglect can be accounted for in part by the controversial nature of the subject matter. But it may also be the result of a superficial clumsiness and sentimentality in Herbert's handling of the central relationship between Smitty and Mona. These faults are especially evident in two crucial scenes, the one a rehearsal for a Christmas party and the other the last encounter between the two boys before the end of the play. Both of these scenes depend for much of their significance on Shakespearian quotations which Herbert (somewhat improbably) has incorporated into the action. It is clear from a study of the revisions he made in the script during rehearsals and early performances that Herbert had considerable difficulty with these passages. That trouble almost certainly reflects a tension between his vision and the form he has chosen to express it. It may also reflect his inability to separate himself completely from Mona, the character in the play who seems to express most clearly his own particular view of life.

During much of the early part of the play, Mona remains a shadowy figure, kindly but apparently weak and consequently victimized by the others. In the rehearsal scene he shows a streak of stubborn fanaticism which reveals another side of his character. The scene in question begins with Queenie giving a wickedly funny female impersonation looking like

> A COMBINATION OF GORGEOUS GEORGE, SOPHIE TUCKER, AND MAE WEST. HE WEARS A PLATINUM BLOND WIG, SPANGLED SEQUIN DRESS, LONG BLACK GLOVES, LARGE RHINESTONE JEWELRY ON EARS, NECK AND WRISTS, HEAVY MAKE-UP, AND IS CARRYING A LARGE FEATHER FAN. (70)

With characteristically poor judgement, Mona has decided to attempt something more serious and has memorized Portia's "mercy speech" from *The Merchant of Venice*. In the original version of the play, presented as a studio production by members of the Stratford Festival Company in Stratford, Ontario, Mona appears in

> THE TRADITIONAL COSTUME FOR PORTIA'S COURT SCENE …
> IT IS OF RED VELVET AND BECOMES HIM WELL, BUT CON-
> TRAST [sic] BETWEEN THE GRACEFUL, CLASSIC COSTUME AND
> QUEENIE'S GLITTERING ENSEMBLE SEEMS INCONGRUOUS.
> (typescript 35)

Ignoring the interruptions of the other boys, Mona directs the speech entirely to Smitty, "feeling the words and meaning completely." The seriousness of the moment is underlined by Mona's intensity, by the fact that his "performance would be worthy of any Shakespearian actor—or actress," and by the slow blackout which concludes the scene immediately following the recitation (typescript 37).

The published text differs from this earlier version in a number of interesting ways. The costume is described as "makeshift," made from "a converted red velvet curtain" and it becomes Mona only "somewhat." Mona's delivery is much less effective. He "begins very hesitantly, stuttering (with comic pathos and badly spoken) —as others giggle and roll eyes etc." Finally, Herbert has written a short bridge between this and the following scene thereby eliminating the blackout. Instead of the scene ending impressively on the Shakespearian lines, it declines into burlesque as Queenie unceremoniously ushers Mona out of the cell in a parody of "Gone With the Wind" saying

> Laws has muhcy, Miss Melanie – de Yankees is hyeah. Ain' you skeered
> dy gonna find yoah sissy brudder in dat closet? (PROPELLING MONA
> TOWARD CORRIDOR AND CONCERT) Run foh yoah life; all Atlanta
> am on fiyah. (typescript 73–77).

Amusing as this interlude is, it seems to confuse rather than clarify the scene. By deliberately changing the whole tone of the moment, Herbert has made it difficult if not impossible for an audience to take seriously either the content of Portia's speech or the relationship between Mona and Smitty. Mona is stripped of whatever vestige of dignity he might have retained beneath his ridiculous costume and reduced to a pathetic clown. The revision has all the appearance of a concession to public response. It is more than likely that early performances convinced Herbert that audiences could not be made to take Mona's act seriously and that the only way to save the scene (and the actor's ego) was to play it for the laughs that would inevitably come.

A very similar ambiguity of tone resulting from revisions of the original script occurs in the scene in which the boys read from the Shakespearian sonnet which gives the play its title. In the Stratford version, Smitty and Mona are left alone in the cell. Smitty makes an awkward attempt at seduction by boasting of his dominance over Rocky and Queenie and by promising Mona protection in exchange for sexual favours. When Mona tells him that physical intimacy between them would destroy rather than enrich their relationship because Smitty is simply trying to blot out the memory of a summer he spent with his girlfriend, Smitty turns on him in a fit of frustration and anger, then runs to the bars shouting to be let out. The remainder of the scene is as follows:

> **MONA.** There will be other summers — for you, Smitty.
> **SMITTY.** Go screw yourself!
> **MONA.** I wanted — too much — a friend. (SMITTY TURNS
>   SLOWLY, LOOKS AT MONA, AND FINALLY GOES QUIETLY
>   TO PLACE AN ARM ABOUT HIS SHOULDER)
> **SMITTY.** Between us, here, there can be no secrets — no silly barriers.
>   I need a friend. (THEY BECOME ENFOLDED IN EACH OTHER'S
>   ARMS) Do you know, "When in disgrace with fortune and men's
>   eyes?"
> **MONA.** I, all alone beweep my outcast state,
>   And trouble deaf heaven with my bootless cries,
>   And look upon myself, and curse my fate,
>   Wishing me like to one more rich in hope,
>   Featur'd like him, like him with friends possess'd,
>   Desiring this man's art, and that man's scope,
>   With what I most enjoy contented least;
>   Yet in these thoughts myself almost despising,
>   Haply I think on thee, and then my state
>   (Like to the lark at break of day arising
>   From sullen earth) sings hymns at heaven's gate;
>   For thy sweet love remembered such wealth brings,
>   That then I scorn to share [sic] my state with kings.
>   (SMITTY IS BRINGING HIS FACE CLOSE TO THE
>   MOTIONLESS ONE OF MONA'S WHEN QUEENIE AND
>   ROCKY ENTER....)   (typescript, Insert Act III, sc 2, p 4)

During rehearsals, all of the above dialogue with the exception of the poem, was eliminated and presumably some stage business introduced in its place to bridge the transition in feeling. The Shakespearian text seems originally to have been intended as a declaration of love on the part of Mona and as a counsel to rely on inner resources rather than on the opinion of the world. Far from being an invitation to bed, it seems to be a continuation of Mona's argument that physical intimacy between them would destroy their relationship. It is an affirmation of the superiority of "remembered," that is non-physical, love over depersonalized sex.

In the Grove Press edition of the play, the scene has been considerably altered. Smitty runs to the door of the cell and

> *Bangs wildly on the bars with his fists. Mona follows to stand*
> *behind Smitty, puts out a hand gently, but not touching him,*
> *then with difficulty, punches him on the shoulder. Smitty reacts*
> *violently, turning on Mona.*

> **MONA.** No! Wait a minute! *(Goes to Smitty's bunk, picks up a book and holds it out.)*
> Look—listen—you read it.
> *Smitty goes slowly to sit beside Mona and begins to read, clumsily, haltingly. They laugh, embarrassed, and continue to read until they are in a slight hysteria of laughter that causes them to break up and fall against each other. [By the end of the sonnet] Smitty and Mona are laughing, heads close together, when Queenie and Rocky enter.* (90)

The relationship of the two boys has been completely reversed in the published text. Whereas previously they had established some sort of communication through the sonnet, here they remain ironically detached from the sentiment in the poem. Furthermore, it is not at all clear what they are amused by. Is it Smitty's reading? The sonnet itself? Or is their laughter simply the result of released tension? Whatever the explanation, the shared experience does not seem to be of the kind that would either justify or explain Smitty's extreme reaction later in the scene. Once again Herbert's changes in the text seem less designed to clarify relationships than to avoid unsympathetic laughter.

One may legitimately wonder why, if he felt dissatisfied with their effect, the author did not remove the Shakespearian quotations altogether rather than try to pretend they were not to be taken seriously. The reason, I suspect, is that the passages are far too important thematically to be eliminated and much too specific to allow a satisfactory substitution. For both quotations express in different ways an ideal of sexless femininity which Herbert seems to be trying to embody in the character of Mona. Something of this quality is suggested by the description in the *dramatic personae*. According to that description, Mona

> seems to hang suspended between the sexes, neither boy nor woman. He is slender, narrow-shouldered, long-necked, long-legged, but never gauche or ungainly. He moves gracefully, but not self-consciously. His nature seems almost more feminine than effeminate because it is not mannerism that calls attention to an absence of masculinity so much as the sum of his appearance, lightness of movement, and gentleness of action. His effeminacy is not aggressive ... just exists. The face is responsible for his nickname of "Mona Lisa." Features are madonna-like, straight-nosed, patrician-mouthed and sad-eyed. Facial contour is oval and the expression enigmatic. (8)

It seems clear, however, that Herbert despaired of finding an actor who could project all this or that his ideas could be conveyed in a purely contemporary context. Accordingly he has attempted to associate with Mona other qualities suggested by the Shakespearian quotations—the charity and intelligence of Portia, the grace and wit of Shakespeare's boy actors, the bisexual love of the sonnets.

Mona thus functions in the play as a middle way between the extremes represented by Rocky and Queenie. Rocky is what might be called a caricature male. He prides himself on his aggressiveness and toughness. He is the Jungle King who rules by force, is suspicious of soft or gentle feelings, and is incapable of anything but stereotype thinking. Queenie, on the other hand, is the caricature female. He is completely self-centred and hyper-aware of his effect on others. He uses his attractiveness as a weapon rather than as a gift and has come to think of himself almost exclusively as a sexual object (or sexual manipulator). He is incapable of affection and achieves his ends by using a subtle and vicious intelligence. Mona could be said to be a synthesis of their opposites. He is not strong but he uses what strength he has to endure hardship rather than to inflict it. With his intelligence he seeks sympathy and understanding rather than control. Where Rocky and Queenie are animated by hatred and sex, Mona expresses forgiveness and love.

Fortune and Men's Eyes is therefore not about homosexuality in the tabloid sense suggested by the majority of critics and producers. Neither is it the story of the "depraving" of a heterosexual. It is, as Herbert himself summed it up, about "the cruelty and stupidity of force and violence" (qtd. in Daly). It asserts quite simply that the "feminine" qualities of passivity, gentleness, forgiveness, mercy and charity are superior to the "masculine" virtues of aggressiveness, violence, vindictiveness, competitiveness and lust. Furthermore, Herbert goes on to argue that this superiority is not the result of their respectable heritage but of their effectiveness. Resentment, violence, and hostility are not only bad in themselves, they are ultimately self-defeating.

In this context it is interesting to contrast the fates of Mona and Smitty. Mona is shown to be imprisoned in a double sense. Not only is he trapped behind the locks and bars of the reformatory, but he endures a more frightening imprisonment inside his own body. He has a physical appearance "*that arouses resentment at once in many people, men and women*" (8). He is in prison on a trumped up morality charge made plausible by that same appearance. Even his punishment at the end of the play is brought about in part by the guard's poorly masked hostility. In spite of the shackling effects of both fortune and men's eyes on Mona, he nevertheless manages to retain a sense of his own identity and a reasonable control over his own destiny. He does this, as he explains to Smitty, by separating his body and his mind. Thus Mona chooses the torture of gang rape above the greater torture that would result from his loss of self-respect. Like some of the inmates of the Nazi work camps described by Bruno Bettelheim, Mona has a clear conception of what he can give to the environment without compromising his inner self. He is able to recognize that in a threatening environment, "much that on the surface seems protective is actually self-destructive." Thus Mona never loses what Bettelheim calls "the last freedom"—the freedom "to decide how one wishes to think and feel about the conditions of one's life" (263–65).

Smitty, on the other hand, never makes the distinctions necessary to preserve his autonomy. His rise through the prison pecking order is accompanied by a gradual loss of real freedom as he acts more and more in response to external coercion or out of a sense of resentment. By fighting according to prison rules, Smitty ends up accepting prison values. At the opening of the drama he is described as "*a good-looking, clean-cut youth of clear intelligence and aged seventeen years .... The face is strong and masculine with enough sensitivity in feature and expression to soften the sharp outline*" (7). By the final curtain he is completely transformed. His face "*seems to be carved of stone, the mouth narrow, cruel and grim, the eyes corresponding slits of hatred. He speaks in a hoarse, ugly whisper ... [He has a] twisted smile that is somehow cold, sadistic and menacing*" (96). Smitty's transformation begins when he is forcibly raped by Rocky. He learns that social and sexual contacts in prison are devoid of human feeling and that it is impossible to relate to others on a personal level. As he sees that he is being treated not as an individual but as a sexual object, "a piece of goods," he feels that his sense of identity is threatened. It is partly to get a reaction to himself as a person and not simply as a body that he attempts to establish a more human and meaningful relationship with Mona. But Smitty's lack of self-knowledge together with his instinctive selfishness combine to frustrate this attempt. At least this is how I interpret the rather ambiguous scene between Mona and Smitty at the end of the play.

The encounter moves through three stages—an awkward seduction and rejection, an apparent reconciliation, and the final ironic reversal in which Mona is punished for Smitty's actions. If the significance of the Shakespearian sonnet is unclear, it seems to me that the incidents before and after it are fairly explicit. Mona's refusal to allow sexual intimacy with Smitty, although he himself desires it, is based on Mona's clear awareness of his own identity and his equally penetrating understanding of Smitty's real motives. Mona is convinced that Smitty is not interested in him as a person but only as a sexual convenience—a substitute for the girl that he remembers. Such an interest, Mona realizes, is not love but its opposite—indifference. For Mona to yield to Smitty's advances under those circumstances would be to accept Smitty's image of him—the "sight" of him that Smitty "throws back." Rather than surrender his conception of himself, Mona prefers to suffer.

Unlike Mona, Smitty has no conception of himself apart from his actions. Without Mona's strong sense of identity, Smitty is at the mercy of his instinctive responses—responses which in Smitty's case are almost invariably violent and self-protective. His characteristic manner of reacting to confusing or threatening situations is established in his scene with Mona. When he cannot understand the latter's refusal he turns on him in anger. When he is unwilling to admit his own motives he resorts to violence. This tendency to escape from painful introspection through anger or aggression is demonstrated again following the fight provoked by Queenie and Rocky. When he is questioned about his part in the affair, Smitty denies any responsibility and threatens the guard with blackmail. In his frustration, the guard orders Mona taken away to be whipped. Smitty realizes too late the consequences of his action and tries to admit that he "made the pass" but the guard does not or will not hear. In a fury of helplessness and guilt, Smitty turns his rage against the other boys whom he orders into the washroom.

In their haste to get out, the two bump into each other, ridiculous and clumsy in their new roles. Smitty laughs loudly, revealing a cruelty that fills the room with its sound. Suddenly his head turns in another direction as though just recalling something. He steals a quick look toward the shower room, then stealthily and lithely as a cat, he moves to the corner of the dorm where Mona had listened to the sound of Catsolino's beating. From an attitude of strained listening, Smitty suddenly contorts in pain as Mona had done before, but there is no sound from his distorted mouth. He seems to be whipped by unseen strokes of a lash, until he is spread-eagled across the upstage bars. When it seems he can bear no more, he covers his ears with both hands, stumbling blindly downstage. Standing thus, head and shoulders down, he rises slowly out of the hunched position to full height, hands lowering. His face now seems to be carved out of stone, the mouth narrow, cruel and grim, the eyes corresponding slits of hatred. He speaks in a hoarse, ugly whisper.

[**Smitty.**] I'm going to pay them back.

He then walks, almost casually down to Rocky's bunk where cigarettes, which we have not seen him use before, and a lighter, lie on the side table. He picks up a cigarette, lights it, then stretches out on Rocky's bed, torso upright against the back of it. Looking coolly out to the audience with a slight, twisted smile that is somehow cold, sadistic and menacing, he speaks his last line.

I'll pay you all back.

Light fades to black, and there is heard a final slam of a jail door. (96)

Smitty's final actions can be interpreted as revealing his ultimate loss of autonomy. To survive emotionally he must deny his own responsibility for Mona's suffering and project his guilt on to the guards and society. While such a course of action enables him to escape from the tortures of guilt, as Bruno Bettelheim has shown in his study of similar guilt reactions in the Nazi work camps, it also has the effect of hastening the deterioration of the individual prisoner's personality (192). By denying responsibility, Smitty denies his ability to act freely. By denying his freedom he, in fact, imprisons himself. The final slam of the offstage jail door aptly symbolizes Smitty's ultimate imprisonment—his surrender to the feelings of resentment and hatred which have been building up in him throughout the play and which in the end overwhelm him.

Fortune and Men's Eyes is not a great play. It is marred by moments of awkward dramaturgy and by an underlying sentimentality. But neither is it the cheap sensationalism that some tawdry productions have led many critics to suppose. Herbert in this work deals in a powerful way with issues of enduring interest and importance—issues that are by no means confined to our penal institutions. For as Herbert realizes, our prisons are not distorted versions of our society but reflections of it.

As I see it, in this small setting of a reform institution cell block the whole political situation is intensified. The same things are wrong with our society as a whole but they rise to crest in a cell block ... The manipulation and consuming of one human creature by another breaks through the surface. (qtd. Dempsey.)

Like *No Exit*, a play it resembles in other ways, *Fortune and Men's Eyes* uses confinement as a symbol of Man's existential condition to demonstrate the necessity for choosing freedom. [1]

(1972)

Note

¹ Because of the early date of publication, some of the information provided in the Works Cited is incomplete by MLA standards—Ed's note.

Works Cited

Barnes, Clive. "Mineo Stages 'Fortune and Men's Eyes': Revival of Play Heavy on Sensationalism." *New York Times* 23 October 1969, 55.

Bettelheim, Bruno. *The Informed Heart*, 1960. Glencoe Il: Free P, 1963.

Cohen, Nathan. "Prison Drama Softened." *Toronto Daily Star* 17 April 1967, night ed., sec. 2: 22.

————. "Fortune and Men's Eyes Rich in Reality." *Toronto Daily Star* 20 October 1967, daily ed., sec. 2: 23.

Daly, Margaret. Review of John Herbert, *Fortune and Men's Eyes. Star Weekly* (Toronto): 9 March 1968.

Dempsey, Lotta. "John Herbert." *Toronto Daily Star* 6 August 1966.

Herbert, John. *Fortune and Men's Eyes.* New York: Grove P, 1967.

————. *Fortune and Men's Eyes.* Unpublished typescript, 1967, Stratford Festival Archives. Stratford, Ontario.

————. *Variety* 8 October 1969 .

Mineo, Sal. *Variety* 29 October 1969.

Review, *Fortune and Men's Eyes.* London prod. *Variety* 13 November 1968.

Homo Creation: Towards
a Poetics of Gay Male Theatre [1]

by Robert Wallace

In an interview in *Mtl* magazine, Michel Tremblay stated that "*Moi j'ai découvert mon homosexualité très jeune. C'était un problème social plutôt que personnel.*" He went on to say that he believes "*À l'origine de mon talent d'écrivain, il y a un manque évident de communication. Si j'ai commencé à écrire à 12 ou 13 ans, c'est que je confiais à une page blanche ce que je n'étais pas capable de dire à mes parents*" ("Michel Tremblay"). Tremblay's comments in this and other interviews with the media,[2] along with those of his fellow gay playwrights, provide a valuable resource for people interested in determining the nature and effect of homosexuality in the theatre. I say this for two basic reasons: first, these comments document the playwright's acknowledgement that homosexuality has played a seminal role in the creation and development of his work; and second, they do this in public forums. Because such statements position the playwright as an openly gay man (in a predominantly heterosexual society), they irrevocably alter the context in which his work can be read. No longer is he (just) a playwright, a male playwright, or, in the case of Tremblay, a male Québécois playwright: he is a gay male Québécois playwright whose work can be read as a product of the complicated matrix that these words signify.

There are, of course, those who would argue that, in order to understand a text by Tremblay or any other playwright, it is unnecessary or even irrelevant to consider the author's sexuality; the text is a discrete object of meaning independent of the particularities of time, place, and biography. While any text can be read this way, the limitations of this approach have led, for the most part, to its displacement by more sophisticated critical theories arguing that comprehension of the sociohistorical circumstances that shape both the creation and the reception of the text are not only relevant but also necessary. In such approaches, meanings, as Catherine Belsey explains in *Critical Practice*, "circulate between text, ideology and reader"; "the work of criticism," she suggests, "is to release possible meanings" (144). The work of the critic "is to seek not the unity of the work, but the multiplicity and diversity of its possible meanings" (109).

Belsey's view of critical practice is helpful, for it allows that the experience of homosexuality is important to both the playwright and the audience. In her view, ideology is inscribed in the text by the social and historical contexts of both writer and reader, which, of course, include sexual positioning. And, while the meanings of a text are inevitably constructed by its readers,[3] these meanings are informed by the contexts in which readers approach the text. When these contexts include knowledge of the playwright's circumstances, including his homosexuality, as well as a recognition of the reader's own sexual positioning, which may or may not include homosexuality, a gay reading becomes a viable possibility in the plurality of meanings. In such a reading, homosexuality is a central component of the ideological interplay between writer, reader, and text, ideology being accepted in its general sense as the condition in which we experience the world. Surely this provides the foundation for a poetics of gay theatre, for it facilitates a way of reading or viewing the text that accommodates a way of seeing.

II

Tremblay is not alone in his public positioning as a homosexual writer. Many American playwrights since Tennessee Williams have openly acknowledged their homosexuality and its impact on their work—Edward Albee, Harvey Fierstein, and Lanford Wilson being three important examples. In English Canada, other playwrights—including John Herbert, John Palmer, David Demchuk, and, most loquaciously, Sky Gilbert, artistic director of Toronto's well-known gay and lesbian theatre, Buddies in Bad Times—have openly identified themselves as gay men in various media interviews. In Quebec, Tremblay has been joined by a host of other playwrights—René-Daniel Dubois, Normand Chaurette and Michel Marc Bouchard are the ones I will consider here—who, in the last ten years, have announced their homosexuality inside and outside their plays.

Such declarations both reflect and contribute to the changes in homosexual culture that have occurred rapidly since New York's Stonewall riot in 1969. [4] As sociologist Dennis Altman explains,

> The most striking change in the position of (male) homosexuals over the past decade is their visibility. There was, of course, a homosexual subculture in most large western cities as far back as the eighteenth century, and we are only now beginning to discover its history. But it was largely hidden, and elaborate subterfuge was employed in discussing it (as in Proust's À la recherche du temps perdu and Wilde's Picture of Dorian Gray). As late as the 1960s most homosexuals accepted the need to lead a double life, hiding their sexual and emotional feelings from all but a very few. [Mart Crowley's play] Boys in the Band summed up much of the male gay experience just at that point in time when things began to change. ("What Changed" 52) [5]

Charting this change in personal terms, Tremblay's statements about his homosexuality are remarkable, for they not only facilitate but also *validate* readings of his work from a sexual as well as a social perspective, a practice that he criticized in earlier interviews. As Jane Moss points out in her article "Sexual Games: Hypertheatricality and Homosexuality in Recent Quebec Plays," Tremblay "has insisted that the recurring figure of the transvestite homosexual [in his plays] is not drawn from personal experience, but is rather a cultural symbol of Quebec society"

(287).[6] That Tremblay can now explain why he felt it necessary to hide his sexuality until after his mother's death in 1963[7] reveals the effect that changes in gay visibility have had on one man. Today, Tremblay not only acknowledges the centrality of homosexuality to his plays and novels but also connects his early repression of his sexual self to the development of his creativity.[8]

No matter how we view Tremblay's analysis of the origins of creativity, we must accept his early feelings of loss and isolation as conducive to the sense of marginality that he eventually felt. He explains that, after his mother died, "*je suis allé vers une 'famille' qui accepterait ma marginalité*" ("Michel Tremblay"). Such feelings, of course, are common to many artists, not just to those who are gay;[9] this being the case, in order to argue convincingly for the possibility of a gay sensibility connected to feelings of marginality—a sensibility that would inform a gay poetics—it is essential that homosexuality, not marginality, be regarded as the determining characteristic. Discussing the possibility of a gay sensibility, Altman makes this clear: "what must be established is that there is some way in which being an outsider because of one's homosexuality is the source of a particular vision shared by other homosexuals despite differences in nationality, language, and class" (*Homosexualization* 149).

Invariably, any attempt to construct a gay poetics breaks down over conflicting attitudes to the idea of a gay sensibility and its relationship to homosexual identity. In his excellent book *Sexuality and Its Discontents: Meanings, Myths, and Modern Sexualities*, Jeffrey Weeks notes that

> The quest for identity has characterised the history of homosexuality during this century. The finding of it has invariably been described in terms of homing in on an ultimate self buried beneath the detritus of misinformation and prejudice. (188–89)

For many, the theory of an "ultimate self" rooted in an essential homosexuality is appealing, for it is conducive to the construction of gay communities outside of heterosexual culture, communities in which gay identity can be championed as a political cause and celebrated as a distinct lifestyle. There are those who oppose the theory, however, arguing that it not only contributes to the ghettoization of gay experience but also, more importantly, fails to interrogate prevailing attitudes of heterosexual inevitability by admitting to the idea of innate sexuality; they reject, in other words, the virtue of a fixed homosexual identity in favour of a definition of sexuality as a social construction, a definition in which homosexuality, like any other sexuality, is not so much a product of nature as of history.

In many ways, this debate parallels controversies surrounding *l'écriture féminine*, the movement in French feminism that can also be discussed as essentialist. Central to *l'écriture féminine* is the strategy of *jouissance*, in which the institutions and signifying practices of masculinist culture (for example, speech, writing, and image making) are subverted by the creation of texts that reject the rules and regularities of language formulated and used by men. In the theories of Luce Irigaray and Hélène Cixous, for example, women are accorded a sexuality that exists prior to, and in spite of, social experience, a sexuality that, when released into their writing, can reshape language and thus re-create the world, the total pleasure of which is *jouissance*. While such a theory is attractive to many feminists, it has important opponents, chiefly Julia Kristeva, the French philosopher for whom "femininity," if it has a definition at all, is "that which is marginalized by the patriarchal symbolic order" (qtd. in Moi 166). As Toril Moi elaborates in *Sexual/Textual Politics: Feminist Literary Theory*, "This relational 'definition' is as shifting as the various forms of patriarchy itself, and allows [Kristeva] to argue that men can also be constructed as marginal by the symbolic order..." (166). Indeed, for Kristeva, "woman" represents not so much a sex as an attitude that is typified by resistance to conventional culture and language. Without denying the important challenge that *l'écriture féminine* presents to the patriarchal order, Kristeva allows men access to its *jouissance*, [10] as her analyses of such artists as Louis-Ferdinand Celine, Antonin Artaud, and Lautréamont demonstrate. For her, what is important is that sexuality—and, in particular, femininity—be seen as a matter of positioning rather than essentiality.

Inasmuch as Kristeva's identification of femininity as a patriarchal construction is similar to Weeks's definition of homosexuality as a social invention, the two theorists are aligned: for both, sexuality is a historical creation inextricable from the symbolic order of masculinist culture. This alignment is important to the elaboration of a gay poetics, for it suggests that the marginality of gay artists is, in a sense, the same marginality accorded to femininity: the male homosexual, like a woman, is made marginal *because* of his sexual identity, which, like a woman's femininity is (arguably) a social construction. Even more useful is the idea that both homosexuality and femininity, in their similar social positioning, signify the limits of the symbolic order and thus share what Moi calls "the disconcerting properties of *all* frontiers" (167). (The fact that, until recently, homosexuality in men was often typified as femininity certainly supports this idea. [11]) Here, occupying what is perceived by masculinist culture as a borderline on chaos, women and gay men are vulnerable to similar vilification and romanticization, a fact that informs not only their perceptions of themselves and the world but also the ways in which they express these perceptions in their work—in a word, their ideology. Thus, Weeks, while he opposes the essentialist notion of a gay sensibility, must, like Kristeva, recognize the subversive potential of both *l'écriture féminine* and contemporary gay identities, which, "whether they are the out-growth of essential internal characteristics ... or of complex social-historic trans-formations ... are today as much *political* as personal or social identities." He explains:

> By its existence the new gay consciousness challenges the oppressive
> representations of homosexuality and underlines the possibilities for all
> of different ways of living sexuality. This is the challenge posed by the
> modern gay identity. It subverts the absolutism of the sexual tradition.
> (201)

This subversion is the true accomplishment of the gay movement during the last twenty years, and, inasmuch as gay theatre has deliberately asserted the presence of gay identities in our society, it has immeasurably augmented and sustained this subversion. As to the nature of the gay sensibility that differentiates gay male identities from those of women, this must be approached as a manifestation of situational experience, must, like homosexuality or femininity, be reconceived "as a historical, social, political, and economic phenomenon, as well as a psychological one" (Katz 7). Only then can the experience of a gay male in a masculinist culture be understood as genuinely different from that of a female or heterosexual male. As Robert Scholes points out, "Whatever experience is, it is not just a *construct* but something that *constructs*" (215), an idea that Jonathan Katz eloquently applies to the situation of gay men who have been politicized by the events of the last two decades:

> As we acted upon our society we acted upon ourselves; as we changed the world we changed our minds; sexual subversives, we overturned our psychic states. From a sense of our homosexuality as a personal and devastating fate, a private, secret shame, we moved with often dizzying speed to the consciousness of ourselves as members of an oppressed social group. As the personal and political came together in our lives, so it merged in our heads, and we came to see the previously hidden connections between our private lives and public selves. ... Starting with a sense of ourselves as characters in a closet drama, the passive victims of a family tragedy, we experienced ourselves as initiators and assertive actors in a movement for social change. (1–2)

III

> Past resistance has helped open up social spaces in which we have built our own lesbian and gay cultures. The contradiction between our experiences and heterosexual hegemony is a result of this historical and social process. This sense of "difference" is not natural: it has not been around for all time, nor will it last forever. It is itself a historical creation.
> —Gary William Kinsman (219)

If a connection between feminism and radical (*overt*) homosexuality is justified, then a term borrowed from *l'écriture feminine*—"a site of difference [12]—is perhaps appropriate in this discussion of the possibility of a gay poetics. But in using this term to discuss the nature and effect of recent plays by gay men, I wish to switch emphasis from the word "*différence*" to "site," a word equally, if not more, useful because it provides a pun that encapsulates my major points.

Initially, I am concerned with the literal site of theatrical practice, the stage(s) where plays are produced and, specifically, the stages in Quebec that have presented indigenous work during the last two decades. Much of the writing that has addressed the development of Canadian and Québécois theatre during this period has connected theatrical sites with the articulation of regional and local identities. Indeed, the pluralism of Canadian society that defines both the economic and imaginative geography of our theatre is institutionalized in the ad hoc network of regional theatres spanning the country, theatres that accept to varying degrees the responsibility of providing local playwrights and audiences with forums for their concerns. [13] In the most primary sense, these theatres function as sites of difference because they present playwrights whose regional voices belie a national one. Reading (or viewing) a text by Tremblay, for example, we look to it as a site of difference, as a locus of specific identity in the Canadian mosaic: quite simply, we read Tremblay's Montreal as different from George Walker's Toronto or Codco's Newfoundland. While some critics now use historical, political, and linguistic contexts to develop such readings, few utilize sexual ones even when they embrace biographical criticism, a fact that feminist critics have sought to redress. For a gay critic such as me, sexual context is important. My sexual positioning affects my responses to the texts that I read or see, just as I believe it affects the ways in which these texts are created on the page or in the theatre. This is particularly true of the texts by Quebec playwrights that I consider examples of gay theatre, for they utilize the theatrical site as more than the locus of regional difference. Bouchard, Chaurette, Dubois, and Tremblay eroticize the theatrical site through their homosexual gaze, [14] so that it becomes a site of sexual as well as geographical difference.

The eroticization of the theatrical site in contemporary Québécois theatre is one of the features that firmly distinguishes it from its English-Canadian counterpart. In part, this results from treating the physical and imagistic qualities of performance as equal in importance to the written text in the creation of the theatrical event—an attitude not as prevalent in the rest of the country as it is in Quebec. [15] But while we need not look to texts by gay male playwrights to see the extent to which the physicality of the performers' bodies imparts an obvious erotic signification to Québécois theatre (consider, for example, the work of Gilles Maheu, Jean Asselin, Pol Pelletier, and Danielle Trépanier), the repeated (visual) representation of homosexual desire in recent Québécois theatre marks the site as radical. As Moss explains, plays such as Bouchard's *La contre-nature de Chrysippe Tanguay, écologiste* (1983), Chaurette's *Provincetown Playhouse, juillet 1919, j'avais 19 ans* (1981), and Dubois's *26bis, impasse du colonel Foisy* (1982) do more than "theatricalize homosexual experience": they also homosexualize the theatre experience. As a result, "we see representations of sexual difference and desire that challenge traditional, socially constructed models of gender role behaviour" (287).

Utilizing my pun, I would state this another way: the gaze of the gay male playwright inscribes the performance with its specific vision of the world so that the theatrical site becomes a place of homosexual sight. The gay playwright, seeing differently, defines an ideal of beauty that decentres the aesthetic of the heterosexual male gaze. In this regard, Bouchard's *Les Feluettes, ou La répétition d'un drame romantique* is exemplary: the playwright creates homoerotic imagery that is both intellectually and emotionally powerful, a central expression of his gay sensibility. Moreover, he juxtaposes this imagery with other images in which homophobic institutions of the patriarchy are not only rejected but also destroyed. Specifically, the convent and the school—symbols of patriarchal control—are burned at strategic moments in the evolution of the love affair between Simon and Vallier, the Roberval schoolboys whose "burning" passion is given literal representation in André Brassard's innovative *mise-en-scène*. Watching this play, it is difficult to ignore the connection between the expression of homosexual desire and an attack on the patriarchy, for, as in contemporary society, they are constituted as one and the same.

It is easier to overlook another important aspect of *Les Feluettes*, however, one that also situates it as a work of gay sight, if only because it is assumed from the play's outset: homosexuality motivates the play. Here, as in the three plays mentioned earlier, homosexuality is not ancillary to the central concern, either as a situation that complicates something else (as in Jeanne-Mance Delisle's *Un oiseau vivant dans la guele*) or as a metaphor for another issue (as in René Gingras's *Syncope*): it is the controlling force of the play. As a result, these plays can be read as genuinely radical, for, as Derek Cohen and Richard Dyer explain in "The Politics of Gay Culture," it marks them as products of a gay sensibility that is definitely post-Stonewall:

> Whereas much conventional handling of homosexuality in the arts works by introducing gay characters or images into an otherwise heterosexual milieu, radical gay culture defines its own situation … Radical gay culture sees our *experiences* as being central. In a paradoxical sense, as one of the essentials of our experience as gays is our alienation from society, any culture which attempts in some "liberal" way to include us fails to portray our experiences accurately. That very assimilation, as if we were the same as everyone else but different in one minor way, shows a preoccupation with the surfaces, with the physicality of our homosexuality, and not the dynamics of our interaction with the rest of society. For if it were to recognise that interaction for what it is, an oppressive one, it would also have to recognise its own role in that oppression. (180–81)

That homosexuality is the controlling dramatic force is perhaps the reason why Bouchard accords the death of a gay man (Vallier) in *Les Feluettes* a spiritual beauty that ultimately prevents Simon from killing his enemy, Msgr Bilodeau, even when given the chance: it is important, in other words, to establish that homosexuality is not just a sexual orientation restricted to physical preference but also a full way of being, an experience of the world that can be spiritual as well as social. While we can argue that the play's valorization of death represents a romanticization of homosexual love typical of the masculinist cultural imperative, visual signifiers overcome such an argument: we see desire rather than death depicted on the stage. And, more importantly, these images of desire remain chaste at the end of the play because they must: in the social contexts of both Roberval, 1912, and Montreal, 1988, they are constructed as immoral by the family and the church; to remain true to this fact of gay experience, the consummation of homosexual desire must be presented in a context in which it is either denied or defeated. That Jean Bilodeau, the true instrument of Vallier's death, has become Msgr Bilodeau, the church's representative, in the exterior or framing play of 1952 allows for a reading of the text in line more with gay politics than with heterosexual romance. In such a reading, Bilodeau's repressed desire for Simon, a repression that Bouchard connects to the influence of the boy's homophobic mother, leads not only to his murder of Vallier but also to his religious vocation—facts that attack the morality of the church and suggest its complicity in despair, not salvation. Spiritual beauty is conceived and consummated in the secular passion of two young men for each other, not in the religious ecstasy of a martyr such as St. Sebastien for his God. Simon learns, as have many gay men in history, that death is the consequence of love: Vallier does not die because of love (for Simon) but because of Bilodeau's repressed desire. In this epoch of AIDS, this statement—dying because of loving—is both radical and courageous, possibly one that only a gay man would dare to make. [16]

Hence, media disclosures by and about Bouchard are, like those by and about other gay playwrights, of crucial importance: they locate both the author and his work inside a homosexual ideology, which the reader/viewer can (must?) use to construct meaning. Consider the following statement in *Sortie*, a gay magazine published in Montreal, by René-Richard Cyr, who played the young Bilodeau in *Les Feluettes*:

> *Bouchard est notre premier auteur à aborder l'homosexualité sans aucune revendication, sans aucun misérabilisme. Il ne veut pas faire de ses personnages des martyrs. Il fait référence à des choses qui se sont passées et il ne demande à personne de "s'apitoyer" sur le sort des gais. Il lève le voile sur les amours interdits, mais demande de les laisser vivre. C'est une vision nouvelle—et beaucoup plus saine—de l'homosexualité dans le théâtre québécois.* (qtd. in Crête 34)

Such statements allow me to add another level to my pun inasmuch as they *cite* the experience of the playwright as a gay man—cite in the sense of *quote*, which means to extract from sources other than the text and to do so with authority. Thus, the site/sight of difference is also a citing of difference. I'll be less cryptic: by sexualizing the theatrical site according to his own sight, the gay playwright cites his authority not simply as creator but as gay creator, or "homo creator," as *Mtl* magazine termed Tremblay ("Michel Tremblay"). And by both writing the play and defining a context through which it can be perceived, the homo creator contributes to its reception as a gay play, one that presents the male gaze from inside gay culture.

To the gay readers of *Sortie*, such quotations not only promote the dramatic production but also promise to validate their lives by authenticating their experience of the (masculinist) world. Gay men attend a gay play expecting confirmation of what we already know. In the case of *Les Feluettes*, most of us are not disappointed, Cyr makes clear: "*Le fait d'avoir tout à coup un gars en face de soi pour une scène d'amour nous rend heureux. On dirait qu'on peut alors exprimer tout ce qu'il y a d'étouffé en nous*" (qtd. in Crête 34). It is this confirmation of gay experience that makes *Les Feluettes* most completely a gay play—its expression of the fullness of homosexual desire in its interaction with heterosexual oppression. Altman, without calling such work radical, nevertheless identifies it as a product of the political consciousness of contemporary gay culture:

traditional gay culture (that is, the culture associated with homosexuals, largely male, since the consolidation of our status in the late nineteenth century) is associated with survival; contemporary gay culture (that is, post-Stonewall) is about self-affirmation and assertion. In both cases there is a need to express a sense of community with other homo-sexuals and a view of the world based on the particular experience of being homosexual; as that experience is altered by changing self-perception, so too gay culture itself changes. (*Homosexualization* 152)

IV

Vous savez que ma seule fonction ici est de draguer au nom de l'auteur?
—René-Daniel Dubois, *26bis* (48)

While it would be naïve to argue that Bouchard, Dubois, Chaurette and Tremblay proclaim their sexuality solely to establish homosexual authority in their work, the effect of their disclosures is much the same as if they did. Indeed, in the case of Dubois, this argument finds support in his disgruntlement with what he perceives as the refusal of the Quebec cultural establishment to consider his early plays in the context of a homosexual tradition, one in which he implies that he functions like a contemporary Jean Genet. [17] Certainly, the statements by both Chaurette and Dubois published in *Jeu* 32 locate the origins of particular plays in homosexual desire and situate these playwrights outside mainstream culture (see Lefebvre, Dubois, and Chaurette). Their statements valorize their status as different or other—marginal because of their homosexuality—and provide information for gay readings of their work.

Dubois's statement in *Jeu* is particularly interesting in this regard. An excerpt from *26bis*, the piece is an interruption of the play's central activity, a monologue by Madame, a character whom Dubois acknowledges in the "*première note*" to the published text "*a été écrit en l'imaginant joué par un interprète masculin*" (xxvi). When Madame voices this authorial interruption during the play, she is to become "*physiquement et emotionnellement, au 'neutre'*" (xxvi; emphasis added), as if the playwright somehow takes over "her" body at the expense of gender. Because Dubois's *Jeu* article is a response to questions about his creative process, this excerpt is particularly important: it uses the presence of the playwright in the play to explain his creativity, thereby reinforcing a reading in which the text is a revelation of the play-wright's own experience. Furthermore, because the content of the piece is overtly gay—the mental and physical process of "cruising" a young man named Joe Wyoming—it implies that the origin of the playwright's creativity lies in his gay experience: in this case, the urban sex hunt in which the object of desire is presented as a cowboy, a figure traditionally situated on the western frontier. This contemporary prototype of gay desire is also suggested in Dubois's more recent play, *Le troisième fils du professeur Yourolov*, in which the experience of cruising is again integrated into the text as one of the two male characters explains how he met the other (his lover) in an airport, a man who also has the code name "Cowboy."

Chaurette's introduction to the published text of *26bis* adds to the pattern of cross-referencing that runs through all of Dubois's work by using a quotation from yet another Dubois play, *Adieu, docteur Münch ...* , as its epigraph: "*Il doit venir un temps où la femme parle pour elle-même*" (*26bis* ix); and, indeed, that Chaurette wrote this introduction adds to the play's gay contextualization. While the fact that Chaurette's epigraph connects *26bis* to the female voice must surely be ironic inasmuch as Madame is a man in drag, the statement also links this (overtly) gay play to women in an interesting manner, for it recalls the idea that women, perceived as the limit of patriarchy's symbolic order, represent the frontier that separates man from the chaos of the unknown. Thus, the frontier aspect of Dubois's cruising implied by the use of cowboy names has a double signification: the western motif popular in many gay bars (and, by implication, gay fantasy), and the frontier of a "feminized" sexuality that Dubois occupies as a homosexual. That Dubois self-consciously uses a transvestite as his surrogate in this play is, therefore, of considerable significance and, no doubt, one of the reasons why Chaurette uses this quotation to begin his introduction. It allows the playwright to blur gender distinctions with Madame's visual appearance on the stage while transgressing linguistic conventions by having Madame confuse the masculine and feminine gender when she speaks French, a confusion that is exacerbated when she switches to English for her climactic speech. Near the beginning of this speech, she states, "Of course, my mother tongue is not English. You see, I just use it, hoping people will forget me, so totally absorbed in the words I'm looking for." Her strategy of self-effacement quickly becomes more obvious: "I will strip for you. ... First, my name. And then my silence. My silence, and this distance that lies between my name and my silence" (66). This distance, I suggest, is the play's subject and effect: the rupture of sexual signification that is conditioned by using the actor's body as a site of gender confusion. In this site, the binary nature of semiotic signification (male/female) is challenged both visually and aurally as it is in radical feminist writing. Hence, the fact that Dubois considers himself a contemporary Genet is most appropriate; as Cixous asserts, "Thus, under the name of Jean Genet, what is inscribed in the movement of a text which divides itself, breaks itself into bits, regroups itself, is an abundant, maternal, pederastic femininity" (qtd. in Furman 74); or could we say *jouissance*?

It is important to note here that Dubois's construction of his "princess" in *26bis* is radically different from the conventional use of transvestite characters in contemporary Québécois theatre; for instance, Tremblay's drag queens in both *La duchesse de Langeais* and *Hosanna* are never so self-referential as Madame, though they become so in *Damnée Manon, sacrée Sandra*.[18] While it can be argued that both the duchess and Hosanna draw attention to the theatre experience in which they (only) exist by their direct address to the audience, they do not demonstrate an awareness of their construction as characters in the manner of Madame, who repeatedly acknowledges Dubois as her creator. This also makes for radically different endings in *26bis* and *Hosanna* despite general structural similarities. While Tremblay is content to have

Claude and Raymond strip to signify their acceptance of themselves, Dubois has Madame acknowledge that such an act does little to overcome "her" position as a man:

> And then, when I will have taken off everything ... Everything ... Do you hear me? (*Effrayée*:) Do you hear what I am telling you? ... That I will stand completely naked in front of you! And that I already know that it will not be enough. That I will have to strip my skin as well. ... (*26bis* 67)

Madame recognizes that only when she has destroyed both the physical and linguistic signification of gender will the distance between "her" name and silence be effaced. Thus, her lines suggest the utopian position of Jacques Derrida, for whom the most radical challenge to patriarchy is the destruction of gender, particularly as it is represented in language. If such a destruction were possible, "the code of sexual marks would no longer be discriminating," not asexual but "beyond the opposition feminine/masculine, beyond bisexuality as well, beyond homosexuality and hetero-sexuality which come to the same thing" (qtd. in Furman 75).

While the desire to move beyond gender in order to attack masculinist culture is an understandable strategy of revolt, it necessarily defeats the notion of a gay sensibility that could inform a gay poetics, just as it deconstructs the essential femininity of *l'écriture féminine*; and, indeed, it is for this reason that a number of feminist critics have challenged Kristeva's use of *jouissance*. It is also for this reason, I suggest, that Dubois's self-conscious manipulation of intertextuality is so important. While self-referential intertextuality has become a convention of postmodern theatre, Dubois's use of the technique is specifically homosexual, relying for its effect on the audience's knowledge of what might be called a gay code of reference. In *26bis*, for example, Madame refers not only to Tennessee Williams, Marcel Proust, and Tadzio, the androgynous object of the gay male gaze in Thomas Mann's *Death in Venice*, but also, most importantly, to Tremblay's autobiographical play *Les anciennes odeurs*, in which an estranged gay couple confront their problems in a bourgeois situation that contrasts radically with Madame's more flamboyant lifestyle. "*Moi aussi*," Madame remarks, "*j'aime bien* Remember Me, *mais je ne suis vraiment à mon aise que dans le grave ... et puis il y a des limites au plagiat, non?*" (31).

In fact, there are few limits to plagiarism in the work of Dubois if we (mis)define the term as his use of gay themes and texts: this plagiarism, surely, allows him to locate himself in the gay cultural tradition, which, paradoxically, attacks patriarchy by using one of its models—that is, historical continuity. The idea that there is a gay history that is inscribed in the texts of particular writers is as recent as the concept of gay history itself. As Katz explains in *Gay American History: Lesbians and Gay Men in the U.S.A.*, "The common image of the homosexual has been a figure divorced from any temporal-social context" (6). For him, as for Weeks, homosexuality must be historicized so that its evolution as a social construction can be made clear. As he explains, "All homosexuality is situational, influenced and given meaning and character by its location in time and social space" (7). While this position denies an essential homosexuality, it nevertheless recognizes the historical existence of homosexuals, people whose experience of the world is different from that of heterosexual men and women because it is positioned differently. If we accept that the recovery of this history is as much the work of the gay artist and critic as of the historian, then the assertion of a gay cultural tradition in texts by gay men is both logical and constructive: it both reveals the history of homosexuality and expresses the experience of being gay, the ways in which living as a gay man differ from living as a woman, even when the two are viewed similarly by masculinist culture. Again, the site of difference becomes the place of the gay cite.

While the citation of gay culture in Dubois's texts is probably most understandable to a gay male audience, it is also accessible to others, as Moss indicates:

> Intertextuality reinforces the textuality of *26bis* with irony and humor. Some of the "*nombreuses disgressions*" are mock defenses of Dubois' earlier works and sardonic comments on his relationship to naturalism, melodrama, opera, and comedy of the absurd. While these reminders of the play's status as a theatrical text within a cultural tradition serve to demystify its own exaggerated theatricality, it should be noted that many of the intertextual allusions place *26bis* in the specific culture of homosexual art. (292)

For Moss, the most important consequence of such homosexual specificity is its challenge to heterosexual assumptions. For a gay male critic, however, the technique has a second, equally important effect: the continuation and articulation of the tradition to which I also belong. As another gay critic, Robert K. Martin, points out in *The Homosexual Tradition in American Poetry*, "This tradition has been formed partly out of a need for communication ... and partly out of a feeling of exclusion from the traditions of male heterosexual writing" (xv). He explains that "Most writing has traditionally been, heterosexual, not by declaration but by implication," noting that "Men and women are assumed to be heterosexual until proved otherwise." He continues:

> But for the homosexual man, who must repeatedly observe the differences between his own sexuality and the prevailing assumptions about "everyman," sexual definition is a matter of individual struggle and personal decision. ... It is not surprising, then, that gay [writers] have often used their [work] as, among other things, a forum for the exploration of sexuality and a way of speaking to the past and future, creating viable bonds. ... (xv–xvi)

Implicit in Martin's argument is the idea that citing the homosexual tradition creates bonds not only with other writers but also with the audience. Discussing a season of gay plays called "Homosexual Acts," which was programmed for the Almost Free Theatre in London, England, Dyer gives a personal illustration of this bond, explaining that

> A season that was so blatant in its declaration of the subject of the plays was bound to attract a high proportion of gays, and there was a chance

to feel, for that period at least, that there was something of a shared
positive experience among the audience. The characters in some of the
plays enjoined us to share their good feelings and their bad ones. As
I remember, some of the plays involved sequences where the characters
addressed either the audience as a whole or supposed members of it.
(Cohen and Dyer 181)

Because gay theatre such as this presents "bad" feelings or experiences—our victimization, for example—as well as "good," some critics have rejected it as unnecessarily
negative; in their view, gay theatre is destructive unless it explores gay experience in
positive terms. What these analyses overlook is the way in which gay theatre contributes to our "ability to see the social forces regulating our sexuality and identity"
(Kinsman 190). Quite simply, the presentation of only positive images in gay theatre
would negate our experience of the world.

V

The desire to expose or deconstruct the ways in which social institutions create and
regulate human activity is a strategy of postmodern cultural and critical practice;
obviously, it is useful, if not necessary, to the creation of gay theatre. This strategy possibly explains the self-referential nature of the Québécois texts that I am considering.
Moss summarizes the structural process common to these plays: "first experience is
de-realized and theatricalized and then the theatrical illusion is exposed. [The plays]
are theatrical games which point to their own artifice as they replace unsatisfying
reality with performance" (288). This process, of course, is neither new nor restricted
to Quebec, but its preponderance in Quebec dramaturgy since the early sixties is
another feature that distinguishes Québécois theatre from that of English Canada.
While the "unsatisfying reality" of Quebec's political and economic position in North
America during this period has certainly provided a consistent stimulus to self-
referentiality, for gay playwrights the equally unsatisfying oppression of homosexuality by church, state, and family must also be considered as its origin.
Unfortunately, as events of the last fifteen years have demonstrated, this oppression is
as prevalent in Quebec as it is elsewhere. [19]

In this context, the rejection of naturalism by gay Québécois playwrights can
be viewed as both a repudiation of the dominant theatrical mode of the American
cultural hegemony and a defiant assertion of difference. In Tremblay's work during
the seventies, for example, his experience of the street, be it rue Fabre or la Main, is
both derealized and marked as theatrical—that is, as extraordinary, not natural. This
theatricalization does more than represent the argot of a disenfranchised milieu,
however (the reason why most critics viewed Tremblay's earliest work as radical): it
reminds us that language is deliberately constructed by the playwright according to
his own experience, just as all other theatrical signifying systems are constructed and
controlled by his collaborators. Once we accept this premise—which is tantamount to
acknowledging the playwright's presence in his work—it is but a short step to viewing

such "hypertheatrical" plays (to use Moss's term) as part of the playwright's process of self-construction. It is an even shorter step to viewing the patently self-referential text—one that the playwright deliberately positions in the theatre by exposing its methods of illusion—as an extension of this process.

Certainly, this is true of the work of Chaurette who, in *Provincetown Playhouse*, for example, deconstructs the process by which a playwright uses the theatre both to create and reveal his own identity. Although the playwright in question initially appears to be a character—Charles Charles 38, a mental patient who nightly enacts an evening nineteen years earlier when a performance of one of his plays ended in murder—his double nature throughout the play (he both writes and performs his own drama) draws attention to the playwright's position in the act of performance and thereby emphasizes Chaurette's construction of the overall event. The theatricalization, in other words, exposes the constructed nature of the play and is thus doubly ironic. While this structuring resembles that of *Les Feluettes*, in which the elder Simon "writes" the story of his love affair with Vallier forty years earlier for the elucidation of Msgr Bilodeau (and the audience), the structure of *Provincetown Playhouse* is manipulated with greater conceptual sophistication, introducing Chaurette into the event and thus providing for a reading that includes consideration of his own subjectivity. As Paul Lefebvre points out in his introduction to the English translation of the play,

> The traditional play-within-a-play is here replaced by a constant simultaneity between the action of 1919 and that of 1938, which is a partial recreation of what happened nineteen years earlier. The double structure, masterminded by a dual character with a dual name, creates continual tension between reality and representation. (14–15)

Lefebvre's comment is useful because it reminds us that playwrights can never be truly absent from performances of their texts, even when they try to be. As Patrice Pavis has noted, "In the theatre, enunciating the text always means creating tension between it and what is shown on the stage… " (147). Rather than ignore this tension, Chaurette exploits it to his advantage, a fact evident from the beginning of *Provincetown Playhouse* when Charles Charles 38 describes the events that are about to happen:

> *Charles Charles, 38 ans, auteur dramatique et comédien, leur dire que je suis fou. Autrefois l'acteur l'un des plus prometteurs de la Nouvelle-Angleterre. Ma fin de carrière: l'une des plus prématurées et des plus éblouissantes de l'histoire. Depuis je suis seul. Depuis, c'est un one-man-show. Mesdames et Messieurs.* (26)

The constant interpolations of Charles Charles 38 emphasize that "*La pièce se passe dans la tête de l'auteur …*" (24), an ironic reminder to the reader of the published text of a fact that remains obvious in performance. Indeed, in the production by Les têtes heureuses in 1985, Larry Tremblay's scenography—in which the words of the text were written on giant sheets of newsprint that formed the walls of Charles Charles's cell—emphasized Chaurette's construction of the event: as each of the play's nineteen scenes finished, the text for the scene was torn from the set, a literal image of deconstruction that left the actor playing Charles Charles 38—Larry Tremblay—alone at the centre of a bare stage at the play's end. [20]

The distancing effect of such elaborate theatrics allows the audience to focus on production techniques more closely than usual. This has a political consequence in *Provincetown Playhouse* inasmuch as the play explores not only the lie of the theatre but, in the story that Charles Charles 38 narrates, other lies as well—lies that can be read as particularly important to Chaurette as a gay playwright. If we can believe Charles Charles 38 (who, after all, may be mad), he has been incarcerated because of the monstrous event that occurred nineteen years earlier: the murder of a child who was placed inside a prop (a sack) in the production of his play. The two actors, Alvan and Winslow, who unwittingly mistook the prop as fake and knifed the child to death, were subsequently found guilty of murder because they could not explain their where-abouts when the child was substituted for the cotton originally inside the sack. According to Charles Charles 38, however, the two young men were sleeping in each other's arms after making love, a fact that was not only intolerable to him as Winslow's lover of the time but also, of course, unacceptable to the society that put the boys on trial. Rather than admit to the homosexual activity that would have provided them with an alibi, Alvan and Winslow accept death sentences for the crime that Charles Charles 19 committed as an act of jealous vengeance.

Like Bilodeau in *Les Feluettes*, Charles Charles is thus responsible for the deaths in the play as well as his own mental anguish, but his torment—indeed, that of all the gay men in the play—is a direct result of the repressive social context in which homo-sexuality is constructed as both a sin and a crime. That Bilodeau and Charles Charles think they can manipulate existing social structures to serve their own ends is proven false: in the endings of both plays, the characters reject the very institutions—the church and the court—that they have used to control others. In this way, these plays reveal not only the oppression of gay men but also the self-oppression that can result when we internalize the prevailing attitudes of masculinist culture towards homo-sexual behaviour. [21] Alone in his cell at the end of the play, Charles Charles 38 appears to realize this; like Bilodeau, he has come to recognize his betrayal of the social connection that he holds with the men whom he has loved, crying "*qu'est-ce que je suis, moi, si t'es pas là … ? Et Winslow, et Alvan … hé! revenez …*" (113). But just as Simon turns his back on Bilodeau, so Alvan and Winslow no longer exist for Charles Charles 38, except as memories. Both he and Bilodeau can do nothing but turn to the audience at this point for help, an act that Charles Charles 38 acknowledges that he undertakes every night of his performance. It is this undertaking that makes his direct address a political as well as a theatrical act. In this play, like the others that I have discussed, the central character ends by seeking the audience's complicity in forging the future, leaving the audience responsible for his existence in both the good and bad sense.

In theoretical terms, this gesture suggests not only the interdependency of the gay playwright's self-construction and the self-referential structuring of his work but also, finally, his dependency on the audience for the construction of the meanings in which both he and his texts exist—his social as well as aesthetic reality. The success of these Québécois plays suggests that an audience interested in meeting this challenge exists, at least in Quebec. But only when this audience becomes as self-aware and courageous as these authors are—outside as well as inside the theatre—will the site of difference become a place of social as well as artistic transformation.

(1994)

Notes

[1] This essay originated as a ten-page response to three papers delivered at a session of the Conference of the Association for Canadian Studies in the United States held in Montreal in October 1987. The following January, when I was asked to contribute an essay on homosexuality and Québécois theatre to *Jeu*, a widely read and highly regarded Québécois theatre journal, I expanded my conference response by focusing more specifically on Jane Moss's paper "Sexual Games: Hypertheatricality and Homosexuality in Recent Quebec Plays," which she had presented during the session and subsequently published in the *American Review of Canadian Studies*. My ensuing article, "Homo Creation," though completed early in 1988 and translated into French by Jean Cléo Godin soon after, did not appear in *Jeu* until 1990, by which time the journal's editorial collective had convened a series of seminars in which Québécois theatre practitioners and critics had responded to ideas and issues raised by my article, many of which the collective had considered controversial. The substance of these responses is inscribed in the articles published along with my paper in *Jeu* 54 (1990) and provides a telling summary of Québécois critical opinion on the topic of homosexuality and Québécois theatre at the end of the 1980s.

My article, published here [in *Essays on Canadian Writing* 54 (1994)] for the first time in English, remains basically unaltered since its publication in French and should be approached as a product of my thinking in 1988. Then, as an "immigrant" to Montreal from Toronto, I was intrigued not only by Québécois theatre but also by the ideas of French feminists, whose notions of writing the body perhaps held greater currency then among Québécois artists and academics than they do now. Were I to write this essay today, I would theorize my position differently, relying more heavily on constructionist arguments to problematize more completely the idea of "a gay sensibility" and integrating ideas on the performance of gender and sexuality that have circulated in a variety of important works published since my essay's inception—notably, *Diana Fuss's Essentially*

Speaking: Feminism, Nature and Difference, Judith P. Butler's *Gender Trouble: Feminism and the Subversion of Identity,* Kaja Silverman's *Male Subjectivity at the Margins,* and Marjorie Garber's *Vested Interests: Cross-Dressing and Cultural Anxiety.* For some of my recent (published) thoughts on the construction and performance of gay (male) subjectivities by writers and readers of plays, see "Making Out Positions."

    I should also note that, because of the date of its writing, this essay includes references to "recent" publications that date from 1987 and, in the case of *Mtl* and *Sortie,* no longer exist. The demise of *Sortie* is particularly lamentable; a glossy magazine serving Montreal's gay and lesbian communities with monthly coverage of news and events, it invariably featured useful articles on prominent Québécois artists.

2   See, for example, Khalo.

3   Obviously, I am subscribing here to the idea that textual meaning is a product of a reader's activity, an idea that various critical theorists now hold. Terry Eagleton, for example, asserts that "All literary works … are 'rewritten,' if only unconsciously, by the societies which read them; indeed there is no reading of a work which is not also a 're-writing'" (12).

4   On 27 June 1969, New York City police attempted to make a routine raid on a Greenwich Village gay bar, the Stonewall Inn. They were surprised when patrons of the bar resisted this harassment by fighting back. Over the next couple of days, the protest grew through the distribution of leaflets and demonstrations in the streets. This event is widely considered to mark the birth of the contemporary gay liberation movement in North America.

5   For a useful discussion of the "subterfuge" employed by gay playwrights, and the breakthroughs made in the sixties and early seventies, see Jackson.

6   It is interesting that David Mole, a Toronto gay critic, in reviewing the English-Canadian production of Tremblay's *Hosanna* in 1977, concluded by saying: "As far as I can see, this play has nothing whatever to do with the struggle of the people of Quebec for their national rights" (110).

7   C.V. – *Quand as-tu arrêté de te cacher?*
    M.T. – *Ben … j'ai probablement inconsciemment attendu que ma mère meure.*
    C.V. – *Tu ne lui as jamais dit.*
    M.T. – *Non. Ni à mon père. Tant que je suis resté avec mes amis d'enfance. On n'en parlait pas. C'est quand j'ai changé de gang—je suis allé vers une "famille" qui accepterait ma marginalité.* ("Michel Tremblay")

8   In an interview quoted by Marianne Ackerman in *Saturday Night,* Tremblay states: "I really think a person becomes an artist, and a writer in particular, when there is a communication problem in the family. There were so many things I couldn't tell my mother, father, brothers. Any talent comes from suffering, or something missing in childhood" (43).

[9] Indeed, one of the factors central to the development of a strong Québécois cultural identity in the last twenty years has been Quebec's marginality to both English Canada and the United States, a marginality that many Québécois artists have exploited as an overt strategy of cultural survival.

[10] In his introduction to Kristeva's *Desire in Language: A Semiotic Approach to Literature and Art,* Leon S. Roudiez discusses the *totality* of enjoyment that distinguishes Kristeva's use of the word from its everyday usage: "'*jouissance*' is sexual, spiritual, physical, conceptual at one and the same time" (16).

[11] "Camp," the characteristic style and humour of homosexual subcultures until the seventies, showed what Richard Dyer calls "a great sensitivity to gender roles as roles and a refusal to take the trappings of femininity too seriously" (qtd. in Weeks 190). Weeks goes on to note that "In recent years we have seen a sharp break with this historic identification of male homosexuality and effeminacy," and he suggests that "There is some evidence that the [new] macho-style in male gays *arouses* more hostility than effeminacy in men. It gnaws at the roots of a male heterosexual identity" (191).

[12] The term plays upon the word *différence* and has evolved particularly in relation to *l'écriture féminine.* As Ann Rosalind Jones points out, " … Irigaray and Cixous … emphasize that women, historically limited to being sexual objects for men (virgins or prostitutes, wives or mothers), have been prevented from expressing their sexuality in itself or for themselves. If they can do this, and if they can speak about it in the new languages it calls for, they will establish a point of view (a site of *différence*) from which phallogocentric concepts and controls can be seen through and taken apart, not only in theory but also in practice" (362).

[13] See Czarnecki.

[14] Inasmuch as I use this word to refer to the act of seeing, it is integrally connected to my idea of the gay sensibility. The gaze constitutes not only *what* is seen but also *how* it is seen.

[15] See Wallace, "Towards an Understanding."

[16] We can only speculate about the impact of AIDS on the gay imagination. The linkage of homosexuality and death in this play and other recent works by gay playwrights (for example, Gilbert's *Theatrelife: A Modern Melodrama* or Fierstein's *Safe Sex*), however, suggests the indelible impact of the problem on the gay writer. That a gay man may die of love is now a literal possibility; the spiritual elevation of a gay man's death because of love—and the refusal to grant death to one unworthy of such elevation—is thus logical.

[17] Dubois says: "*Il y a des producteurs qui se flattent la bedaine en montant du Genet, parfois sans même comprendre de quoi ça parle, et qui, s'ils se trouvaient devant un Genet d'ici et d'aujourd'hui, lui feraient subir un sort pire que celui qu'on a fait subir au premier du nom en France*" ("Vivre" 12).

[18] *Damnée Manon, sacrée Sandra* (1977) concludes by having the characters acknowledge themselves as creations of "Michel" (65). For me, this authorial intrusion is much more significant than Tremblay's use of Claude to question the ethics and responsibilities of the playwright in *Le vrai monde?* (1987), considered by many to be his most self-referential work. Certainly, Tremblay's "appearance" in the earlier play is more directly connected to the public construction of his homosexual identity.

[19] Montreal police throughout the seventies conducted raids on gay bars and steam-baths, and gay organizations experienced persistent problems with obtaining liquor licences for community events. Official harassment reached a peak on 22 October 1977 when police raided Truxx, a local gay bar, and arrested 146 people who were charged with being found-ins in a common bawdy house. A few weeks later, perhaps embarrassed by the outrage generated by this police action (at that time the largest mass arrest in Canada since the imposition of the War Measures Act seven years earlier), the Quebec government quietly altered the province's human rights legislation to prohibit discrimination on the basis of sexual orientation. Although this change made Quebec the first political jurisdiction in Canada to afford protection to its gay citizens, it clearly did not eliminate the homophobia that still infects Québécois culture.

[20] Indeed, this production was conceived as a one-man show in which Larry Tremblay played not only Charles Charles at both ages but also Alvan and Winslow—a device that made the production appear even more the product of one imagination.

[21] For a useful discussion of this idea, see Hodges and Hutter.

Works Cited

Ackerman, Marianne. "Sweet Jesus! Who's That, Ma?" *Saturday Night* June 1988: 40–47.

Altman, Dennis. *The Homosexualization of America: The Americanization of the Homosexual.* New York: St. Martin's, 1982.

———. "What Changed in the Seventies?" Gay Left 52–63.

Belsey, Catherine. *Critical Practice.* London: Methuen, 1980.

Bouchard, Michel Marc. *Les Feluettes, ou La répétition d'un drame romantique.* Montréal: Leméac, 1987.

Chaurette, Normand. Introduction. *Adieu, docteur Münch ....* By René-Daniel Dubois. Montréal: Leméac, 1982. i–xxv.

———. *Provincetown Playhouse, juillet 1919, j'avais 19 ans.* Montréal: Leméac, 1981.

Cohen, Derek, and Richard Dyer. "The Politics of Gay Culture." Gay Left 172–86.

Crête, Jean-Pierre. "Un homme de théâtre en pleine ascension." *Sortie* November 1987: 33–35.

Czarnecki, Mark. "The Regional Theatre System." *Contemporary Canadian Theatre: New World Visions.* Ed. Anton Wagner. Toronto: Simon & Pierre, 1985. 35–48.

Dubois, René-Daniel. *26bis, impasse du colonel Foisy.* Montréal: Leméac, 1982.

———. "Vivre de sa plume au Québec: Entrevue avec René-Daniel Dubois." *Lettres québécoises* 43 (1986): 10–13.

Eagleton, Terry. *Literary Theory: An Introduction.* Minneapolis: U of Minnesota P, 1983.

Furman, Nelly. "The Politics of Language: Beyond the Gender Principle?" *Making a Difference: Feminist Literary Criticism.* Ed. Gayle Greene and Coppéia Kahn. London: Methuen, 1985. 59–79.

Gay Left Collective, ed. *Homosexuality: Power and Politics.* London: Alison, 1980.

Hodges, Andrew, and David Hutter. *With Downcast Gays: Aspects of Homosexual Self-Oppression.* Toronto: Pink Triangle, 1977.

Jackson, Graham. "The Theatre of Implication." *Canadian Theatre Review* 12 (1976): 34–41.

Jones, Ann Rosalind. "Writing the Body: Toward an Understanding of l'Écriture Féminine." *The New Feminist Criticism: Essays on Women, Literature, and Theory.* Ed. Elaine Showalter. New York: Pantheon, 1985. 361–77.

Katz, Jonathan. *Gay American History: Lesbians and Gay Men in the U.S.A.* New York: Crowell, 1976.

Khalo, Michel. "Michel Tremblay, ou l'art de la pudeur." *Fugues* January 1988: 63–64.

Kinsman, Gary William. *The Regulation of Desire: Sexuality in Canada.* Montreal: Black Rose, 1987.

Lefebvre, Paul. Introduction. Trans. Barbara Kerslake. *Quebec Voices: Three Plays.* Ed. Robert Wallace. Toronto: Coach House, 1986. 9–16.

———, René-Daniel Dubois, and Normand Chaurette. "Chaurette et Dubois écrivent." *Jeu* 32 (1984): 75–86.

Martin, Robert K. *The Homosexual Tradition in American Poetry.* Austin: U of Texas P, 1979.

Moi, Toril. *Sexual/Textual Politics: Feminist Literary Theory.* London: Methuen, 1985.

Mole, David. "*Hosanna*: A Review of Michel Tremblay's Play." *Flaunting It! A Decade of Gay Journalism from The Body Politic.* Ed Jackson and Stan Persky. Vancouver: New Star; Toronto: Pink Triangle, 1982. 109–10.

Moss, Jane. "Sexual Games: Hypertheatricality and Homosexuality in Recent Quebec Plays." *American Review of Canadian Studies* 17 (1987): 287–96.

Pavis, Patrice. *Languages of the Stage: Essays in the Semiology of the Theatre.* New York: Performing Arts, 1982.

Roudiez, Leon S. Introduction. *Desire in Language: A Semiotic Approach to Literature and Art.* By Julia Kristeva. New York: Columbia UP, 1980. 1–20.

Scholes, Robert. "Reading Like a Man." *Men in Feminism.* Ed. Alice Jardine and Paul Smith. New York: Methuen, 1987. 204–18.

Tremblay, Michel. *Damnée Manon, sacrée Sandra.* Montréal: Leméac, 1977.

———. "Michel Tremblay: Homo creator." With Carole Vallières. *Mtl* November 1987: 19.

Wallace, Robert. "Making Out Positions." Introduction. *Making, Out: Plays by Gay Men.* Toronto: Coach House, 1992. 11–40.

———. "Towards an Understanding of Theatrical Difference." *Canadian Theatre Review* 55 (1988): 5–14.

Weeks, Jeffrey. *Sexuality and Its Discontents: Meanings, Myths, and Modern Sexualities.* London: Routledge, 1985.

"That's Why I Go to the Gym":
Sexual Identity and the
Body of the Male Performer

by Reid Gilbert

It becomes impossible, in Judith Butler's words, "to separate our 'gender' from the political and cultural intersections in which it is invariably produced and maintained" (3). "Gender," suggests Butler, "is the repeated stylization of the body, a set of repeated acts within a highly rigid regulatory frame that congeal over time to produce the appearance of substance, of a natural sort of being" (33).

Such a definition of gender approaches a definition of theatre itself and suggests that the portrayal of gender on stage is not only mimetic, but, indeed, part of the collective cultural description of sexual identity; if theatre is myth-making (as it has traditionally been held to be) it is also gender-making, and the making occurs first at the level of the body. If theatre is itself an act of desire, then the object of the audience's desire is, at base, the bodies of the actors, which are also the essential sites of gender identity. Jan Kott has called the actor's body "the basic [theatrical] icon" (19), and others have agreed that it is at least the "locus of multiple interconnecting sign-systems" (Aston and Savona 105). The actor's body, then, would appear immediately to announce biological gender, especially in theatre performances where the body is seen naked. But if the body is a tool of the actor, its biological configuration may, indeed, be as much a prop for the establishment of one of a set of available sexual identities as are the clothes and mannerisms in which it dresses itself, the vocalizations it produces, and the actions it is assigned.[1] In such a viewing of the actor's body as sign-vehicle for established or resistant sexualities—or for the construction of the very idea of sexual differentiation—a polarity emerges between the assumption of the body as a mere psychic space upon which an iconography may be written and as a physical being who feels the role and feels it within his or her "skin."

Ed Cohen points out that "while Butler assiduously abjures any recourse to an essentializing model of gender that is predicated on the ontological or metaphysical priority of the body," her analysis does so "precisely by invoking a parallel somatic idealization" (82). For Butler, "the body is not a 'being' but a variable boundary, a surface whose permeability is politically regulated, a signifying practice within a cultural field of gender hierarchy and compulsory heterosexuality" (139). Cohen finds much that is "congenial" (82) in Butler's analysis, but worries that her "problematic"—relying, as it does on a Freudian paradigm and on Lacan's "disso[lution of] the (e)motions of embodied experience in the diaspora of language"—threatens to "evacuate ... (e)motion from the 'space' of its inquiry," eliding somatic individuation (84). Looking for movements for political change, Cohen points out that "idealizing the 'difference' that 'the body' makes to 'identity' politics" imposes a new set of limitations and may erase the collective feeling that urges those engaged in resistance to "put their bodies on the line" (84). If Cohen is right, it is literally the bodies of the actors that must be put on the line. Jill Dolan also points out that identity is a felt experience, arguing that "As much as she might empathize or do visualization exercises to project herself into a lesbian role, a heterosexual woman will never know, in her body, what it feels like to be queer in a homophobic culture. She has not developed the survival instincts that would teach her the signals lesbians use to break the code, to signify and to read what dominant representations suppress" (158). [2]

To be able to "get under the skin," in these terms, does not signify skill in realist performance. Indeed, realism may act against the discovery of sexual identity by substituting a set of available *personae* approved by the dominant and—important in this context—patriarchal culture; the plays I will be discussing consistently offer such *personae*. Rather, to "get under the skin" is to achieve a vital identity with a particular projection of gender object or—more powerfully—a sharing of that object.

Lacan has suggested (in *Seminar I*) that at the centre of the unconscious being is the *je*, devoid of form and object; we seek through fantasy to project onto a *moi* a "fictive object for a fundamentally aobjectal desire" (Silverman 4). At base, we project our own bodily image as what Kaja Silverman calls the "first and most important of all ... objects ... The self, in other words, fills the void at the centre of subjectivity with an illusory plenitude" (5). Jean Laplanche and J.-B. Pontalis suggest that through this fantasmatic the *je* acts out a script "of organized scenes which are capable of dramatization, generally 'in a visual form' and in which 'the subject is [itself] invariably present'" (*The Language of Psycho-Analysis* 318 qtd. in Silverman 5). As Silverman sums up the concept, "it is only in the guise of the ego that the subject can lay claim to a 'presence' ... ; the *mise-en-scène* of desire can only be staged ... by drawing upon the images through which the self is constituted" (5). The body of the actor must, then, convey not only biological differentiation but formulations of sexual identity by which the inner subject seeks to objectify itself in order to behold itself. The audience participates with the ego of the character (and, perhaps, of the actor or director) to achieve a sense of "being there," becoming a collective ego engaged in a representation, or a dream, by which it fills the void in each spectator's *je* by substituting a sort of collective *nous* (my term) which parallels the character's *moi*—and is just as illusory. In the process, the body of the actor projects this object into reality so that the spectators can also view "him" or "her." In plays like Robert Lepage's *Polygraph*, Terrence McNally's *Lips Together, Teeth Apart*, and David Drake's *The Night Larry Kramer Kissed Me* this process of psychic projection also functions within a collective psychoanalysis.

The force with which the collective will-to-exist resists or impels the fictionalization of the dramatic *moi* is more keenly felt, and the dramatic *persona* of the *moi* more powerfully drawn, in spectatorial processes at either extreme of experience, when the dramatic *moi* is either less similar to each individual spectator's pre-existing, individual *moi* (as in a heterosexual audience viewing *The Night Larry Kramer Kissed Me*, where the *moi* appears, in fact, *comme eux* [my term]) or when the *moi* is more similar to each spectator's previously established *moi* (as in a male, white, urban homosexual audience viewing the same play, where the *moi* feels like "*nous-mêmes*" [my term]). When the audience is mixed or when the images of the sexual *moi* are various within the production—when the "writings" are "many," as in *Polygraph*—complex processes of projection occur in which the audience is offered a set of objects upon which to gaze and from which to choose and is, in the process, rendered the subject of its own analysis. As Michael J. Sidnell points out, we see in *Polygraph* not only the lie detector machine in operation but "also the relation it helps constitute between its operator and its subject. And the play itself, as its title declares, is another such machine" (47). The apparati of this machine are the bodies of the actors: sinuously entering the psychic field; nakedly exposing their vulnerability and their dispassionate voyeurism; displaying their sexuality, tightly denying their sexuality; dominant, abused, reduced to objects; dressed and undressed: collectively seeking a *moi* to view in the literal and psychological mirrors held up to the audience.

In *Polygraph*[3] notions of guilt and punishment are bound up in notions of sexual desire and identity. By presenting two men, one gay and one straight, the play immediately invites comparison between these two identities, self-images which in post-industrial societies have become less descriptors of sexual preference than categories or "lifestyles" (itself a term which implies the adoption of a fictive self-contained in a series of indices and postures). In the co-production by Pink Ink Theatre and Théâtre la Seizième in Vancouver, this comparison was exaggerated by indexing the homosexual waiter, François, in 501 jeans, white tee-shirt, and leather jacket (the uniform of the urban, homosexual man of the period, and a strong marker of the masculine in mainstream iconography) and the criminologist, David, in jacket, tie, and trench coat (the uniform of the urban, heterosexual man and a sign of the detective, the spy, the dangerous agent of the establishment). That the criminologist speaks with a German accent, attends a conference in East Berlin, and has memories of a lost love in Germany adds another intertext, inscribing him under the signs of the KGB, the Nazi, the torturer—codes essential to the hermeneutic of the police investigation, but, more important, metaphoric of the splitting of personality under stress and the central question of what constitutes a true self, of what is to be found on the other side of "The wall which separates truth from fabrication [and is] sometimes paper-thin" (63).

David's marked self-control, even when confronted by the admission of his lover, Lucie, that she has also slept with François, underlines the masculine ideal of emotional stability but betrays the emptiness of this pose. Early in their relationship, Lucie urges David to cross over the wall into the theatrical by putting drops in his eyes to make him cry. The chemicals work best when the subject also recalls a sad memory, just as the polygraph works best when the subject believes "the mystique" of its power to disclose (64). David's memories of Anna's love letter lead him to tears—

or the drops do—but he denies the emotion: "This stuff really burns ... it's like getting soap in your eyes" (56). His reading in German while he cries, in counterpoint to the English subtitle, "I can see it in your eyes," brings about the intersection of a series of signifiers of his character and a series of inscriptions of the male as contained, in denial, fluent in the languages of international power but unable to feel. As his affair with Lucie develops, David is finally able to "understand" her urging, "if you want to cry, cry. If you want to hold me, hold me," and to "accept" emotion (63). But he is able to do so only after he has measured himself against François and satisfied himself that to feel love is not to picture himself as the despised Other, the homosexual:

> **Lucie.** Did you hear me? I, I made love with François. (*She is both compassionate for and irritated by David's non-reaction*) Say, do something. (*David pretends to have something in his eye; he washes it out in the basin.*) Can't you allow yourself your own emotions?
> **David.** What do you want me to do? You want me to be jealous of a homosexual? (63)

David's incredulity underscores an axiom maintained by many men—that the straight man is superior to the homosexual male, in that the homosexual occupies a position closer to the female, and therefore further from the apex of power. The question bespeaks a deeply held belief—a belief the dominant culture must maintain in order to frame its definitions of sexual identity—that the homosexual lacks, and hence must be an object of scorn rather than envy. As we shall see, this attitude is so deeply structured in a male view of self that it is also exhibited by homosexuals. It is this double viewing of self as object of desire and of scorn that creates much of the confusion in male subjectivity.

In Terrence McNally's *Lips Together, Teeth Apart,*[4] two straight men spar through a weekend spent with their wives at the Fire Island beach house of a gay brother-in-law. Ostensibly a play about AIDS, the piece also exhibits another collective self-analysis as each man reflects on his relationship with his own wife, with the other women (sister or lover) and with the unseen but always felt presence of house parties of gay men offstage on either side of the beach house. The two men prefer to ignore their neighbours, but one of the women repeatedly engages them in conversations of which we hear only her side, and the other woman projects onto them—and onto a solitary swimmer bent on suicide—the love, guilt and fear prompted by her brother's illness and death. Invisible, the groups of gay men become a very real presence on stage as they offer what each actor rejects and yet, somehow, craves. And it is in the unseen bodies of these men that the psychoanalysis situates itself as the four antagonists seek a reflection of self to clothe each unsatisfied *je*. For the garrulous wife, the healthy, muscled bodies of the men next door suggest an image of male beauty which her own husband does not provide. "Don't straight men think we have eyes?" she asks (32). For the introspective wife, the still healthy body of the swimmer suggests a horrible irony as he swims to his death, perhaps to escape a ravaging illness. For the two men, the bodies represent physical competition, objects to envy, but only if they are regarded; for most of the play the two refuse to look next door. In a central scene, however, one brother-in-law takes a shower on the elaborately naturalistic stage and the other, bringing him a towel, remarks that he didn't know his brother-in-law had a mole, admitting (in a very off-hand manner) that he has viewed the naked body (63). In the same scene (64–65), the sister tells her brother that she hasn't seen him naked since he was a boy and shamelessly insists that he open the shower door to her gaze (playing off the audience's desire or embarrassment that his nakedness might actually be shown). When he finally relents, opening the door outward, across stage, so the audience cannot see him and investing his sister as audience agent, she remarks that he is much better endowed than her husband, complimenting him by attacking the husband who has recently rejected her. The audience does not view his genitals, though it has seen him washing his torso and legs. It has, however, been confirmed that he is an appropriate fantasmatic heterosexual *moi* with which to identify or to desire; indeed, he has been assigned the synecdochal sign without risk that the actor may not live up to it. Culturally imbricated signifiers do not rely on physical reality; in fact, they prefer to avoid it. The audience is, after all, seeking to view itself in a literary and iconic mirror, not a real one.[5]

Now, a complex quadrangle is set up: the wife who finds the gay men beautiful has indexed her brother as more "male" than her husband, who himself has admitted looking at the brother, but who immediately attacks the neighbours verbally. Gradations of male power present themselves in the forms of these potential bodies: the naked brother who emerges at the top of the pyramid is, as a result, freed to be tender (for a moment)—just as David is freed to cry when he apologizes for his defamation of François. Clearly marked as clean, male, and potent,[6] he now attempts a reconciliation with the brother-in-law with whom he has been fighting all day. More important, he also narrates, with considerable surprise at his own lack of revulsion, a scene of male lovemaking offstage. He remarks that he hears sexual murmurings, but no statement of emotion and then, as a number of strands come together in simultaneous dialogue on stage, he "hears" and repeats the climax of the sexual encounter offstage: "I love you" (86). In one of the few understated moments in this rather heavy-handed play, this heterosexual man actually views other men, allows their bodies to be sexual actors and admits that their physical actions express love. But his brother-in-law, who has opened the door for such a revelation by first peeking at his brother's nudity, is revealed to be dying of cancer. Like the gay man in the water, like the brother who has died, like the toned bodies next door which may all carry the virus which will emaciate and destroy them, this heterosexual is punished for having broken the taboo, for having viewed another male body. Once again, the warning is clear to the heterosexual male spectator: if the *je* admits the possibility of its own body as sexual object, the *moi* it conjures will be stained and it will be punished. Once again, the warning is clear to the homosexual male spectator: As the *je* has accepted its own body as sexual object, the *moi* created, no matter how well formed, is doomed and must destroy itself before it can pollute the essential *je*—just as the dead brother has polluted the swimming pool on stage into which the heterosexuals will not step lest it infect them with HIV. Significantly, it is this brother-in-law who finally leaps into the pool and floats face down in a 'dead man's float' (85).[7]

Although the play has been well received by some gay critics, it seems another negative statement of denial; the characters do come to some self-understanding and some fairness in their dealings with each other and the other residents of Fire Island, but nothing changes at the heart of self-identification. The iconography of the body as presented only perpetuates the prevalent mythology. The heterosexual is still presented as the norm against which all is to be measured, though this norm is shown to be distorted. While the women's *personae* are, to some extent, read as culturally induced (and the nervous sister is clothed and reclothed to index this putting on and taking off of identity), the men are read as biologically entire, though needing to explore a wider range of expression. Had it grasped the potential the beach setting offered, the play might have moved away from realist portraiture to work directly with the series of male bodies discussed but never presented and, in the interaction of these bodies, have offered a set of mirror images of value to the spectator's own self-analysis. But to do so would, of course, have been to allow the exposure of the male body which is not available for view, too essential is it to the deepest vision of the collective *moi* and too holy within the culture. As Silverman points out, "our 'dominant fiction' or ideological 'reality' solicits our faith ..."; "'exemplary' male subjectivity cannot be thought apart from [this] ideology, not only because ideology holds out the mirror within which that subjectivity is constructed, but because the latter depends upon a kind of collective make-believe in the commensurability of penis and phallus" (15).[8]

When it is put on view as sexual object, the male body is most often punished. In the 1990s, this point requires precision: today, the male body can be displayed as icon of power and of the sexuality of power—advertising and male pornography often render the body in this way. In these cases, the body is read as desirable but in control, not only returning the spectator's gaze but overwhelming it with a more arrogant, or uncaring, or sexually potent gaze. In these cases, the viewer becomes, her- or himself, the secondary object of the gaze of the primary object; in Lacanian terms, the *je* locates itself as subservient to the fiction it projects onto its own *moi*. Women have been told this constitutes for them a double submission, as the *moi* returns to them the falseness of the fiction by saying "you are not as strong as me and you cannot ever resemble me, since you lack." But just as this is nonsense for women, it is equally distorting for men. The message of the *moi* to its fellow man is complicated: "You could be like me if you become as strong as me, but you cannot really *be* me if you are looking *at* me, and you must, therefore, inevitably fail; I remain the desired Other you either must love or from whom you must hide." Trapped by a belief that the fiction of the culturally induced *moi* is true and that it holds some biological *a priori*, men of all sexual persuasions view the male body with deep fear (and covert or overt longing).

If, on the other hand, the male body is displayed not as icon of power and completeness *qua* subject but as pure object incapable of staring down the spectator, it takes on the signification previously assigned to the female, but it also adds to this scorn a sense of culpability: while the female cannot be held responsible for failing to be male (though she is to be despised for her failure), the male can be held responsible and can, and must, be punished. Much current advertising plays with these notions by showing a male body with averted eyes or acquiescent to the viewer, but as Norbert Ruebsaat points out, this object is probably just "another man in sheep's clothing" (C4). Certainly in drama—even gay drama—the myth continues and the objectified male body is routinely punished.

In *Polygraph*, François commits suicide, as does the swimmer in *Lips Together, Teeth Apart*. But before he does so, François is shown as masochist, punishing himself at the hands of the desired but silent mystery man he picks up in a bar. The scene is titled "The Flesh"—reminding the audience that this exchange takes place directly at the level of the body. In the Vancouver production, François was displayed at the outset of this scene as iconographically gay male—lounging against the omnipresent wall, drinking a beer, bare-chested in a black biker's jacket. Although he is surveying the men in the bar, it is important to note the stage direction: "Soon he realizes one of the crowd is assessing him" (54). The object of the audience's gaze is also the object of the gaze of a fictional subject. What does the sadist see? Clearly the man he views is garbed in the indices of maleness, yet the true man is able to intuit that François is weaker than himself—or, more important, is prepared to act out a role as weaker. This man, of course, is never seen: he is a projection by François of the man he desires but feels unable to resemble and by whom, therefore, he must be punished. He is a creation of the fantasmatic. A complex treatment of masochism and its role in male homosexuality lies beyond the scope of my discussion: Kaja Silverman's book treats the subject at length; Jonathan Dollimore argues that masochism functions within the mythological history of homosexuality. The point I am raising is that the audience, collectively analyzing identities of the male and female in this play, participates in the creation of this mystery man—indeed, *is* him as he beats François. Regardless of the revulsion any given spectator may feel in watching François "recoil against the wall" with "each sound of the whiplash," the audience becomes Lacan's ego-subject, observing François as object "very sensuously dropping to a kneeling position with one eye on [it]" (54). And by constructing the imaginary act in tempo to its sound, the audience becomes the lover François conjures and projects onto stage. But, as the audience also creates the fiction of François (through the agency of the actor), it actually comes, on a collective level, to desire itself and yet to flagellate itself for failing to be the Perfect Male it seeks to view in the psychic mirror.

On an individual level, responses will vary. I set aside female responses, which I am not qualified to assess. Heterosexual male viewers may reject the entire situation, but they are also complicit in the punishment of the body they were forced moments earlier to view lounging seductively within their gaze and toward which they may feel superior. Homosexual male viewers are caught in a complicated semiosis: some will identify with the scene but generally not with its sadomasochism; some, having identified with François, will now distance themselves from his fetish; others will now associate their own desire with François's pain; some will experience a composite of these responses. Victimized by the projected *moi* of power and yet desirous of him, they are faced with a self-analysis stripped of its fictive guise. As Lucie says later of her audition, "I think I felt a bit—well, silly ... I found the director quite ... *aggressive* with his camera ... And ... oh ... I felt more observed by the crew, and the director himself, than by the voyeur in the scenario. I was being watched. Me, not the character. Do you know what I mean?" (58). The gay spectator knows exactly what she means.

Being observed is the essential *mise-en-scène* of David Drake's *The Night Larry Kramer Kissed Me,* produced at the Perry Street Theatre in New York in the fall of 1992. [9] Assuming a largely gay audience, the one-man show makes direct use of the actor's body, of the audience's sexual response to it, and of the complex self-identification/self-rejection which Lepage also employs.

The show is a series of vignettes in which Drake remembers his boyhood—caught playing with his girlfriend's dolls by her brother, a prototype of the brothers-in-law in *Lips Together, Teeth Apart*—his arrival in New York, where he learns how to live within the urban, gay subculture, his afternoons at the gym, and his late nights cruising in bars. Throughout the show, Drake balances, once again, the binary opposites of male identity: the sissy and the muscled hunk. In this show, even more than the others under discussion, the site of his analysis is the body itself.

The two most powerful vignettes—the gym and the bar—vividly portray aspects under discussion: the creation of masculinity in the fiction of a *moi* which is muscled, sexually potent, and well-endowed, and the reflection of that *moi* back onto a *je* which views it as normative and yet unattainable. This reflection is, for the *je,* both itself and the impossible Other, who is at once the object of sexual desire and the punishing Male of cultural definition, simultaneously attractive and yet false. Disturbing in the politics of this play—given that it is a vehicle for ACT UP and the Queer Nation approaches to gay rights, and despite the optimistic ending—is the continuing depiction of the protagonist as submissive to the image of the straight man or as determined to fight him but with his own arsenal. In an early childhood memory, the protagonist recalls that Brad, his friend's brother, threw his Barbie doll away, and ridiculed his gift of a Village People album, telling the children that the Village People were "Fairies." Seeking an image, an infantile "*je-idéal*" (Lacan, "Mirror" 2), the boy remembers that "they don't look like fairies on the record cover. They look really tough ... really cool" (29). The child's fear of the bully is coupled with self-hatred. In a wonderfully overlapping image pattern he creates objects in which his subject-child seeks self-identity: as child, as butterfly encased in a paperweight, as sissy chased by tougher boys, as gay icon from the Village People. Always, however, he is viewing himself, if only in projection, as the bully, now pinned inside a paperweight on his desk to whom he can shout, "See ... See what happens when you mess with me!" Always he is subject and object simultaneously, recognizing the falsity of the iconic projections and yet desperate to locate himself in them. And always, his recognition that the images of the dominant culture are false reminds him that he has no image he can validate, that he can view himself (as the audience views him, whether in empathy or derision) only as lacking; he picks up the paperweight which ostensibly contains his tormentor, but contains his own desired *moi* as well, and screams at it "with deep, primal rage: 'FAIRYYYYYYYYYYYYY!'" (30).

This same mixing of hate and desire permeates the rest of the play, as the mature boy presents a series of representative moments in single, urban gay life. Repeatedly, the protagonist exposes his desire for and his repudiation of "Them" (37)—straight men whom the culture tells him are the norm and whom he encounters everywhere, including in that sanctuary of the body, the gym. Repeatedly, he creates for himself images of maleness which he compares to "Them."

The gym scene is a chanted narration and enactment of the ritual of working out. The rap is redolent of maleness: the "whiff of Old Spice Lockers, damp white towels, musk, steam, soap, cream . . . and pubic hairs dried to the strangest places" (32–33). Undercoded in the "back channel" [10] are separate signifiers of gay maleness: gray cotton Calvin Klein shorts, a "spandex-spread-dick," condoms. The scene begins with Drake stripping on stage, exposing a finely toned body which signifies success in the ritual of body building and which presents to the audience an object of desire and a *moi* whom spectators might well emulate. It also presents the male body as highly erotic object, a condition which, we have seen, prefigures punishment.

The reasons for going to the gym are immediately presented in a set of parallel statements accompanied by mimed action: To view the "guys you've wanted since the day you first feared the sensations they gave you in the junior high showers. Only now … you can 'do it.'" (33). To enjoy the workout—"Felt that burn. MMMmmmm, yeah. That's why I go to the gym";

> to-please-the-by-er-I-don't-have-so-I-can-get-one/
> to-fuck-one/
> with-a-con-dom/
> to-pro-tect-one/
> from-the-stalk-ing/
> that-is-go-ing/
> down-on-my-street/
> a-ttack-ing-dykes-&-fag-gots-who-are-dy-ing-as-they're-ly-ing-
> down-on/
> my-street/
> Yeah/
> That's why I go to the gym;
> [to become strong enough to fight off the gay-bashers]
> who are knoc-king-me-down/
> on-my-street,/
> arm-in-arm-in-packs-that-roam-my-street/
> roam-my-street/
> roam-my-street /
> hun-ting-down-my-kind-of-meat/
> …/
> That's why I go to the gym. (39, 38)

In the movement from narcissism to militancy the dual value of a muscled body is presented, but so is the confusion built into this notion of masculinity. In order for gay men to "have the final laugh" they must have "that membership card that lets you into ... *The Warrior Room*. Where the men dress like boys. But it's an outfit for the transformation: turning the boys ... into men" (31). But the "men" into whom they are turned still weigh identity in terms of bulk and "blue / veins / sna-king-up-my-fore-arm / to my / bubble- / knot- / bi-cep. Mmmm, yeah. That's why I go to the gym" (35–36). The goal is to overcome fear of the straight men, the "Them" who interrupt his narcissism to cut in on the machines—" Sure. Go ahead" (37)—and over whom Drake stands—"Yeah, I'll spot you" (38)—while he chants his defiance against those who would bash him. The imagery becomes a war cry, but it expresses the same aggression it repudiates, for Drake knows that in our society such terminology carries the audience's measure of the male:

> When-we be-gan-the-pumping/
> and-the-pul-ling
> and-the-curl-ing/
> and-the-cut-ting/
> and-the-lunging-and-the-reping-and-the-crunching-
> and-the-pressing-towards-the-day-we-win-the-
> FI-
> NAL-
> WAR-

And Drake knows—"(*removing pants, noticing audience*) Amongst the other guys snapping snaps, belts, and elastic straps against their naked buttocks"—that the "hushed" and "concentrated effort" of the audience, like that of his fellow athletes (both straight and gay), is "with or without attention paid to the size ... of your cock" (32). Once again, the final measure of manhood is viewed or pointedly ignored—but it is, once again, a presence on stage defining the *moi*.

The result of his afternoon in the gym is a body prepared to cruise. And in the following vignette, Drake announces himself now ready to be viewed: "Girth is everything. / Inches count. 6 inches / by 6 inches / equals 12 inches / equal me" (43). He is now defined entirely in terms of image: he is a walking sign-vehicle: "G-W-M; 29; 5'9, 150 lbs, blond-slash-blue. / A 12 inch single, smart, smooth, swimmer seeks ... you. And you. And you" (44). And he now "seeks" the audience even while he seeks his fantasy lover. The scene echos the bar scene of *Polygraph*. Rejecting body types which do not measure up and repeating his own self-defining talisman—"I'm a 12 inch Single. / Play me once, flip me over, play me twice" (47 *et pass.*)—*he* seeks a man to:

> Fill me
> Take me.
> Hit me.
> Hit me.
> Hit me.
> Hit me.

Hit me, hit me, hit me, hit me
HIT
ON
ME. (46–47)

The phrase "hit me" occurs seventeen times in the scene while the protagonist seeks "a man's PUNCH" (50) and at the same time cautions that "Straight-Acting, Straight-Appearing ONLY need apply" (50) to "Choose me. / Abuse me. / Lose me" (53). The scene is highly ironic; but the deep seated identification with a hard body, violence, and punishment as emblems of the male overwhelms the gay activist writing to reflect onto the audience another set of damaging reflections of the *moi* society tells us we should seek. When a "soldier" in the bar looks away from him, the protagonist attacks in bitter self-vilification: "Hey, don't divert your eyes from me. Hey, look here … QUEEEEEEEEEEEEERRRRRRRR!" followed by a page-long list of pejorative slang terms for homosexual (53). The soldier, after all, is a male icon and is not supposed to gaze upon another man; but this soldier is found in a gay bar, where his refusal to do so reinforces the protagonist's self-image as that which must not be seen, while at the same time exploding the myth of the soldier as necessarily heterosexual.[11] The scene also admonishes the spectators to continue to gaze upon the hero, and in doing so to see images of themselves. In the end of the scene, the protagonist finds his fantasmatic lover: again, he is sadistic (or certainly aggressive) and silent. While chanting "MMMMMM-you- / sick … / yeah" five times (56–57), Drake mimes a seduction of and by the lover who pulls a knife and inscribes on Drake's perfectly fabricated torso a deep imprint of his threatening power and potential violence. The image of the actor tracing a knife line around his own chest, pressing the point of the knife into his own pectoral muscle, displays exactly the composite of desire and self-mutilation which gay men appear in these plays to read into their bodies as the texts upon which a culturally induced masculinity is written.[12]

If a new society, like the utopia described in the final scene of *The Night Larry Kramer Kissed Me* at "five minutes" to the end of the century (81) is to come to be— a culture in which traditional images of the male no longer frame male or female bodies or senses of self—it will be essential for theatre to present new images, a multiplicity of images, upon which the *je* of its spectators may gaze in search of potential, and perhaps provisional or momentary, identities. If theatre is gender-making, it has a political responsibility to recognize that role and to take action. Much feminist theatre is reinscribing the woman; male theatre needs to address the constricting armour it has created to hide the various male bodies beneath.

(1994)

Notes

[1] This assertion is illustrated by performances which feature cross-dressing (of which there are many examples), or the appropriation of gender—as, for example, in Peggy Shaw's body in *Belle Reprieve*, a co-production of Split Britches Company (New York) and Bloolips (London) which reinvents Tennessee Williams's *Streetcar Named Desire.*

[2] Dolan has modified this view in later essays; cf. her *Presence & Desire: Essays on Gender, Sexuality, Performance.* Ann Arbor: University of Michigan P, 1993.

[3] The performance under discussion was a co-production of Pink Theatre and Théâtre la Seizième, Vancouver, October 1992.

[4] The production under discussion was at Vancouver Playhouse, January 1993. Dir. John Cooper.

[5] Cf. the necessary erection on stage of a male actor in Theatre Passe Muraille's *I Love You, Baby Blue* (Erin, ON: Press Porcepic, 1977). Here, the male actor must demonstrate what Keir Elam calls "iconic identity" (22) rather than simply invoking the phallic icon and cannot rely on what Silverman calls "collective make-believe," a notion to which I will later refer. Even though the show presented the "Human Levitation Scene" ironically, it was always risky theatre: it changed the position of the actor as fantasmatic male to that of real man, which threatened to deny his superiority. When the effect was successful it overlapped the fantasmatic with the real, "proving" that the power of the erect male is truism rather than artifice, and then it was very powerful theatre.

[6] Cf. Richard Meyer.

[7] In the Vancouver Playhouse production, Norman Browning exploited the effect brilliantly by holding his breath just longer than the audience expected, raising noticeable jitters in the audience that the actor was actually at risk of drowning and intensifying the symbol of the pool as a place of death, and as an intersection of the theatrical and "real."

[8] Cf. the treatment of the naked male body in Jane Campion's film, "The Piano." Here, a female writer and director exposes her male subjects' bodies repeatedly, even alone on screen as the only object of the gaze. It is interesting to note the treatment by this writer of the male body as object of touch, including her exposure of the buttocks as field for touch. The antagonist, not surprisingly, is unable to allow his body to be used in this manner; he twice reacts against the caressing of his buttocks, pulling up his (indexing) long underwear and attempting to become "active"—to touch the woman and to employ his penis. Work by women playwrights is beginning to subvert the "collective make-believe" of "exemplary" male subjectivity.

[9] This New York production, with Drake as the actor, is the staging under discussion.

[10] See Victor H. Yngue.

[11] Current controversy about the visibility of homosexuals in the United States military underlines how powerful this set of icons is in the American psyche. Military figures rarely appear in the drama in Canada, where the icon has less currency; interestingly, the Canadian armed forces accepted homosexual military personnel some years ago, with little objection.

[12] Cf. René-Daniel Dubois's *Being at Home with Claude* (Montréal: Leméac, 1986) where a knife falling between two lovers at the culmination of their most honest lovemaking becomes a phallic fetish/phobic object which requires a death (and causes one). A film version of this play (produced by Films du CERF and the National Film Board of Canada, 1991) is available on video.

Works Cited

Aston, Elaine and George Savona. *Theatre as Sign-System: A Semiotics of Text and Performance*. London: Routledge, 1991.

Butler, Judith. *Gender Trouble: Feminism and the Subversion of Identity*. New York and London: Routledge, 1990.

Cohen, Ed. "Who are 'We'?: Gay 'Identity' as Political (E)motion (A Theoretical Rumination)." *Inside/Out: Lesbian Theories, Gay Theories*. Ed. Diana Fuss. New York: Routledge, 1991.

Dolan, Jill. "Breaking the Code: Musings on Lesbian Sexuality and the Performer." *Modern Drama* 32 (1989): 146–58.

Dollimore, Jonathan. Keynote Address. Conference of the Association of Canadian College and University Teachers of English. Carleton University, Ottawa. 30 May 1993.

Drake, David. *The Night Larry Kramer Kissed Me*. New York: Anchor, 1994.

Elam, Keir. *The Semiotics of Theatre and Drama*. London: Methuen, 1980.

Kott, Jan. "The Icon and the Absurd." *The Drama Review* 14 (1969): 17–24.

Lacan, Jacques. "The Mirror Stage as Formative of the Function of the I as Revealed in Psychoanalytic Experience." *Écrits: A Selection*. Trans. Alan Sheridan. New York: Norton, 1977.

Lacan, Jacques. *The Seminar of Jacques Lacan, Book I: Freud's Papers on Technique, 1953–1954*. Trans. John Forrester. Cambridge: Cambridge UP, 1988. 141.

Lepage Robert and Marie Brassard. *Polygraph* [*Le Polygraphe*]. Trans. Gyllian Raby. *Canadian Theatre Review* 64 (1990): 51–65.

McNally, Terrence. *Lips Together, Teeth Apart.* New York: Plume, 1992.

Meyer, Richard. "Rock Hudson's Body." *Inside/Out: Lesbian Theories, Gay Theories.* Ed. Diana Fuss. New York and London: Routledge, 1991. 259–90.

Ruebsaat, Norbert. "New Males: It's the same game in a different guise." *Vancouver Sun* 13 February 1993: Saturday Review, C4.

Sidnell, Michael J. "*Polygraph*: Somatic Truth and the Art of Presence." *Canadian Theatre Review* 64 (1990): 45–48.

Silverman, Kaja. *Male Subjectivity at the Margins.* New York: Routledge, 1992.

Yngue, Victor H. "On Getting a Word in Edgewise." Papers from the 6th Regional Meeting of the Chicago Linguistic Society. Chicago: U of Chicago P, 1970.

Only in Alberta?:
Angels in America and Canada

by Susan Bennett

> Homosexuals are men who know nobody and who nobody knows. Who
> have zero clout.
> Does this sound like me, Henry?
> > (Roy, *Angels in America: Millennium Approaches* 45)
>
> Is homosexuality intolerable? – that is the ultimate question.
> > (Sinfield 276)

1. "America has rediscovered itself. Its sacred position among nations" (Joe, *Angels in America: Millennium Approaches* 26)

Tony Kushner's *Angels in America*, the 1993 winner of the Pulitzer Prize for Drama, enters theatre history as certainly the most successful play of the decade and it is not surprising, then, that there has been in Canada almost a stampede to get production of the two-part epic onto our stages. Not since John Osborne's *Look Back in Anger* (1956) has any play been so widely regarded as a barometer of the times (especially in North America but elsewhere in the world, as well) and, in this context, the production and reception histories of *Angels in America* merit particularly close attention. From Kushner's sub-title for his text, "A Gay Fantasia on National Themes," the play is marked as imbricated in two of the most freighted and controversial identifications in a positionality-saturated world; it asks explicitly: "what does it mean to 'be' gay" and "how does that mean in a 'theme' that is 'America'"? Whatever its geographic specificity, these are the questions that a production of *Angels in America* brings to its audiences' attention and there is, apparently, a fluctuating, variable relation between these two critical components: gay and/in America. More generally, performances of *Angels in America* interrogate the very "notion of gay ethnicity" (Sinfield 290) and its operations in contemporary cultural experience. What I want to address is the play's critical reception in a Canadian context as one response to Alan Sinfield's provocative inquiry that opens this paper.

First, then, it is useful to mark the expeditious and literally far-reaching production history of Kushner's landmark play. *Millennium Approaches* (the first part of *Angels*) was originally workshopped by the Center Theater Group at the Mark Taper Forum in Los Angeles in May of 1990. Several full professional productions (involving some very prestigious venues and directors) followed over the next three years (The Eureka Theatre Company of San Francisco in May 1991; the Royal National Theatre in London under the direction of Cheek by Jowl's Declan Donellan, January 1992; the Mark Taper Forum in November 1992; the Sydney Theatre Company at the Wharf Theatre under the direction of playwright Michael Gow in February 1993; and the Walter Kerr Theatre in New York in April 1993, under the direction of George C. Wolfe).[1] With so many early, significant productions, it is no wonder that Robert Brustein noted that *Millennium Approaches* "may very well be the most highly publicized play in American theater history" (29)[2] and even Frank Rich, who admits he "reached voting age just after the heyday of Miller and Williams and Albee," calls *Angels in America* "the most thrilling new American play of my adult lifetime" (6 June 1993). Almost all the major reviewers of the London and New York productions of Kushner's drama gush in their enthusiasm for the epic, including overtly conservative critics more or less conceding the play's brilliance, so that by the time *Angels* reached New York in 1993, Rich could comment: "This play has already been talked about so much that you may feel you have already seen it, but believe me, you haven't, even if you actually have" (5 May 1993).

So what of *Angels in America* in Canada, its performance venues and its critical impact? The Manitoba Theatre Company (MTC) staged a coup in securing its first production in this country. As Kevin Prokosh reports in the *Winnipeg Free Press*, MTC's prescience in getting the rights for Kushner's play translated, seemingly, into very good box-office: "The inclusion of *Angels* on the Warehouse playbill is credited with sending season subscriptions shooting up 38 per cent this year to 2,903" (D1). Equally enthusiastic was Linda Rosborough's review of the production for the Winnipeg newspaper. Granting *Angels* four and a half out of five possible stars, Rosborough starts her review:

> When a play is touted as the best of the last 50 years, that's a heap of hype. But with the vast, passionate and witty *Angels in America*, the gush of praise is well-earned. The capacity crowd was on its feet Wednesday night at the MTC Warehouse, following the Canadian premiere of the intensely funny and sad play. (D4)

Rosborough's review dwells on the humanity of Kushner's text, calling the writing "the real star of the show" and the cast "exceptional." Only as a penultimate paragraph does she issue any kind of warning to potential spectators and then rather factually and as a springboard for her final praise:

> *Angels in America* contains strong language and frank discussions about sexuality, but nudity is minimal. Far more naked are the characters, who, despite their failings and weaknesses, are hopeful in their quests for love and acceptance. For all the sadness, sickness and greed in his story, Kushner still believes in angels. (D4)

In both Prokosh's preview piece (based on a one-hour phone interview with the playwright, as well as conversations with MTC's artistic director Steven Schipper and University of Winnipeg theatre professor Per Brask who had recently edited a volume of critical essays on the play) and Rosborough's review, there is a low-key but confident endorsement of *Angels in America* as both a timely and relevant play. While both writers mark this as a gay play, both contextualize this constituency in the larger scheme of apparently shared cultural experience: "The play covers all the bases: life, death, love, hate, religion and politics" (Prokosh D1).

Much more critical of MTC's premiere production is Kate Taylor, reviewing the play for the *The Globe and Mail*.[3] Content to award a more measly two and a half stars, Taylor concludes: "MTC is the first Canadian theatre with the courage to mount *Angels in America*, and there are courageous moments in this production, but generally it is one that exposes Kushner's few weaknesses without glorifying his many strengths" ("Angels Needs").

Taylor's consideration of the MTC production dwells on characterization; it is evident that she believes that it is the characters who are at the heart of Kushner's text (though how Taylor ever manages to see Joe and Harper as a "straight" couple I cannot quite imagine) and that MTC does not fulfill her expectations in this area.

Since Canada's premiere production of *Angels* in Winnipeg, there have been several others: Edmonton's Phoenix Theatre (Part I, October 1996) and Citadel Theatre (Part II, October 1996); Toronto's Canadian Stage (Part I, September 1996; Part II, November 1996), Calgary's Alberta Theatre Projects (Part I, September 1996; Parts I and II, May/June 1997); and Halifax's Neptune Theatre (February 1997). The Centaur Theatre production in Montreal opened in May 1997. Critical reception of these various productions is, generally, benign: Vit Wagner for *The Toronto Star* concludes that Canadian Stage's production "does what every production of a great play should do. It leaves little doubt that the play is indeed great"; Liz Nicholls in *The Edmonton Journal* gives perhaps the most rounded and sensible of any of the Canadian critics drawing positive attention to the play's political emphasis and seeing the representation of gay lives within that overtly drawn politics;[4] Kate Taylor, *The Globe and Mail*'s reviewer for the Winnipeg production, returns to preview ("On") and review the Toronto version. Persuaded on this occasion to raise her approval rating to four stars, she has, moreover, revised her account of Joe and Harper as a couple who are "nominally straight" ("Angels Mixes"). Most recently, Elissa Barnard in the *Halifax Chronicle-Herald* describes the play as the theatrical event of the 1990s, a bold exploration of "issues of politics, spirituality and sexuality" (B4). But, alongside all this Canadian critical acclaim, there is, as Barnard notes, the controversy of the Calgary production: "When the play was staged at Alberta Theatre Projects, Calgary, a few MLAs tried to pull government funding from Alberta Theatre Projects because of their production of a 'gay' play, something that was spoofed on 'This Hour Has 22 Minutes.' The play was sold out every night" (B4).

Calgary, then, seems the logical site on which to stage an interrogation of Alan Sinfield's question of tolerance and homosexual identity.

2. "What's it like to be the child of the Zeitgeist?" (Louis, *Angels in America: Millennium Approaches*, 71)

Perhaps the best indicator of the depth and duration of the media attention given to the Alberta Theatre Projects production of *Angels* might be given in a citation from an encomium to Calgary published in *Maclean's* some five months after the play's opening. The cover of *Maclean's* February 24, 1997 issue proclaims "Calgary: On Top of the World. The nation's centre of gravity is shifting to the 'new' West," but within the piece's opening paragraph, such splashy claims are modified: "And yet when a local theatre company stages a play with gay themes and nudity—even a Pulitzer Prize-winning one—it sets off something of a tempest" (13). Even—or perhaps especially—measured against the attack on *Angels* delivered by a fundamentalist minister in Charlotte, North Carolina (where the production also went ahead successfully), Calgary alone in its response to Kushner's play seems to stand as evidence within Canada of an intolerance for homosexuality, or even its on-stage representation. [5]

The reaction of staunch conservatives within the Alberta Legislature was, of course, not unprecedented. Similar outrage and threat had been expressed in response to an Alberta College of Art show "Bound to be Tongue Tied—Gagging on Gender," the New Gallery's installation "Fantasmagoria: Sexing the Lesbian Imaginary," and, most notoriously, Maenad Theatre's presentation of American performance artist, Holly Hughes. [6] At the time of the protests against Hughes's performances, then Community Development Minister Gary Mar said: "There have been some Alberta Foundation for the Arts [AFA] supported shows recently which many Albertans have objected to seeing government dollars going towards funding. I've looked at the situation, reviewed it, and I've asked the AFA to end project-specific funding." [7] In the end, of course, no such action was taken, but the threat was, at least at the time, taken seriously. [8] In this context, it could be argued that Alberta Theatre Projects would have anticipated both the media and legislature attention and, indeed, their public relations and sponsorship strategies for the play suggest that they had done precisely that.

The Calgary story starts even before *Angels* had opened at the Martha Cohen theatre in the centrally-located Centre for the Performing Arts. Peter Stockland, a regular columnist for *The Calgary Herald*, described the play as, among other things, "offering all the benefits of left-wing enlightenment provided by wobbly bare male bottoms, simulated homosexual copulation, and language that would sear the ears of a sailor's parrot" (A12). The other city newspaper, *The Calgary Sun*, was in the fray two days later with its own description provided by Steve Chase of their Legislature Bureau: "a seven-hour gay epic including sex scenes between men, frequent partial nudity and plenty of swearing." On the same day (September 13, 1996), the paper's editorial took *Angels* as its subject with a headline "Curtain down":

> Alberta Theatre Projects is about to stage a seven-hour homosexual epic at the prestigious Calgary Centre for Performing Arts that depicts simulated sex scenes between men and with obscene language for sound effects.

What great family entertainment for the company that just months ago gave us *My Fair Lady*!

…

Due to cutbacks, hospitals are closing and nurses are losing their jobs, teachers have been laid off, schools are overcrowded, and the elderly are caught in a vise.

Yet taxpayers are still having to hand over hundreds of thousands of dollars to a company that stages a self-indulgent production many feel is abhorrent. It is simply not right.

And five Tory MLAs (Lorne Taylor, Jon Havelock, Heather Forsyth, Judy Gordon and Ron Hierath) had already pitched in to demand, in an echo of Gary Mar, the withdrawal of government support to Alberta Theatre Projects. [9]

This, by any account, is a public display of intolerance, especially given that ATP's production did not even open until September 15. By the time I saw the production, a couple of weeks into the run, ATP had "opinion boards" up in the lobby for audience members to contribute feedback as well as a programme insert which sought contributions towards a $50,000 goal for underwriting costs of the production of both parts of Kushner's epic. The insert, which had attached to it copies of *The Calgary Sun* condemnation of the play as well as Peter Stockland's original piece for *The Calgary Herald*, asked

> Despite the outcries from certain members of this community who believe that it is wrong for ATP to present these plays, many Canadians have responded with their support. Currently we are at 52% of our goal. Do you believe in Angels? Please read the attached newspaper articles and decide for yourself. We are looking for people to join our roster of Angels by contributing to one of our nine choirs [donation levels].

Moreover, *The Calgary Herald* returned to the production some two weeks after opening night with an almost full page coverage, divided between two regular columnists: Peter Stockland (again) and Don Martin who had attended a performance with one of the Tory MLAs, Jon Havelock. (ATP had offered complimentary tickets to any MLA who wanted to see the show.)

Quite surprisingly, Don Martin was able to describe a conversion of Jon Havelock to the cause of Kushner's play:

> By the end of the show, Havelock was so caught up in the plot he was describing his disappointment that an AIDS victim's gay lover had left for another man. If that sounds like a bizarre conversation with an Alberta Tory, you're right.
> Okay, let the record show there was an apparent act of anal sex deep in the shadows. For about two seconds. Two men kissed. Once.
> As for the nudity, *puhleeze*, an actor dropped his shorts and allegedly exposed himself while completely covered with a night shirt.

> As for Havelock's reaction, it was a refreshing display of a politician
> entering a debate with his eyes open and his judgment on hold.
> He was enthralled. After one hilarious, insightful dialogue on racism in
> America, the MLA for Calgary Shaw actually felt compelled to applaud.
> And he did. Solo.

Don Martin's intervention in the debate is obviously to be applauded. His attention
to how small detail had been overstated in the hostile press, not to mention his
willingness to accompany Havelock to the theatre, was undoubtedly useful to those
proposing a more open viewing of the play. And even if Havelock's enthusiasm might
have been that of a naive and infrequent theatregoer, his change of heart did much,
I think, to dampen the spirits of the protesters and give weight to the claims made
elsewhere in the world for Kushner's drama. On the other hand, on the same newspaper page, Peter Stockland repeated his original criticism and then some, under the
heading "Pump vigor into the arts—let's all boo and hiss": "Seen and heard, what's
truly alarming about *Angels* is not its omnipresent profanity and vulgarity, but its
reduction of the art form of Sophocles, Shakespeare, Molière and Oscar Wilde to the
depth and breadth of a cast-off T-shirt." The call to return to canonical dramatic
literature—which is to say, so-called "good art"—is altogether another tactic, and one
to which I'll return, but here one wonders if Stockland remembers the fact that
Oedipus slept with his own mother, has heard the profanities that punctuate
Shakespeare's English, realizes Molière was denied a Christian burial, or knows that
Oscar Wilde wrote *The Picture of Dorian Gray*.[10] If he's tongue-in-cheek about all this,
and I find that unlikely, then it's a subtlety that would be completely lost on his
supporters. His conclusion is that the audience must take back the boo and be
prepared to hiss at the end of every performance of the play, a recommendation that
Calgary audiences failed to seize upon.

On October 7, *Alberta Report* endorsed Stockland's attack, running the Calgary
and Edmonton productions[11] of *Angels in America* as its cover story. Kevin
Michael Grace leads off his cover story article as follows: "Live theatre is very much
a minority taste in Alberta. Few attend, and despite generous government support,
most theatre companies hover perennially on the verge of insolvency" (34) and then
turns specifically to the first part of *Angels*:

> *Millennium Approaches* is an artistic failure but it bears a powerful
> revolutionary message. While it elevates the belief current in the 'AIDS
> community' that victims of the disease are holy martyrs, homosexuals
> and AIDS victims are only one division of Mr. Kushner's vaster army:
> one that seeks to destroy the very concept of the law—on earth and in
> heaven. (34)

At first glance, it would appear that *Alberta Report* has realized that its frequent attacks
on homosexuality have not been particularly effective and that they have changed
their approach to look not at the representation of a minority identity (here, gay)
but to focus instead on the explicit politics of the play: "Playwright Tony Kushner,
however, is not interested primarily in sex. His obsession is politics" (35). And there is

a way in which the *Alberta Report* gets the point—and the play—in a way that other Canadian critical responses seemed determined not to. Sex is not sequestered in order to give way to praise for the play's humanity, spirituality and universality; instead *Alberta Report* makes gay sex the avatar of Kushner's left-wing agenda. Ironically, they point precisely to the strength of *Angels* to enact the intolerances of contemporary North American culture, one of which circulates around the visibility of homosexuality.

Moreover, *Alberta Report* astutely observes the economic benefits that can accrue to a theatre company in the kind of controversy Stockland had stimulated. The piece claims "[c]onsidering *Angels'* true lack of novelty, Alberta Theatre Projects, and its producer Michael Dobbin, must be pleased with their success in using scandal as a marketing tool. ... Mr. Dobbin anticipates that *Millennium Approaches* will fill the theatre to 90% capacity during its run" (35). Theatregoers may or may not have been brought to the theatre by all the deserving praise and awards that Kushner's play has received, but there does seem to have been an unmistakable advantage for any Canadian theatre box office in adding an apparently controversial choice to a production season. Whereas Ian Olorenshaw comments of early Australian productions that audiences were around the 50% capacity and cites the audience development manager at the Melbourne Theatre Company, "the subscription audience for *Millennium Approaches* was low and that most of the general public ticket sales came from university ranks and the homosexual community" (67), the Canadian audiences have been far more mainstream and far higher in percentage attendance. While I don't mean to suggest that the *Alberta Report* is right (or, perhaps more accurately, I do mean to suggest they are right but for the wrong reasons), there is the question—important, I think—of what *Angels in America* offers to mainstream repertory companies and their audiences. How, then, does intolerance—to use a theatrical metaphor—get "performed"?

Rather than see the opposition to the play in Alberta as symptomatic of the province's dinosaur mentality and its ultra-conservative politics—something that would rely on an all too easy cliché—it might be more useful to see these declarations as the overt and unselfconscious statements of the assumptions and fears that attach to any mainstream production of *Angels*. It is not a case, then, of "only in Alberta" but, more accurately, "clearly in Alberta," and, I think, instructive as such.

3. "Your problem, Henry, is that you are hung up on words, on labels, that you believe they mean what they seem to mean." (Roy, *Angels in America: Millennium Approaches*, 45).

To return to Alan Sinfield's provocative question and gay "ethnicity," it is worth remembering, as Sinfield himself suggests, that "it is not that existing categories of gay men and lesbians have come forward to claim their rights, but that we have become constituted as *gay* in the terms of a discourse of ethnicity-and-rights" (272). As he continues:

There are drawbacks with envisaging ourselves through a framework of ethnicity-and-rights. One is that it consolidates our constituency at the expense of limiting it. …

Also, fixing our constituency on the ethnicity-and-rights model lets the sex-gender system off the hook. It encourages the inference that an out-group needs concessions, rather than the mainstream needing correction. (272–73)

It is precisely this kind of performance of ethnicity-and-rights which prompts Gordon Rogoff to offer an ironic assessment of *Angels*:

[I]f Kushner wished merely to be current, he would have had to be more inclusive, offering a rainbow coalition of super-shifts and sappy saints— more WASPs, surely more fundamentalists, one real Lesbian at least, a Native American to go with the Eskimo who passes through the Mormon wife's fantasy, and no doubt some country-western twangers, Hispanics, CEOs, students, seniors, and maybe even a token president or Supreme Court justice or car salesman, real estate agent, talk-show host, or perhaps David Schine, the forgotten man in the real Roy Cohn saga. (28)

But Kushner knows exactly the "trap of the visual field," as Peggy Phelan has described it. Phelan argues the trap lies in the seeming "promise to show all, even while [the visual field] fails to show the subject who looks, *and* thus fails to show what the looker most wants to see (24). And this is true. So, to enter the specular economy "as a" gay man (or any other "ethnicity" under the rights model) provides a very limited political opportunity. More likely, it is limited to and by the very conditions of heteronormative reception processes which Tom Waugh has usefully elaborated in the context of gay male film:

[N]on-gay spectators, one can speculate, attach their voyeuristic fix on the gay subject himself, shaped through discourses of stereotype, freak-show, and pathos/victimization. … Meanwhile, straight critics actively stifled gay discourses around these films, either through homophobic panic, liberal tolerance ("I'm so matter-of-fact and cool that sexual orientation doesn't have to be mentioned"), or allegorical exegesis ("This film is not about gayness, it's about fill-in-the-blank"). If the built-in ambiguity of the narrative codes of the art cinema allowed gay authors space to create, it denied them the chance to nurture a continuous and coherent gay audience. Instead, we remained invisible and covert spectators, a divided and discontinuous audience. (156)

In the Canadian reviews of *Angels*, there is plenty of evidence for liberal tolerance and allegorical exegesis—indeed, it is encouraged by the play itself. Homophobic panic, something the play lays bare in Joe's own horror at his sexual desires, is, too, evident in the narratives that attempt to make sense of Kushner's project for a mainstream theatre-going public. Consider, in this regard, Elissa Barnard's preview piece for the Halifax press. While on the one hand, she quotes actor Peter Hutt's criticism of the real Roy Cohn and his refusal in a "60 Minutes" interview to admit to either homosexuality or AIDS, she is also at pains to point out that Hutt will celebrate finishing his run as Kushner's Roy Cohn with a Caribbean holiday "with his wife, who'll come to see him in *Angels*, and two young daughters, who won't" (B4). Also, we're told, that Jordan Pettle (Louis in the Neptune Theatre production) got into acting in high school because acting, rather than sport (his apparent first choice), made it easier to meet girls.

An effect, then, of making gay identity visible and to find that project garnering mainstream recognition is, inevitably, "yet another measure of the power of liberal pluralism to neutralize oppositional practices" (Savran 226). Where the liberal pluralism is a little less liberal (which is to say, in the Canadian context, Alberta), the specificities of that effect become just a little better focussed. The attack returns here to the notion of "good art" (in itself, always already a dangerous territory because of its attractiveness as a career choice to gay men and promiscuous women). In our contemporary moment, Alberta dares to say out loud what most Western societies have been practising: cut funding for art because it is undeserving and only of interest to a small percentage of the population. And the New Right assumes the right to say what small percentage of society that can be (those who, in the most conservative sense, can afford it). This is a political issue that continues to confront artists in all media. Related and relevant is the introduction of H.R. 122 in Congress by Sam Johnson (a Republican from Texas) on 7 January 1997; H.R. 122 would amend the National Foundation on the Arts and the Humanities Act of 1965 to abolish the National Endowment for the Arts and the National Council on the Arts. Equally germane is a critical practice, explicit or implicit, that would elide sexuality under the banner of politics (akin to Sinfield's attention to "letting the sex-gender system off the hook"). Once again, the New Right sets the agenda, claiming "their" art is above and beyond politics (and therefore, ironically, "good"), leaving the Left scrambling to defend itself and its own art. Furthermore, a recourse to the generalized category "politics" denies the particulars of gay history. This is absolutely what *Angels in America* seeks to avoid.

In a foreword to John Clum's anthology of gay male plays, Kushner describes "having arrived as a community with a history—of both oppression and liberation" (ix) and it is the hybrid experience of oppression and liberation that makes *Angels* such an important and such an impressive drama. As well as contributing to a liberal pluralist economy (which can only ever re-affirm the *status quo*), the play's success, David Savran rightly claims, "also suggests a willingness to recognize the contributions of gay men to American culture and to American literature, in particular" (226). [12]

Finally, then, it might be said that homosexuality, as it is made visible in *Angels in America*, is tolerated rather intolerantly. And that, in the end, is not altogether a bad thing. The play falls into the trap of the visual field with a self-conscious fashioning. It performs a hybridity of oppression and liberation that cannot ever quite be subsumed by liberal humanism or related homophobic panic precisely because it assumes a relation to these expressions of mainstream Western cultures, a relation that is pliable and contingent. At the end of his powerful argument, Sinfield concludes:

> One inference from anti-essentialist theory should be that we cannot simply throw off our current constructions. We are consequences of our histories—those that have been forced upon us and those that we have made ourselves—and we have to start from there. The notion of gay ethnicity is intuitively powerful and therefore we have to remain in negotiation with it. At the same time, it is because we believe that culture constructs the scope for our identities that we may believe those identities to be contingent and provisional, and therefore may strive to revise our own self-understanding and representation. Subcultural work is our opportunity to support each other in our present conditions, and to work towards transforming those conditions. 'Together, we will learn and teach'—'Go West.'

Sinfield's reference is, of course, to a hit song from 70s disco stars and gay icons, the Village People (and, more recently, the Pet Shop Boys' remake of the same), but he might as well be referring to *Angels in America* in Calgary. In the subculture of theatre in this particular West, the very premises in which art and the ethnicity of identity are conceived and regulated strain at the limits of liberal tolerance. At the same time, both somehow exceed their prescribed conditions. How, then, could it be any surprise that the very province that has made so much fuss about *Angels in America* and Canada is expecting to host Tony Kushner as a 1998 Markin-Flanagan Writer-in-Residence at the University of Calgary. Go West, indeed.

(1996)

Notes

I am grateful to my assistant, B.J. Wray, for the excellent research on *Angels in America* she produced. Her help has been made possible through a grant awarded by the Social Sciences and Humanities Research Council of Canada.

[1]   *Angels in America* has also been widely produced in many other countries; according to David Savran, there would be productions in seventeen countries during the 1994–95 theatre season (129). His interview with Kushner—as well as essays about Danish, German and Australian productions of the play—can be found in Per Brask's *Essays on Kushner's Angels.*

[2]   Brustein's article on *Angels* entitled "Angels in America," which contained some speculation on some fighting between Oscar Eustis (the director of the Los Angeles production) and the playwright, brought about a swift and angry response from

Kushner. And, in turn, Brustein responds, concluding that "Kushner wants to be both a radical non-conformist and universally loved." Kushner's letter and Brustein's riposte are in *The New Republic* 14 June 1993: 4–5.

3 The preview piece and review in *The Globe and Mail* for the Toronto production some eight months later were also authored by Kate Taylor—her rather more animated discussion in these columns is discussed later in my article.

4 Nicholls writes:

> The arguments are big, and extravagantly put. They restore theatre to the kind of central hotspot in American political life it hasn't occupied for years, not to say *decades*. And they locate, and empower, the gay community in the larger context of American history and politics (B9).

She, better than any other reviewer, understands Kushner's interweaving of social and sexual issues in *Angels* and doesn't for a moment recuperate the play for a liberal humanist agenda: "And it's no mere liberal apology, though Kushner has puckishly said that it's easier to come out of the closet as a homosexual than a socialist in modern America" (B9).

5 See Kate Taylor's piece for *The Globe and Mail* (September 26, 1996: C1–2). Accounts of protests in Charlotte seem to be centered, not surprisingly, on the opinion of one fundamentalist minister and in opposition to general opinion in the town—a town, it might be noted, with only about half the population of Calgary.

6 Hughes had achieved international notoriety as one of the four performance artists defunded by the National Endowment for the Arts. As she puts it, "When Congress passed restrictive language in 1989, equating homosexuality with obscenity, I knew that as one of the few lesbians to get NEA funding for 'out' work presented in publicly funded spaces, I was skating on thin ice" (*Clit Notes: A Sapphic Sampler.* New York: Grove Press, 1996, 19).

7 The backlash against Holly Hughes's performances in Calgary I have discussed in a piece co-written with Maenad Artistic Director, Alexandria Patience. "Bad Girls Looking for Money" is in *Canadian Theatre Review* 82 (Spring 1995) 10–13. For the discussion of Hughes and the government reaction, see especially 13.

8 The truly puzzling aspect is why the Legislature seems to scrutinize Calgary's theatre much more avidly than Edmonton's, at least beyond the capital city's general anxiety about its faster growing competitor to the south.

9 Alberta Theatre Projects was the recipient of about $500,000 from the Alberta Foundation for the Arts towards the 1996–97 operating season.

10 Tom Waugh writes of *Dorian Gray* that the play "may not have been the first work to posit artistic representation as some kind of metaphoric analogue of gay identity, and the artist-intellectual as the gay prototype, but it is undoubtedly the Ur-text of the third body [implied gay subject] narratives" (149).

[11] Calgary's production was still on stage; Edmonton's was soon to open.

[12] Savran goes on to ask:

> What is one to make of the remarkable ease with which *Angels in America* has been accommodated to that lineage of American drama (and literature) that focuses on masculine experience and agency and produces women as the premise for history, as the ground on which it is constructed? Are not women sacrificed—yet again—to the male citizenry of a (queer) nation? (226)

This seems like an important, and disturbingly accurate, observation. That *Angels in America* is *all* about men is probably the best reason there is for its success. A more recent tirade in *Alberta Report* came in the form of an attack on the University of Alberta's "doctrinaire feminism" (by which they referred to the appointment of a new woman chairman of the Political Science Department involving for "her close personal friend and colleague" an assistant professorship in women's studies) and gestures tellingly through some faux graffiti in their cover illustration that this means "Death to Dead White Males"—hardly, one would have thought, much of a threat. See *Alberta Report*, 30 September 1996.

Works Cited

Barnard, Elissa. "Angels among us." *Halifax Chronicle-Herald* 6 February 1997: B1+.

Bennett, Susan and Alexandria Patience. "Maenad Making Feminist Theatre in Alberta." *Canadian Theatre Review* 82 (1995): 10–13.

Brask, Per. *Essays on Kushner's Angels.* Winnipeg: Blizzard, 1995.

Brustein, Robert. "Angels in America." *The New Republic* 24 May 1993: 29–31.

Chase, Steve. "Anger rises over gay play." *The Calgary Sun* 13 September 1996: 7.

Clum, John M. *Staging Gay Lives: An Anthology of Contemporary Gay Theatre.* Boulder, CO: Westview, 1996.

Gever, Martha, Pratibha Parmar and John Greyson. *Queer Looks: Perspectives on Lesbian and Gay Film and Video.* Toronto: Between the Lines, 1993.

Grace, Kevin Michael. "The Lawless Millennium." *Alberta Report* 7 October 1996: 34–37.

Kushner, Tony. *Angels in America: Millennium Approaches.* New York: Theatre Communications Group, 1992.

———. "Foreword." Clum, vii–x.

Mar, Gary. *Alberta Hansard* 26 May 1994: 2126.

Martin, Don. *The Calgary Herald* September 27, 1996: A15.

Nemeth, Mary. "On Top of the World." *Maclean's* 24 February 1997: 13–20.

Nicholls, Liz. "The Angels' bandwagon." *The Edmonton Journal* 16 October 1996: B9.

———. "Part II Angels." *The Edmonton Journal* 27 October 1996: D1.

Olorenshaw, Ian. "*Angels* in Australia." Brask 63–86.

Phelan, Peggy. *Unmarked: The Politics of Performance.* London: Routledge, 1993.

Prokosh, Kevin. "Arts community says farewell." *Winnipeg Free Press* 17 January 1996: C8.

———. "Outspoken Angel." *Winnipeg Free Press* 12 January 1996: D1.

Rich, Frank. Rev. of *Angels in America. New York Times* 5 May 1993: C15.

———. Rev. of *Angels in America. New York Times* 6 June 1993: 2.1.

Rogoff, Gordon. "*Angels in America,* Devils in the Wings." *Theatre* 24.2 (1993): 21–29.

Rosborough, Linda. "*Angels in America* earns its praise." *Winnipeg Free Press* 19 January 1996: D4.

Savran, David. "Ambivalence, Utopia, and a Queer Sort of Materialism: How *Angels in America* Reconstructs the Nation." *Theatre Journal* 47.2 (1995) 207–27.

Sinfield, Alan. "Diaspora and hybridity: queer identities and the ethnicity model." *Textual Practice* 10.2 (1996):271–93.

Stockland, Peter. "Playwright breaks old ground." *The Calgary Herald* 11 September 1996: A12.

———. "Pump vigor into the arts—let's all boo and hiss." *The Calgary Herald* 27 September 1996: A15.

Taylor, Kate. "Angels Mixes Poetry, Comedy, Hard Realism in Epic Sweep." *The Globe and Mail* 27 September 1996: D8.

———. "Angels Needs Some Divine Intervention." *The Globe and Mail* 19 January 1996: C2.

———. "On the Side of Angels." *The Globe and Mail* 26 September 1996: C1+.

Wagner, Vit. "Millennium solid top to bottom." *The Toronto Star* 27 September 1996: C3.

Waugh, Tom. "The Third Body: Patterns in the Construction of the Subject." Gever, Parmar and Greyson 141–61.

Queer(y)ing the Canadian Stage:
Brad Fraser's *Poor Super Man*

by Marcia Blumberg

Brad Fraser's *Poor Super Man*, a sexually explicit investigation of diverse friendships and erotic relationships set in Calgary, is a powerful vehicle for queer(y)ing the Canadian stage. The world premiere, early in 1994 in Cincinnati,[1] overcame obstacles threatening closure and then achieved a sold-out extended run at the Ensemble Theatre. Edinburgh's Traverse Theatre mounted an acclaimed production in 1994, which transferred to London after a successful run at the Edinburgh Fringe Festival. Brad Fraser directed the Canadian premiere in Edmonton (1994) and another staging in Vancouver (1996) while a joint production by the Manitoba Theatre Centre and Canadian Stage played to packed houses in Winnipeg and a twice-extended season in Toronto from February to June 1995. Pierre Bernard's *Poor Super Man* in Montreal in May 1995 was judged by Fraser as "the best production yet ... even if [as Conlogue notes] he doesn't understand a word of French" (D2). At the same time successful productions were mounted by local directors and actors in Sydney, Australia and Wellington, New Zealand.

Fraser's acknowledgment of the global entrenchment of American pop culture highlights an inflammatory issue since Canadians often feel swamped by an influx of American television channels, fast food outlets, and Disney artifacts. Even though this list offers a limited view of the diversity of American culture, many Canadians argue for cultural autonomy yet are often themselves hard-pressed to define a diverse and changing Canadian culture.[2] In addition, *Time* magazine's rating of *Poor Super Man* as one of 1994's ten best plays in America raises the question whether an American or international stamp of approval is required before Canadian audiences risk material that challenges the status quo and expressly aims to revitalize English Canadian theatre, which Fraser claims is boring and out of touch. For that matter, Fraser's assertion provokes the much debated theatres of Canadian identity, nationalism, and Quebec separatism on and off the theatrical stage,[3] a significant and complex topic that I merely signpost in this analysis as I traverse another route.

Instead, my exploration focuses on another aspect, the queer(y)ing of the Canadian stage, which Robert Wallace has insightfully analysed in other Canadian contexts. He quotes John Palmer's representative remarks of 1975: "Nobody minds that you are gay....As long as it isn't mentioned" ("To Become" 5). Wallace's recent assessment indicates a transition over almost two decades that still leaves much to be desired:

The dominant sensibility of Canadian culture is as anti-sexual as it is homophobic ... Because Canadian theatre also is reluctant to produce work that deals openly with gay interests and behaviour, texts by lesbians and gay men still enter Canadian culture through the back door. Canadian playwrights who openly declare a same-sex preference still are subject to enormous prejudice—systemic homophobia that works to silence voices that offer alternatives to the heterosexual norm. ("Making" 16, 28)

Whilst gay playwrights in Canada occupy differing subject positions and situate themselves in complex relations with the staging of their theatrical work and their gayness, Brad Fraser is, in his words, a gay playwright who deliberately engages with the diversity of gay communities and their positioning in an avowedly heterosexist society. He also strongly resists the relegation of himself, his work, and those classed as outsiders (notably those identified as members of the gay community), to the margins:

There is a dignity and a power and an importance to all human experience ... [T]he marginalized segments of our society... that's where history is changed, it's never done by the complacent middle-class, it's done by the people who have to struggle and have to fight to be heard ... [M]y message is about those people and those things. (Bailey np)

No doubt the constructions of male and female characters in *Poor Super Man* will disturb and challenge audience members in different ways depending on their positionings, their politics, and the particular production they are viewing, yet the play presents complex interactions that mitigate against blanket denunciations, the surety of heroes, and an ongoing denial of societal issues at the nexus of gender, sexual orientation, cultural difference and the AIDS pandemic; the play, moreover, interrogates the fixity of categories in discursive, performative, and societal domains. Fraser writes out of an awareness that theatre is hardly a popular form of entertainment for many spectators, who prefer viewing movies, rock videos and television. Consequently, in keeping with the rhythm of the sixty-second sound-bite and the fast pace and clashing concerns that typify urban living, he structures the play as a myriad of short scenes that pile one upon the other at breakneck speed. Comics and cartoons are another generational source that inspires this dramatic structure; the playwright not only "keeps a collection of 10,000 comic books" (Johnson 60) but asserts their importance during his miserable childhood: "Television and comic books were my touchstones ... Pop culture became our physical landscape" (61). *Poor Super Man* utilizes the Superman intertext to remind spectators of the more than five-decades-old Action Comics hero but concomitantly enacts Adrienne Rich's notion of "re-vision: the act of looking back, seeing with fresh eyes, of entering an old text from a new critical direction" (35). While Rich considers that this process "is for women more than a chapter in cultural history: it is an act of survival," I extend her rubric to argue that *Poor Super Man* provokes women and men to explore the emergence of new possibilities that not only interrogate the conventional reception of the popular intertext but also undermine traditional viewings of seemingly entrenched societal norms.

The title's rupture of the conventional designation of the comic hero renders problematic the glorification of a masculine stereotype representing brute strength, corporeal superiority, and the invincibility implied in Superman's epithet, "Man of Steel." This appellation resonates on many levels with Klaus Theweleit's *Male Fantasies*, an extensive study of the dynamics of the fascist unconscious. Theweleit juxtaposes a photograph of a painting of a discus thrower by a German artist with a drawing of a superhero from the comics—in this instance, Spiderman—and links these two images with the notion of the new man as a perfectly functioning machine:

> The most urgent task of the man of steel is to pursue, to dam in, and to subdue any force that threatens to transform him back into the horribly disorganized jumble of flesh, hair, skin, bones, intestines, and feelings that calls itself human .... The new man is a man whose physique has been machinized, his psyche eliminated. (160, 62)

Poor Super Man acknowledges the wretchedness and deficiency of a society where the operative dynamics have valorized those attributes of masculinity. Fraser argues that the title signifies the "unrealistic role models" for boys as well as girls and their effects:

> so many men have trouble being vulnerable or dealing with their feelings ... they are so afraid of failure ... [There is] a real potential in our society for self-hatred because "men never live up to the expectations of the society." (Stein 1B)

The titular format also questions the necessity for the construction of heroes in a manner reminiscent of Brecht's Galileo, who counters his assistant's indictment of betrayal, "Unhappy the land that has no heroes" with an apposite rejoinder, "Unhappy the land where heroes are needed" (98); the title, consequently, foregrounds the impoverishment of a society that relies on the viability of superheroes, whether they emanate from the comics or are constructed as such in a present-lived reality or in history.

Umberto Eco's analysis of Superman's performance of heroic powers and his defence of "Truth, Justice and the American Way" interrogates aspects of the comic hero which are implied in Fraser's play:

> Superman *could* exercise good on a cosmic level, or a galactic level, and furnish us in the meantime with a definition that through fantastic amplification could clarify precise ethical lines everywhere ... In Superman we have a perfect example of civic consciousness, completely split from political consciousness ... The paradoxical waste of means ... astound[s] the reader who sees Superman forever employed in parochial performances. (22, emphasis added)

Written over two decades ago, Eco's ideological critique of limited individual good deeds versus a lacunae of group action, and by implication a preservation of the status quo, forms an important *caveat* for Fraser's *Poor Super Man*. Is Superman so ethically impoverished and collectively ineffectual that his death should be welcomed rather than mourned?

Querying the *Poor Super Man* stage picture demands engagement with an unstable urban Canadian 1990s locale synonymous with fragmentation. Over two-hundred shifts in spotlighting evoke the frenetic pace, instability, and bombardment of urban living. In addition, these multiple sites foreground a short-lived present and signify past and future scenarios to stage both ruptures and connection. The title and subtitle, "A Play with Captions," generically mark a liminal space between the worlds of theatre and the comics. Spectators require a simultaneous engagement with the stage—a raked wooden floor signifying a tenuous grounding for five characters—and the backdrop—panels intermittently overlaid with lettering. These captions represent thought bubbles in counterpoint to staged action or speech. Flashing by like frames of a cartoon, they situate scenes, emphasize issues, and highlight the continuum of negotiation between reality and wish-fulfillment, truth and lies, or euphemisms and personal desires; mostly, however, they stress impermanence and an intellectual and/ or emotional contestation of expectations, all of which demonstrate one mode of queering the stage.

Stage locales (an artist's studio and a bedroom) serve as spaces for straight and gay coupling as well as a place for dying. The Edinburgh production partitioned the bedroom space into three adjacent floor areas covered with similar duvets and pillows, where repeated sexual acts and a suicide occurred in designated sections; this compo-sition invites us to compare the complex juxtaposed actions. In Vancouver, the three areas worked differently: straight coupling and death occurred in beds on each side of the stage, while gay coupling took place in the centre of the stage on a geometric-shaped area that served multiple purposes, such as the table in the cafe. Perhaps this production points in its very staging to the fact that gay sex refuses the putative convention of the bedroom setting in the same way that gay relationships resist the fixity and conformity of heteronormative structures. In Toronto, however, the single bed used for straight and gay coupling as well as suiciding makes visible in a more obvious but perhaps simplistic manner these complicated dynamics. The apparently minor variation, however, lays itself open to a reactionary reading that unproblematically equates sex with death for gay men at a time when AIDS in North America has undoubtedly wreaked enormous loss in the gay community; this aspect of the Toronto staging, therefore, risks perpetuating the homophobic stereotype that not only suggests the possible hearkening back to moralistic judgments of perversity and punishment in an act of scapegoating but also offers a potential interpretation of the containment of AIDS within specific risk groups such as the gay community, which is both patently false and counterproductive to the provocative reassessment of societal mores that the drama text stimulates.

Poor Super Man also refuses the apparent dichotomy of the straight/gay binary with its assumed privileged and devalued terms. Neither does the play invert the hierarchy even though a gay artist is the central character. Instead it enacts Eve Kosofsky Sedgwick's broadening of the term to explore the plethora of possibilities that comprise gender, sexuality, and other "identity-constituting and identity-fracturing discourses" (9). The unfixity of relationships in ever-changing scenarios relentlessly challenges perceived norms and inspires re-visionings. Speech acts mediated by the captions as well as the coupling of bodies express a desire to relate meaningfully across regulated norms and keep loneliness as well as alienation at bay. Poignant and witty evocations of loss, pain, intimacy, and renewal articulate the dynamics of a pre-operative transsexual, who is living with AIDS and re-casts the entire scenario in a new time-space that defies the mythic invincibility of Superman and, more importantly, foregrounds the limitations of "superheroes" of science and medicine. Despite the violent juxtaposition between the comic book world and issues of life and death on the stage and in society, the curtain-line caption, "beginning," invests the stage picture with transformative potential and suggests affirmation over despair.

In moving across various formulations, whether these be national boundaries, genres, media, genders, or sexualities, the play celebrates what Sedgwick terms

> the moment of Queer.… [S]omething about queer is inextinguishable. Queer is a continuing moment, movement, motive.… The word "queer" itself means across … multiply transitive.… It is relational, and strange. (xii)

A continuing movement of queerness inflects *Poor Super Man*. Sonic characters perform difference to resist the reification of sexual identities and demonstrate and expose, by way of contrasting perspectives and behaviour, the effects of homophobia and a potential for change. The play, moreover, disturbs what Jauss terms "the horizon of expectations" of the spectators since it continually crosses boundaries and relates strange and even antithetical generic modes and assumptions. David Halperin's definition of queer also informs the play:

> *whatever* is at odds with the normal, the legitimate, the dominant. *There is nothing in particular to which it necessarily refers.* It is an identity without an essence. "Queer," then, demarcates not a positivity, but a positionality vis-a-vis the normative.… [I]t describes a horizon of possibility whose precise extent and heterogeneous scope cannot in principle be delimited in advance … a variety of possibilities for reordering the relations among sexual behaviours, erotic identities, constructions of gender, forms of knowledge, regimes of enunciation, logics of representation, modes of self-constitution, and practices of community—for restructuring, that is, the relations among power, truth, and desire. (62)

Although some constructions and characters in the play reiterate what Michel Warner terms "a heteronormative understanding of society" (xi), these are problematized by the spectator especially when they are contrasted with the queer dynamic as explicated by Halperin that fuels the play.

The age-old trope of the quest for self-knowledge which motivates the narrative structure contrasts with the fragmented postmodern dramatic structure. These occupy a generic configuration of comedy that employs the mechanisms of triangular relationships with a blocking figure, typically associated with Classical New Comedy, as well as the convention of the happy ending, which in the play translates for this spectator into a powerfully affective and complex but ultimately affirmative finale that refuses closure. Another crossing juxtaposes the descriptor urban comedy with many serious issues: fragmentation, loss, broken relationships, mourning, and the immense challenges for people living with AIDS. While witty repartee, the lingo of a hip generation, and the sexual explicitness and forthright dialogue usually induce the laughter of recognition in Fraser's audience, the play also utilizes, but at the same time significantly re-visions, conventional generic markers of comedy.

Poor Super Man comprises two sets of triangular relationships: one constituted by sexual desire, another performing the love of friendship. Both triangles stage the traversal of apparently rigid categories using characters that effect this crossing with varying degrees of success. In both sets of relationships the pivotal character is a gay artist, who performs the pursuit of self-knowledge and a meaningful relationship to rekindle his creativity and well-being. David is also the main reference point for the intertext, naming himself Superman (88) and Clark Kent (98), and confessing his out-sidership: "I don't know anyone who's like me. I'm a fucking alien" (153). In contrast with Superman's unrequited love triangle constituted by an inept Clark Kent, who loves his colleague, Lois Lane, who in turn desires the hero who will never form an attachment, David's sexual relationships refuse the societally constructed boundaries of normative heterosexuality. This context of difference, nevertheless, also offers similar structural mechanisms. Countering the accepted Superman lore, David Mamet calls "the man of steel"

> the most vulnerable of beings…. His power is obtained at the expense of any possibility of personal pleasure…. *He cannot tell [Lois] his secret, for to do so would imperil his life*…. He can have adulation without inti-macy, or he may long for intimacy with no hope of reciprocation. Superman comics are a fable, not of strength, but of disintegration…. Superman's personalities can be integrated … only in death. Kryptonite is all that remains of his childhood home…. It is … fear of those remnants, which rule Superman's life. (177, 78)

David, an out gay man, wrestles with secret alienation or what the play depicts as a lack of knowledge that propels him towards relationships with straight men. Whether an abusive relationship with his cousin who reappears in his paintings or the urgency of desire in his relationship with Matt, the young restaurateur who is his temporary employer, David structurally occupies a position similar to that of straight men with whom he becomes involved, and this involves a possible misogyny.

Unlike the conventional love triangle, which stereotypically posits two men in pursuit of a woman, Fraser's revisioning offers two men in a relationship of mutual desire and Matt's wife, Violet, as the betrayed victim still firmly entrenched in hetero-sexist assumptions. David and Matt's burgeoning relationship initiates the artist's creativity and Matt's awareness of a new path of desire, different sexual practices and a depth of intimacy. Yet while Matt succumbs to a fear of societal castigation, "You think I want people saying I'm a fucking queer.... I don't want to be a famous fag" (147, 158), Violet discovers in David's paintings a different Matt. Although her own sense of failure as a woman and a wife remain intact, her admission, "he loved you as much as I did" (174) acknowledges difference and validates David's conviction: "I don't believe all relationships are the same ... I don't think we have to love only one person ... I think love needs to be redefined" (132, 33). Matt's attraction to David is, however, soon overshadowed by an inability to situate himself outside rigid traditional structures. On the strength of another broken relationship, David resolves "to find someone like me—instead of trying to create him" (176). This confrontation with his secret vulnerability acknowledges the difference between the limitless creative potential he stages as an artist and the boundaries of the roles he performs in a lived reality; it also forms one of his rationales for cutting ties with Superman, taking control, and making his life anew.

The friendship triangle occupies more stage time and significance than the love triangle. David's feisty friend, Kryla, regrets her single status and obsessively and unsuccessfully searches for a male partner. Work provides no compensation for the lack of significant relationships, which leaves her bitter and jealous of David's absorption with Matt. Fraser's construction of Violet and Kryla problematically exposes the always already oppressive positioning of women in patriarchal culture and reinforces the pervasive entrapment of gender stereotyping. Kryla's recognition of her role model, "Lois Lane is the reason I entered journalism" (28), emphasizes the inter-textual *caveat*.[4] The play confines both women's potential for transformation, which forms a central attribute of feminist theatre[5] (Keyssar xiii), to the final moments and their break with past dynamics. Yet the play does invest transformative potential and a model of compassion in the relationship between David and his roommate, Shannon, a pre-operative transsexual denied the fulfillment of her dream of becom-ing a woman because of AIDS. Shannon's distress at the impossibility for a crossing of this sex/gender border evokes David's unconditional affirmation: "I love you no mat-ter who you are" (79).

Their witty and forthright banter signifies the closeness of an abiding friendship and forms a central structuring of the play. It also reminds us of Michel Foucault's concept of friendship:

> A way of life can be shared among individuals of different age, status and
> social activity. It can yield intense relations not resembling those that are
> institutionalized. It seems to me that a way of life can yield a culture and

an ethics. To be "gay," I think, is not to identify with the psychological traits and the visible masks of the homosexual, but to try to define and develop a way of life. (207)

The dynamic of their intense friendship performs an ethics that is revealed in Shannon's confrontation with AIDS, which engages David in her philosophy of living and dying and inspires greater self-awareness and courage. Shannon's answer to the first caption of Act Two, "Why People Cheat On Their Lovers," significantly follows the other characters' one-liners:

Cheating's a relative concept. Tom [Shannon's lover] fucked other people all the time. But he was completely up-front about it and—once I got over those suck ass morals our lying, cheating parents foisted on us—I realized his other sexual partners had nothing to do with his love for me. It was okay. It was great. Christians are liars. (104)

Whilst some spectators may regard this speech as shocking or even blasphemous, Shannon's mourning for her dead lover and the performative actions of a loving friendship with David make visible her convictions. In challenging the pervasive rectitude of societal norms, Shannon also questions institutional structures, belief systems, and, by association, the veneration of superheroes. Their final exchange before Shannon's suicide tellingly reinvokes the inter-text. David's desperate attempt at dissuasion, "I'll use forgotten Kryptonian technology to suck the virus out of your body," is met with Shannon's sobering reminder, "You're not Superman, David" (166). Her determination to make the final decision about the diminished quality of her life signifies her choice of suicide as an act of empowerment that transgresses juridical prohibitions. Moreover, throughout the play Shannon enunciates her sense of death as a process of renewal (43, 85) which she appears to perform in her final utterance, "Wow" (171). This exclamation marks the inextinguishability of queer life and celebrates Shannon's agency rather than victimhood in the face of the pandemic; at the same time, its juxtaposition with David's elegy for the many friends who have died of AIDS refuses a romanticization of her death.

In this time-space of AIDS, the problematic role of a diminished eponymous hero is evoked in references and marked by physical absence, except in the Montreal production where the director "theatricalizes the metaphor by projecting panels from Superman comics on the backdrop at crucial moments" (Conlogue). In the concluding dialogue, Kryla presents David with Action Comic No. 500 celebrating Superman's rebirth. David's refusal of this peace offering, which he drops on the ground, visually reinforces his final word, "Goodbye" (179), a reiteration of all the characters' farewells to a child-like innocence and an allusion to their collective relinquishing of their superhero. The ending foregrounds the gap between the myth and the present moment, a time when even Superman cannot prevail.

Despite the violent juxtaposition between the comic book world and issues of life and death on stage and in society, the final caption, "Beginning" (179), invests *Poor Super Man* with a measure of affirmation in a generically typical comic ending of renewal. This final tableau vigorously counters reliance by children or adults on a powerful superhero to fix the world, and the play in its entirety simultaneously demythologizes Superman and emphasizes the imperatives of self-knowledge and empowerment. Moreover, in performing and negotiating various queerings, *Poor Super Man* refuses the fixity of socially constructed norms and offers in its place a critique of regulative divisions and a challenge to instigate change.[6]

(1996)

Notes

[1] Cincinnati is the city notorious for the debacle with the Robert Mapplethorpe photographic exhibition. Chris Jones contextualizes the play within this political climate:

> The people of Cincinnati passed a resolution in early November [1993] denying civil rights protection to gays and lesbians. In the unfriendly environment the theatre's 28-member board initially voted to cancel the production. (32)

Fraser reacted perversely to the notion of opening the play there: "It's important to invade enemy territory" (Jones 33).

[2] See Reid Gilbert's article, "Mounties, Muggings and Moose: Canadian Icons in a Landscape of American Violence," and others in a collection that explores aspects of Canadian culture: *The Beaver Bites Back.* Ed. David H. Flaherty and Frank E. Manning. Montreal: McGill/Queen's UP, 1993.

[3] In *Producing Marginality* Robert Wallace asks "Why is theatre in English Canada suffering a debilitating crisis at exactly the time that Québécois theatre companies are travelling the world to rave reviews, and packing houses at home?" (15)

[4] The objectification and diminution of women in comic books has continued unabated. William Savage reminds us that

> Lois Lane demonstrated that it was perfectly all right for a professional woman to behave like a moron while mooning over the man of her dreams .... [While] women were out to marry ... marriage was out of the question for heroic males because it cramped their styles. (78)

[5] Fraser's play has provoked strong reactions from some feminist critics who are justifiably disturbed at the constructions of women in the play: a witty but cynical and complaining almost middle-aged woman whose life is characterised by empti-ness, absence, and missed opportunities and a naive, young wife who is a victim of betrayal. Other feminist academics, who actively participate in turf wars, decry the growing interest in gay and lesbian issues and the burgeoning field of queer theory,

which they feel "steals the limelight" and deflects attention from the multiple feminist fields of inquiry. Engagement with these theories and practices is more helpful and is the subject of the Summer-Fall 1994 issue of *Differences*, entitled "More Gender Trouble: Feminism Meets Queer Theory," with an introduction by Judith Butler. As a feminist spectator and academic whose work is primarily directed at feminist approaches to theatre and texts by women playwrights, I am also committed to the nexus of theatre, AIDS, and activism. Whilst I problematize the constructions of women and other aspects of *Poor Super Man* I pay attention to a play which has achieved sold-out runs internationally and locally and raises multiple issues; most particularly it has proved an affirmative experience for many people who are HIV+ or are living with AIDS and has brought new insights to many people who have had no exposure to the issue other than in newspaper headlines or TV programs.

[6] I acknowledge with much appreciation a Postdoctoral Fellowship from the Social Sciences and Humanities Research Council of Canada. Sincere thanks to Reid Gilbert for insightful comments about this work and a warm debt of gratitude to Stephen Oldenburg-Barber for ongoing dialogue.

Works Cited

Bailey, Tonya. "'Superman' explores sexuality." *The News Record* 27 April 1994: np.

Brecht, Bertolt. *Life of Galileo.* Trans. John Willett. London: Methuen, 1986.

Conlogue, Ray. "Stereotypes sap strength of *Poor Super Man.*" *The Globe and Mail* 12 May 1995: D2.

Eco, Umberto. "The Myth of Superman." *Diacritics* (1972): 14–22.

Foucault, Michel. "Friendship as a Way of Life." *Foucault Live: (Interviews, 1966–84)*. Trans. John Johnston. Ed. Sylvere Lotringer. New York: Semiotext(e), 1989. 203–10.

Fraser, Brad. *Poor Super Man.* Edmonton: NeWest, 1995.

Gilbert, Reid. "Mounties, Muggings and Moose: Canadian Icons in a Landscape of American Violence." *The Beaver Bites Back.* Ed. David H. Flaherty and Frank E. Manning. Montreal: McGill/Queen's UP, 1993.

Halperin, David. *Saint Foucault: Towards a Gay Hagiography.* Oxford: Oxford UP, 1995.

Johnson, Brian D. "Brad the Impaler." *Maclean's* 13 February 1995: 60–62.

Jones, Chris. "I'll Take Cincinnati." *American Theatre* 11.4 (1994): 32–33.

Keyssar, Helene. *Feminist Theatre.* New York: Grove, 1985.

Mamet, David. "Kryptonite: A Psychological Appreciation." *Some Freaks.* New York: Viking, 1989. 175–80.

Rich, Adrienne. "When We Dead Awaken: Writing as Re-vision." *On Lies, Secrets and Silence.* New York: Norton, 1979. 33–49.

Savage, Jr., William W. *Comic Books and America, 1945–1954.* London: U of Oklahoma P, 1990.

Sedgwick, Eve Kosofsky. *Tendencies.* Durham: Duke UP, 1993.

Stein, Jerry. "'Poor Super Man': Controversial play about men and love." *The Post* 25 April 1994: 1B.

Theweleit, Klaus. *Male Fantasies.* Vol. 2 of *Male bodies: Psychoanalyzing the White Terror.* Trans. Erica Carter and Chris Turner. Minneapolis: U of Minnesota P, 1989.

Wallace, Robert. *Producing Marginality.* Saskatoon: Fifth House, 1990.

———. *Making, Out: Plays by Gay Men.* Toronto: Coach House, 1992.

———. "To Become: The Ideological Function of Gay Theatre." *Canadian Theatre Review* 59 (1989): 5–10.

Warner, Michael. Introduction. *Fear of A Queer Planet: Queer Politics and Social Theory.* Ed. Michael Warner. Minneapolis: U of Minnesota P, 1994. vii–xxix.

Wrestling with a Double Standard [1]

by Darrin Hagen

When Tony Kushner's play *Angels in America* was produced in Alberta two seasons ago, the public outcry was enormous. Politicians stepped on each other to criticize a play that, even though it won the Pulitzer Prize, 'questioned the validity of a belief in God,' promoted a homosexual, antifamily agenda, and featured more than one scene involving gay sexual situations. The *Alberta Report* featured a cover that had poster boy Mark Bellamy, dressed as a studly, buffed angel, covered in painted-on Kaposi's sarcoma. [2] The right-wing called (again) for an end to arts funding (when the art in question reflects same-sex issues). When the dust cleared, *Angels in America*— Parts One and Two—outsold almost every other theatrical production in Edmonton and Calgary.

When singer and performer Marilyn Manson toured his dog and pony show through Alberta last year, the Calgary business community (fueled and encouraged by religious groups) canceled his one Cowtown performance, citing unsubstantiated rumors of onstage sacrifices, devil worship, and anti-establishment lyrical content. The scandal was front page news in Edmonton, where Manson played to far more people than he would have, had the scandal in Cowtown not made him more notoriously infamous than he already was.

Two pieces of high profile entertainment were challenged in this province strictly based on content (or rumors of that content). The amount of negative press *Angels* and Manson received was frightening: journalists wringing their hands in mock horror at the decay of our Albertan society.

The funny thing is, a show just traveled through both Calgary and Edmonton that featured onstage man/man sexual situations, an obsession with the Dark Forces, an open challenge to the authority of God, mock rape, and, dare I say it, necrophilia, symbolic dismemberment of women, nudity, foul language, and—gasp!—really loud rock and roll. And it got nothing in the way of religious outcry, moralizing or political comment.

Is Marilyn Manson starring in *Angels In America?* Is the Jim Rose Freak Circus back on the road?

No. Last Sunday I went to see WWF (the World Wrestling Federation).

I, three friends (my partner and a straight couple), and thousands of screaming families converged on Edmonton's Skyreach Centre to watch Stone Cold Steve Austin, The Undertaker, The Brood, New Age Outlaws, Val Venus, Mankind and Golddust 'wrestle' in front of a sold-out crowd of children and ladies and gentlemen of all ages. Let me tell you, until you've heard eight-year-old girls screaming things like "Break his leg!" and "Finish him off!" you haven't really witnessed how low society can scrape.

First off, I have to say this: the show is actually quite entertaining, for about fifteen minutes. WWF shows have a lot more in common with the big annual Drag Ball than with any 'sporting' event. In fact, the reams of media coverage the WWF received while it was in the province (almost all positive or, at least, tongue-in-cheek) was in the entertainment section of the newspaper. The 'show' consists of lots of introductions, lots of big entrances, lots of swaggering with an exaggerated sense of self-importance, lots of cheesy music cues, lots of larger-than-life personas, and the occasional prop. 'Titles' are read as the stars enter the room and stroll down a long ramp to their pounding music, a spotlight on them the whole way.

Once the actual 'wrestling' starts, it becomes even more like an overlong drag show: the numbers all start to sound and look the same after a while. Every match is almost identical in execution, utilizing the same pallet of moves and choreography, with occasional 'personality' variations. The Undertaker, for instance, generally relies on the piledriver move to stun his opponents into pretend unconsciousness. Val Venus enters to vampy burlesque sax music, wearing a towel, wiggling his derriere like a stripper at a stag party. The opponents generally insult each other, attacking such important topics as whose appendage is larger, the quality of a female partner's breasts, etc., until one is driven mad by the teasing and attacks. The audience cheers, then grows distracted as the 'fight' progresses. The success—entertainment-wise—of each match depends entirely on how skilled the performers are in making the violence look real. If I can tell from the nosebleed section of the Skyreach Centre that kicks or punches aren't connecting, I'm not going to care much about who wins. What keeps people watching is when the gimmicks start.

Every wrestler has a gimmick tied to his character's history or plot line. Al Snow carries a female mannequin head by the hair (AL: "What do we want?" CROWD: "Head!"). 'Head' talks to him and tells him who to take down. The Brood, consisting of pretty-boy heart-throb Edge and his also pretty Goth-vampire buddies Christian and Gangrelle, wear sexy pirate shirts and PVC pants, and flip their luxurious blond hair around more than a babe in a Bon Jovi video. Val Venus's striptease entrance relates to his history as a porn star. The New Age Outlaws (with Team De-Generation X) consist of Outlaw Jesse James (a.k.a. Road Dogg, "'cause he likes it doggy-style") and Badass Billy Gunn (who likes flashing his bum to get the other team fightin' mad). Every time Jesse James gets a male opponent into a hard-to-get-out-of hold, he humps him from behind, or pretends to eat him out. The crowd goes wild at every sexual suggestion. Somehow, watching two boys having fake anal intercourse on stage is fine, as long as one of the men is being held in that position against his will. Or Jesse and Badass, in a perfectly choreographed oral gang rape, place two pseudounconscious opponents in opposing corners, then climb up on the ropes, pretend to fuck their faces, then pummel their heads with punches (all timed) while the audience counts the toll.

Of course, there are the women: Sable, Tori, Ivory, Jacqueline, all dressed for success in string bikinis, silver jumpsuits, and hair that flies around as they fight. Implant versus implant in this fight to the finish.

Who won? Does it matter? A half billion people (including three million Canadians) tune in each week to see the televised version of this road show. There is a recording studio being built to issue the release of WWF CDs, which are mostly "themed" collections of dinosaur heavy metal bands. There are theme hotels and amusement parks in the works. Stone Cold Steve Austin, the current smash fave (whose motto is on banners and T-shirts all over the Coliseum: "AUSTIN 3:16 Do Unto Others Before They Do Unto You"), is the merchandising king, selling 25,000 t-shirts a month. The ticket sales, the pay-per-view rights, the videos, the action figures all add up to an unstoppable commercial enterprise. Wrestling is huge business.

Supporters call it "a mock-violent soap opera that interacts with its crazed audience" and "escapist entertainment." And I suppose, on one level, that's true. The success of the WWF or of the TV show "Jerry Springer" proves that there is a rabid audience for the stuff that you can scrape out of the gutter. But when escapist entertainment is built on a bunch of thugs exhibiting Grade 8 locker room bullying, waving dicks in each other's faces to prove their masculinity, I have a problem with that. When an audience cheers they want 'Head' and they're talking about a symbolic decapitated female on stage, I have a problem with that. When the crowd goes wild while the New Age Outlaws pretend to assault the two men they just finished raping, the message is loud and clear: As long as you're the one doing the poking, you're not a fag. But make sure you beat up the fag you just fucked, so that you'll still be a man. People will cheer.

I have a serious problem with that.

And the worst part of all is that this sideshow is marketed mainly at children. I watched little boys and girls, supported by their parents, cheering the *demasculinization* of men who were held in positions in which they couldn't defend themselves against their rapists. As a gay man, I sat and listened as tens of thousands of people (mostly families) cheered simulated forced man-on-man anal sex and the subsequent beating of the victim.

Adults can watch what they want. But children all over the world are consuming this product. Forget the Backstreet Boys, the Spice Girls. When an ACCESS reporter asked a bunch of ten-year-old boys in Calgary what they wanted to see at the show, they screamed "We want to see the sluts!" In Edmonton, the hottest selling item at the merchandise stand was a baseball cap bearing the New Age Outlaws' motto: "SUCK IT!"

The media wasn't silent. Many are concerned with the effect wrestling has on the younger fans. But most of the press coverage the WWF received in Alberta was about its popularity. Not one journalist mentioned the homophobia or the sexism within the show. 'Everyone knows it's not real.' Yet when *Angels in America* was produced in

Alberta, did the fact that everyone knows it's not real save it from being skewered as immoral? No. The image of two men in a gay relationship kissing was enough to draw fire from extremists all over the province. It was labeled as "perverted," or "anti-God."

Where is the WWF headed? Is there any line it won't cross? Rumor has it that partial nudity (female, I assume) will play a big role. A little T&A will send viewing figures through the stratosphere. But ultimately, the WWF and the hysteria that makes it so popular rely on one thing: the preservation of the myth of straight white male power. And in that context, it's perfectly correct. Its symbols of masculinity—brute force, fake violence, bravado, posturing, drawing your power from the *disempowerment* of others—are tried and traditional. It's a brilliant symbol of the last bastion of the old guard clinging to the tattered shreds of its former glory and power. That's why the claims of escapist entertainment are so disturbing. It's not escapist entertainment to the people who have to face that attitude in their lives on a daily basis. It's real. There's no escape. And there's nothing entertaining about it.

(1999)

Notes

[1] A version of this article was first published in the June 1999 (Pride) issue of *Outlooks Newspaper* under the title, "Wrestling With a Double Standard." It was originally written as a warm-up research exercise for Hagen's fringe theatre play *PileDriver!* Hagen reports, "The story caused quite a commotion … it was linked to Xwrestling.com, which connects to all news about wrestling, and it received an astonishing—to me—6,000 hits a day. Then, *Outlooks* received a few nasty letters to the editor taking me to task for 'hetero-bashing,' claiming they—as gay men—had been watching wrestling for years and had never seen anything like the stuff I mentioned." *Outlooks* submitted the article to the Gay Press Association, where Hagen won second place in the Best Opinion/Editorial/News Analysis category in the regional division of the Vice Versa Awards. On his achievement, Hagen declares, "Caught me very much by surprise. I didn't even know I had been entered … Wait, I should probably rephrase that!" Editor's Note: This commentary was used as the foreword to another version of the article, "Why I Hate Wrestling (the Sport, Not the Foreplay!), which appeared in *torquere* 1 (1999): 114–19.

[2] Mark Bellamy is the Calgary-based actor who posed for the *Angels in America* poster. Alberta *Report* used the photograph from the poster as the basis for its offensive cover.

Hosanna! Michel Tremblay's Queering of National Identity

by Elaine Pigeon

In 1968, Michel Tremblay made history in Quebec when he electrified audiences with his audacious play, *Les belles-soeurs*. No one had ever seen or heard anything like it before on the Quebec stage. Shock waves reverberated throughout the community, sparking unprecedented debate. There was also much cause for celebration: *Le théâtre Québécois* had finally been born. Tremblay's spectacular career took off, and for the next quarter of a century his work continued to arouse greater critical controversy in Canada than that of any other dramatist in or out of Quebec (Usmiani, *Michel Tremblay*, 2). Although his recent plays have lost their original political bite, to date Tremblay remains Quebec's most important playwright.

Les belles-soeurs introduced one of Tremblay's renowned theatrical innovations: his controversial use of *joual*, the term used to describe the particular variety of street French or slang commonly used in Quebec. By incorporating various Anglicisms and religious expressions, or "*sacres*"—such as "*crisse*" and "*tabarnac*" ("sacred"—such as "Christ" and "tabernacle")—along with the use of phonetic contractions, *joual* carries important religious and socio-political connotations. Renate Usmiani, who has written extensively on Tremblay, rightly points out that, at the time, young radicals "hailed the use of *joual* as a major step through which Québécois culture was finally asserting its independence from centuries-old bondage to the culture of France, the mother country, a partial liberation on the level of language which carried strong political overtones" (*Michel Tremblay*, 4). Clearly, Tremblay achieved a significant breakthrough in making the spoken language of his people acceptable as a dramatic idiom. But the initial effects of Tremblay's use of *joual* were of even greater import, for the cultural identity of a people had been galvanized. Consequently, the presentation of *Les belles-soeurs* can be viewed as a political marker, signifying nothing less than Quebec's first step towards decolonization and liberation (47).

Yet some critics were less than enthusiastic about Tremblay's use of *joual*, arguing that it was "a symptom of defeat: a language whose very texture expresses the alienation, lack of identity, inability to communicate and tragic impotence of Quebec society" (4). A heated debate over the correct usage of the French language in Quebec ensued, in which one writer, Jean Marcel, even went so far as to publish a book entitled *Le Joual de Troie* (*The Trojan Horse*), a pun on *joual*, the dialect pronunciation of *cheval*, meaning horse. For Marcel maintained that *joual* "constituted yet another pernicious instrument of colonization, encouraged by Anglophones to bring about the total destruction of Francophone culture" (Usmiani, *Theatre*, 97). Subsequently, some Quebec intellectuals began to insist that Québécois writers utilize a universal language—namely, standard French—in order to distance themselves from a regional dialect associated with underdevelopment and an illiterate working class. In part, their efforts succeeded.

Thus it is somewhat ironic that Tremblay's early plays—collectively known as *le cycle des belles-soeurs*—all depict members of the Quebec working class grappling with an oppressive family life: *la maudite vie plate* (the blasted boring life). But, in the sixties, the stereotypical Québécois was working class. Tremblay, moreover, was particularly vexed by the advent of a consumer society, one of the more insidious effects of Quebec's "Quiet Revolution." With the death of "*le chef*" (the boss), the autocratic Premier Maurice Duplessis, in 1959, Quebec rapidly underwent the final stages of modernization, shifting from an essentially agrarian culture to industrial urbanization, complete with a massive working class, the majority of whom were rural Québécois who had migrated to the cities in search of jobs and a better life filled with material prosperity. As Tremblay's plays so poignantly demonstrate, the good life that Quebec's modernization promised often translated into a tragic version of the American dream.

During this period, Quebec artists and intellectuals all began to focus on their unique social situation, summing up the problem as nothing less than total alienation on the political, economic, and cultural fronts. In 1963, the radical journal *Parti pris* was founded by a group of creative writers and political activists, including many Marxists. In the wittily titled "Fear of Federasty," Robert Schwartzwald—one of the few scholars who publishes in English on francophone Quebec culture—notes that the journal defined: "the specific tasks of Quebec's Quiet Revolution with a social program and a political objective that took its inspiration from the anti-imperialist and anti-colonial struggles of the period: national independence in Africa, revolution in Cuba, and the civil rights movement in the United States" ("Fear of Federasty," 177). The goal of *Parti pris* was nothing less than "an independent, socialist Quebec," but first the people had to be "free of political influence from the Catholic Church" (Forsyth, 159).

Previously the Church had taught Quebec's agrarian nationalists "to be satisfied with a lesser lot in life, to believe that they had been '*nés pour un petit pain*' (born for a little bread roll), which, Schwartzwald points out, is "a reference to the buns given out on the feast of Saint John the Baptist, the patron saint of French Canada" ("Fear of Federasty," 178; "Symbolic Homosexuality," 269). Under the old regime, "messianic ideology sought to turn Quebec's underdevelopment into a virtue," by which Quebec was to exemplify its "spiritual, Latin" ancestors in the New World ("Symbolic Homosexuality," 268). In contrast, modern nationalism sought to expose the self-deception behind this degrading subjugation, which further reinforced the collective sense of failure that had haunted Quebec's colonized consciousness ever since the "Conquest," the defeat of the French on the Plains of Abraham in 1759 ("Symbolic Homosexuality," 268-69; "Fear of Federasty," 176). Thus, the rise of Quebec's new nationalist movement also meant rejecting the second-class status of being Canada's Other, the so-called "French"-Canadians. So the task of Quebec artists, writers, and playwrights "became to denounce the past and to liberate—as well as create—a sense of identity" (Usmiani, *Michel Tremblay*, 13). In short, the Quiet Revolution finally "laid to rest the century-long ideological representation of Quebec as a piously Catholic, agrarian society" ("Fear of Federasty," 177) and thereby prepared the ground for the emergence of a new nationalist consciousness.

While the Quebec population discovered their "imagined community" or "nation-ness" through print culture—the process described by Benedict Anderson in his attempt to clarify the modern nation as a cultural formation—theatre audiences in Quebec also found their cultural identity reflected on the stage, which of course helped foster the construction of a new national identity. Therefore, to view Tremblay simply as a product of his time is not adequate; it is far more important to grasp how he participated in shaping Quebec's nationalist project, for Tremblay wrote in response to the momentous transformation that Quebec society was undergoing. By dramatizing individual efforts to break free of the family and to liberate the self from the repressive effects of the Catholic Church, Tremblay created allegories suggestive of national liberation. At the same time, he emphasized the pernicious influence of American consumerism on an emergent community, an issue that was then a major national concern, but even more pressing for a vulnerable Quebec.

Following *le cycle des belles-soeurs*, Tremblay went on to portray characters who had managed to escape from the tyranny of the family but were now surviving on the fringes of society, the social outcasts who frequent Montreal's demimonde (fringe society), the downtown core locally known as "The Main." "The setting itself, and the choice of this particular milieu," Usmiani writes, "is a plea for marginality, for freedom of the individual from the pressures of society, as well as for the freedom of marginal societies," such as the Francophone community in North America (*Michel Tremblay*, 22). Tremblay's comments support this view. In discussing his predilection for marginal characters, Tremblay asserts: "If I choose to talk about the fringes of society, it is because my people are a fringe society" (Anthony, 283).

In *Hosanna*, Tremblay's most notorious play, he presents a vivid glimpse into the life of two homosexuals who have become part of that *demi-monde*. *Hosanna* was first performed at the Théâtre de Quat'Sous in Montreal in 1973. Initially its blatant homosexuality created such a sensation that the political implications of the play were largely overlooked. Because of its wild, exotic appeal, *Hosanna* was translated into English almost immediately, and the following year it was produced at the Tarragon Theatre in Toronto, where it instantly became a major success. *Hosanna* then opened on Broadway where, unfortunately, it achieved only a lukewarm reception; nevertheless, it went on to be staged in Vancouver, Amsterdam, Paris, London, Cologne, and Glasgow. In the early 1990s, a significantly modified version of the play was produced in Montreal in French; this version merits further consideration, since it also addresses nationalism's gender politics. While the original production bravely embraced homosexuality, by essentializing sexual identity, it reinscribed Quebec's marginal position, inadvertently replicating Quebec's feminization in relation to the rest of North America. Somewhat paradoxically, the 1991 production of *Hosanna* more readily lends itself to a queer reading of nationalism, since this version takes yet another step forward and attempts to deconstruct the heterosexual gender categories that privilege the masculine ideal.

HOSANNA IN THE SEVENTIES

Hosanna deals with the anguish of two aging homosexuals caught in the trap of identifying with heterosexually-defined gender roles as a means of sustaining their relationship. By night, Claude, a hairdresser, transforms himself into the drag queen, Hosanna, while Raymond, a biker, complete with black leather and studs, is the macho lover who goes by the name of Cuirette. The play opens in Hosanna's cramped bachelor apartment on Halloween night. Cuirette and Hosanna, who is still in full drag, return from the annual costume party at Sandra's transvestite bar, where Hosanna had hoped to realize her lifelong dream and outdo Elizabeth Taylor's rendition of Cleopatra. As a transvestite, Hosanna wanted to emulate the most desirable of all women. However, to teach Hosanna a lesson for being such a bitchy queen—that is, for thinking herself better than all the other drag queens—Cuirette had them all show up dressed as Cleopatra as well. Of course, Hosanna was devastated. Hurt and humiliated, she has it out with Raymond, who wants Claude to stop pretending to be a woman. Finally, by the play's end, Claude declares that Cleopatra is dead; he removes all his makeup and strips down naked, boldly asserting: "Look, Raymond, I'm a man ... I'm a man, Raymond ... I'm a man ..." (87). They passionately embrace and the lights fade.

One of the most remarkable aspects of the critical response to *Hosanna* is that the two primary interpretations tend to cancel each other out. On the one hand, numerous critics focused on the play's ostensive homosexuality, thereby eschewing a political interpretation. For example, immediately following *Hosanna's* opening night in Montreal, Martial Dassylva, the theatre critic for *La Presse*, restricted his discussion to the play's homosexuality. He noted that this play offered the first time two of Tremblay's characters actually achieved a mutual understanding. While Dassylva expressly chose to defer a political analysis, a few days later, in *Le Devoir*, Albert Brie dismissed the possibility of any political message, claiming the play had no real theme: "*Il est à cent lieues du théâtre à these.*" Instead, Brie, in a gesture that appears to be an attempt to assuage his own sexual anxiety, clearly identified himself with straight audiences—"*Nous autres, normaux*" (We normal people ...)—but encouraged them to see the play on the grounds that their assumptions about homosexuality would be dispelled. On the other hand, political readings of *Hosanna* see it as an allegory, but for the most part deny its homosexuality by interpreting Claude's feminization as a consequence of colonization by the English and his final declaration of manhood as an assertion of Quebec nationalism. Precisely because of the heterosexist bias that pervades western discursive practices, including nationalist discourse, the homosexuality intrinsic to the play simply vanishes.

An instance of such a reading can be found in Renate Usmiani's otherwise comprehensive study, *Michel Tremblay*. Rather than explore the significance of the play's homosexuality, she proposes that *Hosanna* also functions on a psychological level, in that "it offers a gripping insight into the complex workings of a lovers' relationship," which of course it does, but she then hastily concludes "that both happen to be male becomes irrelevant" (89)! To support her point, Usmiani quotes from an interview published in Geraldine Anthony's *Stage Voices*, in which Tremblay himself tends to privilege a political reading of the play:

> My play, *Hosanna*, deals in a symbolic way with the problems of Quebec. Although *Hosanna* concerns two homosexuals, one an exaggerated masculine character, the other a transvestite, it is really an allegory about Quebec. In the end they drop their poses and embrace their real identity. The climax occurs when Hosanna kills Elizabeth Taylor and at the end he appears naked on stage and says he is a man. He kills all the ghosts around him as Quebec did. We are not French but we are Québécois living in North America! (284, emphasis added)

The play itself, however, shows that homosexuality is integral to *Hosanna*. As Schwartzwald remarks, in the second act, when Cuirette returns from his frustrating walk through Parc Lafontaine, he laments that "the newly installed floodlights have obliterated the shadows in which he used to cruise and have sex with other men. His response to this municipal act of moral zeal is a defiant one: 'From now on we're gonna do it in public, goddamn it!'" Schwartzwald deftly suggests that Cuirette's "refusal to seek new shadows and relegate his desire to the realm of the hidden sets the stage for Hosanna's own moment of enlightenment" ("From Authenticity," 499). Schwartzwald argues that *Hosanna* is a coming-out play, and in more ways than one, since on the level of political allegory, Claude is also coming out in terms of his cultural identity. In Schwartzwald's reading, homosexuality figures in the articulation of that identity, underscoring Quebec's position as a minority. While the repudiation of feminization still provides the key to a political interpretation of the play, Claude's avowed homosexuality significantly complicates his assertion of manhood and, by extension, Quebec's status within North America.

Even though Usmiani dismisses the play's homosexuality, she does offer some pertinent comments on Hosanna's transvestism and notes the prevalence of transvestite characters in Tremblay's work. She suggests that "these can be seen as inverted and caricatured versions of the sex symbol, a central element in the consumer society much hated by Tremblay. They also carry heavy overtones of political symbolism: the transvestite par excellence represents loss of identity, as well as impotence" (*Michel Tremblay*, 22). Indeed, Claude is powerless because of his marginal position as a Francophone in a Canada dominated by Anglophones. Culturally, however, Canada is marginal in relation to its more powerful neighbour, the United States. Thus, Claude's identification with Elizabeth Taylor, the British-born actor who became a major American movie star, brilliantly illustrates just how far removed Claude has become from his own cultural identity. Not only is Claude attempting to appropriate an English heritage—the cultural roots of the colonizer—his assumption of Elizabeth Taylor's star persona reveals the extent to which he has been overwhelmed by American culture. The fact that these identifications are played out under the guise of Cleopatra, the *femme fatale par excellence*, serves to highlight Claude's loss of a masculine identity. In this sense, Claude's feminization clearly signals his emasculation, his having been "conquered" by a dominant power.

However, Claude's sense of powerlessness is further exacerbated by his homosexuality, since it excludes him from heterosexual society, including Francophone Quebec, in which homophobic males dominate. In other words, Claude's feminization is pushed to the limit, so that drag becomes a means of empowerment, for, as Hosanna, Claude can assert his desirability by mimicking the heterosexual feminine ideal, even if he is restricted to society's margin. But in the process Claude is reduced to a sex object. Whereas the drag queen's often campy magnification of femininity highlights the performative aspect of gender, it also suggests how gender has been both reified and commodified. Yet, as a female impersonator, Claude takes his performance very much to heart, which signals the extent to which he has been alienated from his "true" or "essential" self. Usmiani suggests that as a theatrical device the transvestite embodies a universal archetype of alienation that exceeds the boundaries of any one nation or language (81). In her reading, Claude's final declaration of his manhood provides him with the strength necessary to assert his true cultural identity and thereby reclaim his humanity. But, in accordance with the humanist tradition upon which Usmiani draws, the subject is assumed to be a male heterosexual, constructed through the repression of the possibility of homosexuality.

What complicates a humanist reading of the play is that at the very moment Claude finally repudiates his feminization and asserts his manhood, he actually finds the courage to accept his homosexuality. By removing his makeup and stripping down naked, Claude reveals that he is indeed fully human, with needs and desires of his own: he is a man who loves other men. When viewed through a heterosexual lens, however, Claude's assertion that he is a man confounds the possibility of homosexuality precisely because "to be a man" is assumed to mean, "to be a heterosexual male." In *Sexual Dissidence,* an illuminating study of homosexuality's symbolic centrality to modern society, Jonathan Dollimore states, "the opposition masculine/ homosexual is a conflation of two other classic binaries: masculine/feminine; hetero/homosexual" (236). Homosexual relations are assumed to entail feminization for at least one of the males involved, since only one can physically penetrate the other, who must submit, thereby assuming the subordinate feminine role in relation to the dominant male. In terms of the binary logic that underpins this traditional definition of heterosexuality, the very logic that informs and drives the "violent hierarchies" of colonial discourse, the dominant male is privileged. That Raymond wanted to claim this role is made explicit by his macho posturing, even if it is an exaggerated masculinity suggestive of overcompensation. More to the point, however, by honestly confronting their homosexuality, Claude and Raymond are attempting to escape the trap of heterosexually-defined sex roles and to love each other as equals, in this case, as two human beings who are homosexual males. Tremblay himself maintains that as a political allegory his play means that the people of Quebec must "embrace their real identity," suggesting that despite their minority status within North America, Québécois, while different, are nevertheless entitled to full equality.

In his astute reading of the play, Schwartzwald is one of the few critics to explore Tremblay's convergence of discourses of sexual and national liberation, a convergence, Schwartzwald notes, that Tremblay makes appear *almost natural*. Precisely because Claude must accept that it is as a man that he desires other men before he can feel *bien dans sa peau* (comfortable in his own skin), "sexual desire is thus posed to perform as a more naturalized and radical arbiter of authenticity than gender, which for Tremblay is already encoded as more performative and therefore 'artificial'…" ("From Authenticity," 504). For despite Cuirette's macho posturing, it is he "who does all the cooking, cleaning, and housework and who is financially dependent upon '*her*'" (506); conversely, Hosanna, as the professional hairdresser Claude, is actually the bread-winner. Quite rightly, Schwartzwald argues that "the inconsistencies of Cuirette's gender performances, when compounded by their inevitable interaction with Hosanna's own, tend to underscore just how inoperative a category gender finally is for Tremblay" (506). In Foucauldian terms, Tremblay privileges sex as the measure of truth; in other words, it is the assertion of Claude's male sex, combined with the acceptance of his (homo)sexuality, that reveals the truth of his being—his essential, authentic identity.

Nevertheless, the deployment of the category of the homosexual as a means of stabilizing cultural identity proves problematic, since it creates a seeming paradox: as Schwartzwald notes, Claude's "rapprochement with his homosexual essence permanently marginalizes him as a sexual minority even as it authenticates him" (504). It was, moreover, the intolerably oppressive minoritizing dynamic of Quebec's relation to the rest of Canada and Quebec's vulnerable position within North America that fuelled the nationalist argument in the first place. Is Tremblay then suggesting that Quebec embrace its uniqueness, its inherent "*Québécité*," and accept its marginal status, even as this minority position stubbornly reinscribes Quebec's feminization in relation to the rest of North America? Or, as Schwartzwald puts it: Does Hosanna's reconciliation with the authenticity of his sexual desire imply that Quebec "was to be a permanently countercultural society, and consequently excluded from easy integration into the extended family of modern nations"? ("Symbolic Homosexuality," 265) Conceptions of the modern nation rely on the heterosexual model of the patriarchal family as a means of naturalizing nationalism.

In his study of French nationalism during the first half of the twentieth century, David Carroll observes that if "organic unity" is to characterize the form of the modern nation, "the origin of the nation and its model is the *patrie* conceived as the primal family, the original and natural community or society" (84). As nationalism gained prominence over the course of the nineteenth century, the rhetoric of empire building replicated the rigid gender divisions that privileged heterosexual men. Mary Louise Pratt concisely sums up the predicament of women by pointing out that their "value was specifically attached to (and implicitly conditioned on) their reproductive capacity. As mothers of the nation, they are precariously other to the nation. They are imagined as dependent rather than sovereign. They are practically forbidden to be limited and finite, being obsessively defined by their reproductive capacity" (51). While women were relegated to the domestic or private sphere, men presided over the public sphere, which included business, the military, and of course politics, a realm in which they sought to consolidate and expand the power of the nation. Most significantly, men's privileged position was predicated on the maintenance of homosocial relations; to transgress this social code meant to lose the privileges of heterosexual male entitlement and, hence, to be excluded from society, becoming, like women, other to the national project. Ideologically, even as it exists today, nationalism is closely imbricated with what Adrienne Rich has adroitly called "compulsory heterosexuality." Thus, the figuration of a national entity as homosexual as a means of authenticating its identity virtually excludes it from "the extended family of modern nations."

While Benedict Anderson claims that "in the modern world, everyone can, should, will 'have' a nationality, as he or she has a gender" (14), it is vitally important to recognize that national identity is already imbued with gendered significance. In an engaging analysis of queer belonging in Quebec, Elspeth Probyn astutely notes that what is less evident in Anderson's "formulation is that the type of nationality one will 'have' is dependent on the way in which gender is locally articulated" (36). For the centre and its margins are conceived as respectively masculine and feminine through the interpretative grid of heterosexuality. For instance, traditionally Canada has figured as feminine in relation to the United States; in addition, prior to the Quiet Revolution, Quebec figured as a marginal female in relation to the rest of Canada. It was precisely this oppressive configuration that Tremblay drew on for *Les belles-soeurs*. Usmiani, who aptly describes the play as "a contemporary domestic tragedy," notes that when read as a political allegory, Tremblay's presentation of an all-female society, "a powerless, exploited and almost marginal group in traditional society, effectively parallels the position of Quebec as a whole versus the rest of the North American continent" (*Theatre*, 45). However, to further complicate things, Probyn reminds us that "the French 'minority' comprises, in actual fact, 82% of the population within Québec which then allows some anglophone rights groups to position themselves as marginal and in need of protection. This then produces a discourse of anglophones as 'emasculated' in relation to the Québécois strongman" (50).

More relevant though is Probyn's observation that "the general troping of national identity as gendered and heterosexual can break down" (50). For the shifting power relations between various nations or "imagined communities" that give rise to the figuring of gendered positions illustrate how heterosexual binary categories are not stable, since the dominant masculine position can collapse into the feminine, while the feminine can assume a masculine position of dominance. By exposing the absence of an immutable essence around which each of these binary opposites can cohere, these transformations highlight the abstract conceptions on which traditional definitions of gender have tenuously been grounded. At the same time, the persistent articulation of nations in terms of their gendered positions betrays the extent to which a heterosexist bias shapes nationalist discourse, which of course continues to privilege the heterosexual male.

In asserting its difference, homosexuality radically challenges conceptions of the nation based on the traditional familial model. As Schwartzwald remarks, it is not difficult to see how Tremblay's "construction of homosexual and national identity as adequate metaphorical substitutions for each other could seem scandalous to those nationalist ideologues who saw independence as the goal in a developmental narrative deployed around a trope of infantilism and maturity" ("From Authenticity," 504). In Freudian terms, maturity means the assumption of male heterosexuality: identification with the father; Freud considered homosexuality "to be a variation of the sexual function produced by a certain arrest of development" (Dollimore, 196), identification with the dreaded mother. Burdened with the mark of effeminacy, homosexuality perturbs the link between traditional notions of masculinity and post-colonial conceptions of the nation that derive from a normalizing or regulatory model of the patriarchal family. As a stigma, effeminacy, or feminization, further suggests just how far removed we remain from accepting the sexes as equal. During the not-too-distant nineties, western nations consistently devalued democratic ideals traditionally associated with the "feminine," such as the notion that society is responsible for its disaffected, since in western discursive practices the feminine continues to be equated with frivolousness, weakness, and subservience. Indeed, for women to be taken seriously, they must deny their difference and conform to the masculine "norm." In contrast, because the feminine has been so denigrated in the western imaginary, when it "penetrates" the heterosexual male ideal, it contaminates it, rendering it abject. That the feminization of the masculine systematically evokes abhorrence demonstrates how misogyny drives homophobia, thereby revealing how the two are intimately related. By differing from the norm, the white heterosexual male, *all others* are deemed inferior, even if they comprise a majority. Yet, despite its privileging of the male, what was so remarkable about the original production of *Hosanna* was Tremblay's attempt to counter the devaluation of difference by having two men accept and love each other with dignity and mutual respect. Significantly, this only becomes possible once Claude and Raymond drop their heterosexual posturing and its attendant power dynamics, a move which enables them to recognize each other's sameness, their essential equality.

In *Epistemology of the Closet*, Eve Kosofsky Sedgwick brilliantly argues that "thought and knowledge in twentieth-century Western culture as a whole are structured—indeed, fractured—by a chronic, now endemic crisis of homo/heterosexual definition, indicatively male, dating from the end of the nineteenth century," when the category of the homosexual first emerged in medical discourse. As a result, "an understanding of virtually any aspect of modern Western culture must be, not merely incomplete, but damaged in its central substance to the degree that it does not incorporate a critical analysis of modern homo/heterosexual definition" (1). While not unique, Quebec nationalists have proven particularly resistant to just such incorporation. Their analyses of the failure of the nationalist project evince a typically homophobic response, which however provides valuable insight into their underlying assumptions and projections.

However, as Schwartzwald points out, "One of the most salient features of modern intellectual (self-)representation in Québec turns out to be that the homophobic elements of its *learned* discourse on identity are largely inconsistent with both liberal legal discourse and popular attitudes" ("Symbolic Homosexuality," 266). Ironically, "Québec was the first state jurisdiction in North America to adopt anti-discrimination legislation on grounds of sexual orientation, and this was done by the *nationalist* Parti Québécois government," which was elected in 1976 ("Fear of Federasty," 180). Far from stigmatizing homosexuals as emblematic of "national alienation," at that time, the government, under the leadership of the late René Lévesque, "spoke of wanting to protect and further the interests of all communities in an inclusive figuration of the nation" (180). Nevertheless, following the defeat of the 1980 referendum on sovereignty-association, the analytic trend of Quebec nationalists proved to be especially sensitive to "homosexually inflected articulations of identity, which [were] compulsively read for clues that might explicate the identitary impasse of the Québécois subject-nation" ("Symbolic Homosexuality," 267). Drawing on the coming-of-age trope common to postcolonial discourse, "a developmental narrative in which Québec's independence would be the culmination of a process leading from 'infancy' to 'maturity'" was consistently produced (265). Consequently, Quebec nationalists all too readily assumed "the homophobic assignation of homosexuality as *arrested* development" in support of their "explanations of Québec's long, halting progress toward self-determination" (267).

While "the formation of a viable Québécois nation implicitly depended upon the forging of a new, emancipatory social contract," which was "one of the most powerful discursive ruptures initiated by the Quiet Revolution," Schwartzwald concludes that:

> the overarching persistence of a developmental model for nationhood within this contractual paradigm and its particular claims to modernity reveals an enduring reliance upon heterosexually ordered and ultimately archaicizing familial models when constructing the national 'body' itself. Subjecting contractual models to pressures as great as the defeat of a popular referendum on sovereignty is perhaps a sad but effective way of demonstrating how the attendant figures of a familial model never entirely disappear, but are instead held 'in reserve' until a disastrous conjuncture resuscitates them. (270)

In his analysis of the discursive practices of Quebec nationalists, Schwartzwald goes on to show how homosexuality persistently figures as central "to the identitary matrix of the subject-nation" but becomes "the repressed whose return portends only disruption and signifies failure" (270). It is, however, the heterosexually ordered familial model of the nation/state that is doomed to failure. Precisely because heterosexuality is predicated on the denial of homosexuality, the latter underpins the very foundation on which masculine identity is precariously constructed, creating an unstable structure. Whereas homosexuality is an internally repressed difference, for the insecure or threatened heterosexually identified male, through the process of unconscious projection, homosexuality is perceived as an external threat, an unsettling recognition of denied otherness. In his book, *Homos,* Leo Bersani suggests that "homophobia may be this fearful excitement at the prospect of becoming what one already is" (28). Of necessity, a successful model of the modern nation must dispense with heterosexual rigidity. A new, more inclusive national configuration is now needed; such a model must be expansive and diverse in its conception, allowing for difference rather than assimilation, which only leads back to the reinstatement of an exclusive, self-defeating norm. While the appropriation of a heterosexual model inflects the queering of nationhood with developmental failure, in order to arrest this interpretive trend, it is imperative to recognize how homophobic anxiety inevitably undermines the very model it seeks to impose.

Dollimore determines that the "associations of sexual deviation and political threat have a long history sedimented into our language and culture" (236–37). By way of example, he cites the term "buggery," the origin of which apparently "derives from the religious as well as sexual nonconformity of an eleventh-century Bulgarian sect that practised the Manichaean heresy and refused to propagate the species. The *Oxford English Dictionary* tells us that it was later applied to other heretics, to whom abominable practices were also ascribed" (237). In addition, Dollimore finds that "social and political crisis provokes renewed urgency in the policing of sexual deviance" (237). He then refers to Arthur N. Gilbert, who reports that in England "[d]uring the Napoleonic wars the numbers of prosecutions for sodomy increased. To understand why," he continues, "we need to understand the construction of the sodomite, his association at that time with evil, rebellion, and insurrection, and the belief that to tolerate his sin was to court the possibility of divine revenge (as with Sodom and Gomorrah)" (237). During this period the mythology surrounding the sodomite found an immediate focus: he "was perceived as an internal deviant who refigured a foreign threat, in this case the threat from the French" (237). The displacement of non-sexual fears onto the sexual deviant, Dollimore concludes, "are made possible because other kinds of transgression—political, religious—are not only loosely associated with the sexual deviant, but 'condensed' in the very definition of deviance"; that this process of displacement succeeded attests to "the paranoid instabilities at the heart of dominant cultural identities (237).

In "Fear of Federasty," Schwartzwald explores the homophobic tropes deployed by Quebec nationalists during the 1960s and 1970s, tropes that evoke the mythology that connects sexual deviance with political threat. He suggests that for these nationalists, "homosexuality signifies metonymically ... that is, as the *presence* of an earlier intellectual elite composed of or tied to the clergy that entered into a compact with Anglo-Canadian capital to divide supervision over the colonized body of the Québécois..." (180). In their attempts to effect a radical break with the conservative nationalism of the past, the homophobic anxiety of the new nationalists was articulated by characterizing "those found to be traitors or sell-outs to the cause of national revolution ... as passive/seductive men" (179). Such a man was labelled a *fédéraste,* a play on *pédéraste,* the French word used to signify homosexuality, although its primary definition concerns the love of men for boys. For to be called a *fédéraste,* Schwartzwald duly notes, meant to be one of those who are "first the victims, then the corrupted perpetrators of what is figured as a permanent violation by a salacious 'fully grown' Canada against the waifish, innocent Québec" (179). Because the term *pédéraste is* not usually used in Quebec, "its foreignness as a continental French signifier for homosexuality underlines the 'exotic' or unrooted personality of the traitor/violator"; in addition, "the activity to which *fédérastes* give themselves over is compulsive, repetitious, and unproductive" (180). Thus, the figuring of Quebec as a homosexual came to assume a doubly vexed position. As a consequence, even those who considered themselves among the most progressive of the new breed of nationalists were primarily interested in reasserting conventional gender definitions, in which Quebec would assume the position of a dominant heterosexual male.

Schwartzwald cites an essay that appeared in *Parti pris* in 1964, tellingly titled "The Colonial Oedipus," in which Pierre Maheu, in a fit of blatantly sexist rhetoric, urged fellow nationalists "to accept that we are sons of women. This will lead us to make of women both our lovers and wives while we liberate ourselves from the Mother by surging forth once again from her breast, well armed for a new combat, a new confrontation: that of the free man who attacks concrete enemies head on ..." (188). Quebec's nationalist project was not unique; rather it situated itself "within the universalizing discourse of all the great anti-colonial movements of the epoch in question" (179). Schwartzwald proposes that it was "the preoccupation with unified subjectivity that led to a profound sexual anxiety in Quebec's anti-colonial discourse, an anxiety which *is already* borne within the attempted synthesis of Marxist, existentialist, and Freudian theory that underlies the anti-colonial writings of the post-war period" (178).

Freud's writings, given their complexity and contradictions, offer various possibilities for a counter-discourse. Of particular relevance is Freud's acceptance of Wilhelm Fliess's view that human beings are inherently bisexual. In *The Ego and the Id,* Freud maintains that the most important way in which bisexuality influences the vicissitudes of the Oedipus complex is in its complete form, which is two-fold, both positive and negative, meaning both same-sex identification and opposite-sex identification. Surprisingly, Freud then suggests that the positive or "simple Oedipus complex is by no means its commonest form..." (279). The more complete Oedipus complex, he writes:

> ... is due to the bisexuality originally present in children: that is to say, a boy has not merely an ambivalent attitude towards his father and an affectionate object-choice towards his mother, but at the same time he also behaves like a girl and displays an affectionate feminine attitude to his father and a corresponding jealousy and hostility towards his mother. It is this complicating element introduced by bisexuality that makes it so difficult to obtain a clear view of the facts in connection with the earliest object-choices and identifications, and still more difficult to describe them intelligibly. (279)

Freud's characterization of the boy's affection for the father as feminine is a key. As Judith Butler points out, "for Freud *bisexuality is the coincidence of two heterosexual desires within a single psyche.* The masculine disposition is, in effect, never oriented toward the father as an object of sexual love, and neither is the feminine disposition oriented toward the mother.... Hence, within Freud's thesis of primary bisexuality, there is no homosexuality, and only opposites attract" (61). While this highlights a fundamental flaw in Freud's thinking, which of course reflects the much larger problem in western conceptual systems, Freud's reinscription of hetero-sexuality is symptomatic of his own sexual anxiety and evidence of the regulatory pressures of compulsory heterosexuality. Freud acknowledges these pressures elsewhere, indicating that the predominance of heterosexuality is driven by cultural attitudes.

For instance, in 1915, Freud added to his *Three Essays on the Theory of Sexuality* an extraordinary footnote that extends over four pages, in which he argues against "separating off homosexuals from the rest of mankind as a group of a special charac-ter" (56). To support his argument, he makes the astonishing statement that hetero-sexuality is *also a problem* that is not fully understood:

> [F]rom the point of view of psychoanalysis the exclusive sexual interest felt by men for women is also a problem that needs elucidating and is not a self-evident fact based upon an attraction that is ultimately of a chemical nature. A person's final sexual attitude is not decided until after puberty and is the result of a number of factors, not all of which are yet known; some are of a constitutional nature but others are accidental.... But in general the multiplicity of determining factors is reflected in the variety of manifest sexual attitudes in which they find their issue in mankind. (57)

In recognizing the limits of his knowledge, Freud makes a generous allowance for cultural determinants and their diverse manifestations.

Although Dollimore maintains he is not interested "in recovering the authentic voice of psychoanalysis," he is particularly interested in Freud's "deconstructive assault on normality" (182). Dollimore argues how, via Freud, "we can see that the concept of perversion always embodied what has now become a fundamental deconstructive proposition: whatever a culture designates as alien, utterly other, and incommensu-rably different is rarely and perhaps never so" (182). Drawing on Freud's concepts of repression, disavowal, negation, and splitting, Dollimore elaborates on what he calls "the perverse dynamic": how perversion "destroys the binary structure of which it is initially an effect" (183). Freud recognized that the development of culture inevitably led to the production of the effects it sought to repress (188). As Dollimore remarks, at this point Freud anticipates Michel Foucault.

In *The History of Sexuality,* Foucault makes his now famous argument that the intensification of the regulation of sexuality over the course of the eighteenth and nineteenth centuries did not lead to the repression of same-sex activity; on the contrary, it led to the production of the category of the homosexual. "Homosexuality," Foucault writes, "appeared as one of the forms of sexuality when it was transposed from the practice of sodomy onto a kind of interior androgyny, a hermaphrodism of the soul. The sodomite had been a temporary aberration; the homosexual was now a species" (43). While the end product may appear to be qualitatively distinct, Robert May points out that "analysis shows that the determinants are only different in degree" (163). Citing Freud's remarkable footnote, May draws attention to Freud's admission that there are no "constitutional peculiarities" that can be attributed to the homosexual that are not present, "though less strongly, in the constitution of transitional types and those whose manifest attitude is normal" (163). In other words, for Freud, heterosexuality and homosexuality are not discrete categories, but overlap, thus destroying their binary structure. So, if masculinity and femininity are merely elaborate cultural fictions deployed to promote heterosexuality in the interests of empire building, what then does it mean to be a man or a woman? But even more disturbing, can the differences between the sexes and sexual difference be articulated without recourse to the heterosexual matrix?

HOSANNA IN THE NINETIES

Within its specific historical context, the deployment of sexual binaries provided Tremblay with a unique means of authenticating Claude's cultural identity. In 1991, however, a new production of *Hosanna* was staged in Montreal, in which the emphasis on an essentialized conception of sexual identity shifted to foreground gender roles and their performative character. As previously noted, while discussing the original production of the play, Tremblay stated, *"Hosanna* concerns two homosexuals, one an exaggerated masculine character, the other a transvestite ..." (Anthony, 284). In a note in the 1991 program, Tremblay proceeds to describe the play as an exploration of the crisis of *"two* transvestites, not only Hosanna but her lover Cuirette ..." ("From Authenticity" 502). Tremblay's comment, Schwartzwald observes, "reminds us that these issues were present in the original version, but remained largely illegible when set against the overarching, virtually compulsory reading of *Hosanna* at that time as an allegory of national oppression" (502). In addition, in the 1991 stage production, Claude is no longer in drag; instead, Hosanna's bright red dress glares out at us from the open closet, and Cuirette's macho posturing is also exposed as an exaggerated gender performance. Even Claude's final line, "I'm a man," no longer resembles an affirmation of an authentic identity; rather it has become a profound interrogation charged with ambivalence, creating a gaping uncertainty ("From Authenticity" 501). The new version of *Hosanna* engages a Quebec that has undergone profound cultural changes, including a confrontation with the developments of French feminism and deconstruction. "To those who yearn to be part of a stable, homogeneous majority," Schwartzwald concludes, the new *"Hosanna* responds with another allegory, this time mocking the self-delusion that underwrites the self-confident 'putting on' of gender roles that appear more natural, but whose performative character is denied" (505).

In *Gender Trouble,* Butler argues that while there is no abiding substance or immutable gender core that derives from morphological sex, gender is not a set of free-floating attributes that can be assumed at will, but "the substantive effect of gender is performatively produced" over time by the demands of a regulatory discourse that encodes masculinity and femininity within the heterosexual matrix (24). Because gender categories have been organized to coincide with and promote heterosexuality, for a male to become a "man" requires the repudiation of an identification with the feminine, a repudiation which "becomes a precondition for the heterosexualization of sexual desire and hence ... its fundamental ambivalence" ("Gender Melancholy," 26). It is this fundamental ambivalence—a haunting doubt that must constantly be appeased—that produces sexual anxiety for the heterosexual male. While the misogyny underpinning the privileging of male heterosexuality fuels homophobia, leading to aggression, intimidation and even violence, it also perpetuates the oppression of women, who, in assuming the masquerade of femininity, obediently conform to the inferior position and thus provide a mirror that enables masculine dominance.

As a homosexual attempting to assert his desirability, Claude emulates the ultimate woman, but once he removes his costume and makeup—as Hosanna presents himself to the audience in the 1991 production—he reveals himself as a male, and as such, from an already gendered position. It is precisely at this point that Butler's analysis becomes most relevant, for she points out that there is no one prior to this *naturalized* performance of gender. Gender itself proves to be performative, "that is, constituting the identity it is purported to be" (25), even if its performative character is not evident. As Hosanna laments, "the show must go on ... and on ... and on ... and on ..." (62). The question now becomes where to go from here: Once the masks have been removed, how are Claude and Raymond to articulate their identities as gay men?

In rethinking gender performativity, Butler refers to Jacques Derrida, who emphasizes that it is necessary to understand performativity "*as* citationality, for the invocation of identity is always a *re*invocation" (Rajchman, 132). This means that a subject can be produced only "through the citing of a norm, a citing which instantiates and institutes the norm" (134). How then can gay men articulate their masculinity and not efface their homosexuality? It seems that a specifically gay male identity can be produced only by queering the norm, by marking it with an exaggerated expression of femininity or masculinity. This of course is not to suggest blind adherence to heterosexual gender positions, the positions which Cuirette and Hosanna initially tried to inhabit before accepting their homosexuality. Rather, the self-conscious reinvocation of these gendered markers can be used with deliberation, to signal the incoherence of heterosexual gender binaries while simultaneously producing a queer subject position.

Since the emergence of queer theory in the late 1980s, the term "queer" has taken on new significance. Embraced as a site of resistance, "the desanctioning power of the name 'queer' is reversed to sanction a contestation of the terms of sexual legitimacy"

("Critically Queer" 18). Butler's translation of queer theory into praxis envisions a new form of political activism. She elaborates:

> Paradoxically, but also with great promise, the subject who is 'queered' into public discourse through homophobic interpellations of various kinds *takes* up or *cites* that very term as the discursive basis for an opposition. This kind of citation will emerge as *theatrical* to the extent that *it mimes and renders hyperbolic* the discursive convention that it also *reverses*. The hyperbolic gesture is crucial to the exposure of the homophobic law which can no longer control the terms of its own abjecting strategies. (18)

Not only does the performance of queerness enable the articulation of a specifically homosexual subject position, it also provides the ground on which to develop an oppositional movement. By mocking the incoherence of its antagonists' position, queerness undermines the very ground from which the attack was launched. Thus queer politics instantiates what Dollimore defines as the "perverse dynamic," for the queer dynamic activates the deconstruction of the binary structure that not only produced it, but also attempts to contain and oppress it.

Even though queer theory is anti-essentialist, queer politics remains a form of identity politics since the modern political realm is dominated by the notion of a coherent or essential self. Nevertheless, it is identity politics with a difference: its potential lies in queerness as a political identity. As Jeffrey Weeks puts it, in its broadest sense, the organizing principle of queer politics "is not an assumed sexual identity based on orientation or practice, but identification with the forms of politics and patterns of transgression that define queerness" (112). In addition, Michael Warner argues that queerness "rejects a minoritizing logic of toleration or simple political interest-representation in favor of a more thorough resistance to regimes of the normal" (xxii). Specifically, it is the privileging of the white heterosexual male that is being contested. This makes for a potentially inclusive political movement, one which covers a broad spectrum, including gays and lesbians, bisexuals, transsexuals, single mothers, feminists, sympathetic heterosexuals, and ethnic minorities. Indeed, it covers all who embrace the ambiguity of culturally produced identities and want actively to challenge the ways in which categories such as gender, sexuality, race, and nation are constructed by powerful cultural narratives in order to protect and promote the existing norm by marginalizing difference.

Bersani questions queer theory's effectiveness as praxis and thus proposes an alternate strategy—what he calls "homo-ness"—arguing that it is a more radical possibility, since "*it necessitates a massive redefining of relationality*" (76). Bersani remarks that "[i]t is not possible to be gay-affirmative, or politically effective as gays, if gayness has no specificity" (61). He then reminds us that in a heterosexual society women have played an important role in teaching gay men how to frame and stage their sexuality (61). Referring to Kaja Silverman's *Male Subjectivity at the Margins*, Bersani reiterates her queer argument that "the gay man's deployment of signifiers of the feminine may be a powerful weapon in the defeat of those defensive maneuvers that have defined sexual difference. This goal," he adds, "is also served by the instability of the deployment" (61). But, as he sees it:

> The gay man's identification with women is countered by an imitation of those desiring subjects with whom we have been officially identified: other men. In a sense, then, the very maintaining of the couples man-woman, heterosexual-homosexual, serves to break down their oppositional distinctions. These binary divisions help to create the diversified desiring field across which we can move, thus reducing sexual difference itself—at least as far as desire is concerned—to a merely formal arrangement inviting us to transgress the very identity assigned to us within the couple. (61)

In other words, the assumption of heterosexually defined roles *at will*—alternating between mimicry and reversal—will inevitably strip these roles of their power.

Quite rightly, Bersani proposes that we can also all learn something from the experience of homosexuals. Rather than privilege difference, which the dominant power perceives as the inferior term, he recommends we begin to privilege our "*near-sameness*" or, as he prefers to call it, our "homo-ness," which, however, does not mean "the perfect identity of terms" (146). For, "identities," Bersani adds, *always* "spill over." So, instead of focusing on difference, he suggests we first acknowledge our likeness, not necessarily the essentialized sameness of gender, sexuality, or race, but shared characteristics, such as the fact that we are all living, breathing, feeling, thinking beings, in short, equal. "To recognize universal homo-ness," Bersani writes, "can allay the terror of difference, which generally gives rise to a hopeless dream of eliminating difference entirely. A massively heteroized perception of the universal gives urgency to a narcissistic project that would reduce—radically, with no surplus whatsoever of alterity—the other to the same" (146). Bersani's proposal is worth considering, for its implications are far reaching.

For instance, the 1991 production of *Hosanna* suggests that we can extend the questioning of heterosexual gender categories to that of national identity; specifically, we can ask what it means to be a Québécois or a Canadian. In an attempt to rewrite the narrative of the nation, the postcolonial theorist Homi K. Bhabha effectively argues that the ambivalence that haunts the articulation of gender positions parallels the ambivalence that haunts the idea of the modern nation. According to Bhabha's timely argument, in the discursive production of the nation, "there is a split between the continuist, accumulative temporality of the pedagogical," the people as an *a priori* historical presence, an ideal, and the people constructed in the performance of narration, the enunciatory present (297–99). In Quebec, the pedagogical ideal of a homogeneous mass, the people as one deriving from old Québécois stock—*la souche*—creates the imaginary boundary that marks the nation's selfhood: "the people as 'image' and its signification as a differentiating sign of Self, distinct from the Other or the Outside" (299). But within the postmodern context of mass migration, the pedagogical narrative is disrupted, introducing a temporality of the "in-between," what Bhabha defines as a liminal "space of representation that threatens binary division with its difference" (299). The opening up of this "in-between" space, where the external threat of the other is now perceived as having infiltrated the nation/state, creates intense anxiety, often leading to xenophobia. However, the enunciation of cultural differences within a nation, Bhabha points out, can only be agonistically articulated. Although it is doubtful that the agony of this postmodern articulation can be avoided, as Bersani suggests, the terror of difference can be allayed by privileging our "near-sameness." It is here that his concept of "homo-ness" reveals its broadest applicability.

While heterogeneous figures now proliferate on the streets of Montreal, the obsession of Quebec nationalists with *la souche*, Probyn pointedly remarks, "continually threatens to asphyxiate their movement" (63). Referring to C. Philo, Probyn adds, "it is deeply insufficient to think that we can comprehend forms of belonging by seeking to refer them to an underlying structuring principle, a stable and guaranteeing referent" (17). As she notes, when the Parti Québécois resumed power in 1994, one of the first statements premier Jacques Parizeau made was "that it is now time to make Quebec into a normal country" (n65), meaning of course a patriarchal nation-state based on the white male norm. Sadly Parizeau's response to the failure of Quebec's 1995 referendum confirms Bhabha's assertion that such a model is no longer viable within a postmodern context. For Parizeau, overcome with bitterness, firmly placed the blame on "money and the ethnic vote," money here referring to the English minority in Quebec, who are for the most part no longer wealthy, since the money migrated west. And why immigrants would vote for a sovereign Quebec that bars them from participating in that society poses a serious question these nationalists must now address. As Bhabha concludes:

> Once the liminality of the nation-space is established, and its 'difference' is turned from the boundary 'outside' to its finitude 'within,' the threat of cultural difference is no longer a problem of 'other' people. It becomes a question of the otherness of the people-as-one. The national subject splits in the ethnographic perspective of culture's contemporaneity and provides both a theoretical position and a narrative authority for marginal voices or minority discourse. (301)

Somewhat ironically, in Quebec, the narrative authority of marginal voices has actually succeeded in asserting its presence. But here, as elsewhere, the issue of identity remains an ongoing preoccupation. Perhaps, then, in rethinking the Canadian experiment in the face of the "perplexity of living," there remains the possibility of imagining a new, postmodern community.

(2001)

Works Cited

Anderson, Benedict. *Imagined Communities: Reflections on the Origin and Spread of Nationalism.* London: Verso, 1983.

Anthony, Geraldine, ed. *Stage Voices: Twelve Canadian Playwrights Talk about Their Lives and Work.* Toronto: Doubleday, 1978.

Bersani, Leo. *Homos.* Cambridge, MA: Harvard University Press, 1995.

Bhabha, Homi K. "DissemiNation: time, narrative, and the margins of the modern nation." In *Nation and Narration.* Ed. Homi K. Bhabha. New York: Routledge, 1990. 291–322.

Brie, Albert. "Tremblay joue et gagne." *Le Devoir* (15 mai 1973): 10.

Butler, Judith. "Critically Queer." In *Playing with Fire: Queer Politics, Queer Theories.* Ed. Shane Phelan. New York: Routledge, 1997. 11–29.

———. *Gender Trouble: Feminism and the Subversion of Identity.* New York: Routledge, 1990.

———. "Melancholy Gender/Refused Identification." In *Constructing Masculinity.* Ed. Maurice Berger, Brian Wallis and Simon Watson. New York: Routledge, 1995. 21–36.

Carroll, David. *French Literary Fascism: Nationalism, Anti-Semitism, and the Ideology of Culture.* Princeton, NJ: Princeton UP, 1995.

Dassylva, Martial. "Des éclaircies de tendresse." *La Presse* (11 mai 1973): 12A.

Dollimore, Jonathan. *Sexual Dissidence: Augustine to Wilde, Freud to Foucault.* Oxford: Clarendon, 1991.

Forsyth, Louise H. "Beyond the Myths and Fictions of Traditionalism and Nationalism: The Political in the Work of Nicole Brossard." In *Traditionalism, Nationalism, and Feminism: Women Writers of Quebec.* Ed. Paula Gilbert Lewis. Westport, CT: Greenwood, 1985. 157–72.

Foucault, Michel. *The History of Sexuality: An Introduction.* Vol. 1. Trans. Robert Hurley. New York: Vintage Books, 1990.

Freud, Sigmund. *On Sexuality: Three Essays on the Theory of Sexuality and other Works.* Vol. 7. Trans. James Strachey. London: Penguin, 1977.

———. *The Ego and the Id.* Excerpt in *Freud on Women: A Reader.* Ed. Elisabeth Young Bruehl. New York: Norton, 1990. 274–82.

May, Robert. "Re-reading Freud on Homosexuality." In *Disorienting Sexuality: Psychoanalytic Reappraisals of Sexual Identities.* Ed. Thomas Domenici and Ronnie C. Lesser. New York: Routledge, 1995. 153–65.

Pratt, Mary Louise. "Women, Literature, and National Brotherhood." In *Women, Culture, and Politics in Latin America: Seminar on Feminism and Culture in Latin America*. Ed. Emilie Bergmann et al. Berkeley: U of California P, 1990.

Probyn, Elspeth. "Love in a Cold Climate." *Queer Belongings in Québec*. Montreal: GRECC, 1994.

Rajchman, John, ed. *The Identity* in *Question*. New York: Routledge, 1995.

Schwartzwald, Robert. "Fear of Federasty: Québec's Inverted Fictions." In *Comparative American Identities: Race, Sex, and Nationality in the Modern Text*. Ed. Hortense J. Spillers. New York: Routledge: 1991.175–95.

———. "From Authenticity to Ambivalence: Michel Tremblay's *Hosanna*." In *American Review of Canadian Studies* 4th ser. 22 (1992): 499–510.

———. "'Symbolic' Homosexuality, 'False Feminine,' and the Problematics of Identity in Québec." In *Fear of a Queer Planet: Queer Politics and Social Theory*. Ed. Michael Warner. Minneapolis, MN: U of Minnesota P, 1993. 264–99.

Sedgwick, Eve Kosofsky. *Epistemology of the Closet*. Berkeley: U of California P, 1990.

Tremblay, Michel. *Hosanna*. Trans. John Van Burek and Bill Glassco. Vancouver: Talonbooks, 1991.

Usmiani, Renate. *Michel Tremblay*. Vancouver: Douglas & McIntyre, 1982.

———. *The Theatre of Frustration: Super Realism in the Dramatic Work of F.X. Kroetz and Michel Tremblay*. New York: Garland, 1990.

Warner, Michael, ed. *Fear of a Queer Planet: Queer Politics and Social Theory*. Minneapolis, MN: U of Minnesota P, 1993.

Weeks, Jeffrey. *Invented Moralities: Sexual Values in an Age of Uncertainty*. New York: Columbia UP, 1995.

The Elephant, the Mouse,
and the Lesbian National Park Rangers

by B.J. Wray

The relationship of nationalism to lesbianism has never been a monolithic one. Although it is easy to compile a lengthy account of the ways in which state-sanctioned nationalism has coerced, pathologized, and terrorized lesbians as sexual "deviants," and although it is easy to recount innumerable occasions on which the agents of national borders consistently police lesbian desire through the confiscation of sexually-explicit material, the ideology of nationalism has frequently and repeatedly been invoked as a paradigm for lesbian community-building. Nationalism— especially the sense of connectedness, unity, and commonality that its discourses convey—holds a certain appeal for an otherwise amorphous community whose members do not share a single geography, passport, or currency. In the succinct phrasing of legal theorist Carl Stychin, "[s]ocial movements ... deploy the language of nation as a means of constituting and reinforcing their own identities" (7).

This vexed connection between national discourses of belonging and lesbian identity provides the backdrop for Shawna Dempsey and Lorri Millan's 1997 site-specific performance, *The Lesbian National Park Rangers*.[1] I have chosen *The Rangers* from Dempsey and Millan's extensive oeuvre because of the ways in which this performance demonstrates a complex interaction with, and intervention in, the operations of normative national and sexual discourses.[2]

Dempsey and Millan humourously interrogate the "unnaturalness" of lesbian sexuality from within the confines of the state-sanctioned "naturalness" of Banff National Park. The relationship between national citizenship and lesbian sexuality hinges upon an ever-shifting politics of representation, and Dempsey and Millan's strategies of lesbian representation, while cognizant of the pitfalls attached to visibility politics, employ parody and hyperbole to resight/site a lesbian subject within a national setting.

My examination of *The Lesbian National Park Rangers* is framed by contemporary discussions of rights discourses and sexual citizenship. Lesbian activism specifically and activist theory generally, within the Western nation-state, is most often driven by a desire for the rights that full and equal national citizenship promises. As one of the most tangible markers of belonging, full and equal citizenship is held up as a guarantor of minority recognition within the nation-state. Lesbian theorist Shane Phelan is representative in her assessment of the road to "democratic empowerment": "Clearly, new rights are needed if lesbians are to be full citizens"

(129). Phelan's linkage of full citizenship with the procurement of rights characterizes contemporary mainstream sexuality activism. Both "rights" and "citizenship" are understood, in this equation, as concepts that must be expanded to include lesbian subjects. This form of mainstream activism takes for granted the liberating power of full and equal citizenship and fails to consider the ways in which the discourses of national citizenship actively materialize sexual identities, histories, and cultures.

As categories of identification, citizenship and sexuality engender certain representations of the identities at hand. The rights discourses associated with full and equal citizenship *compel* the narrativization of lesbian history, culture, identity, and desire along the homogenizing trajectory of national belonging. A rights discourse works to the extent that it both constitutes and articulates the existence of an identifiable, marginalized group of people. Calls for full and equal citizenship must grapple with the potential reiteration of normative notions of identity that are always already present in the national discourses at hand. Lesbian sexuality is imagined within the parameters of these activist calls for full and equal citizenship, and lesbian identity cannot be separated from discourses of national belonging. In other words, an analysis of the style in which identity is imagined—its discursive materialization—exposes the structuring power that national citizenship has on figurations of lesbian community and identity.

Critics of the power that citizenship wields over non-normative subjects and communities have tended to focus on the illusory nature of citizenship's apparent inclusivity. Specifically, the notion of "universal" citizenship has come under fire from feminist scholars for its implicit privileging of white, heteronormative subjects. Political theorist Iris Marion Young outlines the problematic foundation of conventional citizenship:

> Founded by men, the modern state and its public realm of citizenship paraded as universal values and norms that were derived from specifc-ally masculine experience: militarist norms of honor and homoerotic camaraderie; respectful competition and bargaining among independent agents; discourse framed in unemotional tones of dispassionate reason. (266)

Citizenship is produced as a productive and disciplinary category that is regularly deployed within formal and informal relations of power. David Evans further clarifies this process: "Behind the rhetoric of universal rights of privacy, dignity, religious and cultural beliefs, there stands a citizenship machinery which effectively invades and corrals those who by various relative status shortcomings are deemed to be less than fully qualified citizens" (5). Non-normative sexual identities fall outside the realm of "universal" rights, and the "citizenship machinery" that Evans identifies actively curtails the representation and recognition of these identities within the nation-state.

In direct opposition to this process of delimitation, erasure, and exclusion, feminist and lesbian-rights activism often seeks to transform citizenship into an inclusive category of identification. On the other hand, separatist-based politics wants to be rid of the category altogether. In the words of Canadian historian Gary Kinsman, "[T]raditional concepts simply cannot be stretched to cover our experiences. We must step outside the dominant discourses—as must women and other oppressed groups—if we are to create a body of knowledge to help us in our struggle" (31). Rather than replicate either an assimilationist or a separatist approach towards imagining sexual citizenship and the new constitution of universality that these models tend to promote, I am interested in the types of citizenship that are forged where identification and misidentification overlap.

My usage of citizenship extends beyond state-sanctioned definitions and narrow legal and political applications. Rather, I understand citizenship as a malleable model of performed affiliations whose contours are discursively constituted and, therefore, continually reiterated within the nation-state, or as political theorist Terrell Carver notes, "citizenship is a movable metaphor of 'belonging' and 'inclusion'" (16). In the words of Lauren Berlant: "It [citizenship] is continually being produced out of a political, rhetorical, and economic struggle over who will count as 'the people' and how social membership will be measured and valued" (20). Citizenship, as we will see in *The Lesbian National Park Rangers*, is not a static delineation of national belonging, but is an active, ongoing performance that can never be fully or finally conferred. Conceptualized as performance, citizenship becomes newly accessible for resignification by minority subjects.

The Lesbian National Park Rangers begins this process of resignification through an exploration of the ways in which national identities come to be "naturalized." Dempsey and Millan's spectacular, hyperbolic performance transforms lesbian invisibility within discourses of Canadian nation-ness into a showy, campy display of "official" lesbian presence. The "naturalness" of national and sexual identifications is taken to task by Dempsey's and Millan's parodic invasion of a significant site of Canadian nationalism, Banff National Park. *The Lesbian National Park Rangers* interrogates the exclusionist operations of nation-making and exploits the signifiers of normative national belonging as the newly configured sites/sights of lesbian sexuality. Dempsey and Millan's performance does more, however, than simply expose the quotidian operations of nation-making. Instead of reiterating the representational difficulties associated with an oppositional approach to activism, the spectacle offered by *The Lesbian National Park Rangers* insists upon a mode of lesbian activism that critiques conventional discourses of national and sexual identification through *direct engagement* with these dominant paradigms.

Banff National Park is Canada's postcard to the world. Perhaps the most recognizable of Canadian scenery, Banff's wildlife, snow-capped mountain peaks, landmark hotels, European-inspired townsite, and five million tourists a year guarantee the international representational cachet of this National Park. My academic home, the English department at the University of Calgary, banks on the allure of this National Park to entice guest lecturers and job candidates to our University: a day of lectures and a weekend in Banff, it sells well. Established in 1855, Banff is Canada's oldest National Park and the anchor in a countrywide chain of thirty-eight federally created and regulated "natural areas of Canadian significance" (www.parkscanada.pch.gc.ca/np/english/nptxt_e.htm).

Banff alone functions as Canada's Ur-Park. It acts, within an international and Canadian imaginary, as a tangible marker of Canadian geography and, more importantly, of Canadian identity. I hardly need remark upon the prestigious role ascribed to this so-called "wilderness" in the making of a Canadian national identity. Margaret Atwood's highly influential 1972 thematic guide to Canadian literature, aptly entitled *Survival*, informs readers that "[t]he central symbol for Canada ... is undoubtedly survival ... For early explorers and settlers, it meant bare survival in the face of 'hostile' elements ... For French Canada after the English took over it became cultural survival .... And in English Canada now while the Americans are taking over it is acquiring a similar meaning" (32).[3] The commodification of Banff National Park into an irresistible tourist destination is a testament, then, to our triumphant "survival" in the wilds and, following Atwood's logic, while ignoring the Disney-like packaging of the Park, Banff's iconographic status also testifies to Canadian "cultural survival" in the face of what is commonly referred to in Canada as the threat of America.[4]

Canadian cultural commentator, Kyo Maclear, wryly summarizes Banff's contribution to Canada's "not-American" identity:

> Those Canucks who fear our very identity is in danger of obliteration by the juggernaut to the south—those who fear that McBanff burgers and Mount Rundle Dairy Queen sundaes are just around the corner—can leave Banff flush with local colour, "authentic" Indian curios and, perhaps most important, a sense of BIGNESS. (13)

"Bigness" is, indeed, most useful when the dominant trope of Canadian/ American relations, first proposed by the late Pierre Elliot Trudeau, depicts Canada as the mouse asleep in the shadow of the American elephant. The precariousness of Canada's position within this analogy often extends into the academic realm where the ambivalence associated with this relationship is readily apparent. Linda Hutcheon remarks in the May 1999 issue of *PMLA*:

> For Canadians ... the MLA, like the nation in which it is based, is perhaps not distant enough. Spatial and cultural proximity to the United States, a large and influential force, has had diverse effects on Canada-based academics, ranging from *fear* of what the media refer to as 'American cultural imperialism' to *pleasure* at participating in a larger professional context. (311–12, emphasis added)

These simultaneous and contradictory responses to the American academy are symptomatic of the instabilities that characterize the ongoing production of English Canadian national identity. Coerced *and* seduced by the Americanization of our identity, the strength of the Canadian/American coalition does not depend upon a simplistic territorialization of the margin by the centre but, rather, this coalition holds because Canadian nationalist sentiment remains inextricably and complexly bound to a "not-American" status. Marking and remarking upon differences (even, perhaps especially, where they do not exist) ensures the articulation of an English Canadian imaginary in the face of an otherwise invisible "otherness."

The complicated relationship between sameness and difference that defines Canada's link to America corresponds to the ambivalence that characterizes contemporary notions of sexuality. Andrew Parker comments that "if modern philosophies of the nation have had to negotiate between the contradictory requirements of sameness and difference, of universalism and singularity, these are also the (equally unstable) terms that have shaped modern conceptions of sexual orientation" (212). The concurrent existence of both universalizing and minoritizing discourses of homosexuality resonates with the tenuousness of national identities. The boundaries of Canada, like those of homosexuality, are internally and externally unstable. English Canadian national identity and homosexual identity share the structuration of incoherence, and activist identity-making strategies in each of these areas have frequently aimed to contain this incoherence by stabilizing, unifying, and rendering intelligible (therefore legitimate) a singular, monolithic paradigm of existence.

In particular, the grafting of lesbian identity onto a nationalist framework, as I have already touched upon, has proven to be a particularly durable as well as vexed linkage. Jill Johnston's now famous description of lesbian community as a "Lesbian Nation" first appeared in a 1971 *Village Voice* article and, since then, the association of nationalism with lesbian community building has been unshakable. The utopic ideals of Lesbian Nation continue to inform current mainstream activism in that lesbian identity is accorded legitimacy through an appeal to the nationalist rhetorics of citizenship. The belief in full and equal citizenship, and the attendant reliance on a discourse of rights, has permeated to the core of mainstream lesbian political organizing in North America. One's rightful place within the national body politic is delineated by asserting one's claim to certain rights.

Alan Sinfield astutely problematizes the agency assumed by rights advocates when he writes, "For it is not that existing categories of gay men and lesbians have come forward to claim their rights, but that we have become constituted *as gay* in terms of a discourse of ethnicity and rights" (271, emphasis in original). It is not that citizenship and equality rights legitimize pre-existing identities, but rather the contours of identity are shaped by the demands of citizenship and rights models themselves. Sally Munt characterizes this process as the "Americanization of identity politics" (172). This Americanization signifies, for Munt, a non-reflective usage of national citizenship paradigms that, unwittingly, reinforces the homogeneity of identity politics. In other words, the tactic of shrouding sexual identity in a cloak of full and equal citizenship ignores the incoherencies at the heart of nationalism in favour of exploiting the legitimizing and coalition-building powers of a nationalist rhetoric. In doing so, rights activism ironically mimics and upholds the means by which national incoherencies are sutured through the tactics of "othering" and coercion into "proper" citizenship.

Given the obvious pitfalls of working within national conceptions of sexual identity to obtain rights and establish coalitions, and the equally problematic refusal to engage in the struggle for full and equal citizenship, is it possible to transform this ambivalence into a critically reflective alliance with nationalism for activist ends? By way of answering this query, we must journey back to the rather unlikely site of lesbian activism: Banff National Park.

In July of 1997, the Banff Centre for the Performing Arts invited eight performance artists to participate in "Private Investigators," a three-week long exhibition that took place in and around the Banff townsite and at the Walter Phillips Gallery in the Banff Centre. Among the performers invited were Dempsey and Millan. For the "Private Investigators" exhibition, the Winnipeg-based video and performance duo created the fictitious organization, Lesbian National Parks and Services, and they donned the khaki uniform of the Lesbian National Park Rangers. For three weeks, the Lesbian National Park Rangers patrolled the streets of Banff politely handing out pamphlets on the Lesbian Flora and Fauna in Banff National Park while courteously dispensing directions and other Park information to unsuspecting tourists. The Rangers paddled the canoe routes and roamed hiking trails of the Park and they staged, in the centre of the townsite, a particularly successful Lesbian National Park Ranger recruitment day, complete with official induction ceremonies, pink lemonade for the Junior Rangers, and posters proclaiming: "Lesbian National Parks and Services WANTS YOU!"

With the splendour of the Banff scenery always in the background, Dempsey and Millan's performance offers a multi-layered commentary on the interlining of sexuality and nationalism in both state-sanctioned discourses *and* queer activist practices. Their parody of Canadian National Park Wardens is an insightful indictment of normative notions of identities. Kyo Maclear notes: "The first thing [Dempsey and Millan] want us to know is that nothing is what it seems: not the mythical 'lesbian' (demonized as a social threat, target and outsider), or the equally fictionalized 'ranger' (celebrated as a front-line guardian of the Canadian Wilderness)" (57). When these identities merge in the figure of the Lesbian Ranger, the signification process takes a very queer turn that requires a double- or triple-take on the part of the viewer. It is in this momentary disruption that Dempsey and Millan's performance gently coaxes viewers out of the accepted, even expected, passive and unengaged consumption of the landscape that scenic tourism tends to promote.

The Lesbian Rangers' critique of tourist consumption continues in their information brochure where readers are assured that they will discover the uniqueness of the Banff Wilderness by hiking down Banff Avenue and trekking into Cascade Mall. The accompanying Banff street map directs tourists to such lesbian landmarks as the "Invisible Plaque Dedicated to our Founding Foremothers," the "Invisible Museum of Homosexual Mountain History," the "Invisible Lesbian Heritage House and Gardens," and of course the "Lesbian National Parks and Services Information" booth.

Attentive to what is hidden by national maps and histories, the Lesbian Rangers intervene in the production of a national imaginary by re-mapping "invisible" lesbian sites. That these places are marked as "invisible" suggests an unwillingness by Dempsey and Millan to replicate the problematics of representation often associated with mainstream visibility politics. This tongue-in-cheek depiction of lesbian activity in Banff crucially gestures towards the social amnesia encoded within the "happy trails mentality" (Maclear, 10) of Canada's National Parks System. Just as the "official" guidebooks to the area refuse to acknowledge anything but a heterosexual history so, too, they establish a specifically white-colonialist-national-narrative-of-progress by conveniently "failing" to mention that Banff National Park is part of a Siksika Nation land claim and that "the Canadian Rockies served as a physical and symbolic border for Japanese Canadians who were not allowed west of the mountains until the late 1940's" (Maclear, 10). Neither do these guidebooks mention that "the [mountain] peaks are unmarked graves for Chinese railroad labourers who died in the thousands" (Maclear, 10). Although the Lesbian Rangers expose the (hetero)sexual logic governing Banff National Park's "management" of the wilderness, their performance leaves intact the racial exclusiveness underpinning Canadian national belonging.

Arun Mukerjee powerfully sums up the exclusive operations of Canadian nationalism: "Canadian nationalism, for us non-whites, is a racist ideology that has branded us un-Canadian by acts of omission and commission" (89). The ongoing production of Canadian nationalism in opposition to the threat of American domination reveals the exclusionary, racist practices perpetuated by an unexamined nationalist discourse. As Mukerjee continues, Canadian nationalists of the sixties and seventies "did not produce an ideology of national liberation that would include all Canadians on equal footing. Instead, they constructed a Canada that was being savaged by American domination ... Their Canada was an innocent victim" (89). This "innocent victim" mentality continues to dominate Canadian nationalist sentiment, especially in the realm of cultural nationalism. Dempsey and Millan intervene in the operations of this uncritical Canadian nationalism by hyperbolizing this traditional oppositional relationship to America, and by situating minority history within the parameters of a national institution. Their spectacular visibility within Banff National Park places lesbians at the heart of the nation-making process and begins to dismantle the binary of normative and non-normative sexual citizenship.

In a quirky homage to Lesbian Nation activism, Dempsey and Millan's performance takes up nationally inflected activist strategies. With their uniforms, slogans, maps, and historical information campaign, the Rangers exploit the material renderings of nationalism and, in doing so, they tap into the legitimacy, authority, and sense of respect that those trappings command. However, the parodic edge of their spectacle insists upon a self-reflective relation to the discourse of nationalism and, in particular, its impact on the style and content of lesbian mainstream political activism. Rather than strategize around lesbian minority status or assimilationist politics, the Rangers address and exploit those right-wing fears by explicitly confirming the existence of a "homosexual agenda."

The Rangers actively promote recruitment as well as the homosexualization of "the heterosexual wilderness" (55). In their daily Field Notes, they outline their goals and methodology for implementing an intensive homosexual overhaul of Canada's scenery and they note with much delight that "Ranger Envy" has inflicted many of their onlookers. In their Final Report, the Rangers conclude that: "The introduction of homosexual species to the area might also lead to exponential multiplication, transforming the gay-wasteland-that-is-Banff into a virtual Galapagos of homosexual wildlife" (55). With this hyperbolic flourish, the Rangers queer not just the nation but the entire ecosystem into a world-renowned site of oddities and "unnatural" creatures.

In their *The Rangers* performance, Dempsey and Millan appropriate a myriad of authoritative discourses. Margot Francis, in her review of *The Lesbian National Park Rangers,* assesses this tactic: "Throughout all the LNPS brochures, reports and performances, Dempsey and Millan inhabit the booming voice of the (white, male) 1950s 'expert'—and use it for their own ends. But never have we heard an expert talk about the desirability of achieving 'explosive homo growth'" (42–43). Dempsey and Millan's exploitation of "expert" voices works as an act of resignification that queerly inhabits these pathologizing discourses.

Dempsey and Millan also take on Canada's ambivalent relationship with America through a similar parodic appropriation of national registers. The often overwhelming presence of American cultural products in Canada and their subsequent influence on Canadian national identity, as either that which must be resisted *or* embraced, is, in Dempsey and Millan's performance, self-reflectively resisted *and* embraced. The resignification in their performance and literature of recognizably American slogans such as "The Lesbian National Park Rangers WANT YOU!," and "Wherever you go, whatever you do, ask not what lesbianism can do for you, but what you can do for lesbianism" is juxtaposed against the iconography of Banff National Park and the folk hero mythology accompanying the Park Wardens. This somewhat irreverent redeployment of American nationalist sentiment exposes the constructedness and yet pervasiveness of this American identity framework. The Rangers make use of these "Americanisms" to re-imagine Canadian ambivalence as a potentially playful, provocative national culture.

The critical cultural activism of Dempsey and Millan provides viewers with the opportunity to unravel the connections between national and sexual identities. The Lesbian National Park Rangers attack on several fronts at once and insinuate a lesbian presence into the quotidian operations of national culture. I want to remain mindful, however, of the extent to which the success of their performance hinges upon the "'benign,' white body of the ranger" (Francis 41) that Dempsey and Millan each inhabit. Margot Francis situates the easy consumption of the Rangers performance by their Banff audience within the context of a "manageable, albeit risky, difference" (43). Francis reads Dempsey and Millan's whiteness as integral to the performance's reception:

> Importantly, the rangers' image of innocence, reminiscent of Girl Guides (or, Boy Scouts) only works for a majority white audience when it is materialized through whiteness, specifically Dempsey and Millan's white female bodies. Girl Guides, park rangers and many other icons can

only be seen as benign, normative symbols if they are racialized as 'just people,' which, in a Canadian context, representations of people of colour have never been. (43–44)

There can be no question that Dempsey and Millan's whiteness, and the innocence—even dorkiness—of their appearance, lends legitimacy to their performance. However, Francis's analysis cannot account for the ways in which the Rangers resignify the whiteness they inhabit. The normative identities upheld by national citizenship (white, heterosexual, male, and so forth) are intimately linked and I would suggest that Dempsey and Millan's performance, through their historical revisions, parodic interventions, and focus on the *performativity* of nation-making, gestures towards the necessity of re-imagining *all* of these normative markers. The Rangers' interventions onto the "naturalization" process of national belonging have implications, then, for an explicitly anti-racist project.

The power of national discourses to materialize certain, acceptable bodies and elide "others" comes to the fore through their performance. *The Lesbian National Park Rangers* provides a critical commentary on the ongoing *processes* of nation-making, and although they do not literally embody a racialized other, Dempsey and Millan's performance initiates an examination of the operations of whiteness in national spaces. They reinvigorate the activist potentials of nationalism by reminding us that "whether you live in a large urban centre or a small rural community, on a mountainside or the vast, open prairie: Lesbian National Parks and Services depends on the commitment of all citizens to create an ecosystem better suited to the diversity of lesbian wildlife."

(2001)

Notes

¹ At the time of this writing (October 2000), Dempsey and Millan are putting the final touches on a video "mockumentary" of their Lesbian National Park Ranger performance. Order inquiries may be directed to Finger in the Dyke Productions, 485 Wardlaw Ave., Winnipeg, Manitoba, R3L 0L9.

² Dempsey and Millan have collaborated on feminist performance art since 1989. They are well known for pieces such as *Mermaid in Love*, 1990; *Mary Medusa*, 1993; the 1994 videotape "What Does a Lesbian Look Like?", which played in rotation on MuchMusic; their film "Good Citizen, Betty Baker", 1996; and their site-specific performance of *The Lesbian National Park Rangers*, 1997. Between 1989 and 1994 they completed a series of performances using the dress as metaphor: *Object/Subject of Desire*, 1993; *The Thin Skin of Normal*, 1993; *Arborite Housewife*, 1994; and *Glass Madonna*, 1994.

³ I invoke this outdated text by Margaret Atwood only to demonstrate the formative power of the "wilderness" within the historical constitution of a Canadian literary canon. Atwood's text solidified Canada's position as the colonized in relation to America, and this notion continues to permeate mainstream media discussions of Canadian identity. A number of Canadian writers have since provided excellent critiques of this hegemonic understanding of Canada. See, for instance, the writings of Arun Mukerjee, Fred Wah, Richard Fung, Thomas King, Dionne Brand, Roy Miki, and Marlene Nourbese Philip. In the words of Mukerjee, "Canadian literature, created, published, taught, and critiqued under the aegis of Canadian nationalism, promotes the settler-colonial view of Canada" (83).

⁴ The most recent discussion of this threat is found in *Maclean's Magazine* year-end poll on Canadian identity wherein fifty per cent of Canadians surveyed fear we are becoming more like Americans (*Maclean's Magazine*, December 20, 1999, 22).

Works Cited

Atwood, Margaret. *Survival: A Thematic Guide to Canadian Literature*. Toronto: Anansi, 1972.

Berlant, Lauren. *The Queen of America Goes to Washington City: Essays on Sexuality and Citizenship*. Durham, NC: Duke UP, 1997.

Carver, Terrell. "Sexual Citizenship: Gendered and De-Gendered Narratives." In *The Politics of Sexuality: Identity, Gender, Citizenship*. Ed. Terrell Carver and Veronique Mottier. New York: Routledge, 1998. 13–24.

Dempsey, Shawna and Lorri Millan, perf. *Lesbian National Parks and Services*. Finger in the Dyke Productions, 1997.

———. "Lesbian National Parks and Services." In *Private Investigators: Undercover in Public Space*. Ed. Kathryn Walter and Kyo Maclear. Banff: Banff Centre, 1999.

Evans, David T. *Sexual Citizenship: The Material Construction of Sexualities*. New York: Routledge, 1993.

Francis, Margot. "Unsettling Sights …" *Fuse* 22.4 (2000): 41–45.

Hutcheon, Linda. "Academic Free Trade? One Canadian's View of the MLA." *PMLA* 114.3 (1999): 311–17.

Kinsman, Gary. *The Regulation of Desire: Sexuality in Canada*. Montreal: Black Rose, 1987.

Maclear, Kyo. "The Accidental Witness." In *Private Investigators: Undercover in Public Space*. Ed. Kathryn Walter and Kyo Maclear. Banff: Banff Centre, 1999. 9–17.

Mukherjee, Arun. "Canadian Nationalism, Canadian Literature, and Racial Minority Women." *Essays on Canadian Writing* 56 (1995): 78–95.

Munt, Sally. *Heroic Desire: Lesbian Identity and Cultural Space.* New York: New York UP, 1998.

Parker, Andrew. "Grafting David Cronenberg: Monstrosity, AIDS Media, National/Sexual Difference." In *Media Spectacles.* Ed. Marjorie Garber, Jann Matlock, and Rebecca Walkowitz. New York: Routledge, 1993. 209–31.

Phelan, Shane. *Getting Specific: Postmodern Lesbian Politics.* Minneapolis: U of Minnesota P, 1994.

Sinfield, Alan. "Diaspora and Hybridity: Queer Identities and the Ethnicity Model." *Textual Practice* 10.2 (1996): 271–93.

Stychin, Carl F. *A Nation By Rights.* Philadelphia: Temple UP, 1998.

Young, Iris Marion. "Polity and Group Difference: A Critique of the Ideal of Universal Citizenship." In *The Citizenship Debates: A Reader.* Ed. Gershon Shafir. Minneapolis: U of Minnesota P, 1998. 263–90.

"Performing Femininity"
On Stage and Off: Confronting
Effeminaphobia Through Drag Performance

by David Bateman

> What would Miss Carr say if she knew you carried on correspondence
> with me, a homosexual, a female impersonator ... You had better keep
> quiet on that score, she may think you are imagining pathos.
>
> Margaret Gibson ("Making It" 99)

Coming of age in Toronto in the late seventies has had a particular effect upon the re-presentation of my body, on stage and off, as a drag performance artist, an educator and a creative writer. The "performing" bodies of internationally-acclaimed Canadian female impersonator Craig Russell and Toronto-based writer Margaret Gibson emerged during a formative period in my development and provided me with bold physical and textual images that informed my representational strategies over the next two decades. As an effeminate young man I was simultaneously frightened and titillated by the very self-reflective sight of a gay male, in drag, displaying his femininity for a paying audience. Writing about it in a very open, bittersweet way, as Gibson did in her short story "Making It," was equally engaging for a young, aspiring drag queen with literary ambitions. Through these experiences, among others, I have come to view gender behaviour as largely constructed and citational (citing masculinity and femininity through a variety of culturally conceived bodies and texts). Subsequently, the intersecting sites of gay male effeminacy, and the kind of femininity culturally enforced upon the biological female strike me as prime locations for an interrogation of gay men as women, women as women, and women as men— on stage, on the page, and off.

The recent appearance of a new Canadian drag musical (*Outrageous, A Musical,* Canadian Stage, Winter 2001) based, in part, on Gibson's "Making It," prompts me to include an excerpt from her text. Gibson's close friendship with Craig Russell in the seventies is reflected, in semi-fictionalized form, in the story. The extreme emotional bond between the two characters suggests the very strong yet delicate connections that often occur between gay men and straight women. Liza, the protagonist, opens the narrative with a letter to her drag queen roommate Robin, and incorporates into her letter drag signifiers such as Joan Crawford and Bette Davis—both staples of many drag queen's repertoires. The letter reveals an arduous search for a sense of identity in the face of emotional and mental instability.

Dear Bette,
Did you fumble your way up the long staircase with eyeless fingers ...
are you someone else today? Joan Crawford married to a lunatic ...
leaves falling to the ground ... I know who you are but I will pretend
I don't just to confuse anyone else who might read this letter. All that
matters is that you know who you are ... Is God in the snowflakes? I am
looking for a God. It seems a sensible thing to do now that I am going to
have this baby ... so today I will say that God is in the snowflakes.
Yesterday he was Caliban. Tomorrow if the snow is gone I will assume
that God is dead – again. Perhaps he is always Caliban. (Gibson 96)

The emotional landscape developed by Gibson, where drag-related images of Joan
and Bette are interspersed with the central character's exploration of herself as
someone reliant upon God as Caliban, God as snowflake, God as saviour, suggests a
relationship between a search for, and an impersonation of, a multiplicitous self.
While craving emotional sustenance, the pregnant woman in Gibson's short story
does not have at her disposal the same kind of self-reflective impersonation available
to the man in drag. Nevertheless, both subjects share a kind of commonality through
a repressive cultural order of femininity that restricts the development of a multi-
gendered body. The drag queen disguises the self and pretends to be a woman in order
to succeed. The woman, often culturally marked by what can become a form of
repressive femininity, may be hard put to find a hiding place, especially in the case of
Gibson's protagonist, the pregnant Liza. Both subjects are often the subject of ridicule
and/or public scrutiny. Some gay men and some straight women feel simultaneously
in union with, and separated from, their bodies when confronted by a culture (and a
paying audience) that consistently finds their often not-so-chosen social and cultural
positions or professions hilarious, entertaining, light comic fare, or, at the worst of
times, unstable and ultimately pathologized—as seen in Gibson's central character in
"Making It." Gibson and her fictionalized female character become, in a sense, within
the broad concept of all gender as innately imitative and citational, representatives of
biological woman as drag queen. Liza's struggle in particular becomes an attempt to
convince the outside world, comprised by her social worker, the father of her child,
and her drag queen best friend, that she is "real."

Like you and Eric he did not think me real. I did not like him at all ...
I was not real to him and did not like him for the half laces littering the
kitchen table. (Gibson 114)

Defining Margaret Gibson, or any biological woman, as a kind of drag queen may
summon the idea of drag as misogynist insult. On the contrary. As famed Australian
drag queen Dame Edna Everidge would say, "I meant that lovingly, not the way it was
intended." Indeed, traditional culture may have intended to posit the concept of
woman as drag queen as an insult when in fact what drag does is reveal the artificiality of particular gender codes. As performative gestures, any given drag performance
may ultimately serve to alleviate strict conformity to any gender binary. In her writing, Gibson's attraction to the drag queen as citational "female" representative has

established her as an articulate creative spokesperson for the ways in which women and gay men may see aspects of themselves in each other.

> You could not divide the he-she in your being and I – I could not stop the bone splitting, dividing into nightmares and hallucinations and breathing floors. Somewhere in the void you and I met, walking and wounded and collapsed into each other's arms ... (Gibson 115)

Given these problematized intersecting sites (i.e., mental health, effeminacy, drag), it seems only fitting that a notorious queer playwright (Brad Fraser), with the aid of a brilliant composer (Joey Miller), should take a stab at setting it all to music. *Outrageous, A Musical,* based on the seventies film version (*Outrageous* starring Craig Russell) of Margaret Gibson's story, successfully represents the many forms drag can take, on stage and off, from Marilyn Monroe to blues artist to airline stewardess to Wonder Woman. These iconic images are woven into the music and the book in an enlightening and thoroughly entertaining manner. Liza's struggle with mental illness, as it intersects with the larger-than-life presence of a truly gifted drag performer, was somewhat overshadowed by the breakneck pacing, the flashy musical numbers, and the exquisite costumes. Nevertheless, *Outrageous, A Musical* stands as an exciting addition to a general lexicon of North American drag performance and reveals a fundamental aspect of femininity as culturally constructed, and an act, much like masculinity, that is performed daily by both men and women, on stage and off.

As a popular form of entertainment, drag has tended to locate itself historically within two distinct areas: lip-sync and live female impersonation. The suspect, and somewhat effeminaphobic notion that drag insults biological women is a subjective discourse based upon particular aspects of some drag performances. Discovering examples beyond this restrictive ideology that dismiss transgendered experiences is up to the urban drag tourist. The fairly recent popularity of *Drag Kings* throughout North America reverses the drag queen aesthetic, in a sense, when the biological woman resists feminine make-up and turns to a masculine version of the made-up self through applied, or grown, facial hair, and lip syncs to the likes of Tom Jones. Jones is an especially prime location for male impersonation, as his masculinity has existed in excess within mainstream culture for decades.

Toronto, in particular, provides the gender-curious viewer with an array of spectacular drag performance. Clubs scattered along Yonge Street near Wellesley, and the nearby Church Street "gay ghetto" area, offer regular events where fine examples of lip sync performance can be found. Female impersonation that does not utilize lip-sync technique includes such luminaries as Bitch Diva (Michael Fitzgerald), a formidable talent who has reinvented himself, over the past ten years, as drag torch singer extraordinaire, moving from a blurred "gender fuck" persona relying upon his own hair and his own ambiguous gender, into a more traditional bewigged glamour drag contrasted by a deep, rich, only slightly feminized singing voice. Along far more traditional lines, Ryerson alumnus Christopher Peterson has taken on the title of "Canada's foremost female impersonator" and crafted an internationally acclaimed one-man/woman show (*Eye-cons*). The basic difference between Fitzgerald and

Peterson as drag performers is that Peterson, like the late Craig Russell, impersonates a variety of celebrated female vocalists, while Fitzgerald represents a version of himself as a "woman" through his "own" voice. Both artists impersonate a traditional, "made-up" idea of woman as glamorous and iconic. My own performance work shifts sideways from these forms and into a representation of man as man, and man as woman, simultaneously, without the physical "hiding place" that full drag, in a sense, provides.

My most recent performance piece, entitled *A Particular Class of Cross-Dresser*, utilizes a form of characterization that attempts to provide the audience with a look at the various environments that cross-dressed males find themselves within when they confront their desire to wear "women's clothing." Ranging from a white-collar worker in Sudbury who finds solace in the expropriation of female garb within a natural setting (i.e., the forest, the Big Nickel, the crater-like surroundings of Sudbury) to the more urban circumstances of a gay male stripper saving money for an actual sex change operation, the piece utilizes text written on various costumes and set pieces as a way toward a consciously anti-appropriative voice. In a sense I try to channel, through interviews tailored into my own fictionalized versions, the voice of the varied cross-dresser through my own body. By doing so I engage in what could be considered an impersonation of an impersonation. [1] The presence of the written text on stage, partly memorized and partly recited, attempts to show the audience that I, as a performer, am attempting to take some responsibility for my use of the appropriated voice. The problematic nature of any form of appropriation relates to the general idea of drag as an art form that, as Judith Butler has suggested, "characterizes the wishful performative of gender ... the production of 'identity' through an imitation that is always already expropriated and elsewhere. Hence, 'Women' who perform femininity are as much 'in drag' as 'men'" (*Gender* 89).

My particular form of drag performance intersects with a general analysis of the ways in which the world of gender performance relates to effeminaphobia, a near relation, and bonding agent, to both homophobia and misogyny. My work is located somewhere between the work of Craig Russell as a traditional impersonator of female celebrities, and Margaret Gibson's penchant for the re-presentation of the struggling feminine voice existing in a misogynist world. Part of my "recovery" from this struggle to find a feminine and a masculine voice has been the reconstruction and performance of texts that blend fantasy and realism in order to contribute to the possibility for other bodies to exist beyond repressive hierarchies concerning strictly gendered behaviour. In my first full-length performance piece I dressed in a powder blue gown that exposes a decidedly male chest. The narrative attempts to recuperate the past through a re-telling of a fantasy that I constructed as a boy in order to psychically challenge codes that restricted my daily gender behaviour.

> When I was in grade school I had a very long walk home. Almost forty minutes. It seemed like forever. On the way home, to pass the time, walking alone, I used to like to fantasize about what I would be wearing, if I were a girl. In grade eight, the class slut, just because she was beauti-

ful and dated every good-looking boy in the school. I wasn't beautiful, not like her, and I wanted to date every good looking boy in the school. I guess I was the class slut too. She had these beautiful powder blue earrings in a kind of a mod teardrop shape that I would stare at for whole periods. I often think that's why I never learned to speak French or read music because I would literally lose myself in her fabulous earrings. For awhile they were concerned that I was becoming autistic. But no. It was just that everything was powder blue. I wanted to wear all powder blue, and white vinyl go-go boots and a matching head band, and best of all, I wanted it to rain a lot so I could wear a transparent rain-coat and carry a matching umbrella so that everybody, short or tall, could see through to my beautiful powder blue world. And I would be so pretty that no one could touch me. I could only touch them. And it would never occur to them to laugh at me or make fun of me, or call me "girly" or "sissy." Instead they would just date me, to death. Women and faggots. We have some pain in common. (Bateman 21)

As well as forms of entertainment, the variety of drag performances that I have discussed may also be viewed as symptoms of a healthy gendered body reclaiming modes of self expression denied during formative periods of self-discovery. In a darkly comic and culturally-reflective moment Margaret Gibson reveals, in "Making It," a common notion that the body that performs drag is in fact the false body, and in a sense, a diseased mind.

Anne says that you are merely acting out your sickness through your nightclub act like the way Fellini puts his sickness on the screen. (Gibson 108)

On the contrary, drag performance can be, as Judith Butler eloquently suggests, an attempt to understand how what has been banished from the proper domain of "sex"—where that domain is secured through a heterosexualizing imperative—might at once be produced as a troubling return and not only as an imaginary contestation that effects the failure in the workings of the inevitable law. Instead, drag performance can be an enabling disruption, the occasion for a radical re-articulation of the symbolic horizon in which bodies come to matter at all. (Butler, *Bodies* 23).

As troubling returns, and enabling disruptions, we drag performers—men and women alike—continue to "fumble [our] way up the long staircase with eyeless fingers" each time we attempt, consciously or otherwise, to re-present the gendered body on stage and off (Gibson 96). We are the constant revisionist physical reinventions of the multi-gendered body caught in an over-stabilized gender universe. By performing our gender, on stage, on the page, and off, we are caught in the act of exposing our bodies and our selves as living, viable, and complex artifacts that attest to a highly theatrical commingling of culture, biology, glamour, and everyday life.

(2002)

Note

¹ After a performance of *What Dreadful Things To Say About Someone Who Has Just Paid For My Lunch* Professor Veronica Hollinger (Cultural Studies, Trent University) commented that the particular kind of performance art that I take part in could be considered "a representation of a representation."

Works Cited

Bateman, David. *What Dreadful Things to Say About Someone Who Has just Paid for My Lunch.* Ennismore, ON: Ordinary, 1993.

Butler, Judith. *Bodies That Matter.* New York: Routledge, 1993.

———. *Gender Trouble.* New York: Routledge, 1990.

Gibson, Margaret. "Making It." *The Butterfly Ward.* New York: Vanguard, 1976.

The Configurations of Gender in Tomson Highway's
Dry Lips Oughta Move to Kapuskasing

by Susan Billingham

> Recovery is not an act that ignores the disease. Recovery is becoming stronger *than the disease.*
>
> —Beth Brant, *Writing as Witness* 44; emphasis in original

Tomson Highway (Cree, Brochet Reserve), the first Native playwright to achieve recognition in mainstream Canadian theatre and literary criticism, has opened a lot of doors for those who follow. Combining pragmatism with idealism, his work unflinchingly exposes conditions on the reserve but retains hope for positive, cross-cultural transformation. This article undertakes a close analysis of gender dynamics in Highway's second published play. *Dry Lips Oughta Move to Kapuskasing* was conceived as the second in a projected cycle of seven plays about the fictional Wasaychigan Hill reserve. [1] In the course of the action, seven rez men are forced to come to terms with the consequences of past and current events. Performed on two levels in three languages, the play revolves around two iconic moments: the re-enactment of the birth of Dicky Bird Halked seventeen years earlier, in 1973—the same year as the stand off at Wounded Knee—to a mother drunk nearly senseless in a bar; and the rape, with a crucifix, of Patsy Pegahmagahbow/Nanabush by Dicky Bird. A connection is implied between the two moments, in that the victim of the first incident (Dicky Bird suffers from foetal alcohol syndrome) becomes the perpetrator of the second crime. This paper examines the configurations of masculinity and homosocial relationships in the play, giving particular attention to the homosexual subtext and the extent to which this subtext subverts conventional gender roles. My consideration of the complicated interplay among colonization, political disenfranchisement, shifting gender roles, and same-sex desire aims at an understanding of the play in light of both the Cree/Ojibway [2] context and Euro-American theoretical paradigms. Gender roles and sexual practices vary across cultures. Despite the colonial imposition of legal and social institutions, it is inadvisable to assume that Native constructs of gender and sexuality are completely identical with Western ones. Thus traces of practices known as *berdache* [historically, roughly, people inhabiting a "third gender"], as well as the notion of the two-spirit more recently adopted, must be taken into account alongside gay or queer politics and subjectivity.

In *Dry Lips,* Highway employs a number of tactics that serve to keep the audience off balance. First, despite the traumatic nature of the subject matter, the play is funny, even verging on slapstick. Highway's humour is in keeping with the Trickster tradition as it has re-emerged in contemporary First Nations writing in Canada. Nanabush, the Ojibway Trickster, plays a key role in *Dry Lips*, and Highway's work to date consistently reflects his belief in the importance of this being. Secondly, Highway selects a number of highly charged "cultural icons," both Native and white North American, to magnify the effects of intercultural contact. Examples include the poster of Marilyn Monroe, the crucifix and the Bible, the powwow bustle, Wounded Knee, and Hockey Night in Canada. A third feature of *Dry Lips* is the inversion (if not subversion) of conventional masculine and feminine gender roles throughout. One of the play's chief themes, this cross-gendering [3] also contributes to the situational comedy. Finally, the action is framed as a dream. As the playwright explains in his program notes, "dreams—and the dream-life—have traditionally been considered by Native society to be the greatest tool of instruction" (qtd. in Preston 148). In *Dry Lips*, these complex elements are interconnected, and we cannot fully understand any single aspect of the play without contextualizing it in relation to the others.

The interpretative crux of *Dry Lips* lies in the interrelationship among the Trickster, the humour, and binary versus two-spirited models of gender and sexuality. Highway's version of Nanabush has provoked the most controversy: does s/he function as an object of (male) desire, or as a figure for (female) power (if indeed these choices must be seen as antithetical)? The Wasy men treat much of the potentially empowering resistance by the women—largely offstage—as comic. While numerous critics have entered the debate on misogyny few have noticed that the various sexualities and gender roles at play in Highway's work address homophobia as well. My reading is prompted by a crucial, but neglected, scene in which Creature Nataways reveals his repressed feelings for Big Joey. The introduction of a gay subtext, however truncated, necessarily affects our reading of the play's inversion of conventional gender traits. Ultimately, however, I contend that even the presence of Creature Nataways and Nanabush the gender-shifter do not fully succeed in opening up a space for "third" (or fourth) genders. *Dry Lips* employs a strategy of inversion in such activities as men baking and knitting or women playing hockey, at the risk of re-inscribing an oppositional model of gender.

IN SEARCH OF THE TWO-SPIRIT

Like the word "queer" in contemporary Euro-American culture, "two-spirit" is a recuperated term. It is cross-cultural by definition, first, because many First Nations had specific, intra-cultural words for gender variance, and secondly, because it emerges post-contact. Over the past twenty years, scholars have begun to recover knowledge about gender and sexuality in Native North American societies, notably Walter L. Williams in *The Spirit and the Flesh: Sexual Diversity in American Indian Culture* and Will Roscoe in *Changing Ones: Third and Fourth Genders in Native North America*. [4] Prior to the collapse of traditional socio-economic and cultural systems, many Nations across the continent embraced gender diversity exceeding the dualistic masculine/feminine model. Until recently, 'these third- or fourth-gender roles were known collectively to anthropologists as *berdaches*.[5] Current research suggests that such roles were more widespread than was previously believed, occurring in every region of the continent, among speakers of every major language group, including the Cree and Ojibway.[6]

The *berdache* was a biological male (or female) who identified with and adopted the social functions and activities more typically associated with the "opposite" sex; in Western terms, the *berdache* crossed conventional gender distinct category. *Berdaches* often had clearly defined roles and an accepted social status,[7] sometimes confirmed in the Nation's mythology. They were viewed as mediators, not only between men and women, but also between the physical and spiritual realms, frequently fulfilling a ceremonial function (e.g., shaman, visionary, healer, or artist). Both Williams and Roscoe argue that sexual-object choice was a secondary consideration in the emergence of the *berdache*. In many of the Nations studied, the tendency to identify as *berdache* became evident before puberty (for example, through play and social activities or through dreams). According to Roscoe, "The primary characteristic of third gender sexuality in the native view was not its same-sex nature, but the fact that it was non-procreative. That is, rather than an opposition of heterosexuality to homosexuality, native beliefs opposed reproductive to non-reproductive sex" (*Changing Ones* 10). In other words, where sexual pleasure was valued in its own right, same-sex practices were not necessarily viewed as unnatural. Furthermore, not all same-sex activity necessarily involved a *berdache*. Sexual-object choice and practice, therefore, remained a less important consideration for defining someone as a *berdache* than has become the case for contemporary gays and lesbians in Western societies.

Characters in Highway's plays, like Emily Dictionary in *The Rez Sisters* and Creature Nataways in *Dry Lips*, are not *berdaches* because the socio-economic, cultural, and ideological conditions that made this role possible no longer exist on modern Canadian reserves. The suppression of the *berdache* tradition formed part of the broader policies of colonization and assimilation of First Nations. Throughout North America, Euro-Americans destroyed the basis of Native economic and social structures by killing the game, forcing Nations onto reserves, and removing traditional means of subsistence and relations to the land. Governments attempted to inculcate agricultural pursuits in place of hunting. They removed children from their parents and attempted to eradicate Native languages and cultural practices in residential boarding schools. They forbade key religious practices by law, while missionaries converted many Natives to Christianity, producing rifts between old and new ways within communities. In short, every aspect of bureaucratic, legal, educational, and religious policy combined to undermine pre-existing cultural customs. Sexual and marriage practices among First Peoples were subjected to criticism and regulation by church and state alike. Male *berdaches*, particularly those who (to European eyes) "cross-dressed" or engaged in same-sex marriages, presented an obvious target. Generations of Native peoples absorbed the (hetero)sexist, homophobic messages of the establishment. Knowledge of traditional third- and fourth-gender roles went underground, where they were not lost or disowned completely. Only in the last twenty to thirty years has the "two-spirit," as it has come to be called, (re)-emerged.

Despite a tradition of acceptance of and respect for third-gender individuals in many Native cultures, gay and lesbian Natives have faced a history of double oppression in the twentieth century. In addition to racial discrimination from without, lesbian and gay Natives often encounter silencing and hostility, if not outright violence, within their own communities. Many believe this situation has developed as a result of contact:

> For many natives today, homosexuality is completely "other," a phenomenon imagined to belong to the urban white man and categorized with the other catastrophes attributed to him—disease, alcoholism, emotional dysfunction.... [G]iven the associations of homosexuality as constructed by Western medical and psychiatric discourse—as weakness, depravity, and compulsion—it is not surprising that some natives fail to perceive any connection between it and traditional third and fourth genders. (Roscoe, *Changing Ones* 102)

Some migrated to larger urban centres to find support. Inevitably, post-Stonewall gay and lesbian rights movements and Euro-American identity politics have impacted on Native individuals.

More recently, First Nations have been re-connecting their contemporary experience of being gay/lesbian with *berdache* traditions, reviving the notion of being two-spirited. "Two-spirit" is a transliteration of the Anishinabe expression *niizh manitoag* (Roscoe, *Changing Ones* 109) and, as such, recalls one of the tribally specific terms for gender variance. Encompassing both men and women, it is also pan-Native and contains an element of renewed ethnic or racial pride. As such, it should not be considered merely as a synonym for gay, lesbian, or queer. Two-spirits do not want to return to a past way of life that is no longer possible; rather they seek to accommodate remnants of cultural customs and attitudes to the new social conditions. According to Roscoe, the designation two-spirited was adopted at the third annual gathering of American Indian Gays and Lesbians in Winnipeg, 1990, and in 1992, the Toronto-based group Gays and Lesbians of the First Nations officially changed its name to Two-Spirited People of the First Nations (109). Since these events took place contemporaneously with the production and publication of *Dry Lips Oughta Move to Kapuskasing*, it is possible to read the play in light of such cultural knowledge and traditions—but cautiously. It should be pointed out that there are no positive models of two-spirited existence in Highway's work, whether traditional or contemporary (at least prior to his novel, *Kiss of the Fur Queen*). Creature Nataways is a troubled and confused character, and the environment in which he finds himself is hardly conducive to coming-out narratives. [8] Yet Highway himself has begun to reclaim third-gender or two-spirit tradition as a way to clarify his own position. In his version, "The third gender acted as a buffer between the other two, who were unfortunately at war a great deal of the time. We call this gender the Two Spirited people. In English they are called homosexuals. So in Native culture there is a circle of genders as opposed to a straight line" (Interview with Farrell 88). Highway also associates "in-between people" with artists, shamans, and visionaries, whose role was to deal with Nanabush and the spirits ("Twenty-One" 23). [9] Just as Highway juxta-poses Cree/Ojibway cosmology with Christian and Greek mythologies or blends Western and Native musical forms, constructions of gender in the play might best be understood by means of a cross-cultural approach.The interrelationship between colonization, (dis)empowerment, and shifting gender roles must be held in mind when considering the significance of the "homosexual" subtext in *Dry Lips*.

TRIANGLES

The opening scenes of *Dry Lips* establish the rivalry between Big Joey and Zachary on both economic and sexual levels. Zachary is caught naked on Big Joey's couch, giving Joey an opportunity to pressure him to withdraw his bid for Band Council funds. In the course of their argument, Joey alludes elliptically to the events of seventeen years before in Espanola: the night when Black Lady Halked, drunk in a bar, gave birth to Dicky Bird, Big Joey's illegitimate son, and Big Joey, sick at the sight of the blood, ran away and shirked his responsibility. This incident clearly marked a moment of estrangement between the former friends. As the play unfolds, *Dry Lips* explores, not merely dysfunctional families, but dysfunctional communities, particularly, with regard to gender relations and the breakdown of homosocial bonds. Twenty-one years ago, Zachary, Joey, Creature Nataways, Spooky Lacroix, and Eugene Starblanket cut their wrists and swore blood brotherhood for life (106); the events in Espanola four years later tore the group apart, and the wounds from that time have never healed. Significantly, in the opening scene, Joey interprets a quarrel between his lover Gazelle Nataways and Zachary's wife Hera, as a reflection on his own reputation: "[addressing Zachary] *You* gave me one hell of a slap in the face when *your wife* gave *my* Gazelle that kick in the belly. I overlooked that" (23; emphasis added). The possessive pro-nouns indicate that the relationship between the men is most important to Big Joey.

The third player in the opening scene is Creature Nataways, and his role mirrors his nickname. Creature reinforces Big Joey's position, by recording Zachary's predica-ment on Polaroid, jumps to obey Joey's snapped fingers and retrieve Zachary's shorts, and teases Zachary with singsong taunts: "Here doggy, doggy. Here poochie, poochie woof woof!" (19). Even the stage directions reinforce the idea of this character as Big Joey's "Creature," describing his laughter as "tittering" and his "yelps" from the back-ground as being "like a little dog" (19-20). The close of this initial scene and segue into the next is also revealing, in light of Creature's subsequent disclosure of his feelings for Big Joey:

> *The moment Zachary is gone, Creature scurries to the kitchen door, shaking his fist in the direction of the already-departed Zachary.*
>
> **CREATURE.** Damn Rights! (*Then strutting like a cock, he turns to Big Joey*) Zachary Jeremiah Keechigeesik never shoulda come in your house, Big Joey. Thank god, Gazelle Nataways ain't my wife no more ...

> Big Joey merely has to throw a glance in Creature's direction to
> intimidate him. At once, Creature reverts back to his usual
> nervous self. (25)

Creature's "cocky" behaviour once the danger of actual physical violence is over, followed by a quick reversion to his usual, "nervous" manner, suggests the classic representation of a man who wants to appear tough but is coded as weak or "unmasculine." Throughout the exchange that follows, Joey ignores Creature, who chatters away while attempting to clear up some of the mess by shoving things back under the couch—in spite of the fact that he is in Big Joey's house, not his own. Creature's actions here verge on the domestic, with a hint of parody of the stereotypical scene between husband and wife, the former watching the hockey game on television and ignoring the latter's conversation and activity around him. [10] The speech accompanying this stage business reveals the further details that Gazelle left Creature four years ago, leaving behind the children [11] but taking the television: "I don't mind, Big Joey, I really don't. I tole you once I tole you twice she's yours now. *It's like I loaned her to you,* I don't mind. I can take it" (25; emphasis added). Initially, the viewer might assume that Creature protests too much, that he *does* mind. But in retrospect, the whole situation may be interpreted according to Sedgwick's concept of the homosocial continuum.

In the triangle created by the exchange of a woman between men, the intensity of the bond of (male) rivalry may be as strong as the bond of (heterosexual) love. Such rivalry is structured by the play of emulation and identification. By using the term homosocial *desire*, Sedgwick draws attention to the possible presence of an erotic element in the bonds between men. In the current instance, both friendship and rivalry are implicated, as well as power dynamics. The situation is only slightly complicated by the fact that Gazelle has chosen to abandon Creature—since retroactively, Creature has reconstructed the event as a *loan* from himself to Joey. The triangle takes on a new dimension, however, once Creature admits his repressed desire for Joey. This confession of love occurs towards the end of the play and is embedded amongst a variety of other serious issues and complicated strategies that serve to transgress boundaries and undermine simple binaries. These layers must be unpacked before the key scene can be approached.

My description above of the three-cornered exchange between Zachary, Big Joey, and Creature as the opening scene is slightly misleading. The discovery of Zachary asleep on Big Joey's couch, and the ensuing conflict, constitutes the first *spoken* scene. But the play has already begun before Joey utters the first line of dialogue. The details of the stage set, along with the wordless stage business, introduce most of the key motifs to be explored in the play. These elements include the life-size pin-up poster of Marilyn Monroe prominently displayed on one wall (15); the spotlight focused on Zachary's naked butt; Nanabush, as Gazelle, slipping into her stockings, putting on the false, oversized rubber breasts, planting the lipstick kiss on Zachary's bare butt, shimmying into the V-cut hockey shirt, and turning on the television with a bump; and Dicky Bird's mute voyeurism and evident fascination with Big Joey.

According to the stage directions, "[t]he first thing we see when the light comes up—*a very small 'spot,' precisely focussed*—is Zachary's bare, naked bum" (15). The spotlight initiates a chain of (homo)erotic images that reverberate throughout the action. The naked butt is then marked by Gazelle/Nanabush's kiss and lipstick trace and re-marked when Creature calls attention to the stain: "Lipstick on your arshole, tole da tale on you-hoo" (19). As Gin Burnham points out, "Creature's [...] remark reiterates the anal/oral connection of the marks" (22). In my opinion, the fact that the ambivalent Creature speaks the line reinforces the homoerotic tension underlying the exchange. Burnham goes on to link this reference to Pierre St. Pierre's later misidentification of a Johnny Cash song as "Rim of Fire" ("Cash's ring has become a rim that carnivalizes the already burlesque country song" [22]), extending the chain of anal signifiers. To this I would add Pierre's punning allusion to that famous hockey player "*Gay* Lafleur" (68; emphasis added). Later, during Gazelle's striptease in Act Two, the watching men are literally "caught with their pants down" when the lighting returns to normal, underlining "the fixation on male buttocks signalled from the opening scene" (Dickinson 185). At the end of the play, with Zachary once again naked on the couch, Hera's kiss recalls Gazelle's more mischievous gesture. While this final kiss "effectively takes the play out of the realm of gay fantasy and back into the conventions of bourgeois domestic realism," Peter Dickinson argues, "the 'anality' of *Dry Lips*, whether prosthetic or otherwise, is sufficient enough to signify an extension of the notion of a 'crisis of authenticity' ... to include not only patriarchal constructions of gender and racialist constructions of ethnicity/aboriginality, but also (hetero)normative constructions of masculinity/sexuality" (185). A homosexual subtext is thus introduced from the first scene of the play.

TRICKSTER LOGIC

While this strand of images and business running throughout *Dry Lips* can be read as homosexual subtext, the anality hinted at is just as characteristic of Trickster narratives as it is of homoerotic ones: "The Trickster was a very sensual character—making love, eating—all those bodily functions, he celebrated them, he lived for them. The Trickster's most frequent conversational partner was his anus" (Highway, qtd. in Wigston 8). The scene following the accidental death of Simon Starblanket is a typically equivocal one. Nanabush appears "*sitting on a toilet having a good shit. He/she is dressed in an old man's white beard and wig, but also wearing sexy, elegant women's high-heeled pumps.[...] [S]he/he sits with her legs crossed, nonchalantly filing his/her fingernails*" (117). Emblematic of scatological Trickster humour and the Trickster's self-absorption (marked by seeming indifference to human affairs, except when his/her own interests are involved), this scene also depicts the white male Christian God in drag, blending traits of masculine and feminine appearance in a manner consistent with the gender-crossing of the play. The iconoclastic treatment of the Christian deity enacts resistance to one of the most blatantly hierarchical, patriarchal, heterocentric and ethnocentric institutions of the colonial regime. The scene consequently functions both as part of the homosexual subtext and as an exemplum of Highway's Trickster logic.

What are some of the elements of this trickster logic? For the Anishinabeg, Nanabush has a lineage that is lacking for other audiences. As a cultural figure, Nanabush is known for the power to create and educate, the ability to transform at will, and the ability to deceive and play pranks. Stories about Nanabush illustrate the importance of maintaining proper relationships with members of the community (Christen 148–50). Trickster cycles help to establish taboos and boundaries, often by relating how the Trickster flouted or discovered them: "[H]e attempts to kill his father, the male authority symbol. As a grandma's boy, he has to come to terms with male-dominated culture by trying to do away with his dad.[…] Nanabush also gave an assist to the Creator…. Modern escapades would be impossible to enumerate but some agreement seems to exist that Nanabush is both an honorary Anishinabe and an honoured supernatural" (Baker, "Old Indian Trick" 49).

These stories are especially suggestive for the fractured homosocial world of *Dry Lips*. At the same time, Lina Perkins reminds us that "Nanabush is a character in a play … as well as being a cultural figure," and Highway's trickster is not identical with the ones of Cree and Ojibway mythology (259). Just as the two-spirit is a fusion of recovered tradition and contemporary political needs, "Nanabush is neither a contemporary nor a readily available figure; he is a figure brought back from the past of a culture that no longer exists in any coherent form. The point of Nanabush's presence is that he has been forgotten, at least in part, and needs to be recovered" (260).

Two other key features of Trickster logic emerge from Highway's interview with Heather Hodgson: using humour and teaching by negative example (3). In *Dry Lips*, Highway takes stereotypes created by the dominant culture and re-projects them, intensifying the (white) audience's discomfort. One obvious example of this tactic can be found in his confrontation of the problem of alcoholism: "As an Indian person in this country, you are aware, like it or not, that [the street drunk] is the first and only way most white people see Indians. It's an indictment. That's our national image" (Highway, qtd. in Wigston 8). Through the character of Pierre St. Pierre, the reserve's bootlegger, Highway makes this image comic, while preserving its seriousness, by showing us the devastating effects of alcohol abuse on the community. For example, in the opening scenes of *Dry Lips*, when Pierre rushes in with his news, the stage directions indicate that he is "*[a]ddressing the case of beer directly*" (26). Throughout the scene he grabs and drinks one beer after another, talking out the side of his mouth. Pierre is the one character in the play whose function consists almost entirely of comic relief; unlike the other characters, he does not directly face a personal crisis point. [12] But Spooky is a recovered alcoholic (the only positive consequence of his born-again Christian faith), and Dicky Bird is permanently damaged by foetal alcohol syndrome. We can detect a similar Trickster logic behind the other severe problems Highway tackles:

> Highway's humour is Cree to the core. Historically, and since before the arrival of Christianity, Native peoples did not feel a sense of shame

associated with jokes about the body, and they often use humour to dull the pain, thereby creating an opening through which the wounds of life can be healed. This is crucial: Cree humour is not simply episodic; it is a distinctive way of being in and looking at the world. (Hodgson 3)

In addition to the humour and the powers of deception and transformation associated with these figures, Tricksters typically occupy an ambiguous gender position, particularly in contemporary revisions. (Compare, for example Thomas King's version of Coyote, in works such as *One Good Story, That One* and *Green Grass, Running Water*.) Highway repeatedly links the gender-bending Trickster with the ungendered nature of Native languages like Cree and Ojibway, which he describes as fun-loving and visceral, in his critiques of the hierarchical, cerebral and unfunny English language and the heterosexist Christian patriarchy (see Interview with Farrell 88–91). Within the play, Simon draws attention to the lack of gender in the Cree language, in his drunken dialogue with Nanabush/Patsy, who simultaneously stresses the feminine aspect of the Trickster (110–13). [13] But it should be noted that, except in the toilet scene cited above, Nanabush's gender remains decidedly feminine throughout *Dry Lips*, as she impersonates the spirit of three different women. Nanabush is portrayed with oversized breasts, for Gazelle Nataways, an oversized belly, for the nine-months-pregnant Black Lady Halked, and an oversized bum, for Patsy Pegahmagahbow. This exaggerated sexuality, like the scatological humour and immense physical appetite, conforms to Trickster conventions.

In this instance, however, exaggerated sexuality, combined with the sensitive subject matter, has elicited mixed reactions from audiences. Robert Cushman, reviewing the Royal Alex production for *The Globe and Mail*, described *Dry Lips* as "the most powerful play I have seen about misogyny" (qtd. in Wasserman 319), whereas some women have accused the play itself of being misogynist. [14] For example, Anita Tuharsky (a Métis) criticizes Highway for failing to balance the negative representations and acknowledge the efforts at healing among First Nations: "Highway abused his writing abilities and chose to disregard respect to create pleasures for the public which enjoys these stereotypes and images. It justifies their reluctance to see aboriginal peoples as equals" (qtd. in Filewod 370). The reaction of Saulteaux/Anishinabe poet and playwright Marie Annharte Baker is more mixed: "In *Dry Lips* ... the laughter is unavoidable. All the gags work [...] But why we are laughing and at whom has become an invalid inquiry" ("Angry" 88). While she celebrates the achievement of Native drama, she is mindful of the consequences of internalized racism and sexism. Baker explains that she identified with the *men* in the play, but *not* the women: "I wanted to jump up and say to Hera Keechigeesik, 'Please say something positive about being a Native woman, besides the breeder bit! Please!' Instead she worries that she might get a hockey puck in the left tit, and returns to her domestic bliss" (89). This presumably is the crux of the problem, as women are silenced once more and persuaded to adopt the male point of view: "Although the victim merry-go-round is well depicted, the men's passivity does nothing to change their helpless life cycles. The women in the audience must again feel that it is the men who suffer more.... [I]t is hard to resist the mesmerizing male dogma that is the backbone or wishbone of the play" (88–89).

In retrospect, the reason behind Highway's decision to tackle such painful topics is not hard to find. The rape of Patsy should be read in the context of two related factors. Highway attended junior high school in The Pas in the late 1960s; a year after he graduated, seventeen-year-old Helen Betty Osborne was gang-raped by four white men, stabbed fifty-six times with a screwdriver, and left to die. No one spoke out for sixteen years, despite the fact that most people in the white community knew who was responsible, and only one of the four was ever convicted of anything. Highway explains, "It changed me, and I will write this sort of stuff until the world stops treating women so poorly" ("Twenty-One" 22). Secondly, rape has become a common theme in much Native theatre. As Drew Hayden Taylor observes, "There's mention of a rape in *The Rez Sisters*, there's a rape in *Moonlodge*, there's a homosexual rape in *Fireweed*, there are four or five rapes in *Night of the Trickster*, and I could name more. I'd say in 75 per cent of the Native plays written and produced, there is a rape" (35). Taylor speculates that many Native playwrights may be using their drama to work through persistent, traumatic issues:

> [R]ape represents the horrific amount of sexual abuse that exists in Native communities because of the residential school system, because of alcoholism, because of the breakdown of the extended families, because of adoption. Sexual abuse is cyclical in that the abused becomes the abuser. The dramatic version of rape is also the perfect metaphor for what happened to Native culture. In many communities, culture was matrilinear or matriarchal. Another culture comes in, forcing itself on the community [...] (35–36)

The danger, as Taylor concludes, lies in becoming "fixated" on "dysfunction" (36), to the exclusion of other subjects. And this seems to be the criticism voiced by audience members like Tuharsky and Baker. The common denominator is a perceived lack of balance. The absence of positive representations of Native women risks reinforcement of (sexualized) stereotypes. There are two points to be addressed here: first, the poison is exposed without any tangible evidence of healing; secondly, some women question the *type* of femininity that is apparently upheld as ideal by *Dry Lips*.

An alternative interpretation of Nanabush's appearance and behaviour is offered by Peter Dickinson, in the first reading to give full weight to the differing context produced when we view the play in light of Highway's homosexuality. Although the part of Nanabush in *Dry Lips* was acted by a woman, René Highway was the choreographer for the first production, Dickinson points out. [15] While he acknowledges the objections of feminist critics and reviewers, Dickinson asserts that the "prosthetic devices [worn to portray Gazelle and Patsy], in their obvious signalling of exaggerated femininity, may provide a link with the particular theatrical excesses of gay drag, where female masquerade is perforce performed as a fantasy of the hyper-real" (184). According to Dickinson, Nanabush occupies a position not only of profound gender ambiguity but also of profound sexual ambiguity. I agree that the homosexual subtext in the play must not be ignored. The fact that we watch Nanabush put on Gazelle's fake breasts at the outset, highlighting the performative aspect of gender, might tend to support the notion of drag. But this does not mean that criticisms like Tuharsky's or Baker's can be dismissed without careful consideration (even though they may contain a certain prescriptive element concerning what Native theatre should be or do and the value of positive role models). If the Trickster in the plays, considered *collectively*, demonstrates an ambiguous or shifting gender, the fact remains that, in *Dry Lips*, the sexual traits are exaggeratedly female. The question is: what impact does this incarnation of Nanabush have, when coupled with the play's other strategies of gender inversion? Does Highway go *beyond* mere inversion to offer a genuine challenge to the binary model?

ICONS AND INVERSIONS: MARILYN MONROE, HOCKEY NIGHT IN CANADA, AND WOUNDED KNEE

The difficulty becomes evident upon examination of some of the cross-gendering play and the representations of femininity with which we are confronted in *Dry Lips*. Take, for example, one of the images prominently displayed on the set for much of the action: the poster of Marilyn Monroe.[16] For many, Monroe has come to symbolize the exploitation of women as sexual spectacle in film. In its very conception, the pin-up relies on appearance and depersonalized objectification and taunts ordinary women with an unattainable ideal of beauty and femininity. Monroe was marketed as the archetype of white, blonde femininity, synonymous with sensuality and available sexuality (though she was also associated with innocence and vulnerability). What does the appearance of Marilyn as poster pin-up mean on the set of *Dry Lips*? If we are to assume that the audience recognizes Monroe as an icon of feminine beauty and desirability, if we assume Big Joey has chosen this poster as an object of his desire, what implications does this have for the Native women of the reserve, particularly for Gazelle, who now shares Joey's house? When white womanhood is taken as the norm or standard of female beauty, women of colour are placed at an automatic disadvantage. As many feminists have pointed out, the assumption of racial inferiority has served as the rationalization for a fatal linkage between Native women and sexual availability.[17] It could be argued that Highway reinforces objectification and degradation by his depiction of Gazelle as the dancing girl in the bar at Espanola, seventeen years ago, and by the striptease performed at the beginning of Act Two. But does he also begin to undermine this (racialized) hierarchy, through the subsequent stage business with the pin-up poster?

Towards the end of *Dry Lips*, Dicky Bird attempts suicide, by placing Big Joey's hunting rifle in his mouth and pulling the trigger. The gun fails to fire; as the lights fade out, "*Marilyn Monroe farts, courtesy of Ms. Nanabush: a little flag reading 'poot' pops up out of Ms Monroe's derriere, as on a play gun. We hear a cute little 'poot' sound*" (107). On one level, this is a typical Trickster commentary on the vagaries of human life and death—chance keeps Dicky Bird alive, while, in the next scene, Simon dies accidentally from a self-inflicted gunshot. But surely part of the joke lies in the iconoclastic treatment of the idol of white femininity. In the final scene of the play, when Zachary wakes up on his own couch, the poster has been covered over by Nanabush's large powwow bustle (127). In this gesture, one of the play's key Native icons symbolically conceals, and by implication supersedes, Monroe as icon. It rests with viewers to determine whether this is enough to counter the weight of a graphic, onstage rape of a pregnant woman, a drunken childbirth, and a portrayal of a Native woman as stripper.

If the pin-up of Marilyn represents the feminine norm against which Native women are being measured, then the theme of women playing hockey represents the most obvious instance of cross-gendering in the play. Generally viewed as the national Canadian sport, professional hockey has also been an overwhelmingly (white) male sport. Thus, hockey functions as an icon, simultaneously, of white Canadian culture and of masculinity, evoking associations of toughness, speed, violence, skill, status and so on. The perceived destabilization of gender norms and, by extension, power, caused by the news that Native women are playing hockey, can be deduced from the men's reactions. Big Joey and Creature "*laugh themselves into prolonged* hysterical *fits*" (35; emphasis added); Pierre refers to the phenomenon as a "revolution" (48); and Spooky, after enquiring whether the women are going to revolt against the Chief or the Priest, exclaims "Thank the Lord this is the last year!" (55).

Significantly, to join the Wasy Wailerettes, a woman must either be pregnant or have "piles and piles of babies" (29). With membership in the team linked to women's fertility or sexuality, specifically their capacity to give birth and raise children, playing hockey becomes symbolic of female empowerment. This is made explicit through the character of Simon Starblanket. When Pierre bursts in on Simon and Zachary with news of the team's inception, his confusing allusion to the pregnant Lalala Lacroix leads Simon to offer to fetch Rosie Kakapetum, the reserve's last remaining midwife and medicine woman (46). This juxtaposition aligns the hockey team with Simon's efforts to bring back the drum and revive traditional ways on the reserve (since Simon is seeking to ally himself with Rosie and all she stands for, through his forthcoming marriage to her stepdaughter, Patsy). Pierre later reports Rosie's declaration that "it's a cryin' shame the Wasy Wailerettes is the only team that's not in the Ontario Hockey League" (88), a remark that implies her approval of the venture. Simon functions as a kind of chorus, commenting on the older men's reactions: "You guys have given up, haven't you? You and your generation. You gave up a long time ago. Scared shitless to face up to the fact it's finally happening, that women are taking power back into their hands, that it was always them—not you, not men—who had the power, the power to give life, the power to keep it. Now you'd rather turn your back on the whole thing and pretend to laugh, wouldn't you" (94). This juxtaposition creates a positive power nexus among hockey, motherhood, feminine spirituality and traditional Native medicine; however, the feminine principle being invoked here contains a potentially conservative dimension. Although childbirth remains the one indisputably female function, it is biologically based and is linked with the conventional roles of nurturing and motherhood. Ultimately, this would appear to be a restoration rather than an expansion of women's power and does nothing to disturb conventional gender categories.

A similar ambiguity can be detected in the juxtaposition of images that draw attention to the materiality of women's bodies, on the one hand, with imagery and metaphors carrying more "masculine" connotations, on the other. In the aftermath of the first hockey game, Pierre describes Black Lady's slapshot as "[l]ike a bullet, like a killer shark" (80); the gun as phallic symbol is an old cliché. Pierre also reports that the women decided to suspend play until a "particular puck" has been found, "on principle, no holds barred" (83, 82), a metaphor from wrestling, again a sport more commonly associated with men than with women. Whatever other shortcomings viewers may find in Highway's portrayal of Native women, he certainly cannot be accused of reproducing the stereotype of a co-operative, non-violent "sisterhood." The team spirit (not to mention the normal rules of the game) breaks down, as Gazelle bodychecks Black Lady, who, in turn, deliberately aims a slapshot at her own teammate, with intent to injure. These images are accompanied by a simultaneous emphasis on the physicality of the female body. For instance, Gazelle's huge eyes, after being hit with the puck, exhibit "mascara *stretch marks* [...] perfectly *frightful* [...] to behold" (81; emphasis added). Similarly, the puck disappears down the "horrendous, scarifyin' Nataways bosom crack," sliding "deep, deep into the folds of her fleshy, womanly juices" (81) and is lost. This scene evokes the male fear and horror of the female body, the fear of being swallowed up by the mother, her power to give or withhold human life, and so on. Sheila Rabillard argues that the interplay of absorption and elimination "focuses the audience's attention inescapably upon the female body and, moreover, upon its most taboo aspects: its fluxes, flows, and unstable boundaries, the features that have seemed perhaps most fearful and foreign to a male-dominated culture and that, consequently, have been most firmly associated with feminine inferiority, vulnerability and even uncleanness" (11). [18]

If Highway wanted to invoke a tradition of warrior women, his efforts remain somewhat tentative. Take the name of the team, the Wailerettes. Apart from the use of the "feminine" ending, "ette"—a diminutive shared, incidentally, by the name of the rival team, the Canoe Lake Bravettes—why do the name and the play's "soundscape" emphasize women wailing? Wailing conjures associations with mourning or with the uncanny or eerie; a sinister undercurrent seems to be evoked by this power. After all, if Highway had wanted alliteration, with a positive reference to power and resistance, the team could have been called the Wasy Warriors.

The thematic refrain of women playing hockey intersects with one other significant cultural icon of Native experience: Big Joey mockingly describes the formation of the Wasy Wailerettes as "Wounded Knee Three! Women's version!" (63). Although intended as a joke, the remark, nonetheless, links this motif with a powerful icon of Native culture. The first incident at Wounded Knee, South Dakota 1890—the last battle of the Indian Wars—was a massacre. Estimates of the Sioux dead and wounded ranged from 153 to 300, including many women and children. The second incident took place in 1973, a seventy-one-day standoff between Native activists, on the one side, and the FBI and BIA (Bureau of Indian Affairs) police, on the other. In the third week of February, a mixed caravan of Pine Ridge community members and American Indian Movement (AIM) supporters occupied the church at Wounded Knee. What started out as a local protest quickly escalated, as a mixed assortment of Federal Marshals, BIA police, and FBI operatives closed in. The fire-power of the government forces was vastly superior to that of the Independent Oglala Nation (as they declared themselves). While the eventual victory of the government agents was inevitable, the Oglala won the moral victory, attracting national and inter-national media attention to their cause and airing the long-standing issue of violated treaty rights. No tangible gains resulted immediately from the conflict, but the encounter remains significant; regarded by many as a turning point, politically and psychologically, for Red Power movements. Consequently, Wounded Knee functions, for many contemporary Native writers, as a metonym for the clash of Native and white cultures—and, I would argue in this instance, a metonym for Native resistance. The stand at Wounded Knee was seen, by those who participated, as a fight for the very survival of their people and customs. This seems evident, not only in the heightened rhetoric of the AIM leaders, but in the words of the ordinary people who took part. What emerges most clearly is the feeling of solidarity and community and the belief that something positive would result from the action. One of the Vietnam veterans at Wounded Knee said, "I don't think we will all be wiped out. If we are, there are others who will come take our place. This issue won't die here" (*Voices* 200).

Significantly, however, Big Joey sees Wounded Knee only as a defeat. Initially, recalling his defiant battle cry from the spring of 1973 ("This is the end of the suffering of a great nation!"), he uses imagery that clearly suggests emasculation to describe the outcome: "The FBI. They beat us to the ground. Again and again and again. Ever since that spring, I've had these dreams where blood is spillin' out from my groin, nothin' there but blood and emptiness. It's like ... I lost myself. So when I saw this baby comin' out of Caroline, Black Lady ... Gazelle dancin' ... all this blood ... and I knew it was gonna come ... I ... I tried to stop it ... I freaked out" (119–20). Joey links the blood and violence of the military conflict with the blood and pain of Black Lady's labour and Dicky Bird's traumatic birth. He goes on to confess that he permitted the rape of Patsy because he "hate[s] them fuckin' bitches. Because they— our own women—took the fuckin' power away from us faster than the FBI ever did" (120). Sheila Rabillard argues that Joey's conflation of "political domination and male/female antagonism ... invite[s] the audience to see the opposition between the genders as a hurtful condition analogous to—if not the product of—the sufferings brought about by White colonization" (15). If we adopt Joey's view of Wounded Knee, his equation of women playing hockey with that resistance would amount to an assumption of *dis*empowerment, the futility of inevitable failure—in opposition to Simon's desire to dance with the Rosebud Sioux and his attempt to revive the power of the drum and the powwow bustle.

While Big Joey hates and fears women's power, he turns out to be not only misogynist but also homophobic. This emerges explicitly as Big Joey and Creature watch from a distance while Dicky Bird rapes Nanabush/Patsy with a crucifix. For once, Creature wants to take the initiative and intervene, but Joey physically prevents Creature from going to Patsy's aid (99). Big Joey's homophobia irrupts overtly into his speech at this point: "(*Big Joey suddenly grabs Creature violently by the collar.*) Get out. Get the fuck out of here. You're nothin' but a fuckin' fruit. Fuck off" (100). Creature flees, and Joey continues to watch, "paralyzed." While Big Joey's actions are patently misogynist, they may also contain an element of homosexual panic. Because he is insecure and uncertain about his own masculinity, Joey must "prove" his manhood over and over, with heterosexual conquests and physical violence. He is afraid to risk being perceived as anything other. My reading diverges from Dickinson's at this point. Although he acknowledges the "irony … that in both plays Big Joey, perhaps the one character most associated by Highway with normative patriarchal attitudes, becomes an object of desire for two-spirited characters," he fails to confront directly the implications of "eroticiz[ing] the hyper-masculinity" of a homophobe (180). Surely this amounts to counter-productive self-hatred on the part of the two-spirit.

A few scenes later, Spooky Lacroix asks Creature why he failed to prevent the rape. Lacroix, who assumes Creature is afraid of Big Joey, does not get quite the response he expects, when Creature replies "I love him, Spooky" (104). Note the parallel between Spooky's exclamation, "Lord have mercy on Wasaychigan Hill!" (104) and his earlier reaction to the news of the women's "revolution": "Thank the Lord this is the last year!" (55). Creature's confession of love begins with a simple and forthright declaration. His comments initially seem to be those of a subject gazing at the object of desire: "I love the way he stands. I love the way he walks. The way he laughs. The way he wears his cowboy boots …" (104). But the next speech reveals his confusion "… the way his tight blue jeans fall over his ass. The way he talks so smart and tough. The way women fall at his feet. I wanna be like him. I always wanted to be like him, William. I always wanted to have a dick as big as his" (104). Here Creature shifts from desire to identification: a wish to emulate, specifically directed towards traits conventionally associated with heterosexual constructs of masculinity—toughness, sexual potency, irresistibility to women. Spooky's "[y]ou know not what you say" (104) is an ironically apt description of Creature's confused sexuality. [19] The implication of his "I don't care. I can't stand it anymore" (105) is that Creature has been impelled into this declaration by the shock of Big Joey's behaviour: that is, he has been forced to confront aspects of his own feelings because the man he admires has allowed such an "inconceivable act" (as Zachary calls it [117]) to occur. It remains unclear whether his intention, in proposing to go to Big Joey's house, is to confess his feelings to Big Joey, as well, since he never gets the opportunity.

Spooky's responses in this exchange range from astonishment and disbelief to extreme uneasiness, a milder version of Joey's homosexual panic: "Shut up. You're making me nervous. Real nervous" (105). As the scene unfolds, the issues raised by the emergence of this potential homosexual desire merge into other concerns related to a community dysfunctional and fractured. In his effort to persuade Spooky to accompany him to Big Joey's house, Creature confronts Spooky with his own past (his alcoholism and his rejection of his father's traditional religion) and appeals to the blood-brotherhood sworn twenty-one years earlier by five young men. This evokes the broader homosocial bonds that have been ruptured. As they stare into each other's eyes, Creature insists, "William. Think of your father. Remember the words of Nicotine Lacroix. 'Men who do not worship the Christian way do not automatically go to hell. There are many, many other ways of communicating with the Great Spirit.... Respect us. Respect all people!" (106). Reminded of his dead father's role as medicine man, the Christianized Spooky finally breaks down and swears for the first time in the play. Creature's moment of truth thus transmits itself to Spooky, forcing him, in turn, to confront the damage done by his denial of his father's spiritual beliefs. Taken together with Dicky Bird's quest for a father figure and Big Joey's refusal of paternal responsibility, this crucial scene can be read as part of the broader examination of masculinities throughout the play.

The real problem is what happens to this material afterwards. No further overt reference is made to Creature's revelation, as other events overtake the group. In the next scene where Big Joey and Creature appear together, Creature, at first, seems inclined to continue his supporting role and defend Joey, but then decides to speak of what he witnessed—at which point Big Joey turns on Creature with "you little cocksucker," and Dicky Bird knocks Creature unconscious with Joey's gun (119). The violent silencing of the one member of the community who has expressed a (formerly repressed) homosexual desire, at the very moment of Joey's big confession of misogyny, reminds us of the continuing difficulty, if not impossibility, of speaking two-spirited desire. Dickinson suggests Highway's plays "reveal both the deep gender divisions that have resulted from Indigenous communities' historical experiences of colonization, and the panoply of diverse sexual identities that have thrived and adapted in spite of this shared history" (179). In my opinion, this states the case somewhat too positively, given what happens to Creature. Granted, there are signs of progress and reconciliation at the end: Spooky continues to swear (which I read as a weakening of his over-zealous Christian stance), and Rosie Kakapetum delivers the Lacroix baby; Joey acknowledges Dicky Bird; Hera Keechigeesik is now Captain of the Wailerettes and Creature is cheering for her (suggestive of another new allegiance). But the healing process has barely begun.

CONCLUSIONS

Highway has given us a complex, challenging drama in *Dry Lips Oughta Move to Kapuskasing*. But I would have to conclude that the mediating potential of the tradition of the *berdache* remains potential, rather than actual, in the play as Highway has written it. The play indicates that homophobia, like misogyny, remains a serious problem on the reserve. Highway's position as two-spirited certainly adds another dimension to his drama. The solution to the crisis of masculinity, Highway's oeuvre suggests, is to resurrect the feminine principle—which he consistently links with the goddess, the Earth as mother, and so on. He sees his role as a gay man in terms of the third gender. But for Highway, this role is one of mediating, acting as a kind of buffer between the other two genders. In other words, the third gender, rather than disrupting and breaking down the binary categories, seems to be holding them in place. This can be seen in the play's use of the trope of inversion: women playing hockey, men baking and knitting. Underneath these inversions, a potentially conservative notion of femininity remains in place. A small detail at the close betrays this: Creature has taken up knitting for his new goddaughter, but his insistence that blue is the "wrong" colour for a girl and that he must make pink items preserves conventional gender norms (123). Discouraged violently from taking up an active, open role as a two-spirit, Creature himself remains one of the dispossessed—perhaps even more so than the "beautiful, daring, death-defying Indian women" (124).

The source of my uneasiness and my hesitation to embrace Highway's work fully, then, is similar to that expressed by Tuharsky or Baker: there are no positive counter-images of women—or, I would add, two-spirits—onstage to counterpoise the rape or the gay-bashing. The kind of disruption caused by Highway's Trickster logic has much more to do with the revival of Cree cosmology than it does with the kind of transgression proposed by queer theory and politics. I am reminded of the questions posed by Gary Kinsman in *The Regulation of Desire*: "Why do there have to be only two genders? And perhaps, more radically, why does there have to be gender at all?" (94). Our societies remain trapped by a hierarchical, dualist gender system. We need to (re)imagine what third, fourth, even queer genders might be.

(2003)

Notes

1   *The Rez Sisters*, workshopped with De-ba-jeh-mu-jig (Manitoulin Island), was produced in 1986, by Native Earth Performing Arts. *Dry Lips* was mounted as a co-production, by Native Earth Performing Arts and Theatre Passe Muraille, in 1989, and remounted by David Mirvish, at the Royal Alexandra in Toronto and at the National Arts Centre in Ottawa, in 1991. Highway worked on the third play for years but encountered difficulties getting it mounted because of its ambitious scope. In a 1993 interview, Highway envisaged a cast of twenty-one Native women and seven men (putting "the men and the women [of the reserve] together for the first time" in the cycle), with Nanabush as the ghost of three different women who had died or never been born ("Twenty-One" 25, 17). The musical *Rose* was finally produced in January 2000, by students of the University College Drama Program of the University of Toronto, with a somewhat smaller cast—non-Native, with the exception of Alana Brascoupe, who played the ghost of the unborn baby (see Kenneth Williams). *Rose* was recently published by Talonbooks.

2   "Ojibway" is one of the terms used by white anthropologists and ethnographers for the "Anishinabeg," who have recently reclaimed their own name for themselves. I have generally retained "Ojibway," however, since this is the name Highway uses in his play.

3   Midnight Sun warns that many (non-Native) theorists, when employing cross-cultural (Native) examples to demonstrate the culturally constructed nature of gender and sexuality, isolate one set of cultural phenomena from their wider social and economic contexts. She notes the tendency to use contemporary, Western concepts of gender and sexuality as the standard for comparison, misapplying Eurocentric terms like cross-gender or cross-dressing to Native social practice—often in order to support claims about contemporary Western homosexuality (33). As a white lesbian academic, I recognize my complicity with this motivation. At the same time, the contemporary Wasaychigan rez, as depicted by Highway, suffers precisely because of the superimposition of white gender (specifically patriarchal) norms, so I feel that, in this instance, cross-gendering is an appropriate problem to explore.

4   See also Roscoe, *Living the Spirit*; Kinsman 92–97. For Native women's experience, see Midnight Sun; Blackwood; Whitehead; Brant, *A Gathering of Spirit*.

5   Some scholars believe that "female *berdache*" is a misnomer, that the alternative gender roles adopted by women in First Nations societies did not simply comple-ment those of male *berdaches*—hence the designation fourth gender. Full investi-gation of these roles falls outside the scope of my current paper.

6   Highway's fictional Wasaychigan reserve, inspired partly by the communities on Manitoulin Island, includes both Cree and Ojibway inhabitants.

7   Some Nations, such as the Apache, may have had more negative attitudes towards *berdaches*. Scholars like Williams and Roscoe inevitably focus on those Native societies that integrated gender diversity into established cultural structures.

8   Some viewers may feel that Emily Dictionary is a more positive figure than Creature. Certainly, she is tough and strong and stands up for herself. Equally, her violence, swearing, and anger are symptomatic of internalized misogyny and racism. And like Creature, Emily is subject to prejudice and suspicion: "You have no morals at all. You sick pervert. You should have stayed where you came from, where all the other perverts are," says Veronique St. Pierre to Emily (45). In other words, *The Rez Sisters* betrays pressures and problems similar to those in *Dry Lips*, from a different angle.

9   I have not found any overt references to a third gender or two-spirit in interviews prior to the production of *The Rez Sisters* and *Dry Lips* although, in earlier interviews, Highway does talk freely about how he views the impact of being gay on his work. It is, therefore, difficult to determine precisely when Highway became aware of older traditions—whether he retained such cultural memories personally or encountered them later as Native and queer politics intersected.

[10] When I first read this scene, what came to mind was Archie and Edith Bunker from "All in the Family"; now I wonder whether "The Odd Couple" might not be equally appropriate.

[11] This raises the possibility that Creature is now caring for the children on his own, as a single parent. If my deduction is correct, it represents another reversal of gender assumptions and suggests "unmaternal" behaviour on the part of Gazelle Nataways. (Gazelle's lack of concern for her children is already implied in *The Rez Sisters*; see, e.g., 11, 28.) Gazelle is coded as the feminine counterpart to the bullying Big Joey: she is implied to be sexually promiscuous; she used to be a dancing girl and re-enacts a striptease, etc.

[12] He is, however, trapped in stasis like the other characters—see, for instance, his debate about "hockey" versus "life" (finding the particular puck or stopping Simon from killing Dicky Bird) 103, 107–08. His inability to distinguish between obviously unequal priorities is telling.

[13] In a complex reading of the relation between English and Cree in the play, Randy Lundy argues that part of the solution "lies in the men's returning to a healthy relationship with each other, with the women, and with Indigenous spiritual traditions which are governed by the internal logic of the non-gendered Indigenous languages, rather than gendered English" (111). Of the exchange between Nanabush and Simon, he concludes: "it is clear that Simon has been unable to overcome the gender confusion that the English language has caused and that this gender confusion is largely responsible for his inability to realise his quest" (116).

[14] Highway, predictably, was shocked: "To me *Dry Lips* is about the return of God as a woman [...] I wrote it as a hymn—of pain, yes—but a hymn to the beauty of women and the feminine energy that needs to come back into its own if this world is going to survive" (qtd. in Wasserman 319). In fairness to Highway, much of his early work is women-centred. This does not mean that his views on women and femininity are not conservative, however.

[15] Highway's younger brother René, a dancer, performed the part of Nanabush in the original production of *The Rez Sisters*. He died in October 1990, of AIDS-related illnesses, before *Dry Lips* was re-mounted in mainstream Canadian theatres.

[16] My interpretation of Monroe as icon is indebted to the work of Richard Dyer.

[17] Randy Lundy agrees that the racism and misogyny must be read in the context of the male fantasy Monroe represents: her poster is the single dominant image of Whiteness in the play (106).

[18] It may be significant that, although the boundary between sexual spheres was not fiercely guarded in traditional Native societies, "[o]nly in one respect was male hegemony encoded in 'absolutist' terms: This was in the notion that women's menstrual and parturitional blood was antipathetic to male enterprise, hence to true pre-eminence" (Whitehead 105).

[19] Emily is equally ambivalent in *The Rez Sisters*, swinging between declarations of love for Rosabella Baez and desire for the "hunk" Joey: "That dude's got buns on him like no other buns on the face of God's entire creation. Whooo! Not to mention a dick that's bigger than a goddamn breadbox" (38, 85). In the fluidity of their sexual-object choice, both these characters might be seen as closer to the *berdache/two-spirit* tradition than Western gay/lesbian subject.

Works Cited

Baker, Marie Annharte. "Angry Enough to Spit but with Dry Lips It Hurts More Than You Know." *Canadian Theatre Review* 68 (1991): 88–89.

———. "An Old Indian Trick Is to Laugh." *Canadian Theatre Review* 68 (1991): 48–49.

Blackwood, Evelyn. "Sexuality and Gender in Certain Native American Tribes: The Case of Cross-Gender Females." *The Lesbian Issue: Essays from Signs.* Ed. Estelle B. Freedman, Barbara C. Gelpi, Susan L. Johnson, and Kathleen M. Weston. Chicago: U of Chicago P, 1985. 27–42.

Brant, Beth. *Writing as Witness: Essay and Talk.* Toronto: Women's Press, 1994.

———, ed. *A Gathering of Spirit: A Collection by Native American Indian Women.* Rev. ed. Toronto: Women's Press, 1988.

Burnham, Clint. "Lips, Marks, Lapse: Materialism and Dialogism in Thomson [sic] Highway's *Dry Lips Oughta Move to Kapuskasing.*" *Open Letter* 8.9 (1994): 19–30.

Christen, Kimberly A. *Clowns and Tricksters: An Encyclopedia of Tradition and Culture.* Denver: ABC-CLIO, 1998.

Dickinson, Peter. *Here is Queer: Nationalisms, Sexualities and the Literatures of Canada.* Toronto: U of Toronto P, 1999.

Dyer, Richard. *Stars.* New ed. London: BFI Publishing, 1998.

Filewod, Alan. "Receiving Aboriginality: Tomson Highway and the Crisis of Cultural Authenticity." *Theatre Journal* 46 (1994): 363–73.

Highway, Tomson. *Dry Lips Oughta Move to Kapuskasing.* Calgary: Fifth House, 1989.

———. Interview with Carolyn Farrell. *Questionable Activities.* Ed. Judith Rudakoff. Toronto: Playwrights Canada, 2000. 87–91.

———. *The Rez Sisters.* Saskatoon: Fifth House, 1988.

————. "'Twenty-one native women on motorcycles': an interview with Tomson Highway." Interview with Joanne Tompkins and Lisa Male. *Australasian Drama Studies* 24 (1994) 13–28.

Hodgson, Heather. "Survival Cree, or Weesakeechak dances down Yonge Street: Heather Hodgson speaks with Tomson Highway." *Books in Canada* 28.1 (1999): 2–5.

Kinsman, Gary. *The Regulation of Desire: Homo and Hetero Sexualities.* 2nd ed. Montreal: Black Rose, 1996.

Lundy, Randy. "Erasing the Invisible: Gender Violence and Representations of Whiteness in *Dry Lips Oughta Move to Kapuskasing.*" *(Ad)dressing Our Words: Aboriginal Perspectives on Aboriginal Literatures.* Ed. Armand Garnet Ruffo. Penticton: Theytus, 2001. 101–23.

Midnight Sun. "Sex/Gender Systems in Native North America." *Living the Spirit: A Gay American Indian Anthology.* Ed. Will Roscoe. New York: St Martin's, 1988. 32–47.

Perkins, Lina. "Remembering the Trickster in Tomson Highway's *The Rez Sisters.*" *Modern Drama* 45.2 (2002): 259–69.

Preston, Jennifer. "Weesageechak Begins to Dance: Native Earth Performing Arts Inc." *TDR* 36.1(1992): 133–59.

Rabillard, Sheila. "Absorption, Elimination, and the Hybrid: Some Impure Questions of Gender and Culture in the Trickster Drama of Tomson Highway." *Essays in Theatre* 12.1 (1993): 3–27.

Roscoe, Will. *Changing Ones: Third and Fourth Genders in Native North America.* New York: St. Martin's, 1998.

————, ed. *Living the Spirit: A Gay American Indian Anthology.* New York: St. Martin's, 1988.

Sedgwick, Eve Kosofsky. *Between Men: English Literature and Male Homosocial Desire.* New York: Columbia UP, 1985.

Taylor, Drew Hayden. "Alive and Well: Native Theatre in Canada." *Journal of Canadian Studies* 31.3 (1996): 29–37.

Voices from Wounded Knee, 1973: In the Words of the Participants. Rooseveltown, NY: Akwesasne Notes, 1974.

Wasserman, Jerry. Introduction. *Dry Lips Oughta Move to Kapuskasing. Modern Canadian Plays.* Vol. 2. Ed. Jerry Wasserman. Vancouver: Talonbooks, 1994. 317–20.

Whitehead, Harriet. "The Bow and the Burden Strap: a New Look at Institutionalized Homosexuality in Native North America." *Sexual Meanings: The Cultural Construction of Gender and Sexuality.* Ed. Sherry B. Ortner and Harriet Whitehead. Cambridge: Cambridge UP, 1981. 80–115.

Wigston, Nancy. "Nanabush in the City." *Books in Canada* 18.2 (1989): 7–9.

Williams, Kenneth. Rev. of *Rose*, by Tomson Highway. *Windspeaker* 17.10 (2000): 15.

Williams, Walter L. *The Spirit and the Flesh: Sexual Diversity in American Indian Culture*. Boston: Beacon, 1986.

Brothers' Keepers, or, The Performance
of Mourning: Queer Rituals of Remembrance

by Peter Dickinson

> One cannot hold a discourse *on* the "work of mourning" without taking part in it, without announcing or partaking in death, and first of all in one's own death.
>
> —Jacques Derrida, "By Force of Mourning," 172

> What grief displays ... is the thrall in which our relations with others hold us, in ways that we cannot always recount or explain, in ways that often interrupt the self-conscious account of ourselves we might try to provide, in ways that challenge the very notion of ourselves as autonomous and in control.
>
> —Judith Butler, *Precarious Life*, 23

> But it may well be that theatre and performance respond to a psychic need to rehearse for loss, and especially for death.
>
> —Peggy Phelan, *Mourning Sex*, 3

In *Precarious Life: The Powers of Mourning and Violence*, Judith Butler picks up the threads of an argument first sketched in *Antigone's Claim*; with some political urgency, especially in the wake of 9/11, she asks how one moves beyond the preoccupation with individual human agency implicit in the question, "What *makes for a grievable life?*," to a recognition that "[l]oss has made a tenuous 'we' of us all" (20; emphasis in original). Acknowledging the terrible and terrifying effects of violence to which sexual and other minorities are routinely subjected, Butler nevertheless posits that

> each of us is constituted politically in part by virtue of the social vulnerability of our bodies—as a site of desire and physical vulnerability, as a site of publicity at once assertive and exposed. Loss and vulnerability seem to follow from our being socially constituted bodies, attached to others, at risk of losing those attachments, exposed to others, at risk of violence by virtue of that exposure. (20)

For Butler, then, the more important question becomes how we "transform" or "translate" (to use her words) this loss into a new social ethics and political responsibility, reconfiguring a "model of the human" that accounts for the "you" in "me," and that bears witness to the fact that "I am as much constituted by those I do grieve for as by those whose deaths I disavow, whose nameless and faceless deaths form the melancholic background for my social world" (46, 49).

In this paper, I want to build on Butler's insights here and elsewhere (especially in *Antigone's Claim*), theorizing the political responsibility and social vulnerability that specifically attend queer rituals of remembrance, as well as some of the masculine—and masculinist—teleologies at the heart of these rituals. How do I grieve for the "man" lost in "human," when it is mostly straight white men who have insisted historically that the latter category is one whose loss as a mode of address must be rehearsed over and over again by all the rest of us? How could I ever call such a man my brother? I explore these and related questions by stressing both the *performative* and the *local* applications of a queer theory of mourning. As such, I preface my paper with a brief survey of some spaces of remembrance that in many respects constitute "a landscape of memorialization"[1] particular to Vancouver, and that thus serve as the immediate backdrop to my thinking about the larger issues circulating in the ensuing pages. In suggesting a "nervous mutating catastrophic reach" to these spaces, and the traumatic events they commemorate, a reach that extends beyond Vancouver and, more importantly, my own immediate experiencing of them, I am structuring my paper along the lines of the model for "performative writing" adopted by Peggy Phelan in her brilliant book *Mourning Sex: Performing Public Memories*. There, Phelan notes that "[p]erformative writing is an attempt to find a form for 'what philosophy wishes all the same to say.'" She continues:

> Rather than describing the performance event in "direct signification," a task that I believe to be impossible and not terrifically interesting, I want this writing to enact the affective force of the performance event again, as it plays itself out in an ongoing temporality made vivid by the psychic process of distortion (repression, fantasy, and the general hubbub of the individual and collective unconscious), and made narrow by the muscular force of political repression in all its mutative violence. The events I disclose here sound differently in the writing of them than in the "experiencing" of them, and it is the urgent call of that difference that I am hoping to amplify here. (11–12)

In the main sections of this paper, then, I am likewise seeking to amplify a difference, focussing on four specifically theatrical performances of mourning in order to note how their respective Vancouver stagings speak both to my own evolving memorialization of the city in which I live, and to a communal history of queer witnessing whose narrative lacunae are precisely what constitute the act of memorialization itself. As Butler puts it, "I tell a story about the relations I choose, only to expose, somewhere along the way, the way I am gripped and undone by these very relations. My narrative falters, as it must" (*Precarious Life* 23). To this end, I look initially, and most extensively, at the performance work of Margie Gillis and Paula Vogel, women who have both lost biological brothers to AIDS (Christopher Gillis and Carl Vogel, respectively), and who, moreover, have both sought to memorialize their brothers' lives in specific works of art: Gillis in the solo dance piece *Torn Roots, Broken Branches* and Vogel in the Obie Award-winning play *The Baltimore Waltz*. The public performance of bereavement by these two women, its ritual repetition, is not, I argue, a narcissistic capitulation to grief—as Freud's notion of melancholia would have it—but rather an acknowledgment of community, a symbolic representation of collective struggle in response to an unprecedented social crisis, one that allows for the sharing of loss and the ritualization of remembrance as a precursor to organization and a demand for change.

Here, in theorizing the performance of mourning contra Freud, I will be drawing primarily on the work of two of his more important contemporary interlocutors. In particular, I will be using Butler's influential notion of "gender melancholia," as she has developed and refined the concept over the course of *Gender Trouble, Bodies That Matter* and, most recently, *Antigone's Claim, Precarious Life,* and *Undoing Gender,* and as she has used it to (re)read Freudian (and Lacanian) psychoanalysis in order to demonstrate that homosexual cathexis must precede ego identification and the successful resolution of the Oedipal complex. This will aid in unpacking how performative memorialization overlaps with queer kinship in the texts by Gillis and Vogel. Relatedly, I will also be working from the model for social praxis on offer in Douglas Crimp's important essay "Mourning and Militancy," which takes as its central premise (one that I share) the absolutely necessary connection between mourning/remembrance and activism, especially in the context of the queer community's responses to the AIDS pandemic and decades of unabated anti-gay violence.

I conclude my paper with a very brief analysis of two queer plays which each, in their own way, seek to memorialize—in order to attempt to make sense of—the murder of Matthew Shepard. Terrence McNally's *Corpus Christi,* an intensely homoerotic retelling of the Biblical passion story, was the subject of bomb threats and picketing when it opened at the Manhattan Theatre Club in the fall of 1998. Following Shepard's murder in October of that year, McNally included a preface in the published version of the play that makes a direct link between the crucifixion of the play's fictional gay protagonist, Joshua, and that of the real-life Shepard. Moisés Kaufman and Tectonic Theater's *The Laramie Project* is based on interviews with residents of Laramie, Wyoming in the immediate aftermath of Shepard's killing; a dozen or so actors voice the words of more than fifty distraught, angry, uncomprehending, and media-weary citizens—as well as their own—in an effort to tell the story of this community and, in the words of one resident/character, "say it right" (100). The play was subsequently made into an HBO movie with a who's who of high-profile Hollywood stars.[2]

Both plays are large ensemble pieces that eschew explicit focus on the homosexual victim-as-martyr in favour of a dissection (McNally allegorically, Kaufman documentarily) of the community that produced his homophobic killers. These men, equally our brothers, how do we remember them? I attempt to answer this question by first focussing on a key theatrical convention employed by each play, and then by returning to my opening framing discussion of the specific orientations of queer remembrance in Vancouver via references to local stagings of each play in 2002 (i.e., Hoarse Raven's production of *Corpus Christi* at Festival House in May and Studio 58's production of *The Laramie Project* in October). There, I will offer some final Butlerian remarks on mourning and melancholia—and what remains "unspeakable" in each—

within the context of the Vancouver queer community's determined efforts to remember Aaron Webster, killed by gay bashers in the same park from which an AIDS Memorial has been barred as unsuitable.

The Landscape of Remembrance

This last point refers to a particular confluence of the local and the performative that has necessarily influenced the writing and revising of this paper. I am speaking of the completion (in July 2004) and dedication (on 1 December 2004, in a ceremony that coincided with World AIDS Day) of a long-planned, and long-delayed, memorial to British Columbians who have died of AIDS. The site of the memorial is Sunset Beach West, along a grassy and lightly treed knoll at the foot of Broughton Street and Beach Avenue, in the heart of downtown's West End and a short walk east of English Bay and the Stanley Park seawall. Its design consists of a series of 20 steel panels, each close to a metre in width, cut into and winding through the adjacent landscape like a ribbon unfurling in the wind. The memorial's foundation, like Maya Lin's famous Vietnam Veterans' Memorial in Washington, DC, follows the natural grade level of the site, resulting in a height ranging from 0.75-1.5 metres. Again much like Lin's design, the panels that comprise the Vancouver AIDS Memorial have been laser cut with the names of those who have died from the disease, signifying "their absence from our lives" (Vancouver AIDS Memorial). Small holes have been placed next to each name so that mourners and visitors to the memorial might leave flowers or other tokens of remembrance for lost loved ones. Finally, the following stanza from Spanish-American writer George Santayana's 1896 commemorative verse "To W.P." scrolls above the names, at the top of the memorial:

> With you a part of me hath passed away,
> For in the peopled forest of my mind
> A tree made leafless by the wintry wind
> Shall never don again its green array
> Chapel and fireside, country road and bay,
> Have something of their friendliness resigned;
> Another, if I would, I could not find,
> And I am grown much older in a day.
> But yet I treasure in my memory
> Your gift of charity, your mellow ease,
> And the dear honor of your amity;
> For those once mine, my life is rich with these.
> And I scarce know which part may greater be, –
> What I keep of you, or you rob of me.
> (*Sonnets and Other Verses* 61)

Despite the performance of civic harmony that attended the official ground-breaking ceremony for the memorial in May 2002, and that was likewise featured prominently at the official dedication ceremony in December 2004, public goodwill surrounding the project has not always been very much in evidence. Nor was Sunset Beach, chosen only after an especially arduous and acrimonious two-year public consultation process in June 1998, the site originally proposed for the memorial. Indeed, when the then fledgling AIDS Memorial Committee, working in an ad hoc manner under the auspices of AIDS Vancouver and the Pacific AIDS Resource Centre, first approached the Vancouver Parks Board in 1996 about installing a public monument to the memory of those who have died from AIDS, they proposed a site adjacent Ceperley Park, near the Second Beach entrance to Stanley Park. This proposal was endorsed by the Parks Board at an in camera meeting in November 1996. However, when word of the planned memorial and its proposed location leaked to the press, there was an immediate public outcry. Ostensibly, debate centred around the lack of public consultation surrounding the process, but various media polls conducted during the period repeatedly suggested that what people most objected to was the choice of Stanley Park as the site for the AIDS Memorial—and precisely because the spot was deemed too public (see Fraser).

Ceperley Park, a highly trafficked part of Stanley Park, popular with both locals and tourists alike, and home to a playground and picnic area frequented by young children and families, was deemed inappropriate for a memorial to AIDS victims. Wasn't it enough that the area was annually turned into the start and end point for the Vancouver AIDS Walk every September? A more discreet location should be found for a permanent memorial. Of course what remained unacknowledged throughout this public discourse on the discourse of publicness was that the woods just north of Ceperley Park are highly trafficked in another way—namely, as a late-night cruising ground for gay, bisexual and otherwise identified men seeking sex with other men. In the homophobic equation of "gay sex = AIDS" that frequently subtended the debates around erecting a memorial at Ceperley, what remained palpable—even when unspoken—was the feeling that the gay community wished to flaunt itself in broad daylight yet again, that it was somehow rubbing normal Vancouverites' (and, indeed, the world's) noses in a killing field of its own making, one that had best remain hidden away in the dark. [3] Never mind that the killings that go on in this field in Stanley Park under cover of darkness, killings that remain un—or under—memorialized within Vancouver public discourse, have nothing at all to do with the human immunodeficiency virus, and everything to do with "normal" boys who carry baseball bats—a point to which I will return at the end of this essay.

Vancouver's recent history has been particularly vexed on the subject of public memorials. For example, the fallout attending the December 1997 unveiling of artist Beth Alber's *Marker of Change* memorial in Thornton Park, commemorating the lives of the fourteen women murdered by Marc Lepine at Montreal's École Polytechnique eight years earlier, rehearsed in many ways the same debates around intentionality and appropriateness that have characterized the AIDS Memorial. The conservative local press, led by *Vancouver Sun* columnist Trevor Lautens, and North Vancouver Reform Party MP Ted White, were particularly aggrieved by the fact that the Women's Monument Project (a feminist collective working out of Capilano College overseeing the design competition, fundraising, and eventual installation of Alber's sculpture), like the Vancouver AIDS Memorial Society, saw the *Marker of Change* not merely as commemorative but also as explicitly educative, a way of focussing immediate local attention on the ongoing global phenomenon of male violence against women (see Lautens; Duncan). Clearly the memorial was meant as a feminist indictment of men, the argument went, and, as such, could not be seen as representative of a spirit of shared remembrance in any way. In this regard, critics pointed to the phrase "for all women who have been murdered by men" in the memorial's dedication plaque as unnecessarily provocative.

That same year, Vancouver resident Don Larson angered many in the First Nations community when he spearheaded a campaign to create a monument honouring the memories of the women (many of them Aboriginal sex trade workers) who began disappearing from Vancouver's Downtown Eastside (DES) at a statistical rate of approximately two per year in the early 1980s, a phenomenon that was met with what now seems willful inattention on the part of police and the local media. [4] Despite the fact that the First Nations community had for several years been staging a public performance of remembrance and a call to action for these same women in the form of a "smudge ceremony," accompanied by demonstrations held each Valentine's Day (see Kelley), Larson—who is white—went ahead and unilaterally commissioned the design of a memorial boulder. The boulder was installed in CRAB (Create a Real Available Beach) Park—3.5 hectares of reclaimed land along the waterfront at the foot of Main Street, in the heart of the DES's skid row (a memorial bench was dedicated separately in March 2000). The fact that the monument's dedicatory inscription appropriates a traditional First Nations' "form of address ['All my relations'] … used to begin or end a prayer, speech, or story" (Bold et al. 24) only added insult to injury. In the wake of Robert Pickton's arrest and arraignment on charges of murdering 26 of the more than 60 women currently identified as missing (see note 4), and as Aboriginal and non-Aboriginal artists alike have begun to exhibit with increasing frequency memorial installations to the murdered and disappeared women, [5] family members have begun to discuss—and argue about—plans for a new permanent and official monument.

More recently, Vancouver veterans reacted with outrage when, in the summer of 2003, a loose coalition of youthful protesters wishing to focus attention on homelessness, poverty, and City Hall's repeated delays in converting the abandoned Woodward's Building to social housing, set up an impromptu squat at Victory Square, site of the cenotaph commemorating British Columbians who lost their lives in World Wars I and II. The veterans saw the squatters' actions as a desecration and a violation of public memorial space devoted to the preservation of the past; they also worried that the protest would delay plans by the city to renovate and spruce up the memorial site in time for November Remembrance Day activities. For their part, the squatters argued that their occupation of the square constituted a different kind of (re)memorialization, a protest against the city's active forgetting of its spatial present (see Fong). Ironically, when forced by a police injunction to vacate Victory Square, the protesters split their forces, with half decamping to CRAB Park, and the other half to Thornton Park.

"The Protocols of Mourning"

At the heart of these debates are some fundamentally difficult and necessarily polarizing questions about public memory, memorialization, and mourning: Who gets to publicly remember, for whom, where, in what ways, and how? What constitutes an appropriate (there's that word again) display—psychically, materially—of mourning? When does respectful remembrance cross the line into social activism? And how are all of these rituals further complicated by what Marianne Hirsch and others have called the phenomenon of "postmemory" (see especially Hirsch's *Family Frames*), in which the "performance" of remembrance via internet sites, television shows, and other media technologies designed to remember for us, produces a constant—though necessarily simulacral and ersatz—condition of reminiscence and retrospection that signals not so much a felt connection with the past (including the very recent past) as a profound *dis*connection from it? For Andreas Huyssen, this globalized penchant for instant memorialization—in everything from hurried architectural competitions to rebuild Ground Zero in New York City to more populist expressions of remembrance, such as roadside displays of flowers marking the site of a car crash—has, paradoxically, produced what he calls a "culture of amnesia," whose primary symptom is the "atrophy" of historical consciousness, aided and abetted by a high-tech "media world spinning a cocoon of timeless claustrophobia and nightmarish phantasms and simulation," in which there is "nothing to remember, nothing to forget" (*Twilight Memories* 7, 9). However, as Richard Cavell has recently pointed out, Huyssen's argument is profoundly "normative": "there are good memories and there are bad memories for [Huyssen], and bad memories usually tend to be associated with populist expression—what one might call 'history from below' as opposed to the official or institutional histories most often valorised by the state" ("Histories of Forgetting" 68).

Although Huyssen has since revised his take somewhat in his book *Present Pasts*, even there his critical perspective "is guided by the conviction that too much of the contemporary memory discourse focuses on the personal" (8), especially with respect to episodes of trauma. Such sentiments issue from the statist view that nations, for example, primarily build public monuments to—and organize museums around—great events and great men. These spatial aids to memory (what Pierre Nora has theorized, in the French context, as *les lieux de mémoire*; see his three-volume study of the same name), so the theory goes, in turn help citizens remember iconographically, ensuring that, in the present, we will not forget the past, lest we repeat its mistakes. But this somewhat naively holistic and ameliorative view of historical memory as a collective cultural repository from which humanity progresses forward is, it seems to me, undercut by precisely the more populist, impromptu, localized, and, yes, performative forms of memorialization that Huyssen eschews from his analysis. Take, for example, a queer ritual of remembrance such as the Names Project Memorial Quilt, and its relation to how bodies (as opposed to monuments) remember space, be it the space of a national government capital or the space of history. What the formerly semi-regular unfurling of the quilt on the grounds of the National Mall in Washington, D.C. [6] demonstrated most vividly was that recovering a narrative of collective memory need not be at the expense of all of the individual bodies and personal stories subsumed within that narrative; nor must memorialization's pedagogical function be separated from its political one. [7] Each vibrantly sewn and personalized panel seeks to preserve individual eccentricities and encapsulate the life story of its memorial subject, lest his or her death fade into a roll call of anonymous statistics about AIDS' human toll. At the same time, the display of this individual privation is undertaken as part of a highly theatrical, ritualized, and intensely public act: each panel is laid out for viewing in an elaborately choreographed manner as the names of persons who have died from the disease are read out by alternating participants at a microphone. Carried out in the shadow of a nation's ultimate folly (the hyper-phallic Washington Monument), just a short distance away from the rows of indistinguishable white crosses at Arlington National Cemetery and from the equally white seat of world democracy from which issued the edict "Don't ask, don't tell," such a memorial project is a defiantly personalist resistance of the attempts by governments to muzzle and displace grief through monumentalist abstraction. The Quilt insists not only on telling, but also on showing; it is a performance of mourning that doubles as a political occupation. As Elinor Fuchs notes in a 1993 article originally published in *American Theatre* (and reprinted in her book *The Death of Character*), the whole idea of the Quilt,

> combining monumentality with patchwork, expresses at once the scale of the leaping world AIDS crisis and its assault on humanist faith in order and social continuity. Pastiche and defiant disunity are by now familiar hallmarks of the postmodernist artwork, but here they are returned to a humanism which insists that this exuberant life not be forgotten. In the way it remembers, the Quilt is more relaxed, more inclusive, more sensual, more human, more *theatrical* than anything previously imagined in the protocols of mourning. (196)

I want to link up what Fuchs singles out here as the Quilt's inherent "theatricality," its necessary "imaginativeness," with Huyssen's speculative hand-wringing about the "cultural amnesia" that he sees as a worrisome by-product of such memorial projects. At a physiological level, of course, the cognitive condition of forgetting must in some senses always precede, even prompt, the cognitive condition of remembering. That is, an irony that seems to be lost on Huyssen is that we can only remember something that we have first forgotten. And how do you remember that which official or institutional histories of the sort privileged by Huyssen have refused to record, and thereby literally make impossible to forget? I overstate my case, to be sure, but I do so in order to make an important point about the necessarily performative nature of queer rituals of remembrance and mourning. Phelan puts it this way: "[a]s an art form whose primary function is to meditate on the threshold that heralds between-ness, theatre encourages a specific and intense cathetic response in those who define themselves as liminal tricksters, socially disenfranchised, sexually aberrant, addicted, and otherwise queerly alienated from the law of the father. Queers are queer because we recognize that we have survived our own deaths" (16).

When hate crimes against queers go unreported, when the names of gay men and lesbians killed in Nazi death camps are nowhere to be found at the Holocaust Memorial at Yad Vashem,[8] when the archiving of gay life—let alone gay death—has been and continues to be so scant and piecemeal, how does one remember? One remembers by sewing a piece of fabric onto another, by staging kiss-ins and die-ins at public institutions in major urban metropolises, by placing flowers and placards and talismans in a fence in Wyoming (for a Matthew Shepard) or along a forest path in Vancouver (for an Aaron Webster), by writing plays and choreographing dances for lost brothers. In the absence of built monuments, queer acts of remembrance, witnessing, and mourning necessarily become ritualized through performance, just as they perforce get linked to local manifestations of grassroots activism. Indeed, a key element of the organizational success of groups such as ACT UP, AIDS Action Now, Queer Nation, and Outrage! over the past two decades has been their recognition of the co-extensiveness of activism and memorialization, and their ability to adapt the performance of each to a specific situational context. A march and rally in New York, a charity concert in London, a candlelight vigil in Toronto or Vancouver: at some level, with each event, street theatre segues into social protest, just as the mourning of an individual loss helps to clarify the "fundamental dependency and ethical responsibility" of our participation in a "political community of a complex order" (Butler, *Precarious Life* 22).

Thus, in much the same way that Fuchs has examined how the Quilt necessarily sunders "mourning's ancient links to church, family, class and state" and "re-imagines a connection between politics and the sacred" (197), I want now, in the remainder of this essay, to turn to an analysis of the post-AIDS rituals of grieving, remembrance, art, and social activism in two other performative contexts: dance and theatre. In so doing, I want to link up Butler's theorizing of the relationship between mourning and (queer) kinship with a notion of vigilant remembrance that is both situationally contingent and relationally binding—if not always politically transformative. Christopher Gillis, Carl Vogel, Matthew Shepard, Russell Henderson, Aaron McKinney, Aaron Webster: How am I connected to these men? Why is it incumbent upon me to remember them? How, to use Butler's language, does the rehearsal of their deaths, or the deaths they caused, both constitute me and the other in me? And how does it undo me (see *Precarious Life* 22–23)?

Queer Kinship: Gillis and Vogel

Following the 1993 death of her brother, Christopher, who was himself a member of the Paul Taylor Dance Company in New York, Margie Gillis added two new pieces to her staple of solo dances: *Landscape*, a stark meditation on impending death choreographed for her by Christopher from his hospital bed, and *Torn Roots, Broken Branches*, a frenzied outpouring of grief that she herself created. In the first, Gillis enters the stage down right. She wears a simple white shift reminiscent of a hospital gown and is dragging a bare tree branch on the floor behind her. A solitary strip of torn cloth has been tied to one of the branch's outermost limbs, and before the piece is over Gillis will add another. As the haunting sounds of an Edvard Grieg composition rise and fall, Gillis begins her long painful walk across the stage, progressing slowly, in halting and unsure steps. Her movements, normally Duncanesque in their expansiveness, are here tiny and contained and precise. Indeed, Gillis's solidity as a dancer, the generous shape of her arms and legs, makes the frailty of her gestures in this piece even more powerful and poignant; when, in the middle of the stage, she stumbles and falls, for example, we know that something more inevitable and inexorable than mere gravity is weighing her down. Near the end of *Landscape*, Gillis glances back over her shoulder, measuring the distance she has travelled, trying to bridge the gap between where she has come from and where she is going. The psychological and spiritual isolation that Christopher Gillis has attempted to convey with this piece is encapsulated in this one brief moment and the effect is devastating— knowing this, devastated herself, his sister, Margie, picks up the branch and continues on her journey, exiting the stage upper left.

The image of the broken branch is what links Christopher's vision of his own death with Margie's performance of her mourning. Brother and sister's respective choreographic styles, however, could not be more different. In *Torn Roots, Broken Branches*, the dull grey backdrop of *Landscape* is replaced by one that is blood red. The piece begins with Gillis in the middle of the stage, hands covering her face, dressed head to toe in black: black hat, long-sleeved black bodice buttoned to the throat, full-length black skirt—a formal funereal shroud that will serve alternately as a prop and a shield, parts of which Gillis will gradually shed, throughout the next four minutes. To the keening wail of Sinéad O'Connor's "I am Stretched on Your Grave," a contemporary arrangement of a traditional Irish dirge, Gillis performs her own dance of mourning. As the song picks up speed, particularly in the closing fiddle section, so too does Gillis, whirling about in faster and wider circles, shaking her skirts and hair in fierce fury, her pain and anger and guilt registering ever more profoundly, ever more clearly, on her face—in the wild look of her eyes, the tight clench of her jaw. To label the combined effect as cathartic does not nearly go far enough in describing what both Gillis and the audience have been through by the end of the piece. (I speak from experience, having attended a dance recital by Gillis in Vancouver in 1994 at which both *Landscape* and *Torn Roots, Broken Branches* were performed.) Indeed, as with Gillis's iconic predecessor in the dramatization of sisterly grief, Antigone, cathartic release is arguably replaced by something more akin to empathic identification. And this, to allude to my opening epigraph from Derrida, constitutes the "force" of each sister's mourning, as well as the force of her protest—a point to which I shall shortly return.

Let me speak first, though, to Paula Vogel's *The Baltimore Waltz*, which, as she states in her "Playwright's Note," was written as a direct result of her brother Carl's death from AIDS in 1988. The published play-text reprints a hilarious and touching letter from brother to sister regarding the former's wishes for his memorial service, and Vogel's dedication reads "*To the memory of Carl—because I cannot sew*" (101). The play, which premiered at New York's Circle Repertory Company in 1992 (and received a local Vancouver production the following spring courtesy of Pink Ink Theatre), is set in a Baltimore, Maryland hospital. While sitting in a starkly lit waiting room, "Anna" imagines a final journey to Europe with her brother, "Carl," who is slowly dying in another room from AIDS-related pneumonia. It is this dream voyage that comprises most of the play, and in it Anna, and not Carl, is sick, having contracted Acquired Toilet Disease, or ATD, a fatal illness spread through contaminated potty seats that seems to afflict mostly single female elementary school teachers. Having learned from Anna's doctor about the experimental research of one Dr. Todesrocheln, a Viennese urologist, and having packed, upon the instructions of his old university pal, Harry Lime, his childhood stuffed rabbit, Carl whisks his sister off to Europe for what she thinks will be a final fling, but what he hopes will result in a cure.

In a swift progression of 30 short scenes Anna and Carl hop from Paris to Amsterdam to Berlin to Vienna, all the while trailed by a shadowy figure referred to in the text only as the "Third Man," a composite character who has the disconcerting habit of metamorphosizing, depending upon the specific locale, into either a potential lover for Anna or a possible enemy for Carl. In these scenes Vogel skewers every conceivable stereotype and convention, from the linguistic trials of American tourists to the new age wisdom of Elizabeth Kubler-Ross:

> **CARL.** Calm down, sweetie. You're angry. It's only natural to be angry. Elizabeth Kubler-Ross says that—
> **ANNA.** What does she know about what it feels like to die?! Elizabeth Kubler-Ross can sit on my face. (114–15)

The production notes for *The Baltimore Waltz* call for a lavish, wildly varied, and deliberately clichéd musical score. And, as with Gillis's performance, dance becomes the carapace both of a brother's death and a sister's mourning. In the final three scenes, for example, Vogel carefully choreographs the climax and rapid denouement of the play around the hackneyed violin strains of three successive Strauss waltzes. In the first of these scenes, a conscious homage to the climactic confrontation between Orson Welles and Joseph Cotten in the 1949 film version of *The Third Man*, Carl and his friend-turned-nemesis, Harry Lime, "waltz-struggle" for Carl's stuffed rabbit on the Prater ferris wheel in Vienna. Harry eventually gives Carl a final, and presumably fatal, push and "waltzes off with the rabbit" (128). In the next scene, the urine-swilling Dr. Todesrocheln asks a frightened Anna "*WO IST DEIN BRUDER?*" before transforming before her eyes into the Baltimore doctor from the play's opening scene. Anna, suddenly realizing that she is now "awake," rushes to Carl's bedside, only to find him "stiff beneath a white sheet" (130). To the tempo of "The Emperor Waltz" Anna tries to revive her dead brother, but to no avail. In the play's closing sequence, however, we are briefly transported back to the realm of fantasy. As the stage directions read, "Softly, a Strauss waltz begins. Carl ..., perfectly well, waits for Anna. They waltz off as the lights dim" (132). This final tableau, reminiscent as it is of the scene near the end of Tony Kushner's *Angels in America: Millennium Approaches*, where Prior is permitted one last dance with Louis (114), [9] is of course doubly encoded with meaning. The waltz, traditionally a dance of courtship, is here inverted as the *danse macabre*, in which Anna is literally partnered with death in the form of her brother, their rehearsal of a familiar, repetitive, and circular two-step a moving attempt on Anna's—and Vogel's—part to forestall the return to "reality" that Freud, for one, sees as the normative end point of the work of mourning.

In his essay "Mourning and Melancholia," Freud distinguishes between two types of mourning. What he labels so-called "normal" mourning manifests itself initially in individuals as opposition to the abandoning of libidinal attachment to the deceased or lost object, but whose work is eventually completed through first the hyper-cathecting and then the detachment of "memories and expectations ... bound to the [lost] object," resulting in a return to "reality" (244–45). By contrast, the so-called "pathological" condition of mourning, what Freud refers to as "melancholia," arises essentially from a narcissistic prolonging of libidinal attachment, or ego-iden-tification, with the lost object (see 250 and ff.). As Freud pithily summarizes, "In mourning it is the world which has become poor and empty; in melancholia it is the ego itself" (246). [10]

Following the Freudian model, then, Gillis's addition of *Landscape* and *Torn Roots, Broken Branches* to her repertoire, her apparently compulsive repetition (to allude to another of Freud's famous theories) of them on stages across the world, suggests that she is performing "melancholia" rather than "mourning." Even the lyrics of O'Connor's song—"So I'm stretched on your grave and will lie there forever/If your hands were in mine, I'd be sure we'd not sever"—are suggestive of deeper-than-"normal" attachment. So too with Vogel. In her "Playwright's Note," she states that she began writing *The Baltimore Waltz* as a way of exorcising her own personal demons *vis-à-vis* guilt about not accompanying her brother on his last tour of Europe. But while Freud insists that melancholia "is marked by a determinant which is absent in normal mourning" (250), he also never defines what "normal" signifies in this context (nor even what a return to "reality" might look like). Indeed, as Butler has argued, it is melancholia which is in fact constitutive of normative social relations within Western culture, a process which sees heterosexual genders, for example, institutionalize and memorialize themselves precisely through a refusal of mourning, that is, through the renunciation of the loss of homosexual genders as "a possibility of love" (*Bodies That Matter* 235).

Butler's theorization of heterosexual gender identification as a kind of melancholia, in which unresolved same-sex desire is internalized as a prohibition that precedes the incest taboo, has been articulated in different ways across the body of her work, including most representatively *Gender Trouble, Bodies That Matter*, and *Undoing Gender*. [11] However, it is in *Antigone's Claim*, via her reading of Sophocles' play (structurally the concluding part of his *Oedipus* trilogy, but, crucially in terms of chronology of composition, the first part to be written), and its treatment in Western philosophical discourse, that Butler demonstrates most forcefully how gender melan-cholia has helped structure and hierarchize kinship patterns in our society, patterns whose markers of exclusion only fully emerge in death and the performance of mourning. And, in whose normative constitution we also, per force, witness a perverse negation, or non-consummation of the family romance: as Butler puts it, "Antigone, who concludes the oedipal drama, fails to produce heterosexual closure for that drama" (*Antigone's Claim* 76). At the same time, the prohibition against incest enacted in Sophocles' play, according to Butler, is really something of a red herring. What is more important is how that prohibition has symbolically come to be memorialized as standing in for other socially taboo, morally denigrated, and juridically invalid relationships, modes of gender expression, sexuality, and ways of being and loving in this world, ways that continue to be placed outside the bounds of the normalized nuclear family and the human, and thus subject to social scrutiny, regulation and policing by the state:

> When the incest taboo works in this sense to foreclose a love that is not incestuous, what is produced is a shadowy realm of love, a love that persists in spite of its foreclosure in an ontologically suspended mode…. Do we say that families that do not approximate the norm but mirror the norm in some apparently derivative way are poor copies, or do we accept that the ideality of the norm is undone precisely through the complexity of its instantiation? For those relations that are denied legitimacy, or that demand new terms of legitimation, are neither dead nor alive, figuring the nonhuman at the border of the human. And it is not simply that these are relations that cannot be honored, cannot be openly acknowledged, and cannot therefore be publicly grieved, but that these relations involve persons who are also restricted in the very act of grieving, who are denied the power to confer legitimacy on loss. (*Antigone's Claim* 78–79; emphasis in original)

To put this in more familiar contemporary terms, what if today Antigone were attempting to mourn the death of her common-law husband, a former stepdaughter from a second marriage that had ended but with whom she was still close, a gay male friend she cared for throughout a prolonged illness, her lesbian lover? In this respect, the force of Antigone's protest, like Gillis's and Vogel's, comes through the staging of their *private* sisterly grief in very *public* acts of ritualized remembrance, acting out, and up, performing the personal as political as a direct intervention against a state-sponsored discourse about who can and cannot be mourned, about what, to use Butler's phrasing, remains unspeakable, and unspeakably violent, about any encounter with difference (see *Precarious Life* 48–49). As Phelan remarks, Antigone and—lest we forget—Ismene, both equally caught, in their different ways of mourning, between life and death, point "to a different form of theatre sisters might one day invent. Such a theatre would be more precise than Sophocles's or Lacan's about the distinction between desire and love" (16).[12]

Moreover, as Douglas Crimp has pointed out, "for Freud, [mourning] is a solitary undertaking" (236); at no time does he conceive of it as a shared activity. And it is on this account that I consider the works by Gillis and Vogel to challenge fundamentally the standard Freudian model of mourning. This is also where the concept of performance becomes crucial. For performance, it seems to me, whether we are using the term in a "theatrical" or "theoretical" (i.e. Austinian-Derridean-Butlerian-

Sedgwickian speech act) sense, always requires an audience. Gillis's and Vogel's *public* performance of their bereavement, like Fuchs's description of the public displaying of the Quilt, their invitation to audiences to join the dance, as it were, is not a willful surrendering to the singular oppression of grief; rather, it is an acknowledgment, to return to Butler, that in the spectacle of the self's "undoing" that necessarily attends the process of mourning, also lies the possibility of remaking or refashioning new models of social collectivity, new networks of community action, and new patterns of intersubjective response. [13]

And yet, as Crimp has also pointed out, while collective public mourning rituals have their own affective and even political force, "they nevertheless often seem, from an activist perspective, indulgent, sentimental, defeatist—a perspective only reinforced ... by media constructions of [both mourners and mourned] as hapless victims" (234). Crimp casts aside Freud's interdiction that "any interference with [mourning is] useless or even harmful" (Freud 244), and argues instead for an active—and activist—channelling of grief and loss into the forceful mobilizing of the tenuous collective social body that AIDS has perforce made not just of the queer community, but of us all:

> We can then partially revise our sense ... of the incompatibility between mourning and activism and say that, for many gay men dealing with AIDS deaths, militancy might arise from conscious conflicts *within* mourning itself, the consequence, on the one hand, of "inadvisable and even harmful interference" with grief and, on the other, of the impossibility of deciding whether the mourner will share the fate of the mourned. (237)

As I have already intimated, my only revision to Crimp's comments here would be that I think it's important, in true Greek fashion, to extend the "shared fate" of mourning (and the militancy it might inspire) in this context beyond "gay men dealing with AIDS deaths." What the work of Gillis and Vogel teaches is that every remembering self is inextricably connected to the production and circulation of larger patterns of cultural memory; no act of remembrance can occur without a simultaneous act of empathic identification (meaning, in this context, projecting one's consciousness into the subjective experience of another in order to attempt to comprehend that experience). In *Torn Roots, Broken Branches* and *The Baltimore Waltz*, a sister uses the language of words and the language of the body to reconfigure time and space, imagining herself into the experience of her brother's death, which must also in some senses be her own—and, just as importantly, our own. In the process, the performance of mourning transforms into a performance of protest. In the words of Jill Dolan, Gillis and Vogel are using "the emotion theater inspires to move people to political action, to desire reconfigured social relations, to want to interact intimately with a local and a global community" (90). This harnessing of emotion to action, or even activism as Dolan notes in the subtitle to her book, is what's key. In this sense, it is important to distinguish empathy from what Kushner has identified as the bugbear of catharsis, which, in a neat little capitalist equation, involves an initial expenditure of emotion for a guaranteed return of transcendence ("Notes" 22). By contrast, empathy implies some sense of a relationality on the part of producer and consumer (or actor and spectator), an acknowledgment that both are in the event, that the liveness of theatre creates a space in which we can collectively "engage with the social in physically, materially embodied circumstances" (Dolan 90).

SILENCE = DEATH. The ACT UP activist slogan, like the performances of Gillis's dance movements and Vogel's play, gives voice to our rage and anger and profound sense of loss; but its rhetorical power, again like the work of Gillis and Vogel, is ultimately choric rather than ventriloquized, encouraging us, inducing us, moving us, to lend our voices to the clarion call for action. We are all our brothers' keepers; and we could all do with sisters as keenly vigilant in reminding us of this point as Gillis and Vogel.

Melancholic Spectatorship: McNally and Kaufman

Terrence McNally's *Corpus Christi* recasts the Biblical passion play as a coming-of-age story, set in the small Texas town of the playwright's birth, with the role of Jesus as an initially socially leprous and later progressively more charismatic gay youth named Joshua, who spreads the gospel of love with his "chosen family" of twelve gay brothers, including his sometime lover Judas. Previewing at the Manhattan Theatre Club in late September 1998, the play, by virtue of its subject matter and not least because of the bomb threats, hate mail and picketing that greeted its premiere, became a proleptic and *de facto* memorialization of and performative mourning for Matthew Shepard when the latter's beaten body was found tied to a fence outside Laramie, Wyoming six days before the play's official opening on October 13. Lest we not see the connection, the playwright himself makes it explicit for us in the preface to the published version of the play: "Beaten senseless and tied to a split-rail fence in near-zero weather, arms akimbo in a grotesque crucifixion, [Matthew Shepard] died as agonizing a death as another young man who had been tortured and nailed to a wooden cross at a desolate spot outside Jerusalem known as Golgotha some 1,998 years earlier. They died, as they lived, as brothers" (vi).

The play's central theatrical conceit is that it makes explicit the performative scaffolding of such narrative and historical equations by having the actors in the company "assume" their characters' roles on stage in front of the audience. With house lights still up, and while members of the audience are still finding their way to their seats, thirteen male actors, clad identically in white shirts and khaki pants (blue jeans in the production I saw), slowly make their way to the stage as if for a casual rehearsal rather than an actual performance, pausing to chat with one another, greet members of the audience, check the props table, and limber up with various physical and vocal exercises. At a pre-arranged signal, one of the actors steps forward and speaks directly to the audience, announcing that the story he and his cast mates are about to tell is an "old and familiar one," one we've "all heard over and over, again and again," but that "bears repeating": "The playwright asks your indulgence, as do we, the actors. There are no tricks up our sleeves. No malice in our hearts. We're glad you're here" (1). We then watch as this same actor, who will shortly assume the role of John the Baptist, calls forth each of his fellow actors in turn, blessing them first by their real names before rebaptizing them by the name of one of Joshua/Jesus' twelve disciples.

On a raked proscenium stage, such as the one at the Manhattan Theatre Club, the effect of this opening would, I imagine, be disconcerting enough. In the intimate confines of Festival House, on Vancouver's Granville Island, where I saw Hoarse Raven Theatre's production of the play in May 2002, the whole thing felt painfully voyeuristic: a spare studio space devoid of a raised stage, fixed seating, or anything even remotely resembling wings, means that actors and audience are quite literally on top of one another and—as McNally has staged things—wont to bump into each other in queuing to get into the room. Indeed, it left me, at certain moments, longing for the return of theatre's invisible fourth wall. This is, of course, precisely the point. In watching this play, as intensely moving and romantic and erotic as so many parts of it are, we are meant to feel uncomfortable, to question whether or not the performance has started, whether it has ended, who precisely is part of the action, whether the actors are playing a version of themselves or their characters or both, and how precisely we in the audience are meant to respond to such alienated and alienating transformations.

Something similar takes place in Moisés Kaufman and Tectonic Theater Project's (TTP) play, *The Laramie Project*. Famous for its documentary-style approach to historical moments in queer history, the company had previously scored an unexpected international hit with *Gross Indecency: The Three Trials of Oscar Wilde*. For *The Laramie Project*, which opened at the Denver Centre Theatre Company in February 2000, members of TTP travelled to the Wyoming town, then recently and unwantedly memorialized via the international media as the redneck locus of Matthew Shepard's brutal murder, in order to conduct interviews with its traumatized residents. A narrator who speaks directly to the audience (as, indeed, do all the "characters" in the play) opens by summarizing the process of its creation:

> On November 14, 1999, the members of Tectonic Theater Project traveled to Laramie, Wyoming, and conducted interviews with the people of the town. During the next year, we would return to Laramie several times and conduct over two hundred interviews. The play you are about to see is edited from those interviews, as well as from journal entries by members of the company and other found texts. Company member Greg Pierotti. (5)

The last line of this passage highlights an important feature of *The Laramie Project*'s docudrama—or, more properly, dramatized documentary—narrative aesthetic. That is, the TTP actors, in addition to impersonating on stage the various real-life residents of Laramie whom they interviewed, turning each into a "character" (in both the conventional dramatic sense of playing a part and the broader sense of conveying an individual's distinctive traits or eccentricities through manner of speech, mannerisms, style of dress, etc.), must also deal with the fact that the play likewise turns each of them into a character. This becomes all the more apparent if one attends a production of the play that is being performed by any company or cast other than the original TTP ones. Such was the case when I caught a performance of Studio 58's production of the play in October 2002. A respected actor training program affiliated with Vancouver's Langara College, Studio 58 presented audiences who attended its brilliant staging of *The Laramie Project* with the spectacle of student-actors playing professional actors playing real people, some of whom, as has been the case with many productions of the play across North America since its premiere, could potentially have been in the audience watching their surrogate-selves on stage on any given night.

The use of the narrator throughout the play to introduce both the speech of the actor-characters and the resident-characters is also integral in orienting—or disorienting—the audience's relationships with the action being portrayed on stage. It is akin to Brechtian quotation, in which lines are spoken not as if they were being spontaneously improvised but rather almost in the manner of reading a report. This distancing effect means that we, in the audience, are compelled not to judge the person doing the speaking but rather the words he/she speaks, and the larger social attitudes these words betray. In terms of the work of memorialization and the performance of mourning operating in *The Laramie Project*, such a structural device again functions in two ways—on the one hand, disabusing potentially smug audience members of many of the prejudices they may have held towards the residents prior to the performance, and, on the other, dramatizing the important educational process that the actors themselves must go through in confronting their own preconceptions about the individuals they were going to interview or portray.

In short, McNally and Kaufman, following from Brecht's famous theorization of the Alienation-effect's application to the technique of acting, are asking each actor who speaks their words to "invest what he [sic] has to show with a definite gest of showing," whereby gest refers to "the mimetic and gestural expression of the social relationships between people of a given period" (136, 139). In so doing, these two queer playwrights are, like Brecht, urging both actors and audiences to adopt "socially critical" attitudes: "In his exposition of the incidents and in his characterization of the person [the actor] tries to bring out those features which come within society's sphere. In this way his performance becomes a discussion (about social conditions) with the audience he is addressing. He prompts the spectator to justify or abolish these conditions according to what class [or gender or sexuality or race or nationality] he belongs to" (Brecht 139). "Look what they did to Him. Look what they did to Him," the actor playing James the Less addresses the audience at the end of *Corpus Christi*, coming "out of character" and gesturing to the naked body of Joshua crucified on a cross. The actor's Brechtian transposition of his speech into the third person and the past tense here (see Brecht 138) lets neither the actor playing Joshua nor us in the audience off the hook, as it were. Looking in this context becomes precarious—reinforced by the fact that, in the production I saw, all of the other actors exited the studio shortly after this point as the house lights once again came up, leaving the audience to gaze upon the twisted body of the actor playing Joshua for what seemed to be an excruciatingly long time, wondering this time if the "performance" was over and, if so, whether or not we should clap or continue to sit in stunned silence. Similarly, in the Epilogue to *The Laramie Project*, the actor playing TTP company member Greg Pierotti playing gay Laramie resident Jonas Slonaker frames the question "What's come out of this?" (and presumably this applies in equal measure to the play we are currently watching/reading and to the murder of Shepard memorialized by it) in terms of a juxtaposition between first and third person, past and present:

> Change is not an easy thing, and I don't think people were up to it here. They got what they wanted. Those two boys got what they deserve, and we look good now. Justice has been served. The OK Corral .... The town's cleaned up, and we don't need to talk about it anymore.
>
> You know, it's been a year since Matthew Shepard died, and they haven't passed shit in Wyoming .... at a state level, any town, nobody anywhere, has passed any kind of laws, antidiscrimination laws or hate crime legislation, nobody has passed anything anywhere. (99; second ellipsis in original)

Both speeches force us to interrogate in the present how we have memorialized similar scenes of trauma—in this case, most pertinently, but by no means only, anti-gay and lesbian violence—and our respective identifications or disidentifications with both the "Him" and the "they"—not to mention the "we" and the "you"—of such scenes.

Here I want to link up my all-too cursory redaction of the structural conventions of these two plays to the theoretical ruminations on mourning undertaken in connection with Gillis and Vogel. I suggest that part of the social discussion we in the audience are being asked to engage in by the performers has to do with critically unpacking the complex codes of masculinity operating within the heartland of rural America, and, more specifically, analyzing with whom, in the ritualized violence that all too frequently accompanies the articulation of those codes, we empathize when we mourn. Here, too, I want to bring in the work of JoAnn Wypijewski, who in a 1999 *Harper's* article entitled "A Boy's Life" has written what I believe to be the most critically astute analysis of Matthew Shepard's murder, wading through "the quasi-religious characterizations of Matthew's passion, death and resurrection as patron saint of hate-crime legislation" to zero in on the "everyday life of hate and hurt and heterosexual culture" that constituted the "psychic terrain" of Aaron McKinney and Russell Henderson, Shepard's murderers (62). Following from Wypijewski, then, it seems to me that the crucial question posed by *Corpus Christi* and *The Laramie Project* (albeit retrospectively in the case of McNally's play), is why is it that, in the ritual re-membering of this hate-crime (in the media and elsewhere), Shepard, as passive sufferer, automatically becomes representative of *all* homosexual people, whereas McKinney and Henderson, as violent aggressors, are always discussed in terms of their *individual* predispositions towards delinquency? Why, in other words, aren't McKinney and Henderson seen, why aren't they remembered, as representative of the attitudes of a larger patriarchal-heterosexist culture, a "socially instituted melancholia" that, to adapt Butler, prescribes "how the condemnations under which one lives [e.g. to be gay is to be less than human] turn into repudiations that one performs [e.g. it is alright to kill what is not human]" (*Antigone's Claim* 80)? [14] A similar sentiment is expressed toward the end of *The Laramie Project* by Father Roger Schmit, the Catholic priest whose own attitudes queer TTP writers and cast members Leigh Fondakowski and Greg Pierotti were wont to prejudge upon their initial meeting; Schmit notes:

> I think right now our most important teachers must be Russell Henderson and Aaron McKinney. They have to be our teachers. How did you learn? What did we as a society do to teach you that? See, I don't know if many people will let them be their teachers. I think it would be wonderful if the judge said: "In addition to your sentence, you must tell your story, you must tell your story." (89)

Or, as the "Actor Playing Judas" says about his own character at the close of *Corpus Christi*, "Sometimes I mourn for Judas, too" (80).

Other Brothers

The Vancouver premieres of *Corpus Christi* and *The Laramie Project* in 2002 were all the more compelling because for many of us in the audience the brutal murder of Aaron Webster was still so fresh in our minds. At 2:30 am on Saturday, 17 November 2001, the naked body of 41 year-old Webster was found battered and bleeding by his friend Tim Chisholm in a parking lot near Second Beach in Stanley Park. The victim of a vicious gay bashing, he died a few minutes later in Chisholm's arms as ambulance paramedics tried to save him. The next day, at an impromptu rally at the corner of Denman and Davie Streets, members of the gay community listened as police and politicians labelled the death a hate crime and vowed to act swiftly to apprehend the perpetrators (see Zacharias). In February 2003, a nineteen-year-old male suspect was finally arrested in connection with the crime. Seventeen at the time of the attack, he could not be identified, and pleaded guilty to manslaughter in juvenile court in July. On 18 December 2003 he was sentenced to two years in custody and one year house arrest, the maximum penalty Judge Valmond Romilly could issue; Romilly explicitly labelled Webster's murder a hate crime and berated Crown prosecutors for not trying the case within this context. Another juvenile who also pleaded guilty to manslaughter was likewise sentenced to a maximum of three years in custody on 21 April 2004 (see "Second youth"). Ryan Cran and Danny Rao, two adults also charged in connection with the case, were tried together in December 2004, with BC Supreme Court Justice Mary Humphries sentencing Cran to six years in jail for manslaughter and acquitting Rao due to lack of credible evidence. The verdicts, together with Humphries repudiation of Romilly's previous characterization of Webster's murder as a hate crime, outraged the queer community and prompted renewed protests (see Bellett).

As part of the community programming around Studio 58's production of *The Laramie Project*, Langara College organized a one-day public forum on gay bashing and hate crimes legislation, an issue that has been much in the air in local queer circles since Webster's murder, and especially since Judge Romilly's surprisingly forceful comments. To paraphrase Wypijewski once again, to the extent that "hate-crime laws symbolize a society's values" (74), they can be viewed as a form of cultural memory work, a process of belatedly representing in juridical discourse a hitherto actively forgotten fissure in the social fabric of a community (note, in this regard, how relatively recently anti-gay violence was included under the purview of hate crime legislation in Canada, and how most American states have no legal mechanism to recognize such violence as even constituting a hate crime). This notion of belatedness points, in turn, to the fact that what hate crime legislation actually memorializes is the crime itself, not the culture of hate and violence that produced the crime in the first place. To this end, Wypijewski notes, with characteristic bluntness, that such legislation "means nothing for life and, because its only practical function is to stiffen penalties, everything for death"; it also means, in the specific context of gay-related hate crimes, where "it's always the sexuality of the victim that's front and center, not the sexuality of the criminal or the undifferentiated violence he took to extremity," that "straight people are off the hook" (74, 75). Similarly, as Judith Butler argues in *Excitable Speech*, proponents of hate speech regulation, in focussing on the injury such speech causes to the abjectly governed and agentless individual addressee (be it a woman, a queer, or a racial minority), tend to ignore the ways in which their arguments relocate notions of "sovereignty" and "universality" within a speaker, who not only says what he means, but whose utterances are immediately memorialized by others as simultaneously demarcating and overstepping the borders of what is acceptable. Even more pertinently, for Butler, proponents of hate speech laws fail to recognize how the iterability of such speech is to a large measure coextensive with and institutionalized within much official "state speech" (102).

Towards the end of *Antigone's Claim*, the text that I have been using as my main critical touchstone throughout this paper, and which comes as close as any recent treatise I can think of in articulating a socially relevant theory of queer remembrance and mourning, Butler notes that what remains "unspoken" in Antigone's grief for her brother Polyneices is her shared grief for her "other brother[s]," Eteocles and, not least, Oedipus, both arguably responsible not only for the "crime" of Polyneices' death, but also for the "crime" of Antigone's defiant public mourning of that death. As Butler puts it, "The 'brother' is no singular place for her, though it may be that all her brothers (Oedipus, Polyneices, Eteocles) are condensed at the exposed body of Polyneices, an exposure she seeks to cover, a nakedness she would rather not see or have seen" (79). Likewise, it seems to me that in our vigils for the Aaron Websters and the Matthew Shepards of this world, for the Christopher Gillises and the Carl Vogels, for all our "named and unnamed" queer brothers and sisters lost prematurely to violent death or disease, or simply the violence of heteronormative historiography, we must be as, if not more, vigilant in our remembrance of the un- or underexposed melancholic keepers of that history, our "other" brothers. For, if part of what is enacted in queer rituals of remembrance and queer performances of mourning is a speaking of the unspeakable, then it is incumbent upon those of us who undertake such rituals to utter the silence, to outer the active forgetting, to counter the willful amnesia at the heart of heterosexual melancholia: that, to adapt Wypijewski one last time, Aaron Webster and Matthew Shepard, and Brandon Teena and Sakia Gunn, [15] not to mention the murdered women from the École Polytechnique in Montréal and from the Downtown Eastside in Vancouver, died not because they were queer or feminist or prostitutes, but because their killers were all straight men. And it is this disavowal of brotherly love (of the self, of the same, of the other) at the heart of masculine identity formation that, above all, our culture must mourn.

(2004)

Notes

[1]   I borrow this phrase from Sharon Rosenberg, who coined it in correspondence with me regarding this paper's inclusion in a special issue of the journal *torquere* (Vol. 6, 2004) that she guest-edited. I am extremely grateful to Sharon for the guidance and engaged colloquy she has provided on my work, and on the work of mourning more generally.

[2]   *The Laramie Project* (2002). Directed by Moisés Kaufman. Written by Kaufman and members of the Tectonic Theater Project. Produced by Declan Baldwin. New York: HBO Home Video, 96 min.

[3]   A June 2006 decision by the Vancouver Parks Board to use money donated by the federal government to upgrade the playground at Ceperley Park in memory of victims of the Air India bombing has revived debate around the rejection of the area as a site for an AIDS memorial ten years earlier, with some in Vancouver's queer community accusing the Parks Board of a double standard; see Kittelberg.

[4]   In their article "'How Might a Women's Monument Be Different?,'" Christine Bold, Ric Knowles, and Belinda Leach discuss in more detail the public debates that greeted both Alber's *Marker of Change* and Larson's efforts to remember the missing women from Vancouver's DES, situating those debates within the context of a larger project about feminist memorialization in Canada. Despite substantial evidence and ongoing pressure from the local community and relatives, Vancouver police refused throughout the 1980s and most of the 1990s to acknowledge a connection between the missing women from the DES, or to entertain the possibility that a serial murderer might be preying upon them. It was only in 2001 that the police, in conjunction with the RCMP, set up a special Missing Women Task Force; a year later, in February 2002, Robert "Willie" Pickton, a 53-year-old pig farmer from Port Coquitlam, was finally arrested in connection with the case. A terrible irony is that Pickton had been in police custody back in 1997 on charges of stabbing

a local prostitute; however, the charges were stayed, and Pickton was released (see Joyce; "Vancouver's legacy").

⁵ See, for example, Rebecca Belmore's mixed media installations "Vigil" and "The Named and the Unnamed," which were shown in her solo show *The Named and the Unnamed* at the Morris and Helen Belkin Art Gallery in Vancouver from October–December 2002, before traveling to the Art Gallery of Ontario; see, as well, Kati Campbell's textile installation "67 Shawls," which was shown as part of a group show called *Talking Textile* (which also featured work by Belmore) at the Richmond Art Gallery from December 2003–January 2004.

⁶ The Quilt, which now comprises some 45,000 panels, weighs more than 54 tons, and covers approximately 1,270,350 square feet (or roughly the equivalent of 47 football fields if laid end to end), was last displayed in its entirety in October 1996. While portions of the Quilt continue to tour the U.S. and the world, for obvious logistical reasons there are no immediate plans to assemble and display the whole thing again; see the AIDS Memorial Quilt website at www.aidsquilt.org.

⁷ On this point, see especially the essays collected in Roger Simon, Sharon Rosenberg, and Claudia Eppert, ed., *Between Hope and Despair: Pedagogy and the Remembrance of Historical Trauma.*

⁸ This is not meant to deny the efforts of other memorializations of the Holocaust, both from within and without the queer community, to record this history of persecution. See, in particular, the permanent special exhibit at the United States Holocaust Memorial Museum in Washington, D.C. on the "Nazi Persecution of Homosexuals, 1933–1945"; and Rob Epstein and Jeffrey Friedman's documentary film "Paragraph" 175.

⁹ A further connection between the two plays is that actor/director Joe Mantello originated the roles of Louis and Carl in the initial New York productions of *Angels in America* and *The Baltimore Waltz*. Mantello also directed the New York premiere of Terrence McNally's *Corpus Christi*, discussed below.

¹⁰ To be sure, as Butler notes, Freud was not always consistent in his theorizing of the differences between mourning and melancholia. See Butler, *Precarious Life*, 20–21; and Freud, "The Ego and the Id."

¹¹ See Butler, *Gender Trouble*, 63ff; *Bodies That Matter*, 235–36 and ff; and *Undoing Gender*, 152–60. See, as well, the following comments by Gayle Rubin in "The Traffic in Women": "... the incest taboo presupposes a prior, less articulate taboo on homosexuality. A prohibition against some heterosexual unions assumes a taboo against *non*heterosexual unions. Gender is not only an identification with one sex; it also entails that sexual desire be directed toward the other sex. The sexual division of labour is implicated in both aspects of gender—male and female it creates them, and it creates them heterosexual" (180). And this from Monique Wittig: "The straight mind continues to affirm that incest, and not homosexuality, represents its

major interdiction. Thus, when thought by the straight mind, homosexuality is nothing but heterosexuality" (*The Straight Mind* 28).

[12] In their remarks on Sophocles's play, both Phelan and Butler are drawing on and revising Lacan's famous reading of *Antigone* in his *Seminar VII*. For Lacan, Antigone bridges not only the divide between life and death, but also between the imaginary and the symbolic, her defiance of Creon and the law of the father in death a necessary consequence of her tainted birth.

[13] In this regard, it is important to remember that the dance and theatre communities have been at the forefront of mobilizing in the fight against AIDS: think of the DIFFA Dance and Design Project or Equity Cares/Broadway Fights AIDS in New York; think of Dancers for Life or Theatre Cares Week here in Canada. Likewise, I think that it is also important to note, especially within the context of the argument set forth at the outset to this paper, that I attended and was profoundly moved by local performances of the above works by Vogel and Gillis (in 1993 and 1994, respectively) precisely at the height of my volunteer involvement with the AIDS community in Vancouver. See, as well, in this regard Marita Sturken's *Tangled Memories: The Vietnam War, the AIDS Epidemic, and the Politics of Remembering*, which likewise discusses Freud's dismissal of "the role of collective mourning" (201) within the context of the "conversations with the dead" enacted through the AIDS Quilt.

[14] That our society largely rejects this kind of memorialization is indicated by the negative reaction, noted above, to the inscription "for all women who have been murdered by men" on Beth Alber's *Marker of Change* monument.

[15] Brandon Teena (aka Teena Brandon), a 21-year-old pre-operative transgendered man from Lincoln, Nebraska, was, along with Lisa Lambert and Philip Devine, murdered on New Year's Eve 1993, by former friends Thomas Nissen and John Lotter when it was discovered "he"—at least in the eyes of his homo- and trans-phobic killers—was in fact a "she." Kimberly Pierce's award-winning narrative film "Boys Don't Cry", starring Hilary Swank, chronicles the story, as does Gréta Olafsdôttir and Susan Muska's documentary "The Brandon Teena Story". Sakia Gunn, a 15-year-old New Jersey lesbian returning from a night of partying in New York City with her girlfriend, was stabbed to death at a bus stop adjacent Newark's busiest intersection by 29-year-old Richard McCullogh in May 2003 after she rebuffed his sexual advances (see Smothers).

Works Cited

The AIDS Memorial Quilt. www.aidsquilt.org.

Bellett, Gerry. "Attacker gets six years for role in fatal beating." *Vancouver Sun* 9 February 2005: B1, B6.

Belmore, Rebecca. *The Named and the Unnamed.* Morris and Helen Belkin Art Gallery, Vancouver. 4 October–1 December 2002.

Bold, Christine, Ric Knowles, and Belinda Leach. "'How Might a Feminist Monument Be Different?'" *Essays on Canadian Writing* 80 (2003): 17–35.

"Boys Don't Cry". Dir. Kimberly Pierce. Fox Searchlight, 1999.

"The Brandon Teena Story". Dir. Gréta Olafsdôttir and Susan Muska. New Video Group, 1998.

Brecht, Bertolt. "Short Description of a New Technique of Acting which Produces an Alienation Effect." *Brecht on Theatre: The Development of an Aesthetic.* Ed. and trans. John Willet. London: Methuen, 1964. 136–47.

Butler, Judith. *Antigone's Claim: Kinship Between Life and Death.* New York: Columbia UP, 2001.

———. *Bodies That Matter: On the Discursive Limits of "Sex."* New York: Routledge, 1993.

———. *Excitable Speech: A Politics of the Performative.* New York: Routledge, 1997.

———. *Gender Trouble: Feminism and the Subversion of Identity.* New York: Routledge, 1990.

———. *Precarious Life: The Powers of Mourning and Violence.* New York: Verso, 2004.

———. *Undoing Gender.* New York: Routledge, 2004.

Campbell, Kati. "67 Shawls." *Thinking Textile.* Richmond Art Gallery, Richmond. 5 December 2003–15 January 2004.

Cavell, Richard. "Histories of Forgetting: Canadian Representations of War and the Politics of Cultural Memory." *Mémoire de guerre et construction de la paix: Mentalités et choix politiques: Belgique - Europe - Canada.* Ed. Serge Jaumain and Éric Remacle. Bruxelles: Peter Lang, 2006. 67–80.

Crimp, Douglas. "Mourning and Militancy." *Out There: Marginalization and Contemporary Cultures.* Ed. Russell Ferguson et al. Cambridge, MA: MIT Press, 1990. 233–45.

Derrida, Jacques. "By Force of Mourning." Trans. Pascale-Anne Brault and Michael Naas. *Critical Inquiry* 22.2 (1996): 171–92.

Dolan, Jill. *Geographies of Learning: Theory and Practice, Activism and Performance.* Middletown, CN: Wesleyan UP, 2001.

Duncan, Ann. "Politics threaten massacre tribute." *Montreal Gazette* 10 September 1994: I5.

Fong, Petti. "Veterans demand tenters end Victory Square protest." *Vancouver Sun* 17 July 2003: B3.

Fraser, Keith. "AIDS wall's site at issue." *Vancouver Province* 1 December 1997: A2.

Freud, Sigmund. "The Ego and the Id." *The Standard Edition of the Complete Psychological Works of Sigmund Freud.* Vol. 19. Trans and ed. James Strachey. London: Hogarth, 1961. 12–66.

———. "Mourning and Melancholia." *The Standard Edition,* vol. 14, 1957. 243–58.

Fuchs, Elinor. *The Death of Character: Perspectives on Theater after Modernism.* Bloomington: Indiana UP, 1996.

Gillis, Margie, perf. *Landscape.* Chor. Christopher Gillis. Vancouver Playhouse, Vancouver. 17 March 1994

———, perf. *Torn Roots, Broken Branches.* Chor. Margie Gillis. Vancouver Playhouse, Vancouver. 17 March 1994.

Hirsch, Marianne. *Family Frames: Photography, Narrative and Postmemory.* Cambridge, MA: Harvard UP, 1997.

Huyssen, Andreas. *Present Pasts: Urban Palimpsests and the Politics of Memory.* Stanford: Stanford UP, 2003.

———. *Twilight Memories: Marking Time in a Culture of Amnesia.* New York: Routledge, 1995.

Joyce, Greg. "Pickton hearing adjourned until June 30." *Vancouver Sun* 24 April 2003: B4.

Kelley, Caffyn. "Creating Memory, Contesting History." *Matriart* 5 (1995): 6–11.

Kaufman, Moisés, and members of Tectonic Theater Project. *The Laramie Project.* New York: Vintage, 2001.

Kittelberg, Lori. "Air India tribute proposed for Ceperley Park." *Xtra! West* 6 July 2006: 7, 9.

Kushner, Tony. *Angels in America, Part One: Millennium Approaches.* New York: Theatre Communications Group, 1993.

———. "Notes about Political Theater." *Kenyon Review* 19 (1997): 19–34.

Lacan, Jacques. *The Seminar of Jacques Lacan, Book VII: The Ethics of Psychoanalysis, 1959–60.* Ed. Jacques-Alain Miller. Trans. Dennis Porter. New York: Norton, 1992.

"The Laramie Project". Dir. Moisés Kaufman. HBO Films, 2002.

Lautens, Trevor. "Monument against too many." *Vancouver Sun* 24 June 1993: A13.

McNally, Terrence. *Corpus Christi: A Play.* New York: Grove, 1998.

"Nazi Persecution of Homosexuals, 1933-1945." Special exhibit. United States Holocaust Memorial Museum. Washington, D.C. www.ushmm.org/museum/exhibit/online/hsx/.

Nora, Pierre, ed. *Les Lieux de mémoire*. Paris: Gallimard, 1997. 3 vols.

O'Connor, Sinéad. "I am Stretched On Your Grave." By Phillip King and F. O'Connor. Arranged by Sinéad O'Connor et al. *"I Do Not Want What I Haven't Got"*. Chrysalis, 1990.

"Paragraph 175". Dir. Rob Epstein and Jeffrey Friedman. New Yorker Films, 1999.

Phelan, Peggy. *Mourning Sex: Performing Public Memories*. New York: Routledge, 1997.

Rubin, Gayle. "The Traffic in Women: 'The Political Economy' of Sex." *Toward an Anthropology of Women*. Ed. Rayna R. Reiter. New York: Monthly Review Press, 1975. 157–210.

Santayana, George. "To W.P." *Sonnets and Other Verses*. New York: Stone and Kimball, 1896. 60–63.

"Second youth connected to Webster beating sentenced to three years." *Vancouver Sun* 22 April 2004: B2.

Simon, Roger I., Sharon Rosenberg, and Claudia Eppert, ed. *Between Hope and Despair: Pedagogy and the Remembrance of Historical Trauma*. Lanham, MD: Rowman and Littlefield, 2000.

Smothers, Ronald. "Man arrested in the killing of a teenager in Newark." *New York Times* 15 May 2003: B4.

Sturken, Marita. *Tangled Memories: The Vietnam War, the AIDS Epidemic, and the Politics of Remembering*. Berkeley: U of California P, 1997.

Vancouver AIDS Memorial: A British Columbia Landmark of Hope and Courage. www.aidsmemorial.ca.

"Vancouver's legacy of horror, shame." *Toronto Star* 13 January 2003: A6

Vogel, Paula. *The Baltimore Waltz*. In *Women Playwrights: The Best Plays of 1992*. Ed. Robyn Goodman and Marisa Smith. Newbury, VT: Smith and Kraus, 1993. 99–132.

Wittig, Monique. *The Straight Mind and Other Essays*. Boston: Beacon, 1992.

Wypijewski, JoAnn. "A Boy's Life." *Harper's Magazine* September 1999: 61–74.

Zacharias, Yvonne. "Gays demand action in wake of brutal killing." *Victoria Times-Colonist* 19 November 2001: A12.

Strange Sisters and Boy Kings: Post-Queer Tranz-gendered Bodies in Performance

by J. Bobby Noble

for O.H.D

In and around July of 2004, women's studies in Canadian universities took an interesting turn. That date marks my faculty appointment into the Women's Studies department at the University of Victoria. My presence at the front of women's studies classrooms is utterly confounding to students, whether or not I am out to them as a female to male transsexual man. In fact, outing myself as a tranz man only aggravates their confusion. My body, and all of the institutional and departmental authority it represents in that moment, fails to cohere with the content of our department name. As such, I often have the estranging effect of rendering our program productively incoherent, allowing me an opportunity to mobilize the pedagogical effects of surprise (Johnson) to make gender studies simultaneously defamiliarized and new. While it might be tempting to read this incoherence as solely autobiographical, I want to suggest instead that it marks the beginning of not only a potential transformation in gender studies but also new ways of conceptualizing resistance. As I've indicated elsewhere (see Noble 2005), I am one of perhaps two female to male transsexuals working in Canadian universities, the only working in a women's studies department. While I do have a long history as an active lesbian feminist worker—one that I do not renounce despite repeated pressures from many quarters—that history was part of what made me attractive to a women's studies department. That said, my commitment to women's and gender studies is not without controversy and constant confusion, especially to my non-feminist colleagues who are not aware of my tranz identity. But it is such confusions that render me quite potent in my political inter-ventions. I am as committed for instance to a tranz-politic as I am to ferreting out the misogyny in and racism of both queer and tranz politics and studies of a variety of shapes and sizes.

At its most evocative, "tranz" as I live it is descriptive and intersectional, marking politics lived across, against, or despite always already engendered, sexed, national, and racialized bodies. Often collapsed into "trans-gender," that umbrella term which references almost all of the above practices from one degree to another, the term "transsexual" for instance is thought to mark the use of medical technologies to correct the disjunction between the body and a self which seems at odds with that body. But at its most provocative, "tranz" and the space it references for me refuses the medical and psychological categorical imperatives or coherence through which it has always been forced to confess. But what is also at stake is a politics of self-representation within and often opposed to these violently policed dualistic options. Central to this polemic, then, has to be something of a paradox for tranz-folks seeking images of ourselves: how does one represent oneself when one's self is unrepresentable within current and often conservative categories, forms, practices, and discourses? Hence, I want to argue for the importance of tranz-art and performance artists who have created a space in which to represent the unthinkable overdetermined by binaristic gender schemas but also beyond the celebration of contradiction itself. What I document in this essay, then, is a willful and intersectional political deployment of incoherence against the hegemonies of the white supremacist, sex/gender system. Even as we pull these terms apart, an equally tenacious and conservative set of rhetorics and practices—at the heart of the sex/gender system—continues to fold one back into the other. Sometimes, that folding occurs, quite incidentally, *inside* our movements just as often as outside.

I want to challenge the existing and available categories we have for classifying both our lives but also our social movements. For myself, the oversimplistic and invested categories of "man," "lesbian," "butch," and even "ftm" are not flexible enough to name my experiences. If I call myself, as I do, a "guy who is half lesbian," where does that fit? The realities and lived experiences of those of us who might be verging on incoherent, *post-queer* landscapes are not thinkable within the existing gender economies and lexicons. [1] Hence, the need to move beyond our still young queer vocabularies. Queer is becoming a term marked by both imprecision and fixity; it has the potential to be centripetal or stabilizing the space it marks, or centrifugal, that is, destabilizing of the spaces it flags (as in to pervert, torsion, make strange). While I am convinced of queer's strategic and contingent efficacy, it seems to me its time to call for another—dare I say a post-queer—refinement of our languagings?

This essay will illustrate the effectiveness of a post-queer practice of incoherence through the work of two post-queerly gendered Toronto-based performance artists: one drag king, Deb Pearce (aka "Man Murray" and "Dirk Diggler") and one queer femme spoken word artist and performer, Anna Camilleri. While queer is supposed to function in excess of the equation gayandlesbian and its ideological liabilities, it continues to mark a relation to lesbian and gay as much as it marks distance from it; it also is just not complex enough to hold the lives and bodies of tranz folks either. Calvin Thomas, for instance, argues that such resistances of the regimes of the normal are not exclusive to gay, lesbian, or bisexual practices. Such queerings can be part of anti-heteronormative practices amongst heterosexual practices as well. But cannot a practice of resistance through in-coherence be also a strategy for resistance regimes of racism as well as homo-and trans-phobias? It is harder to place queer in this context, that is, of challenging the coherence that is to accrue between say whiteness and masculinity. To render something in-coherent means three things simultaneously: first, it means a lack of organization, or a failure of organization so as to make that thing difficult to comprehend; but it also means failing to cohere as a mass or entity.

Such failures of comprehension and organization are precisely what an intersectional practice seeks. The reading of a body as "properly" gendered or as racialized "white" involves presenting signifiers within an economy where the signifiers accumulate toward the appearance of a coherently functioning body. Becoming a tranz-sexual white man, for me, however, means occupying the permanent space of not just becoming; that is, it is a permanent place of modulation of what came before by what comes after, never fully accomplishing either as an essentialist stable "reality" but also of permanent in-coherence if I am to matter as a political subject at all. But it also means rendering bodies and subject positions as in-coherent as possible to refuse to let power work through bodies the way it needs to. My question here has been and remains, what happens if we refuse the coherences of gender and practice in-coherence instead? Such a practice, such as that which marks the performances of drag king Deb Pearce/Man Murray, troubles our fantasies of wholeness and singularity in terms of our identities, answering that fantasy with incoherence and multiplicity instead.

What better ground to map that practice onto but the female masculinity as open secret coded onto Canadian songstress, Anne Murray. Deb's "Man Murray" has been a successful feature of the Toronto drag king performance scene for almost nine years. Man takes aim at the gender contradictions of Canadian songstress Anne Murray by layering recognizable performances of female masculinity onto a "failed" performance of heteronormative femininity, queering that which has signified as an open secret for decades: Canada's own butch national icon. What makes Man so pleasurable are the ways in which Deb's performance codes not just irony but layers of irony onto each other. Layering refers to the way that drag kings will map a king persona onto their own gender identities, allowing that identity to show through cracks in the mapping (Halberstam). What Deb draws our attention to is Anne Murray's own layering of genders. Murray has long been rumoured to have a lesbian past; this rumour is virtually unverifiable. But what is far more interesting about this rumour is the degree to which it is fed by a disavowed spectre of masculinity around Murray's gender identity, including her deep baritone voice. Despite the signifiers of femininity that accrue around Murray—make-up including requisite blue eyeshadow, earrings, long gowns, feminine pantsuits, women's low-heeled shoes, and so forth—Murray's performance of white femininity always already seems to fail given it is layered onto a body which reads more masculine than feminine. That is, one could argue that Murray herself, as text, before Man Murray queers her, reads as a very toned-down male to female drag queen.

It is precisely these already existing ironic layerings around Murray that Man Murray foregrounds. Man's performance is choreographed around the many other obvious markers of gender awkwardness around Anne Murray: the short masculine hairstyle, square jaw, broad face and smile, strong hand tightly gripping the micro-phone in a fist; pant suits with slip-on shoes, step-dancing where she moves awkwardly from side to side etc. What makes this performance so effective—that is, what makes the irony so resonant—are the similar facial features that Anne Murray and Deb Pearce share. These are the faces of white butch masculinity, accompanied by what for me, as a young teenage butch, was unequivocally the voice of female masculinity as well. How else might we characterize that deep baritone voice? Only for Anne Murray herself, femininity is layered, quite incoherently onto what can only be read as female masculinity. But Man, on the other hand, is not just layered; he's also queerly camped up. Man is packing a phallus not unlike the microphone Murray grips so tightly. Man draws out the awkwardness of body movements, dancing centred at the knees as they step from side to side, equally awkward facial expressions (the wink, complete with blue eyeshadow, and head nod, for instance), and continues to inhabit Murray's body through some of the crowd favourite songs, such as "Snow Bird."

Clearly, such ironic and simultaneous reiterations of failed heteronormative femininity, disavowed female masculinity, and queered gay masculinity, situate us in a post-queer No Man's Land. But drag kings are not the only inhabitants of No Man's Land. Historically, femme subjectivities have almost always been subsumed by female and butch masculinity. Over 100 years of sexological research, for instance, has rarely, if ever, spent considerable time mapping the powerful existence of queer femininity. Both the fields of feminism and queer theory have also neglected her, the former dismissing her potential while the latter folds her signifiers into pure artifice. I want to explore the work of one queer femme performance artist—Anna Camilleri—who challenges these gender hegemonies through a new kind of "fem(me)inism," post-queer, third wave feminist practices emerging as a viable form of political resistance. Camilleri's work raises compelling questions about femininity, questions that similarly overdetermine femininity on the site where it is thought to be the least self-evident and the most coherent; that is, on queer fem(me)ininity. In many ways, the relation between *trans-gender* and fem(me)ininity has been, to date, a non sequitur. Transgender typically has functioned to mark a space of subjectivity that emerges in contradistinction from the body in which it finds itself eclipsing those who find themselves in the term *femme* as it emerges on what can be (mis)read as a so-called successfully *naturalized* female body.[2] What happens if we refuse the coherence of that neat equation by suggesting that in the case of fem(me)ininity, what one sees is not at all what one gets? The trick, for subjects of fem(me)ininity, is how to stage the gaze as a scene of that incoherence within an economy that apparently binds its subject conventional femininity in the same moment. Can fem(me)ininity resist precisely what femininity is articulated through and contained by?

One of the very recent texts to camp queer femininity is, of course, Lisa Duggan and Kathleen McHugh's "The Fem(me)inist Manifesto." This manifesto is, like other manifestos, an attempt to articulate in the registers of hyperbole and with tremendous irony, a femme call to arms. The piece is written for femmes, directed at masculinity—in equal parts tranz, bio and female—with the goal of destabilizing and, well, ironizing, exactly what we mean by the term femme. Their choice of spelling—fem(me)—is deliberate and works against the self-effacing imperatives of femininity; that is, the spelling, like the spelling of "boi," works as a performative to signal distance and rupture from the sign's each modifies. This manifesto maps economies of resistance, rendering femininity as a result both hyper-performative and strangely defamiliarized. In fact, each of these performance texts that I will consider here signify or perform some kind of violence: the Duggan and McHugh feminist camp manifesto, like any manifesto, shatters habituated thought patterns and over-familiarity on the part of the reader by jarring us into an entirely different stylization of the word. Manifestos, as a public declarative form, make manifest or visible that which habituated thought puts under erasure and by necessity are characterized by elevated diction and tone. Curiously, the term comes from the Latin *manu festus* or "struck by hand," implying the shock of that strike as one way to get attention.

Beyond the sexual ambiguities implied by "struck by hand" the femme subject as trope deliberately plays on the spaces of incoherence between categories: she is both and fully neither lesbian nor heterosexual; she becomes the source of power in the scene by inhabiting, as Duggan and McHugh suggest, normal abnormally. "She" cannot be known and hence contained in categories; her articulations exist in both narrative levels and in both sexual subjectivities (that is, both lesbian femme and heterosexual femme fatale all at the same time). It is precisely her control of what's intelligible or knowable situated as it is within what she knows is unintelligible for the masculinity, which allows the incoherence of the narrative to unfold the way it does:

> Within postmodernism, the fem(me) reappears, signifier of another kind of gender trouble. Not a performer of legible gender transgression, like the butch or his sister the drag queen, but a betrayer of legibility itself. Seemingly "normal," she responds to "normal" expectations with a sucker punch—she occupies normality abnormally. (108)

Fem(me) is, as Camilleri writes in the introduction to *Brazen Femme*, femininity gone wrong; the trappings of femininity gone awry (13). The terms, then, of femme, are both redress and pleasure through the gaze itself, not somehow outside of it (13). While being subjected by the gaze is a consistent part of femme experience, here seeing is the tithe, the price paid for an audacious gaze: "I dared the viewer, the imagined viewer, to look. My legs spread apart, knife gripped tightly, mediating access. Seeing is the tithe, nor the prize. A brazen posture? Yes" (Camilleri 11). This reconfiguration of looking doubles fem(me)ininity relative to femininity gesturing to a productive categorical im/possibility—incoherence—which refuses closure: "What cannot be seen, what cannot be held or pinned down, is where femme is" (12). As we see in the cover image of *Brazen Femme*, she is not either side of the knife blade as a binary opposition; she is its edge: "Femme is the blade—fatally sharp; a mirror reflecting back fatal illusions" (12). The violence of that edge is the redress and the pleasure.

Formerly a member of the performance troupe Taste This (Anna Camilleri, Ivan E. Coyote, Zoë Eakle and Lyndell Montgomery), whose work was collected and published as *Boys Like Her: Transfictions*, Anna Camilleri is now based in Toronto and continues to write and present spoken word performances. *Boys Like Her* was a collection of writings from tours and performances from Taste This, who identify across the spectrum of gender identities. One of the central tensions of Camilleri's work, both in *Boys Like Her* and since, is the representational imperatives and yet impossibilities of fem(me)ininities in both queer and feminist contexts. That is, the subtitle of the collection—*Transfictions*—foregrounds both the form of the work (fictions) but also the location of the performers, including Camilleri. In *Boys Like Her*, subjectivities and gendered desire function as mirrors, especially for fem(me)ininities whose gaze itself is already doubled. What those mirrored reflections, deflections, and refractions reveal is, of course, the ironies and I would argue, the incoherences, of the socially constructed face of femininity, from which fem(me)ininities are redoubled. One of Camilleri's pieces, "Skin to Scar," commands that gaze attend to the processes by which her face was rebuilt when medically necessary and non-cosmetic surgeries became cosmetic. "Look at me," the voice insists:

> Look carefully. Do you see my face? My totally asymmetrical face? My nose is clinically described as a deviated septum. My mandible and maxilla aren't perfectly lined up, and X-rays show that my chin is connected to my jaw with wire. Yes, I'm a head injury patient and a beautiful one at that. A beautifully built woman—I have the doctors to thank for that.... They did a wonderful job, don't you think? ... Look at me.... This face was rebuilt. (88–89)

That invitation becomes a reiterative imperative by the time the second "Look at me" repeats. The double-sightedness that watches from two places at once—from within and from without—watches the watchers to display essentializing and naturalizing Girl-By-Nature machineries (Duggan and McHugh 154). Feminist theorist Camilla Griggers calls these technologies the abstract-machine of faciality, a process in which the face represents an apparatus that, like a machine, constantly produces and re-produces the subject through the signifiers the visual apparatus requires. The face, in other words, is not a natural extension of the flesh, nor is it a signifier of an individuated consciousness. Rather, it is a signifying mechanism, a network of interpretations organizing a zone of acceptable expressions of the signifier and acceptable conductions of meanings to signs and of signs to social subjects (Griggers). Femininity is then overcoded, abstract faciality where the face is a textual space in which meanings can be allowed to proliferate and resonate. The primary means through which this visual regime of signs is produced and consumed is, of course, through the gaze. Camilleri documents this facializing machine in action:

> Beautiful. Yes beautiful.... These words repeat.... The surgeries were needed for medical reasons—and there were "cosmetic benefits." And this, the cosmetic benefits, is what seemed to excite and intoxicate the doctors more than anything else. I remember the calculated, hungry look in the eyes of surgeons who saw me the way an architect might view a partially constructed building. "Lovely foundation, it's a shame that it's not finished." They saw me as incomplete, unfinished and potentially beautiful. And what greater gift could a doctor give to this world than one more beautiful woman? (91)

But there is a way in which faciality can become *de-faced*, re-constructed. Camilleri deploys a similar rhetoric of strategic essentialism to show how fem(me)ininities are grafted from femininity, a so-called source that imagines itself as the original:

> None of the doctors ever asked me how I felt about my face. Go ahead, ask me now ... How do I feel? I can say this: I grew these bones myself, muscle to tendon, skin to cheek. I pushed myself into this world. (92)

That so-called original (yet another assemblage) *loses face* and is even *effaced* in a politic that is ironically played out in the *tranz-gendered* threshold between the perceptible and the imperceptible, and between the imaginary body and the flesh (Hart).

Camilleri's story "Super Hero" stages a similar violent tranz-(re)versal of those subject-forming but also consuming looking practices (1998). "Super Hero" is a fantasy story that the nameless narrator gives herself very late one night when she is unable to sleep. "Furious pounding, screaming inside," writes the narrator, "I know, mean and nasty thoughts aren't going to get me to sleep, but tonight I can't just do some deep breathing [...] No, tonight is different" (131). That difference is one in which the speaker recreates a common experience for women. The scene puts a woman, late at night at the end of her shift, at a bus stop waiting for public transit, harassed by man after man (the "drive-bys") in cars feeling, as the story suggests, like a sitting duck. Those "mean and nasty thoughts," we soon discover, necessitate meeting and returning the gaze of one of the drive-bys as he follows the woman down the street yelling obscenities out his van window. Manipulating the desire of "Dick," the drive-by in the van, the woman climbs into his van, plays equal part seductress and coy, convinces him to return back to her place. Once inside, the woman makes Dick comfortable and retreats to the bathroom to prepare. After returning from the bathroom, pouring a drink, the reader understands exactly what is occurring:

> I pour one shot of Scotch, quietly sort through my cabinet and gather my props. Dick is looking out the window. I hand him the drink and run my index finger down his chest. He smirks and takes a swig. I smile back broadly and bring my right kneecap sharply into his groin. Dick grabs his cock and crashes to his knees.... While he's still down, I cuff him, kick him onto his belly and hogtie him.... A beautiful sight. (133)

Camilleri's "Super Hero" watches the watcher watching and then makes the scene so unbearable that the watcher stops watching and looks elsewhere, all of which is witnessed (by the watched) from two places (both within and without) simultaneously. After tormenting Dick, reminding him that he has only himself to thank for the position he is in, and after reiterating his powerlessness, the woman, who introduces herself as Anna, duct-tapes his keys between his shoulder blades and throws him out of her apartment and watches him stumble down the street naked.

> I walk over to my window, light a cigarette and watch the smoke scatter as it hits the pane. The streetlight is buzzing more loudly than usual.

> Halfway through my cigarette, Dick stumbles out of my building. He's buck-naked, hunching over, trying to cover his cock. (135)

The text is accompanied by the same photograph that appears as the cover of *Brazen Femme*: that of a woman's body, sitting, photographed from the neck down. The woman is seated with her legs pulled up to reveal black leather boots with a very thick high heel, legs clad in stockings held up by a garter belt, arms clasping her knees to her chest, with her only visible hand clutching a knife blade. This image of her body as signifier now draws attention to itself as that which remains, like the image of the knife, in excess of the male gaze. That is, the appearance of the female body is that *object* which was produced by the gaze and yet is the same now *subject* functioning in excess of that same gaze. The gaze that once functioned to secure meaning has simultaneously displaced/deferred the fixed meaning of that signifier and fails to reproduce its power all at the same moment. Like Medusa, the gaze, in other words, is mirrored back onto itself with extremely tranz-formative effects.

The fem(me)ininity in performance, both textually but also when Camilleri performs "Super Hero," stages the failure of the signifiers of femininity to secure a relation between subjectivity and the so-called female body *qua* body. In the earlier bathroom mirror scene, Camilleri stages the female doubled—that is, in-cohering—gaze as both performative, and *productively* self-naming through ritualized speech-acts.

> I lock the bathroom door behind me. I look in the mirror and see myself: a bitch-femme. My eyes are hard and dilated…. I run my tongue slowly along sharp teeth. I silently call on all of the bold bitch-femmes who have come before me, to be here, now. (132–33)

The double-sightedness of fem(me)ininity, which stages a violent assault on both the gaze and the signifiers it productively consumes, does so for both Camilleri from within a number of incoherent places at once: "woman," "bitch," "whore/dominatrix," but also "queer." The male gaze is dependent upon both visibility but also a coherent point of view that provides it with the cloaked machineries of objectification. In the ironically titled "Super Hero," and in "Skin to Scar," that point of view is radically destabilized and shattered, as are the machineries upon which it depends. If Foucault is correct when he argues that "the agency of domination does not reside in the one who speaks (for it is he who is constrained), but in the one who listens [or watches] and says nothing" (64) then for Camilleri those relations of power operative in the gaze are inverted when it is the silent and split spectator of fem(me)ininity who watches a performance of femininity dominate and control the visual exchanges.

These tensions are raised by *Boys Like Her* but it isn't until we get to *I Am a Red Dress: Incantations on a Grandmother, a Mother and a Daughter*, that the disruptural potential of Camilleri's project is fully actualized. *Red Dress* is, as the subtitle suggests, a series of incantations on femininity as it triangulates through three generations of women. Each generation battles violent men, including a paternal grandfather who draws a line between each generation as a sexual predator. Femininity is held to task here, for not stopping him; but femininity is also truncated, interrupted, rendered incoherent by femme, which does not take shape till the final generation. Lyrical, poetic and elegiac in places, *Red Dress* maps that trajectory beautifully. The grammar or lexicon of *Red Dress* are the realities of women's lives, the most potent is the consistent sexual abuse of girl children by a maternal grandfather. Structured by what each generation cannot know about itself—*Grandmother, Mother, Daughter*—*Red Dress* introduces us to the Daughter—"Annina," violently raped by the grandfather for years—as she comes to embody, as femme, the unthinkable rage of each generation of women before her. While Annina's experiences are the same as her mother and grandmother; her choices are not. As a femme, come of age, she files charges against her grandfather, who is imprisoned for his violence, dying shortly after his release.

The book's red cover design signals that incantation. Annina's mother repeats an imperative that she, herself, is unable to actualize: "when your grandfather dies I'm going to the funeral in a red dress" (115). This as possibility repeats endlessly throughout the text like a frustrated desire. "Wearing anything but black to a funeral, to my father's funeral—now that would be a disgrace," her mother confesses. "A red dress is for parties, for celebration" (96). But for the young Annina, that desire and its tenacity not just mark but shatter what seems to be coherent space between femininity and femme. That is, coded into what each generation cannot know— where each is cut from the same hard stone—are the templates for the next generation's work and, in this case, a post-queer third wave fem(me)inist imperative. [3]

> This story is a lexicon between my grandmother, my mother, and I—the stuff that mythology is made of—mother, maiden, and crone. Grandmother notices a red dress. Mother imagines wearing a red dress. Daughter becomes the red dress. The redress. (12).

Camilleri's redress/red dress and the productive failure of femininity to cohere in Man Murray are scenes of what I call post-queer tranz desire whose logic defies even a complex queering. These are identities, desires, and bodies that defy the logic and the grammars of both the sex/gender system and even many of the attempts, well-meaning as they are, to deconstruct "gender" difference. What we are left with, then, is a completely new relation between bodies and identities; one that we might refer to as post-queer genders without genitals. These new incoherent, post-queer performances of gender, I suggest, mark an important paradigm shift within and for feminism. It is that shift we need to promote if these subjects will succeed in remaking incoherently feminist bodies.

(2005)

Notes

[1] This work is part of a much larger book, in press, called *Sons of the Movement: FTMs Risking Incoherence in a Post-Queer Cultural Landscape* (forthcoming, Women's Press, 2006).

[2] The term *naturalized* describes an effect of engendering. While usually referring to a performative moment where an immigrant is conferred Canadian, or indeed, any national citizenship, I use it here to reference a similar performative reading practice which infers a tranzed body, one based on a (mis-)reading of a gender performance, one that is assumed to have emerged naturally out of that body. Femme is often perceived—quite erroneously—as a naturalized gender, a perception that I hope to challenge.

[3] The metaphor of stone—stoneness—is absolutely purposeful and significant. Often used within butch-femme communities to reference butch impenetrability, Camilleri uses this metaphor, as a number of other femmes do as well, to detail a gendered emotional toughness, a kind of similar impenetrability only emotional and not sexual. One chapter details this stoneness; in "Cut from the Same Stone," Camilleri draws lines of continuity through grandmother-mother-daughter through tropes such as "Stone's Throw," "Milestone," "Sticks and Stones," "Skipping Stones," writing, toward the end, "For the longest time, I was concerned about being too soft—a soft touch, soft-hearted, soft-spoken. It wasn't until I was about twenty-four that I realized I had buried that part of me long, long ago. I had grown up into an impenetrable woman, an utterly untouchable femme, just like my mother. I had become a girl, then a woman, living in shadow, who could not bear the weight of her own heart—my heart, sunk as stone, silt cradled at the bottom of a lake" (84).

Works Cited

Camilleri, Anna and Chloë Brushwood Rose. *Brazen Femme: Queering Femininity*. Vancouver: Arsenal Pulp, 2002.

Camilleri, Anna. *I am a Red Dress: Incantations on a Grandmother, a Mother, and a Daughter*. Vancouver: Arsenal Pulp, 2004.

Duggan, Lisa and Kathleen McHugh's "A Fem(me)inist Manifesto." *Women and Performance: A Journal of Feminist Theory* 8.2 (1996): 107–11.

Foucault, Michel. *The History of Sexuality: An Introduction*. Volume 1. Trans. Robert Hurley. New York: Random House, 1978.

Griggers, Camilla. *Becoming-Woman*. Minneapolis: U of Minnesota P, 1997.

Halberstam, Judith. *Female Masculinity*. Durham and London: Duke UP, 1998.

Hart, Lynda. Between the Body and the Flesh: Performing Sadomasochism. New York: Columbia UP, 1998.

Johnson, Barbara. *A World of Difference*. Baltimore: Johns Hopkins UP, 1987.

Noble, J. Bobby. *Sons of the Movement: FTMs Risking Incoherence in a Post-Queer Cultural Landscape*. Toronto: Women's Press (forthcoming 2006).

————. "Sons of the Movement: Feminism, Female Masculinity and FTM Transsexual Men." *Atlantis* 29.1 (2005): 21–28.

Taste This (Anna Camilleri, Ivan E. Coyote, Zoë Eakle, Lyndell Montgomery). *Boys Like Her: Transfictions*. Vancouver: Press Gang, 1998.

Thomas, Calvin, ed. Straight with a Twist: Queer Theory and the Subject of Heterosexuality. Urbana: U of Illinois P, 2000.

Get your "Boy" On!
Politics of Parody and Embodiment
in "Drag" Performances in Toronto [1]

by Frances J. Latchford

On the topic of 'drag kings,' Joy La Chica, who, along with Rose Perri, co-founded Toronto's first drag king troupe, The Greater Toronto Drag King Society, recently said that "in the 1990s, drag was all about parody, politics and critique. We are now living in a post-drag period." "What is absent in today's drag," compared to that of the 1990s, says La Chica, "is a sense of parody" (La Chica, 21 August). Nina Arsenault, actor, writer, and drag aficionado, made a similar observation about Toronto's contemporary drag kings: "The difference between drag today and that of the early 1990s is that drag today lacks irony" (Arsenault). [2]

Why are contemporary drag king performances in Toronto bars, theatres, and at Pride Toronto so different from those of the 1990s? One important reason has to do with a change in the ethos of these performances. Today, drag tends more and more toward an ethos of embodiment rather than parody. Indeed, I think this phenomenon is precisely what La Chica and Arsenault intend when they suggest that current king performances are post-drag and lacking in irony. Maria Popoff recounts that in the early 1970s some lesbian butch women in Toronto did impersonate male singers in bars, and although these performances were called "drag," they were "very, very, serious, not parodic at all" (Popoff). Historically and typically, however, drag, as opposed to impersonation and cross-dressing, is regarded as a genre that is parodic and ironic. [3] It is this tradition out of which La Chica and The Greater Toronto Drag King Society, or dk, emerged.

This paper situates and explores the work of dk in the social and political milieu of the 1990s. It examines the sea change in dyke and queer culture that is transforming female to male drag performance into an increasingly un-ironic imitation of boys and men. At first blush, this may seem to participate in a naive return to a 1970s aesthetic and ethic of impersonation or the kind of drag to which Popoff refers. But drag as embodiment in the first decade of the twenty-first century is not uncritical, taking aim as it does at the meaning of sex in performance. In the final analysis, however, I argue that drag king performances that are designed to be artistic strategies of social and political resistance against gender and sex norms require both parody *and* embodiment to move beyond pure entertainment. It is only by doing so that this form of theatrical performance becomes a powerful vehicle of social critique.

My interest in drag kings, particularly Toronto drag kings, is academic, political, and personal. I am a feminist philosopher who engages with queer theory and sexuality studies. I am interested in how drag king performances can and do shape the cultural, social, political imaginations and subjectivities of sexually diverse peoples and communities in Toronto. Not only have I observed countless drag king performances in Toronto, I am also a performer. I have acted as a drag king in several shows. Like so many Toronto 'bar dykes' who came out in the late 1980s or early 1990s, I witnessed female-to-male drag up-close and personal in pubs, at Buddies in Bad Times Theatre, and annually at Pride Toronto. I love a good "gender-fuck!" and am thrilled by these events, as are several of my friends who established themselves as Toronto's first drag kings in the mid-1990s. It was at their encouragement that I performed drag with Oedipussy Rex, a later incarnation of dk, initially "manned" by Joy La Chica, Suzy Richter, Gumbo Pelly, Nat O'Satchy, Sheila Dietrich, Alicia Salzer, Leslie Miller and myself. We formed in the summer of 2002 when La Chica, having returned from New York, revived a number of campy characters and acts that she originally developed almost a decade earlier. I was the "Leather Man" of "The Village People," a "Gibb Brother," and one of the "Sisters Janet Meat." During this revival, I also performed as a femme background singer and groupie to La Chica's "Don Ho" and "Tom Jones." The whole troupe performed at Pride Toronto 2002 and at a related event at The Reverb. La Chica, Richter, and I also did a number of smaller events at the B Side and Through the Looking Glass over the next few months. [4] In March of 2003, Suzy and Joy brought their "Barry Gibb and Yentl" act to my introductory "Concepts of the 'Male' and 'Female' in Western Culture" course at York University. I also performed solo in the summer of that year for a colleague who teaches the same course. Costumed as a male professor, Ben Stark, I gave a serious lecture on gender and sex before transforming myself surprisingly and humorously into a woman in order to enact the ways in which gender is a construction that entails stereotypical conventions and practices.

According to Linda Hutcheon, parody "is a form of imitation, but imitation characterized by ironic inversion, not always at the expense of the parodied text" (6). In other words, parodic texts, or performances, are essentially "bitextual" and "trans-contextual" (35). In them, there is a "critical distance implied between the back-grounded text being parodied and the new incorporating work, a distance usually signaled by irony" (32). It is in its use of parody that drag's possibility as a kind of performance that critiques gender and sex norms is effectively realized. Parody in performance as dual or multiple textuality means that an audience can, and in a strong performance will, have two or more epistemological experiences that are diametrically opposed and often simultaneous. Where drag takes aim at gender and sex, therefore, parody creates a possibility for the audience to experience an imitation of gender and sex as real or original at the same time that they experience that realness critically as a construction (Butler, Gender 137). [5] In effect, it is parody that underlines drag's subversive quality because it can produce crises in knowledge for the audience. [6]

The subversive nature of drag as gender and sex parody, however, should be distinguished from other types of on-stage gender and sex performance, particularly, male-to-female or female-to-male impersonation, which are types of performance that are often understood as a kind of drag. Compared to drag that employs parody in order to critique gender and sex, the goal of impersonation is to *realize* or embody rather than parody a given gender and sex onstage.

Impersonation, when done well, convinces the audience, unfailingly, that the gender and sex of the performer onstage is real within the context of the performance itself. As Roger Baker points out in a discussion of male-to-female impersonation,

> ...the actor playing a woman is taken by the audience and by the other actors in the play or show as a real woman. This does not mean that the audience and the players are unaware of the actor's real gender. It means that this knowledge is irrelevant to the nature of the drama being played out, or to the effect of the actor's work. (14)[7]

In the 1970s, female-to-male drag appears to have been very much like impersonation. And this type of performance at that time probably would have been considered quite radical simply because masculine women threatened the heterosexual status quo and its assumption that there is a natural affiliation between sex and gender. On the whole, however, drag as impersonation is less subversive than drag as parody insofar as it creates a singular and conflated experience of gender and sex onstage, one which is designed to re-inscribe these social, political and cultural norms as though they are a natural reality. Its measure of success lies entirely in the performer's ability to make the audience suspend disbelief with respect to the experience of such a conflict throughout the performance. In impersonation the audience accepts the sex/gender of the character as real, while in parodic drag the comfort of this fiction is refused. Drag is much more likely to cause a crisis in knowledge because it throws the audience into the precarious and contradictory position of knowing and experiencing gender and sex as simultaneously real and false, thereby focusing the audience's attention on gender and sex as constructions within the performance.

Drag and impersonation both depend on embodiment.[8] Here, embodiment refers to performances in which the actor, physically and phenomenally, inhabits an apparently original gender and sex onstage; his or her performance not only conforms to cultural norms, but is experienced by the audience as doing so. For example, to say that Toronto-based drag king Gricel Severino embodies masculinity means that onstage and for the audience she inhabits the normative meaning of masculinity, even if it is counter-normative for a female to do so.[9] In effect, embodiment is the ontological ethos of male or female impersonators who achieve a sense of reality by adopting gender and sex norms onstage: they literally appear to *be* male or female.

The role of embodiment in drag, as opposed to impersonation, is different. When real gender and sex norms are momentarily inhabited in a drag performance, they force the audience to experience these norms as essentially fleeting and fragmentary. This experience can manifest as identification with or desire for the performer as a real man or woman, but these states are also interrupted repeatedly through the parodying of these norms.

Embodiment of some kind is crucial, therefore, to drag's possibility as a strategy of resistance against dominant gender and sex norms. It is the system of gender and sex signs that denote stereotypical masculine and feminine voices, movements, costumes, and dialogue. It is also the knowledge, produced by these signs, that is thrown into crisis through their parodic critique. In the context of drag that effectively subverts these norms, embodiment is the necessary straight man, forced to take himself much less seriously because he is the repeated victim of parody's rowdy, ironic hijinks.

The emergence of drag kings in Toronto cannot be attributed to any one social, historical, and political moment or force. There were, however, important performative challenges to gender occurring in popular culture which, when conjoined with diverse social, sexual, political and queer discourses of the day, encouraged gender play in this city and contributed to the desire on the part of many women who then identified primarily as dykes to perform male drag. Although new, the idea of female-to-male drag was not entirely alien in the late 1980s and early 1990s. Grace Jones's, Annie Lennox's, and Boy George's daring gender bending inspired many like-minded people to do the same with more frequency, force, and felicity. In Canada, Carole Pope was seducing queer and straight audiences with her naughty butch and leather bravado, which if not drag, was a highly provocative and sexually charged rendition of female masculinity. In Toronto, a group of feminist performance artists The Clichettes dressed in male garb to critique gender and sexual politics in comedic lip-synchs to 1960s songs such as "You Don't Own Me." More specific to Toronto's lesbian and gay punk scene in the mid-1980s, Suzy Richter's gender-fucking performances as "Stevie" in Gloria Berlin's films "Trouble Makers" and "The Yo-Yo Gang," as well as in the "homo-core-punk" zine, *J.D.'s*, edited by Berlin and Bruce La Bruce, caused quite a stir amongst gay fans in Canada and the U.S. who, mistaking "Stevie" for a 'boy,' instead of a 'dyke,' wanted his number figuratively and literally (Richter). In today's terms, however, these once *avant-garde* performances are more properly categorized as androgyne, rather than as drag, insofar as the critique they offered tended toward a rejection of gender. Still, they were provocative and exciting to many queers, starved as we were for images of unconventional women and men like ourselves.

Performances like these also spoke socially and politically to many Toronto feminist lesbians and dykes. By the late 1980s and early 1990s, and across most urban lesbian contexts in North America, androgyny, or the rejection of traditional gender roles, was still a dominant imperative of second wave lesbian feminism (Cruickshank 43, 155; Hart 37; Adam 101). Amongst lesbians, therefore, masculine and feminine drag of any kind was primarily regarded as suspect because it was perceived to be in the service of misogyny and heterosexual normativity (Adam 100–03). Increasingly, however, this imperative, which effectively demanded the erasure of masculine and feminine gender differences, was subjected to fierce critiques from many vantage points. In particular, it was subjected to the critique that it collapsed differences pertaining to sex, race, class, and sexual practice, insofar as each intersects with gender. By the late 1980s and early 1990s, therefore, many Toronto dykes, myself included, no longer deeply identified with androgyny. It was in this context that Suzy Richter and Joy La Chica met and, as members of the Nancy Sinatras' cover band, performed campy, transvestite duets dressed as "Frank and Nancy," "Sonny and Cher," and the "Captain & Tennille" among other characters (La Chica, 29 July; Richter).

At the same time, the AIDS crisis was becoming a central focus of both gays and lesbians in Toronto. [10] It reinforced bonds between gays and lesbians that, prior to, were often tenuous; galvanized organizations; encouraged a large swath of the community to "come-out" (as fags, dykes, bisexuals, transsexuals, HIV positive and/or queer); and enlisted gender performance, indeed, drag, in the social, political, and economic battle against what had become an epidemic. [11] Inevitably, any number of boys and "radical fairies" showed up in drag, or semi-drag, for "kiss-ins" and demonstrations. [12] Toronto AIDS organizations also used drag to raise funds at events like Fashion Cares. [13] The use of drag in response to AIDS by lesbians and gays who increasingly identified as queer activists, coupled with the fact that many queer women now rejected androgyny as a feminist imperative, and comfortably identified as butch and femme, meant that the emergence of male-to-female drag was now less likely to be dismissed as inherently sexist and misogynist.

In 1991, Buddies acquired its first theatre space on George Street in Toronto. Throughout the early 1990s its provocative and queer agenda gave queer drag a home. Buddies' co-founder Sky Gilbert had long stressed the company's interest "in life on the edge, the *avant-garde*, [and] forbidden territory" (Crew). The theatre breathed life into this purpose by staging and hosting a variety of events that dealt with issues ranging from AIDS to queer rights, to questions of gender, diversity, sexual identities, sexual practices, S/M and drag. Its most notorious drag queen was Sky Gilbert's "Jane" who, along with out S/M dyke Sue Golding and lesbian icon Suzy Richter hosted many of Buddies' most memorable parties and, particularly, its "dungeon parties." These parties always featured spectacular costumes, skimpy briefs, leather, skin, spanking, flogging, piercing, bondage, the enactment of sexual scenes and fantasies, and lots and lots of drag. Buddies embraced not only male-to-female drag, however, but full-on female-to-male drag, as naughty women like La Chica, Richter, and Irene Miloslavsky began to arrive at these parties sporting a "five o'clock shadow," a uniform, leather, carrying a cat-o-nine-tails and "packing" a big dildo (La Chica, 29 July; Richter).

Female-to-male drag in Toronto in the early 1990s, however, was not precisely entertainment for its own sake. Many dykes free of the imperative of androgyny, and emboldened by the dissemination of a queer and postmodern feminist cultural politic to define and enact their sexual desires, began to use drag to reclaim and explore not only butch, but S/M identities and practices. Initially, female-to-male drag at Buddies occurred primarily as a component of S/M: "butch, dyke, daddies" used drag as a means of heightening S/M practice and experience as they "topped" or "bottomed" for their femmes in public and private (La Chica, 29 July). [14]

Apart from Buddies' mixed parties in the early 1990s, no bars catered specifically to S/M dykes in Toronto. [15] As a result, some dykes who engaged in S/M, and by proxy, drag, also ventured into gay leather and S/M clubs such as Boots and Buds on Sherbourne Street where, surprisingly, they were welcomed. [16] As La Chica explains, "many of the leather boys enjoyed us and were really titillated by our leather-male drag." "The very first drag I was invited to perform onstage," she recalls, "long before I was a drag king, was in these bars" (La Chica, 29 July). Notably, La Chica was the first and only woman to win the Woody's leather title, "Woody's Guy," in June of 1995, during the Guy to Goddess AIDS Benefit (La Chica, 29 July). [17]

dk was formally organized by La Chica and Perri in the summer of 1995 and it initiated the first wave of drag king performance in the city of Toronto. [18] Informally, La Chica and Perri had been performing female-to-male and female-to-female drag at house parties since 1992. [19] By 1995, they decided to establish a performance troupe that had more "structure and thematic continuity," one which would offer a series of drag acts as a show (Best). The troupe's original players included: Joy La Chica, Rose Perri, Gumbo Pelly, Irene Miloslavsky, Romy Shiller, Dionne Fleming, Alex Bulmer, Louise Basch, Sheila Chevalier, and Deb Pearce, who was asked by La Chica to play "Mann Murray," a character for whom she remains famous. [20] La Chica acted as the troupe's director and primary choreographer, as well as a performer. She was instrumental in developing campy stories and basic characters which the troupe then fleshed out together. Perri performed and served as the troupe's administrator. Daniel Paquette, a fan from the start, acted as their able publicist, helping to secure dk's quick success. The kings staged characters and songs from the 1950s to the 1990s including: "Donny & Marie, Captain & Denial, Sisters Janet Meat, Vanelli-Manelli-Vanilli, Kneel Diamond, ABBA, Man Murray, [and the] Village People." [21] They also ran "the gamut from Buck Nakid, Sure Shot Eddie, [the renamed] M-Ann Murray, and Don Ho to Cowboy Barbie, Jill Jolie, Natasha la Slasha, and Mama Tallulah" (Shiller, *Drag* 24).

Once formed, dk gained a great deal of momentum and its fame quickly exceeded Toronto queer contexts. Within the first year, it garnered the attention not only of local and national gay and lesbian, queer, and alternative presses like *Xtra!*, *Icon*, and *This*, but mainstream presses and television media too: the *Toronto Star*, *The Globe and Mail*, *The Toronto Sun*, *Maclean's Magazine*, and City TV's program "Ooh La La," all of which ran stories about the troupe. The seemingly sudden interest in the troupe was often linked in these articles to the release of films such as "The Adventures of Priscilla, Queen of the Desert" and "To Wong Foo Thanks for Everything, Julie Newmar," as well as to RuPaul's appointment as spokesmodel for MAC Cosmetics ("Girls"; "Royalty"; Giese). dk was being invited to perform with important queer artists such as Carole Pope, Lorraine Segato, Elvira Kurt, and Shelly Mars. Throughout 1995 and 1996, it performed the majority of its shows at Buddies' events such as Strange Sisters, Tinsel and Trash, Viva Vulva, and Pride Toronto, as well as at numerous Toronto bars including Tallulah's, The Horse Shoe, The Opera House, El Convento Rico, and The El Mocambo. [22]

From the beginning, La Chica and her ensemble recognized drag as a popular and powerful conduit for social-sexual-political action in Toronto and articulated this in their original mandate. [23]

> The Greater Toronto Drag King Society is a creative body that seeks to effectively mobilize women with an interest in drag, towards progressive socio-cultural, performance and creative opportunities within the context of camp and humour in masquerade. Through the medium of drag, be it female to female, or female to male caricatures, dk attempts to deconstruct gender and satirize extremes in female and male gender roles, behaviour and stereotypes. …dk recognizes the multiplicity of our own community, and is mindful to the sensitivities intrinsic to our pluralism as women, lesbians and gay individuals of diverse cultural and ethnic backgrounds. (*Crown and Sceptre*)

Toronto's first drag kings clearly identified as political and feminist dykes who consciously critiqued gender through campy, parodic performances of masculinity *and* femininity. [24]

As Roberta Best noted, dk was the "lesbian equivalent to the full-out, over the top, ready-for-Vegas" drag, which had a long tradition in gay male performance but was entirely new for women (Best 14). It also used drag, camp, and parody expressly as a social, political, feminist strategy to deconstruct gender and make explicit the ways in which gender norms and their power relations limited the freedoms of women, lesbians, and gays. [25]

dk's approach to drag would be as provocative today as it was in the mid-1990s, but for different reasons. A decade ago, it was bold simply because it flat-out rejected the assumption that either gender or female-to-male drag was inherently patriarchal and misogynist. [26] dk's approach is still radical because they identified so deeply with the drag queen's sensibility in performance. This is not an approach that is shared widely by today's kings, or by those who theorize about them. For instance, in 1998 Judith Halberstam argued that kings and queens are unlike each other because they "move in opposite directions.…the drag queen expands and becomes flamboyant, the drag king constrains and becomes quietly macho" (259). k. bradford suggests that kings and queens are essentially different because queens' "maleness … locates their parody of femininity in a set of relations built on sexism" (25). Annabelle Willox claims the king "is infinitely more subversive than the drag queen," because his performance undermines "that which society assumes to be a pregiven: masculinity" (280). Willox rejects the idea that the queen's parody of femininity is subversive because of the inherent sexism of a society in which femininity is only ever "derivative" of masculinity (Willox). The idea that the drag king's approach to performance is, or should be, different from the queen's is reiterated today with some frequency and this likely contributes to a predilection for embodiment in contemporary drag king performances. [27] Embodiment, however, was not the main ethic or aesthetic that informed the work of dk. They employed moments of embodiment in performance, but these moments were always undercut by displays of parody and irony which create the doubling that disrupts the audience's experience of the construction of gender and, ultimately, sex as something that is original, material, and/or identical with being.

dk genuinely emulated the drag queen insofar as they regarded parody and camp, above all, to be essential components of a drag performance (Shiller, *Drag* 26; La Chica, 21 August). These kings were nothing if not flamboyant in their campy (re)presentations of both masculinity and femininity—a lack of gender flamboyance was not one of the theatrical differences that separated these kings from queens. If they were distinct from queens with respect to gender flamboyance onstage, it was mainly because they located that flamboyance differently on the body. For instance, they located the excesses of masculinity in their shoulders, as opposed to the queens who located the excesses of femininity in their hips. Of course, dk's identification with the queen's parodic sensibility makes complete sense given that it was in Toronto's gay S/M leather bars and at Buddies' mixed parties that its founding members first became interested in drag and began to perform it in public. It is also linked to the fact that dk took the gay members of their audiences as seriously as they did the lesbians, and so practiced a style of drag that appealed to both. Like the queens, therefore, dk embraced gender parody and reveled in performing campy extremes of masculinity and femininity. And even if their celebration of gender was not always identical with that of the queen, because of their feminist politics, their performances always echoed her mirth, bawdiness, and flamboyance (La Chica, 21 August).

The test of subversion in parodic drag performance is, or should be, its ability to cause an audience to *experience* a crisis in knowledge as it pertains to gender and sex norms. As Roger Baker writes "These are some of the mysteries that surround drag and which sometimes give it an eerie magic,…an unnerving sense of the ground moving beneath one's feet" (14). dk's performances were subversive because they caused the ground of knowledge that composes gender norms to shift for the audience: this epistemological crisis signifies the subversive nature of a performance.

In drag king performances today an important shift is taking place, which distinguishes them from the drag kings of the mid-1990s. While some contemporary drag kings in Toronto such as Deb Pearce clearly do continue to enlist parody as a strategy within performance, many others are tending toward embodiment at the expense of parody. It is in this light, therefore, that I understand La Chica's idea that drag king performance has entered "a post-drag period": drag kings are making less use of parody and so their performances run the risk of being less subversive.

Shows, for instance, in 2005 and 2006 by Toronto based drag kings King Flare, Gricel Severino, and King's Ransom were striking because they embodied masculinity without a great deal of irony, distance, or critique.[28] This is also the case with drag king performances that are being imported by Toronto from the U.S. For instance, the Washington D.C. based troupe Rokett performed at Pride Toronto in 2006. Rokett's soul music performance was remarkable primarily because of their superior voices and choreography, but their performance of black masculinity, which clearly sought to embody recognizable tropes, did not parody these tropes, it merely impersonated them—black women became stereotypes of black men. In so doing, kings such as these render their audiences less likely to experience a crisis in knowledge and more likely to experience their performances of gender and race as a reiteration of these tropes and as a testament to their entrenched reality.

Of course, the social and political context in which contemporary drag kings and their audiences find themselves is very different from the mid-1990s when Toronto's gender and sexual avant-garde primarily identified as "queer," "queer punk," "gender fucker," "bisexual," "dyke," "fag," "butch/femme," "top/bottom" and/or "S/M" and, more rarely, as "trans." In 2006, there is a new gender and sex avant-garde who attends these performances. It is one which is much more removed from (bio-)gay male culture, still identifies somewhat as "queer," but more readily as "transgender," "trans-sexual," "trans," "tranz," "genderfukt," "gender diverse," "boi," "gender boy," "fag" rather than "dyke," "XX queer," "bio-girl," "bio-woman," "femme," and/or "bitch femme" (O'Connor).

Ultimately, these changes in the social and political context in which Toronto drag kings find themselves have implications for their performances. Contemporary drag kings' distance from (bio-)gay male culture suggests they are less likely to identify with the queen's parodic sensibility in performance, insofar as this sensibility and theatrical tradition is often identified with gay male culture. The ethos of drag king performance is subject to further change insofar as today kings are affected by the transgender rights movement and are working with new knowledges of sex, some of which do and do not intersect with feminism and queer theory. What was a parodic and performative focus on the construction of gender in the drag king performances of the 1990s, therefore, has become an embodied and performative focus on sex as a constructed "materiality" (Butler, *Bodies* 2). Indeed, this change underpins the move toward embodiment in performance primarily because the exciting and controversial idea that the materiality of sex is a construction is so new and epistemologically foreign that drag kings, like the rest of us, have yet to identify what it is about sex that is open to parody, in performance and in the world. These changes in the drag king's social and political milieu are what propel him increasingly toward embodied performances.

Assuming that the current ethos of drag king performance has shifted toward the embodiment of sex or maleness onstage, must we conclude that, like impersonation, many contemporary drag king performances are prone to reinscribe sex and, ultimately, gender norms, in so far as gender is folded into embodied performances of sex? To the degree that drag king performances genuinely are moving toward an ethos of embodiment, or fail to achieve parody, I think the answer is 'yes.' An embodied performance of the male sex and gender does not, at the level of audience experience, call enough critical attention to itself as a construction in the way that a parodic performance of sex and gender does. A solely embodied performance fails to be "bitextual," and in not doing so it collapses the simultaneous experience and, thus, knowledge of difference, that makes critique in the form of drag possible.

The move toward an ethos of embodiment in contemporary drag king performance, insofar as it suggests, among other things, that drag king performers, on and off stage, are grappling with a still new and exciting meaning of sex, does not mean that drag cannot retain its subversive possibility. Nor does this tendency toward embodiment mean that parody necessarily has or will completely disappear in drag king performances. For the time being, however, it does mean that performances which emphasize embodiment are less subversive than those which emphasize parody. Nonetheless, the possibility of drag performance in general continues to present feminist, queer and trans performance theorists, drag kings and queens, and their audiences with an enormous opportunity. If drag is most subversive of gender and sex normativity when it employs embodiment *and* parody, then the discovery of the interstices which open up not only gender, but sex, to parody is significant as a social, political, and artistic goal.

(2007)

Notes

[1] My special thanks and gratitude go out to Rosalind Kerr, Kym Bird, and Paul Halferty for their editorial comments and suggestions, as well as their willingness to explore with me in discussion the ideas presented in this paper.

[2] Arsenault writes widely on issues relating to sex, gender, and trans identity in *Fab Magazine* and *The National Post.*

[3] As is well known, the phenomenon of cross-dressing enjoys a very long history in Western theatre. In a context where women were excluded from taking the stage in any guise, male-to-female cross-dressing was a standard theatrical practice from the time of the Ancient Greeks. Female-to-male cross-dressing becomes permissible in the theatre a great deal later, but the length of this history is still noteworthy. In *Redressing the Past*, Kym Bird observes that "[f]emale to male cross-dressing … became a relatively common occurrence when the prohibition against women on-stage was rescinded in England in the mid-seventeenth century" although "in the view of many critics, it predominantly appealed to the sexuality of men." Notably, Toronto has more than a hundred year dramatic history of female-to-male cross-dressing on the stage. Bird examines the first Canadian play to enlist a female-to-male cross-dresser as its main character in the interests of late 19th Century liberal feminism: Sarah Ann Curzon's *The Sweet Girl Graduate.* See Bird 53.

[4] The B Side, Reverb, and Through the Looking Glass are downtown Toronto bars. The Looking Glass, which was on Church Street, is no longer in existence.

⁵ If Judith Butler is right, and the meaning of sex is constructed *as* the 'natural' foundation upon which the meaning of gender *as* a 'construction' is realized, then drag also has implications for the subversion of sex. See Butler *Bodies* 1–2.

⁶ This does not mean that a given parody, just because it is parody, will be subversive. The success or failure of parody in subverting the status quo ultimately depends on the content of the dual texts. As Chuck Klienhans suggests, "there are those who use parody as a means of control and domination. Some maintain their political, economic, and social positions by creating and sustaining parody in the discourses of journalism, advertising, propaganda, and political rhetoric" and, obviously, the same can be said of the theatre, or even drag, depending on the political agenda of a given playwright or performance." See Klienhans 197.

⁷ Baker observes that the highly "disciplined and antique art" of female impersonation "disappeared from the English stage in the late seventeenth century when actresses were finally accepted on the boards." See Baker 15.

⁸ For the sake of clarity in my discussion of embodiment, I use the term 'drag' to refer to gender and sex performances onstage that are parodic and 'impersonation' to refer to those that are not.

⁹ Originally from Venezuela, writer, drag king, director, theatre practitioner and film maker, Gricel Severino is known for her Latin male persona "Papi." See Flores.

¹⁰ Margaret Cruickshank observes that in North America the "AIDS crisis mobilized the gay and lesbian community by concentrating its focus on a single threat and by involving many people who had not been politically active before." See Cruickshank.

¹¹ Miriam Smith locates the origin of the real divide between many gays and lesbians in Canada throughout the 1970s and 1980s to a difference in liberation politics. Gay men typically mobilized around issues of sexual orientation and sexual freedom, whereas lesbian feminists, who often regarded lesbianism as a political choice and response to patriarchy, organized around issues pertaining to sexism and sexual exploitation, such as pornography (see Smith). In the early 1980s, gays and lesbians in Toronto still kept pretty much to their own bars, dances, and events. Of course there was some mixing. For instance, gays, lesbians and heterosexuals who were involved in the alternative punk music scene partied together in bars like the Voodoo Lounge and Katrinas, which were located on St Joseph Street.

¹² Based on my personal knowledge as an activist in Toronto's queer contexts in the 1990s, particularly Queer Nation Toronto, "radical fairy" was a term with which many anarchist fags, who were also involved in AIDS activism and anti-homophobia work, identified. Many of these men were also interested and involved in body manipulation and S/M, but they pursued these interests largely outside the S/M bar scene.

¹³ Fashion Cares is Toronto's largest annual fundraising event for AIDS.

[14] Where 'butch' and 'femme' identifications enjoyed a revival, as often as not they were coupled with S/M identifications of 'top' and 'bottom.' It is also worth mentioning that Joan Nestle, Leslie Feinberg and Pat Califia's works on lesbian butch/femme history and the politics of S/M were becoming popular and treated as required reading by many queer identified dykes at this time. See Nestle; Feinberg; Califia.

[15] This is something that has not changed in Toronto.

[16] Arguably, the welcoming of dykes like La Chica into men's S/M bars signaled something important, especially because Toronto dykes and gay men were primarily unwelcome in each other's bars throughout the 1980s and early 1990s. In the mid to late 1980s, dykes were often barred from entering many gay men's clubs. I was once denied access to a men's bar because the doorman claimed "women have to wear a skirt or dress," a dress code that excluded most lesbians of the day, but included "fag hags." Men in general were also denied access to women's bars, unless accompanied by a female escort, and even that was no guarantee.

[17] Woody's is still a popular gay men's bar on Church Street. Church Street is the main artery of the "Gay Ghetto" in Toronto.

[18] Romy Shiller cites June 1994 as dk's formal date of origin. However, the troupe's publicity material and press kit, as well as La Chica herself date the troupe's establishment in June 1995; Shiller, "Drag King Invasion" 26.

[19] Female-to-female drag refers to the instances in drag king performances where female performers adopt a highly campy female and feminine persona.

[20] A veteran drag king, Pearce's characterization of "Man Murray" continues to please audiences. So does "Dirk Diggler," a more contemporary persona developed by Pearce. It should also be noted that Erin McMurty, Tressa Tadashore, Beth Walden, and Marsha Rak joined dk as players later, for longer or shorter durations, and Diane Flacks made occasional guest appearances.

[21] Taken from an advertisement placed in *Now Magazine* by dk to promote their show *Drag King Invasion II: Festa Rex!*, which took place at the Opera House on November 24, 1995. See "Come."

[22] By 1999, La Chica was living in New York City. Here she would briefly remount the troupe, and many of its old characters, along with new ones she had developed. She invited a number of Toronto and New York dykes to join in on the fun. Out of Toronto, Lynne Crawford, Gumby Pelly, and Suzy Richter joined La Chica, along with Alicia Salzer, Leslie Miller, and Robin Bernstein from New York. The troupe would again garner some media attention for its New York performances in women's bars, such as, *Meow Mix* and *Crazy Nannies*. See Caloz.

[23] To reach potential audiences dk announced its mandate in their publicity posters, audition posters, newsletters, and press kits.

24 It is also worth mentioning that at least some of dk's members were familiar with queer theory, and the work of Judith Butler, where it is concerned with gender, drag and performance. For instance, Romy Shiller was a PhD candidate, whose research focused on drag, at the University of Toronto while a member of the troupe. See Shiller, "A Critical Exploration of Cross-Dressing and Drag," 1999; La Chica also confirms this (29 July).

25 This is not to say that drag queens do not use drag expressly to critique gender. Many queens do use male-to-female drag intentionally and strategically to critique gender norms, as is evident in the work of Toronto drag queens Sky Gilbert and David Bateman.

26 As much as dk wanted to resist gender oppression, they genuinely loved gender and playing with it in performance. This was as clear offstage as it was on in that most of the troupe's members identified openly as butch or femme, performing these identities in the world (La Chica, 29 July).

27 Over-emphasis on the difference that separates the king and queen is problematic if the question, as it is raised, produces a divisive hierarchy between drag performers, rather than an examination of what it is that makes a given performance subversive. Willox and Bradford's arguments ultimately end in such hierarchies. Willox ignores that the meaning of masculinity as "pregiven" is produced through an inter-constitutive and interdependent relation with the meaning of femininity: without femininity, masculinity, as we know it, would cease to be meaningful. To retain meaning in the complete absence of femininity, masculinity would need to be re-constituted in relation to meanings other than femininity, which would entirely alter its meaning, and, thus, expose it as a construction. While the current meaning of masculinity is pregiven and femininity is constituted as "derivative" in relation to this meaning, this meaning is nonetheless interdependent with that of femininity and, thus, it too is a derivative of femininity. The femininity of male to female drag, because it is inter-dependent with the meaning of masculinity, therefore, is always a potential avenue for the parodic critique of both the meaning of femininity and masculinity, just as it is in female to male drag.

In Bradford's argument, something else is going on: essentialism. To say that "maleness," or the biological sex of the drag queen as male, inherently renders the queen's performance less subversive is problematic and simplistic. What renders a queen's or, for that matter, a king's performance sexist is its content, its politics and the presence or lack of gender critique. The idea that biological sex precludes the production of gender parodies by males that are, or are read as, anti-sexist ignores that sexism is something that each of us has, can, and will reproduce at some time, in the company of some or many people, regardless of our sex, politics, or good intentions, simply because we are gendered. Whether we are masculine, feminine, androgyne, or transgender, gender exists, is produced, reiterated, identified with, and/or imposed upon us within a set of patriarchal power relations that currently dominate our culture. This means that, at present, there are no parodies of gender that are absolutely "outside" power relations built on sexism, there are only parodies in which the content is better or worse with respect to exposing the sexism of these relations. See Foucault 218.

[28] King Flare and King's Ransom performed at Toronto Pride 2006. King's Ransom also hosted a bi monthly drag king night, comprised of many participants, at Slack's Bar and Restaurant on Church Street in 2005/2006. Gricel Severino performed at Leslie Feinberg's book launch of *Drag King Dreams*, which was hosted by the Toronto Women's Bookstore, at the University of Toronto, on June 18, 2006.

Works Cited

Adam, Barry D. *The Rise of a Gay and Lesbian Movement.* Social Movements Past and Present. Rev. ed. New York: Twayne, 1995.

Arsenault, Nina. Personal Interview. Toronto, 2006.

Baker, Roger. Drag: A History of Female Impersonation in the Performing Arts. New York: New York UP, 1994.

bradford, k. "Grease Cowboy Fever; or, the Making of Johnny T." *The Drag King Anthology.* Ed. Donna Jean Troka, Kathleen LeBesco and Jean Bobby Noble. New York: Harrington Park, 2002. 15–30.

Best, Roberta. "Camping with the Drag Kings." *Icon: Canada's Gay and Lesbian Magazine* 1995: 14–15.

"Biography for Shelly Mars." 2006. *IMBD: Earth's Biggest Movie Database.* Internet Movie Database Inc. http://www.imdb.com/name/nm0550332/bio.

Bird, Kym. *Redressing the Past: The Politics of Early English-Canadian Women's Drama, 1880–1920.* Montreal: McGill-Queen's UP, 2004.

Butler, Judith. *Bodies That Matter: On the Discursive Limits of "Sex."* New York: Routledge, 1993.

———. *Gender Trouble: Feminism and the Subversion of Identity.* New York: Routledge, 1999.

———. *Undoing Gender.* New York: Routledge, 2004.

Califia, Pat. "From Jesse." *Coming to Power: Writings and Graphics on Lesbian S/M.* Ed. Samois. 3rd ed. Boston: Alyson, 1987. 156–82.

Caloz, Marie. "Long Live the King: Canuck Lesbos Avenge US War of Independence." *Xtra!: Toronto's Lesbian and Gay Biweekly* July 29 1999: 34.

Clipperton, Kelly. "Me My Boys and Their Toys." *Icon: Canada's Gay and Lesbian Magazine* 1995: 21–25.

"Come Join the Feast of Kings." Advertisement. *Now* 16–22 November 1995.

Crew, Robert. "Buddies in Bad Times Theatre". 2006. *The Canadian Encyclopedia*. Historica Foundation of Canada. http://www.thecanadianencyclopedia.com/index.cfm?PgNm=TCE&Params=A1ARTA0012089.

"Statement of Intent." *Crown and Sceptre: The Greater Toronto Drag King Society Newsletter*. 1995. 1.

Cruickshank, Margaret. *The Gay and Lesbian Liberation Movement*. London: Routledge, 1992.

Feinberg, Leslie. *Stone Butch Blues: A Novel*. Ithaca, NY: Firebrand, 1993.

Flores, Alex. "Gatuna Film and Video Collective". 2006. Website. *Gatuna Members and Artist Directory*. Ed. Alex Flores. http://alexarte.com/gatunaartistdirectory.htm.

Foucault, Michel. *Power/Knowledge: Selected Interviews and Other Writings, 1972–1977*. Brighton Eng: Harvester, 1980.

Gibson, Valerie. "Women Who Would Be King." *The Toronto Sun* 23 November 1995.

Giese, Rachel. "King for a Day." *This* 1995.

"Girls Will Be Boys." *The Toronto Sun* 28 November 1995.

Halberstam, Judith. *Female Masculinity*. Durham, NC: Duke UP, 1998.

Hart, Lynda. *Between the Body and the Flesh: Performing Sadomasochism*. New York: Columbia UP, 1998.

Hutcheon, Linda. *A Theory of Parody: The Teachings of Twentieth-Century Art Forms*. New York: Methuen, 1985.

Kenna, Kathleen. "Tonight in T.O." Advertisement. *The Toronto Star* 24 November 1995, sec. Entertainment.

Klienhans, Chuck. "Taking out the Trash: Camp and the Politics of Parody." *The Politics and Poetics of Camp*. Ed. Moe Meyer. New York: Routledge, 1994. 182–201.

La Chica, Joy. Personal interview. 29 July 2006.

———. Personal interview. 21 August 2006.

Nestle, Joan. *The Persistent Desire: A Femme-Butch Reader*. 1st ed. Boston: Alyson Publications, 1992.

Paquette, Daniel. "The Personal Memoir of a Size King." *Xtra!: Toronto's Lesbian and Gay Biweekly* 29 July 1999: 34.

Popoff, Maria. Personal interview. 8 August 2006.

Richter, Suzy. Personal Interview. 26 July 2006.

"The Royalty of Cross Dressing." *Maclean's* 27 November 1995: 12.

Shiller, Romi. "A Critical Exploration of Cross-Dressing and Drag in Gender Performance and Camp in Contemporary North American Drama and Film." Dissertation. University of Toronto, 1999.

———. "Drag King Invasion: Taking Back the Throne." *Canadian Theatre Review* 86 (Spring 1996): 24–28.

Smith, Miriam Catherine. *Lesbian and Gay Rights in Canada: Social Movements and Equality-Seeking, 1971–1995.* Toronto: U of Toronto P, 1999.

Sontag, Susan. *A Susan Sontag Reader.* New York: Farrar Straus Giroux, 1982.

Staff. "Dames in Drag." Arts Link. *The Globe and Mail* 24 November 1995, sec. The Arts.

Willox, Annabelle. "Whose Drag Is It Anyway? Drag Kings and the Monarchy in the UK." *The Drag King Anthology.* Ed. Donna Jean Troka, Kathleen LeBesco and Jean Bobby Noble. New York: Harrington Park, 2002. 263–84.

Making a Spectacle:
The "Danger" of Drag Performance
in Two Canadian Pride Parades

by Judith R. Anderson

> Parades create "passages from one law to another, from one system of rules to another, [which] are, properly speaking, 'outlaw' passages, and thus they betray an element of danger" (Marin 43).

In the Canadian film, "Better than Chocolate" (1999), the transgendered Judy gives a live performance in a gay club of a song entitled "I'm Not a Fucking Drag Queen." The distinction between a performance by a stereotypical drag queen, who only dresses up as a woman on stage, and a performance by a transgendered woman, who identifies as a woman even when offstage, is an important one to Judy, as well as to queer and performance theorists. The film's challenging of the significance of biologically-determined sex is made clear in a scene shortly after Judy's performance of this song: Judy is assaulted in the women's washroom of the club by a woman who rejects Judy's self-identification; Maggie and Kim, the film's two lead characters, come to her rescue and shame the antagonist.

I begin with this film's representation of Judy, and the violence that Judy's performance incites, because "Better than Chocolate" depicts the anxiety about gender identity that drag performances provoke. The anxiety that drag may re-inscribe gender stereotypes and reify heterosexist ideals has been echoed in some feminist critiques of drag. I will argue that, regardless of a performer's chosen or perceived gender identity, and regardless of the distinction (or lack thereof) between identity and performance, drag performance poses a challenge to what Butler describes as the "regulatory fiction of heterosexual coherence" (*Gender* 175). This is accomplished, however, not in the distinction between sex and gender in drag performance, as Judith Butler argues in *Gender Trouble*, but in the spectacle of such a performance.

Following a discussion of Butler's evolving theories about drag,[1] this paper will consider drag performances within the context of the spectacle of Pride parades in Toronto and Winnipeg. In "Better than Chocolate," Judy performs for a small audience in her local queer bar; however, across Canada, thousands of people have attended an annual Pride parade, and for those who have not, images of Pride parades are readily available. Photos of Winnipeg's 2005 Pride parade have been collected in an annual photo album published online by *Swerve*, Winnipeg's monthly queer news-magazine; brief film clips of Toronto's 2003 and 2004 Pride parades have been collected by Gary Innes, Canada Research Chair in Performance and Culture at York University, for his online project on street theatre. [2] Although the subject of this paper, narrowly defined, is drag performance in two Canadian Pride parades, I will go on to suggest that this discussion of the spectacle of drag performance has implications for queer performances beyond that of drag in Pride parades: when drag performance is broadly defined to include any spectacular gender performance, on the stage or in the street, the "danger" of drag, and its ability to subvert the heterosexual imperative in a variety of contexts, becomes evident.

In *Gender Trouble*, Butler positively describes drag as "effectively mock[ing] both the expressive model of gender and the notion of a true gender identity" by parodying "the notion of an original or primary gender identity" (174). [3] Butler's initial goal was to deconstruct the kind of essentialism that feminist critics of drag tend towards, countering contemporary feminist theorists' suspicions of drag: "Parodic identities have been understood to be either degrading to women, in the case of drag and cross-dressing, or an uncritical appropriation of sex-role stereotyping from within the practice of heterosexuality, especially in the case of butch/femme lesbian identities" (174–75). Marjorie Garber notes a similar suspicion of drag in feminist reactions to Dustin Hoffman's cross-dressing performance in the film "Tootsie" (1982). Garber explains that "the subtext [of the film], as argued by Elaine Showalter and others, is that men are better than women" at being women (6). Garber concludes: "What is striking to me about all of these readings of the film ["Tootsie"] is that they erase or look through the cross-dresser" (7) to the performer's biological sex.

Ironically, Butler's representation of drag in *Gender Trouble* could be similarly criticized; the compulsion to "look through" the performer is also evident in her work on drag. In order to argue that drag can serve to deconstruct gender essentialism, Butler relies on a model where the distinctness of sex, gender and performance from one another is key:

> If the anatomy of the performer is already *distinct* from the gender of the performer, and both of those are *distinct* from the gender of the performance, then the performance suggests a dissonance not only between sex and performance, but sex and gender, and gender and performance. As much as drag creates a unified picture of "woman" (what its critics often oppose), it also reveals the *distinctness* of those aspects of gendered experience which are falsely naturalized as a unity through the regulatory fiction of heterosexual coherence. (175, emphasis added)

Here, Butler unnecessarily concedes to critics of drag on two points in this passage: the first, that drag does create a unified picture of "woman"; the second, to borrow Garber's phrasing, that a reading of drag must "look through the cross-dresser" to identify the "distinctness" of sex, gender, and performance.

These concessions prove unnecessary when we consider examples from the 2005 Winnipeg Pride Parade, where we find three markedly different representations of "woman." One shows off slim and smooth legs beneath an elegant white dress, wearing a long wig topped with a tiara (*Swerve* 18); another is stocky, unshaven, and wears a comically colourful and frilly dress with frizzy wig and cat's eye glasses (19); a third wears short shorts with a matching see-through tank top, pink accessories, and feathers in her hair (16). Although recognizable as female stereotypes—the virgin in a white dress, the unattractive spinster, the whorish temptress—these performances are hyper-realist and therefore trade on their own artificiality with no easily-recognizable referent. [4] What this small sampling of performances illustrates is that any proclamation about a unified picture of "woman" is confounded by the multiple possible representations of "woman" in drag performances at an event such as Pride, which range from the glamourous, at one extreme, to the comical, at another, with any number of variations in between.

Although Butler argues that drag "fully subverts the distinction between inner and outer psychic space" (*Gender* 174), deconstructing the false unity and trans-parency of sex and gender, she finds it necessary to "avow the distinctness" of sex, gender, and performance in order to argue against the false unity of these categories. This reliance on the distinctness of the categories in drag performance requires that the sex of the performer be noticeably different from the gender of the performer and the performer's performance. Butler appears to be working with a very narrow definition of drag, one in which a member of one sex dons the outfit and accessories of the other sex. [5] The limitations of this definition are evident when considered in light of performances where the biological sex of the performer cannot easily be discerned. For instance, at the 2004 Pride Parade in Toronto, "fashionably attired drag queens lead the way for a transsexual fairy princess whose stitch-marked breasts reveal her surgically-altered anatomy" ("Queens"). Betrayed in the description of this film clip is the very unknowability of sex and gender in this performance. It may be accu-rate to describe the topless woman in high heels and feathers with stitch-marked breasts as a transsexual; it is, however, presumptuous to identify the fully-dressed women accompanying her as drag queens rather than transsexuals or biological women. The description of the video clip, like the fact of Judy's song in "Better than Chocolate," makes evident that the only way in which biological sex and gender iden-tities can be established with certainty is through the performers' overt declarations, something which Butler's discussion of drag does not fully take into account.

Of course, Butler's primary concern is to discuss gender, not drag, and when she moves to limit the significance of drag in *Bodies that Matter*, it has much to do with this fact. She explains in *Bodies that Matter* that "by citing drag as an example of performativity" in *Gender Trouble*, she made a move that was taken to mean that drag is "*exemplary* of performativity. [However,] if drag is performative, that does not mean that all performativity is to be understood as drag" (230–31). [6] Nevertheless, drag performances do have effects that have been obscured by the recent emphasis on performativity in queer and gender theory. As Laurence Selenick puts it, "perfor-mativity occlude[s] performance," and obscures the fact that "the performing arts provide the most direct, most graphic, often most compelling representations of gender; however, their form and function are often at odds with the concerns of everyday life or even with the common sanctions of society" (6). Drag, which Selenick considers to be an important aspect of the performing arts, does require performers to "put on" their gender; it is not a daily occurrence but an event. And so, if Butler's ideological work is concerned with "everyday life," and is such that there is no room to discuss the exception(ality) of drag, what are some other ways in which we can understand the ideological work drag performance does? The rest of this paper will consider how performances of drag work, outside of the terms Butler has set out, through the spectacle of Pride events.

***

Perhaps the most stereotypical image at any Pride parade is that of a performer sitting atop a float, with nothing to do but wave and be looked at. On one float in the 2005 Winnipeg Pride Parade, two drag performers, similarly decked out in black dresses and holding bouquets of flowers, share a large throne and the spotlight (*Swerve* 18). On another float, belonging to the Snowy Owl Monarchist Society of Winnipeg, two pairs of performers in wedding dresses and tuxedos pose for photographs (*Swerve* 3). [7] In Toronto's parade, another performer, in sequins, and wearing a crown atop a curly blond wig, sits in the back of a convertible with the top down, and gives a royal wave to the crowd ("Pride Queen"). These three examples represent the drag per-formers as royalty or superstars, personages worth stopping in the street to look at. Cross-dressing "invokes aspects of divinity, power, class, glamour, stardom, concepts of beauty and spectacle, the visible contrasted with the unseen or concealed" in addition to concerns about "gendered personal identity" (Selenick 10). Further, their evocation of royalty—the "royal wave" given from a convertible, the throne, and the float carrying members of the local chapter of the Imperial Court System—is an indication of the self-referentiality of drag conventions. [8]

These performers are not concerned with looking like, in a mimetic way, any actual member of the royal family; they are important and spectacular enough to be looked at simply because of the conventions of the parade. Louis Marin's *On Representation* provides a "semiotic note" about the demonstration, cortege, parade, and procession. While these terms all have different specific but overlapping meanings and significations, the term "parade" "intersects with [...] the military domain and the often neighboring domain of aristocratic festivals [and...] the term 'review' [suggests the...] 'inspection of troops lined up to be examined and set to marching'" (39). Perhaps it is the very nature of the parade itself, its blending of authority with its invitation to look or review, that constructs the stereotypical drag "royalty" as an apparently permanent fixture of Pride parades. The "royal wave" offered to spectators simultaneously constructs and is constructed by drag convention at the Pride parade. In much the same way that sex and gender and performance cannot be established as distinct from one another in drag performance, the drag performance (however static or cliché) cannot be separated from the event.

Marin reasons that "a general structure of theatricality or spectacularity seems to link the participants in a parade, cortege or procession" (40). The general structure of the event is also its *raison d'être*; drag performers sit in thrones or convertibles, looking fabulous, waiting to be looked at. The parade creates an audience who participates in the creation of the spectacle. "In the parade, even if it includes an important 'spectacular' component, the spectator is always more or less implicated as an actor [...] whose role and function is precisely to watch the parade go by" (Marin 51). One such spectator can be observed in another video clip of the Toronto Pride parade; he demonstrates his actor status by "us[ing] a balloon as a phallic symbol in emulation of the parade he witnesses, while also attempting to photograph elements of the parade ("Crowd Member"). According to Hal Foster, the spectacle (and the commodity) "fascinate us because they exclude us, place us in the passive position of the dreamer, spectator, *consumer*" (82). In the above film clip, the crowd member is indeed put into the position of spectator and consumer; however, in this case he is not necessarily passive. A crowd member can be interpellated as spectator by the parade, conscripted to be an actor in the spectacle of the parade; by being an actor, however, he is not doing nothing, as his balloon-phallus makes evident. Individual crowd members interact with the parade in different ways, but "the crowd" is, at the least, enabling the spectacle, defining the event as spectacle by the very fact of its gaze.

If, as I have suggested, the drag performance within the parade is entirely self-referential, and if the parade and its spectators are mutually creating the spectacle in which they participate, it would be reasonable to ask how, and in what way, drag can be understood to be doing any subversive work at all. I would like to suggest that the significance of the spectacle of drag performance in Pride parades is its refusal of realist representation and the "everyday" gender about which Butler and others are concerned. Within the spectacle of the parade, the audience and performers effectively break what Tania Modleski calls, in another context, "the vicious cycle whereby the performative and mimetic aspects of texts mutually reinforce each other, representation producing reality and reality affirming representation" (51). Within the spectacle of the parade, gender representation in drag represents only representation.

Foster, reading Guy Debord, provides a useful explanation for how spectacle is able to achieve this effect: "the spectacle works as a simulated reality, a total illusion, a set of effects that consumes the primary event" (80). Foster adds:

> spectacle operates via our fascination with the hyperreal, with 'perfect' images that make us 'whole' at the price of delusion, of submission. [...] This is why for Debord and others spectacle represents the very nadir of capitalist reification: with 'capital accumulated to such a degree that it becomes an image' (Debord), social process becomes utterly opaque and ideological domination assured. (83)

The parallels here are noteworthy. As argued above, Pride parades consist of hyperreal drag performances, where the biological sex of the performers is often undiscernable and therefore beside the point. The parade does, also, invite a kind of submission on the part of the spectator who is invited to watch and wave, further contributing to the spectacle of the event. The social process by which drag performers are selected to appear in the parade could perhaps be described as "opaque," as with the various organizations that enter floats into the parade. The Pride parade itself, finally, could therefore be seen to assure a kind of "ideological domination" for the duration of the festivities. For all of these reasons, as Foster (and Debord) suggest in the above passage, the spectacle in everyday life is problematic.

Notably, the basis of Foster's suspicion of spectacle is its infidelity to a "real." Foster argues that "the simulated world of commodities and spectacles all but defies representation, for representation is based on a principle of equivalence between signs and the real, whereas in simulation signs precede, posit the real" (90). But what does a privileging of the real achieve? How can it be determined, with respect to the representation of gender, without returning to the biological essentialism that feminist and queer theorists have been working to deconstruct? The subversion enacted by the spectacle of drag performances in Pride parades once a year does not lie in its subversion of male and female stereotypes, but in its disavowal of realist representation.

Consider, for example, the drag performers in Toronto who, by virtue of their excessively large breasts, large and rainbow-coloured wigs, strange costumes and colourful accessories, are so far from representing any "everyday" reality that to read them as "citing" or "queering" a heterosexist notion of "woman" seems excessive in itself ("Drag Show"). [9] Where water-balloon sized breasts might be read as an over-signification of the performance's representation of "woman," the masculine voice inviting the crowd to "make some noise" undercuts this illusion. By way of contrast, an androgynous Winnipeg performer in a simple black tank top and blue jeans, blowing bubbles into the crowd from a float, is not "citing" any gender, and yet is garnering similar attention from the audience (Swerve 18). Unlike the performers in "Drag Queen Horseplay" who "put on" the hyper-real, this performer's appearance is decidedly understated and unspectacular in and of itself. [10] The spectacle of the event itself, here reinforced by a very large inflatable green stick figure that waves its arms in the air and dwarfs the performer, is more significant than the degree to which any single performance does, or does not, subvert gender norms. Both performances circumvent the "fiction of heterosexual coherence," not by avowing the distinction of sex and gender, but by resisting any reference to the "reality" of gender altogether. It is the hyper-real of the spectacle that enables this, in the performances that obviously cite a heterosexual imperative as well as those that do not.

Drag performance, by announcing itself as such, by being spectacle, does the subversive work that Butler describes in Gender Trouble, without it being necessary for the audience to look through the performer, or beyond the performance of gender. The hyper-realism of the performances makes biological "reality" irrelevant. In fact, within the spectacle of the Pride parade, gender becomes so irrelevant that sometimes people dress up as objects. It is not uncommon, for example, to find people dressed in fruit costumes at Toronto's Pride, where the term "fruit" is reclaimed by a banana and a kiwi who walk together in the parade.

Unlike a world such as that which Butler theorizes, where the fiction of hetero-sexual coherence is performed repeatedly and inescapably, the spectacle of the Pride parade subverts the notion that gender is always already everywhere in play and inescapable. As quoted earlier, Marin points out that parades create "passages from one law to another, from one system of rules to another, [which] are, properly speaking, 'outlaw' passages, and thus they betray an element of danger" (43). The "danger" of the Pride parade is that, by way of spectacle, it escapes the hetero-sexual imperative that is otherwise always at work, subverting the notion of its inescapability. The parade functions in ways not unlike the Bakhtinian carnivalesque, where a temporary suspension of society's rules can, even after things have returned to normal, have a lingering effect on the world order. An understanding of drag as spectacle enables theorists to talk about the important possibility of escaping (if only momentarily) heterosexual imperatives.

Debord argues that "the spectacle erases the dividing line between self and world [...]; it likewise erases the dividing line between true and false, repressing all directly lived truth beneath the *real presence* of the falsehood maintained by the organization of appearances" (153). His reading of spectacle, like Butler's reading of drag, can be recontextualized. Where Debord characterizes the spectacle as the result of a fall from some ideal, I would like to argue for the spectacle as an escape from ideals which theorists such as Butler have identified as heterosexist and problematic. And where drag is predicated on a narrowly-defined "distinctness" which limits our reading of its subversive potential, I would like, by way of this "spectacular" context, to make room for the subversive potential of all types of spectacular performance, including Judy's in "Better than Chocolate," however exceptional to "everyday" gender performance. Drag performance may not always subvert gender norms, as Butler rightly points out; but, by way of spectacle, drag performance, on the stage or in the street, can represent a subversion of the "real" upon which these heterosexist gender norms are based.

(2007)

Notes

[1] For the purposes of this paper, and its interest in the spectacle of gender per-formance, I will focus primarily on Butler's *Gender Trouble* (1990) and *Bodies that Matter* (1993); while Butler clearly has had more to say on the subject of drag, her move towards broader issues of resignification and public discourse, for instance (see *Excitable Speech* [1997]), is beyond the scope of this discussion.

² All images from Winnipeg Pride 2005 can be found online in *Swerve* magazine's annual Pride photo album, at http://www.swervemedia.org/issues/swerve-2005-07.pdf; film stills and clips of the Toronto Pride Parades of 2003 and 2004 can be viewed online at http://moderndrama.ca/crc/media/streettheatre.php.

³ Here Butler argues that drag serves to represent one way in which gender can be both performative and subversive; however, she later moderates her enthusiasm for drag in *Bodies that Matter*, published three years later in 1993. There she writes: "I want to underscore that there is no necessary relation between drag and subversion [...]. At best, it seems, drag is a site of a certain ambivalence, one which reflects the more general situation of being implicated in the regimes of power by which one is constituted and, hence, of being implicated in the very regimes of power that one opposes" (125). See below for further discussion of this.

⁴ Even the biological sex of these performers is not always clear. One is almost certainly biologically male, another likely biologically female, but the third performer's biological sex is uncertain. The significance of this uncertainty will be elaborated upon below.

⁵ Not only is Butler's discussion of drag predicated upon this distinction, it is described as contributing to drag's entertainment value: "Indeed, part of the pleasure, the giddiness of the performance is in the recognition of a radical contingency in the relation between sex and gender in the face of cultural configuration of causal unities that are regularly assumed to be natural and necessary. In the place of the law of heterosexual coherence, we see sex and gender denaturalized by means of a performance which *avows their distinctness* and dramatizes the cultural mechanism of their fabricated unity" (*Gender* 175, emphasis added).

⁶ Indeed, one of the major ideological imperatives of *Bodies that Matter* is a revision of, and elaboration on, what "performative" means. Butler explains that she does not mean that "one woke in the morning, perused the closet or some more open space for the gender of choice, donned that gender for the day, and then restored the garment to its place at night" (x). Instead, "performativity must be understood [...] as the reiterative and citational practice by which discourse produces the effects that it names" (2).

⁷ The Snowy Owl Monarchist Society (SOMS) is the Winnipeg chapter of the Imperial Court System (ICS). See note 8 below for an explanation of the ICS and "drag royalty."

⁸ The Imperial Court System (ICS) is an international organization founded by in the 1960s in San Francisco by Jose Sarria (aka Her Most Imperial Majesty Empress Jose I, the Widow Norton). The ICS has chapters or "houses" across North America and regulates the election (and number) of title-holders such as Emperor, Duchess, Baron, and so on. The organization's mandate includes fundraising for local causes at its drag shows, and despite its monarchist model, it is run as a democracy where members elect performers to the local branch of the "royal family." "Drag royalty" is a fixture at Pride parades; however, their positions are not determined by the

spectators in the crowd, but by the organizations to which they belong. For a biography of Jose Sarria and the history of the ICS, see *The Empress is a Man* by Michael Gorman.

⁹ Butler writes: "at its best, [...] drag can be read for the way in which hyperbolic norms are dissimulated as the heterosexual mundane. At the same time these same norms, taken not as commands to be obeyed, but as imperatives to be "cited," twisted, queered, brought into relief as heterosexual imperatives, are not, for that reason, necessarily subverted in the process" (*Bodies* 237).

¹⁰ For a discussion of androgyny in drag performance see Judith Halberstam's *Female Masculinity*, especially "Drag Kings: Masculinity and Performance" (Chapter 7).

Works Cited

"Better than Chocolate." Dir. Anne Wheeler. Prod. Sharon McGowan. TVA Films, 1999.

Butler, Judith. *Bodies that Matter: On the Discursive Limits of "Sex."* New York: Routledge, 1993.

———. *Excitable Speech: A Politics of the Performative.* New York: Routledge, 1997.

———. *Gender Trouble: Feminism and the Subversion of Identity.* New York: Routledge, 1990.

"Crowd Member." http://moderndrama.ca/crc/media/interaction.php.

Debord, Guy. *Society of the Spectacle.* Trans. Donald Nicholson-Smith. New York: Zone, 1995.

"Drag Show Horseplay." http://moderndrama.ca/crc/media/interaction.php.

Foster, Hal. *Recodings: Art, Spectacle, Cultural Politics.* Port Townsend, Wash.: Bay, 1985.

"'Fruit' Costumes." http://moderndrama.ca/crc/media/costume.php.

Gorman, Michael Robert. *The Empress Is a Man: Stories from the Life of Jose Sarria.* Binghampton, N.Y.: Haworth, 1998.

Halberstam, Judith. *Female Masculinity.* Durham: Duke UP, 1998.

Innes, Gary, ed. "Street Theatre." *Canada Research Chair in Performance and Culture Website.* http://moderndrama.ca/crc/media/streettheatre.php.

Garber, Marjorie. *Vested Interests: Cross Dressing and Cultural Anxiety.* New York: Routledge, 1992.

Marin, Louis. *On Representation.* Stanford: Stanford UP, 2001.

Modleski, Tania. "Femininity as Mas(s)querade." *Feminism without Women: Culture and Criticism in a "Postfeminist" Age.* New York: Routledge, 1991. 23–58.

"Pride Queen." http://moderndrama.ca/crc/media/satire.php.

"Queens on Parade." http://moderndrama.ca/crc/media/icons.php.

Senelick, Laurence. *The Changing Room: Sex, Drag and Theatre.* New York: Routledge, 2000.

Swerve. http://www.swervemedia.org/issues/swerve-2005-07.pdf.

Wood, Richard F. J. ed. "Swerve's Annual Photo Album for 'I Do ... Pride.'" *Swerve.* July/August 2005. http://www.swervemedia.org/issues/swerve-2005-07.pdf.

Passionate Performances: Pol Pelletier and Experimental Feminist Theatre Beyond Barriers of Language (1975–1985) [1]

by Louise H. Forsyth

Heady, Bawdy Times

Didn't you invite Pol to perform *Night Cows* in Toronto in 1979 or 1980? Didn't she do it at the old Music Gallery? Was it part of a Fireweed Festival? I can't remember exact dates, but I remember they all – Jovette, Pol and someone else – stayed at my place on Queen Street and we stayed up all night talking on the stairs, smoking and drinking plonk. I was smitten. [...] I remember you coming back with the idea of doing a FemCab here at a W[omen's] C[ultural] B[uilding] meeting, and how fucking fabulous it was, changing non-feminist artists into feminists overnight!

—Lynne Fernie [2]

We have to rechart the universe, adjust the sights and focus of our telescopes, and redraw our maps in order to have women's content enter into the fabric of culture.

—Rina Fraticelli (17) [3]

The years between 1965 and 1985 were heady everywhere in Canada for feminist, lesbian and queer activists, for experimental theatre practitioners, for artists in every medium, and, more generally, for those who were passionately committed to real social and cultural change. The drives—psychic, erotic and intellectual—of those who created or got caught up in this ferment were so powerful that linguistic and cultural barriers between francophones and anglophones easily crumbled, thanks to individuals' fresh commitments to their own cultures and identities, to new enthusiasms for bilingualism in anglophone Canada, and to personal initiatives and public programs supporting translation of original theatrical and literary works. People quite literally fell in love with plays, performances, songs, novels, poems, art, films and even comics from places they had not known before. They thrilled to the fresh artistic beauty and felt it resonate in their own lives. They revelled in sharing with new friends and colleagues their love affair with innovative creative forms.

This essay is about trilingual theatre artist Pol Pelletier, whose practice and theories since the 1970s have been remarkably exemplary of this socio-cultural phenomenon. [4] Born in Ottawa, Pelletier began her professional career in the theatre in the early 1970s working in French and in English in major theatres, film and other media in Ontario and Québec. From 1975 on, Pelletier turned her back on mainstream theatre. A unique vision, a flow of spiritual energy, and a powerful anger came to animate every aspect of her work. This vision, energy and anger, which underlie the new theatrical languages, stories, images, forms, and myths she developed, are all rooted in her conviction that the sexed body is every actor's primary instrument. For her, actors' bodies need to be freed from learned behaviour and empowered through physical conditioning so that they discover for themselves the intimate qualities of their relations with things, sounds, other people, and surrounding material space. In particular, actors need to work to rid themselves of internalised constraints that distort or conceal the reality of their own experiences and that cause them to self-censor. For Pelletier all barriers, including the buzz of daily routines, serving to separate creative imagination from sensual and sexual desires must be torn down in order to release suppressed physical and psychic powers. Pelletier created original shows and founded *avant-garde* companies with other experimental theatre artists. By 1985 she was widely recognised for her amazing abilities as an actor, director, writer and teacher, as well as for her compelling presence as a bold and innovative leader in radical feminist theatre practices.

In this essay I provide an introduction to Pelletier during the decade 1975–1985, with particular attention to those aspects of her work which led to encounters and collaborative initiatives with anglophone theatre women. I suggest that feminist social and cultural activists in those heady, bawdy days were convinced that art and its many languages could change the world. They were not about to let linguistic and political barriers, based on patriarchal ideologies that had divided the country into solitudes, stand in the way of their joining together in the richly imaginative exploration on society's stages of what it means to be women.

Hélène Beauchamp has captured the spirit of these transformative times in her description of a defiant Pol Pelletier in an effervescent Montréal at the moment when she first positioned herself as a radical feminist and experimental theatre artist:

> 1975: Montréal. The ebullient years. The fervent years. The creative atmosphere. The streets are alive with cafés, theatres, cinemas, restaurants, people. Art in a fabulous social context. City living at its best. Research and experiment, workshops, texts, questions, debates. Life and its intricacies. Fervour. Love and passion and more questions. [...] Pol Pelletier reborn. Born a woman. (59)

The revolutionary transformation of cultural, linguistic and sexual dynamics had occurred almost overnight in Québec. By the end of the 1960s, this society which had long institutionalised inexorable limitations on the rights of girls and women and exercised harsh control of female sexuality had become the first province in Canada where a handbook on contraception was widely distributed and Morgentaler's first free-standing abortion clinic was opened. Whatever their profession—artists, teachers, militants, social activists, academics, caregivers—women were noisily engaged in creative research applying the tools of their own trade to understanding and representing their very real existence. New feminist associations were formed to demand the recognition of women's rights. Women founded theatres and theatre companies. Increasingly, they created their own shows. Innovative and gifted women writers, musicians, filmmakers, and performers were appearing everywhere. Feminist reports, manifestos, events, movements, publications, periodicals, associations proliferated. Collaborative associations between francophones and anglophones came into being, and publicly funded bilingual bodies nurtured collaboration and communication.

Although Anne Hébert, Marie-Claire Blais and Françoise Loranger also began to write for theatre in the 1960s, writer, singer and founder of Québec's first feminist publishing house Les Éditions de la Pleine Lune, Marie Savard, wrote what I consider the first queer feminist play in Québec: *Bien à moi*, a one-woman show.[5] Dyne Mousso created the role for radio (Radio-Canada) in 1969 and played it on stage at Le Théâtre de Quat'Sous in 1970. This first production of *Bien à moi* occurred on the same program as the first production of Michel Tremblay's *La Duchesse de Langeais*, both plays directed by André Brassard.[6] In *Bien à moi*, the middle-aged, beer-quaffing Marquise/Marie writes and reads aloud love letters to herself as she poetically and hilariously debunks the myths and stereotypes of romantic love and marriage. She extends the affection for herself that she expresses in her love letters to masturbating on stage to the point of orgasm, an action whereby she flaunts her woman's sexed body, gets in touch with herself, regrets her past infidelity to herself, and affirms her intense love for herself.

The Originality of Pol Pelletier's Theatrical Aesthetic

When people come to the theatre
*They should leave with their lives **transformed.***
CHANGE THE WORLD.
Yes, that's my claim.

—Pol Pelletier, *Joy* 52

Susan Bennett has recently recognised the early importance of Québec's feminist theatre for English Canada in speaking of "the innovative and overtly feminist performances that have characterized Québec women's work." Bennett states that "[c]ertainly this has had an important influence on women working in English Canada as well as feminist critical writing." Since Québec is "a location at the forefront of new performance directions in feminist theatre, with a commonality based on a commitment to feminist theory [it] is important [...] to remember the significance of Marie Savard, Pol Pelletier, Nicole Brossard and other Québec women in the landscape of feminist theatre in Canada" (x).

Spurning realism in theatre, Pelletier's experimental work has been a search for a new aesthetic, an aesthetic that would change the world. Rather than simply doing theatre, her practice has been to critically reflect upon the doing of theatre and to dramatise this reflective process. For her, doing theatre while respecting established theatrical conventions and following the norms of realistic representation inevitably perpetuates society's problematic norms, fictions, illusions and delusions. On the other hand, showing the doing of theatre using fresh theatrical forms and languages highlights the creative and performative process and encourages actors and viewers to reflect critically upon why artistic decisions are made. Pelletier's ideas for changing the world have involved an all-absorbing pursuit of transformative beauty for those making theatre and those watching it. Her experimental work in theatre has consistently been the performance of applied research in a broad exploration of the under-exploited potentialities of the body and the spirit. When energised by consciousness that has rid itself of the noise of habit, routine, and learned discourse, bodies and minds are able to let go and produce transformations in ways of seeing, saying, moving and being. Never losing awareness of the physical locatedness of viewers, Pelletier has performatively challenged actors and others doing theatre to explore with audiences that which remains unknown in experiental evidence and so, through new theatrical myths and ritual, to discover new ways of knowing and being.

Pelletier wrote and produced through several versions over the first half of the 1990s an autobiographical and theoretical play, *Joie*. It is the first play of a trilogy, in which she took a retrospective look at her commitment to do theatre that would produce radical social and cultural change. She stated on the back cover of the published script of *Joie* that her acting method has been "*fondée sur l'urgence, la découverte, la jubilation.*"

Le Théâtre Expérimental de Montréal

By 1975 Pelletier was ready to embark on the path that would make her what she soon became: a highly respected—and controversial—actor, director, playwright, theorist, teacher, dramaturg, administrator, founder of training schools and experimental theatre companies. She co-founded in 1975 the Théâtre Expérimental de Montréal (TEM) with Robert Gravel and Jean-Pierre Ronfard. The TEM was a company committed to doing only original collective creations. Pelletier's first initiative at the TEM was to launch a season-long intensive workshop exploring through physical exercise and improvisation alternative acting strategies and roles for women. She wanted to try out with others fresh ways in which women—rid of the trappings of femininity and freed of conventional models for gesture, movement and voice—respond theatrically to experiences such as madness, fear and violence.

Pelletier went on during her more than four years at the TEM to organise additional workshops and collaborate on several bold experimental productions, some with women and men and some with women only. All these collective creations made strikingly, often disturbingly, visual use of stage design and body movement. When Pelletier and other women in the company put on *Spectacle de femmes: Essai en trois mouvements pour trois voix de femmes* (1976, unpublished) and *Finalement* (1977, unpublished), they chose to perform without dialogue in order to bring out their stories using only physical languages. The characters played with vocal sounds and movements involving the whole body, but used no words. Throughout the shows, they wrestled vigorously with forms in geometrical shapes and copious quantities of fabric. Anglophones who attended these experimental shows at the TEM have told me that understanding dialogue in these plays was, of course, not a problem and that their memory of them is of their compelling visual and kinetic qualities.

During her four years as co-director at the TEM, Pelletier took advantage of the improvisational and creative opportunities that reveal themselves when directors and actors turn their backs on single-authored plays in favour of collective creation. She acquired the skills needed to run a young and experimental theatre on a shoestring. Her character has said in *Joie* that this period offered the "heroic" opportunity to acquire the experience and knowledge needed to work in every corner of a theatre where the entire program was original: play development, acting, stage management, set construction, building management, funding, human resource management, administration, publicity, etc. I stress here the importance of acquiring this knowledge and these practical skills at this early stage in Pelletier's career, because she has consistently shown her awareness that creating original theatre is arduous and complex. For many people who were beginning in the 1970s to do experimental, feminist or queer theatre, including Pelletier, the simple fact of speaking out in order to tell one's own story was already an heroic, even monstrous feat. Although necessary, however, this was not a sufficient step. Theatre does not get made just because one speaks one's truths. Pelletier knew from the outset that such truths must be transformed aesthetically, must be *represented* and *mediated* using the languages and spaces of theatre. Such representation and mediation demand practical knowledge and access to technological languages that call upon fields of myths and symbols to make individual experiences collectively significant. Dramatic mediation using the tools of theatre also demands skill, research and experimentation in production and performance. Women have not usually been encouraged to acquire such skill and knowledge, nor to have access to technologies and symbolic spaces. They have most often been assigned their place in shows run by men. Pelletier carried with her this practical knowledge about doing theatre when she co-founded the Théâtre Expérimental des Femmes (TEF), and she showed by example and through teaching to many other women doing theatre, both anglophone and francophone, the importance of having one's eyes and one's hands on the entire operation of theatre. This has been one of her most significant contributions to experimental feminist theatre in Canada.

Other Stages, 1975–1978

In 1975, in addition to co-founding the TEM, Pelletier was working collaboratively with other women who were concerned, as she was, about the distorted representation of women in theatre and the limited artistic and professional opportunities available to them. One of these cultural activists was actor and director Luce Guilbeault, who had co-created the Grand Cirque Ordinaire production of *Un prince, mon jour viendra* in 1973, co-produced with Nicole Brossard in 1976 the NFB feature-length documentary "Some American Feminists," and later played the amazing role of Violette Leduc at the TEF. Guilbeault, working for a year in a process of collective creation with Nicole Brossard and several other feminist writers and actors, directed and produced *La Nef des sorcières* for International Women's Day 1976 at the Théâtre du Nouveau Monde. This radically feminist show at Montréal's primary established theatre was a major cultural and theatrical event. The actors and writers have said that participating in it changed their lives and the course of their careers in theatre.[7]

La Nef is made up of seven monologues (an actress, a menopausal woman, a garment worker, a woman who has lived only to party for the pleasure of men, a lesbian, a writer), each performed by a woman who casts off the trappings of stereo-typed femininity and so reveals to herself and the audience the realities of her body, her feelings, her desires, and her exploited social condition. The Mad Actress, written and performed by Guilbeault, launches the play's subversive project by casting off on stage the wig and costume of the virginally innocent Agnès in Molière's *L'École des femmes*, forgetting her lines and stepping right out of her role, creating the impression that she is urinating right before the eyes of the audience, and revealing that she masturbates, has been sexually active, and has already had an abortion. Such *monstrance* of the female body was quickly condemned in several quarters as both monstrous and untheatrical. The play was, nevertheless, extremely popular with audiences of women.

In *La Nef* Pelletier played the monologues of the lesbian, Marcelle, a character with two visages. In the first monologue, written by Marie-Claire Blais, a tormented and controlling Marcelle has interiorised society's taboos regarding her lesbianism. She suffers from the self-loathing that has made her unable to give love, from the loneliness for which she herself is responsible, from guilt, and from the cruel will-to-power she has developed as a mechanism to protect herself from her own self-doubts and vulnerability. Pelletier played Blais's monologue, but did not wish to leave the character with the negative stereotypes of powerlessness and solitude it conveyed. She decided to write her own dramatic piece, "Marcelle II." She shaved her head and, at the beginning of "Marcelle II," ripped off the feminine wig she had been wearing as Marcelle I, as well as the tablecloth she had set for her lover who failed to show for dinner. In her first words, Marcelle II proclaims, without nuance, her hatred for women, that is hatred for all the women who have been part of her life and who have bought into the heterosexist matrix and patriarchy's devastating representations of women:

> Hate, yes, hate. /I loathe you all. /I refuse, I spit. /Hate, yes, hate for women. /I see my mother and I want to vomit. /You and your long line of humble servants. /You humiliate me, you are deeply humiliating. /You have betrayed me, you have lied to me, /You have made me ashamed, very deeply horribly ashamed. /You have robbed me, do you hear? /You have robbed me of my own sex. And you sold it. To men. (Guilbeault, *Clash* 31)

Pelletier returns in other plays to expressions of hatred for the patriarchal mother and to the link between the mother's hated behaviour and the daughter's loss of her own sex and sexuality. The daughter is powerless to know her own *jouissance* so long as the mother remains a prisoner of the desires of others. The powerful suggestion is that daughters can claim and control their own sexuality only when mothers cease to place themselves and their daughters in the service of men. An extension she makes elsewhere of this urgent need to spit out patriarchal mothers occurs at dazzling moments in her work when mothers and daughters join together to savour in cosmic ecstasy their unbridled sensuality, for example in Jovette Marchessault's *Night Cows*.

Shortly after Marcelle II's defiant outburst at the beginning of her monologue, she makes a symbolic break with the patriarchal mother. She passes to a poetic celebration of the joy of discovering lesbian love and sensuality:

> And then one day a woman put her head on my shoulder. /I feel her cheekbone on my shoulder. /Her hand glides gently over my right breast, /slips inside my shirt. /Her hand on my left breast. [...] What's happening? /I am amazed, overwhelmed [...] My body is delighted, my body is enchanted [...] This is in no way an act of possession. [...] Oh! This long smooth place where bodies can stretch out /under cover! Rustling, hidden, soft and warm. /I remember so well. We were the same length. /A perfect match. /A feeling of complicity and recognition. [...] The unique sensation of feeling /her woman's breasts against my own breasts. /Her woman's body lying on her side, and me facing her, /lying on my side, /the sensation of a woman's skin touching mine, my legs, /oh god! legs, lovely long satin things, /entwined, interlocked, hands on breasts [...]. (Guilbeault , *Clash* 31–32)

Jane Moss has said that "Pol Pelletier [is here] proclaiming her sexual difference. Her poetic description of lesbian lovemaking and masturbation exalt female desire [...]. For Pol Pelletier, lesbianism is an aggressive stance, a slap in the face of male society, and a conscious choice which satisfies, valorizes and liberates her" (22). While I agree with Moss's interpretation insofar as *La Nef* is concerned, I believe that it would be a mistake to generalise from this interpretation in any way that would lead one to classify Pelletier as a lesbian playwright. To do so would be to distort and over-simplify the complex and nuanced approach she has brought to the exploration of gender roles and of women's sensuality and sexuality. Pelletier's dramatic *oeuvre* includes lesbians. It also includes bisexuals, heterosexuals, women of indeterminate sexual orientation, women and girls for whom erotically charged sensuality takes the place of explicit love-making, and gay men. These characters are both glorious and monstrous—bigger than life—frequently taking on mythic proportions in their bold explorations of what women's bodies are capable of and their search for appropriate symbols. They offer some of the undoubtedly infinite number of ways in which women could express and enjoy their sexuality, if only the tenacious and ubiquitous myth of romantic love could be destroyed. Because of this richness of representation of sexuality, sensuality, and sensibility, I describe Pelletier's theatrical and dramaturgical practice as a wide-ranging process of queering the received norms of gendered and sexualised behaviour.

Molly Thom of Toronto's Alumnae Theatre was interested in experimental theatre and focussing on women's plays. Wishing to produce *La Nef* in English, she invited Linda Gaboriau to come to Toronto to work with her on a translation. *A Clash of Symbols* was Gaboriau's first translation and the first translation into English of a feminist Québec play. [8] Directed by Thom, the Alumnae Theatre's performance of *A Clash of Symbols* opened on January 9, 1979 at the mainstage. Pol Pelletier and Nicole Brossard travelled to Toronto for the opening. The sell-out first run, staged in the studio of the Firehall used for experimental purposes, was revived in November on the mainstage with equal success. [9]

La Nef des sorcières was only the second woman-authored play to be staged by the Théâtre du Nouveau Monde (TNM) in its then 24 years of existence. [10] This innovative feminist performance piece opened the doors, however, and was the first of several original productions by feminist writers at the TNM. [11] The second of these feminist plays, Denise Boucher's *Les Fées ont soif*, was probably responsible for raising the greatest awareness in the late 1970s in the anglophone world of the artistry and controversies surrounding feminist theatre in Québec. The three characters in *Les Fées* represent women frozen in their stereotypical roles as mother, whore, and saint and highlight the role played by the Church in creating and preserving these prisons for them. By the end of the play they have violently stepped out of their boxes, cast off their chains, rejected fear, and stand together in facing the harsh realities of women's condition, including the unspeakable violence done to them. While Pol Pelletier was not immediately involved in *Les Fées*, connections were close. Two actors from *La Nef* played the Statue (Louisette Dussault) and Marie (Michèle Magny) in *Les Fées*. The production of *Les Fées* was controversial in the extreme, with formidable political machinations led by the Church, massive street demonstrations, legal actions for injunctions to prevent the representation and sale of the play, and the withdrawal of funds by the Conseil des Arts de la région métropolitaine de Montréal. TNM Artistic Director Jean-Louis Roux was accused by the religious demonstrators of being the devil's "hell-hound," while they predicted that the actors would all lose their hair. The notoriety of this production certainly captured the attention and interest of all, anglophones and francophones alike. The play was given its first English performance at Concordia University in 1981. A mysterious and highly suspicious fire broke out in the theatre shortly after the show opened. The production was transferred to Centaur Theatre, where security provisions had to be included in the budget. [12]

Amazons Playing and Theorising Experimental Feminist Theatre

After the several collective creations at the TEM, and particularly, after the two all-women shows without words there, Pelletier, Gagnon, Laprade and Lecavalier created a third all-women show in 1978 at the TEM, an amazing play entitled *À Ma Mère, à ma mère, à ma mère, à ma voisine*, this time with words and dialogue but integrating many of the experimental techniques, improvisations, and original theatrical languages developed in the earlier experimental shows. In the published text, Pelletier and the three other authors, calling themselves *femmes fortes, guerrières, amazones,* surrounded the words of their text with many photographs from the performance and described their collective improvisational process. Pelletier said in the Introduction: **"je voulais voir sur scène des femmes faire et dire des choses que ne n'avais jamais vues auparavant."** (4, bolded in the original). *À Ma Mère* is a ceremony of exorcism where mothers who conform to "normal" maternal behaviour are condemned to death. Using some 700 yards of white fabric for rolling and unrolling, binding and unbinding, making use as well of clever doubling of roles, the three actors transformed into caricatural performance art the full range of debilitating roles girls and women are called upon to play. In the final tableau after the mother figure has been released from bondage, their powerlessness, fears, isolation and anger are transmuted into a loud and aggressive performance of their physical and emotional strength.

Going even further in their search for a new theatrical aesthetic, Pelletier and several other women working at the TEM also published in 1978 an issue of TEM's journal *Trac:* "Trac. Femmes." This is an amazing theoretical treatise on radical feminist aesthetics where Pelletier published her first theoretical piece on acting and theatre, "*Histoire d'une féministe,*" and where she said that she had been dreaming for ten years of seeing "other" women burst forth on stage, "*des personnages féminins 'autres',*" in an "*explosion d'une mythologie féminine, forte, grande, inédite*" (92). Pelletier believed that this would happen only if women did their own objective analysis of the stupid images they are usually obliged to convey:

> *Il est grand temps qu'on fasse une analyse objective de ce métier, qu'on cesse de l'entourer de mille fadaises romantiques. Que les comédiennes se rendent compte des images de femmes parfaitement rétrogrades et stupides qu'elles véhiculent pour la plupart.* (93)

In an interview published in *Fireweed* in 1980, she explained to Joanne Gormley her conviction that all elements of theatrical production must be transformed. A partial, gradual and compromising approach will not do. It is unconvincing, for example, to have characters make revolutionary demands if in other aspects of costuming, movement and stage design, visual and kinetic messages remain unchanged and standards for judging artistry go unchallenged:

> I want to create a new mythology on the stage with female characters who live by a new code. [...] Visually, you've got all the clichés [...] You need knowledge about your condition and history before you start doing plays about yourself: otherwise you will reproduce the conditions of oppression. The whole concept of what is beautiful in a woman has to be changed; the whole concept of strength in a woman has got to be created; and since it's theatre, it's got to be created physically. This is what I mean by creating a new mythology. (Gormley 94)

Pelletier was the director for the third women's show at the TNM, which celebrated International Women's Day in 1979: *Célébrations*. The show was a collage of women's texts selected by Nicole Brossard and Jovette Marchessault, one of which was Jovette Marchessault's monologue *Les Vaches de nuit*. Pol Pelletier performed *Les Vaches* in *Célébrations* with galvanising effect. This performance was responsible for propelling her as an actor, her method of acting and her theories about doing experimental feminist theatre further into public awareness. The translation of *Les Vaches* by Yvonne Klein, *Night Cows*, and Pelletier's performance of it in English at the Woman's Salon in New York and a short time later at Rutgers University drew international attention to its beauty, originality, and power. Pelletier subsequently performed the play in several national and international locations in both English and French on at least thirteen different occasions, some of which were at the first and third TEF festivals in 1980 and 1983, the Music Gallery in Toronto in December 1980 at the invitation of Atthis, at the Musée d'Art contemporain in Montréal at the time of the exhibition "Art et féminisme" which occurred with Judy Chicago's "Dinner Party" in March 1982, in Factory Theatre Lab's Brave New Works Festival in Toronto in April 1983, at the Women and Words/ Les Femmes et les mots conference in Vancouver in June 1983, and at the conference "Facets of Feminist Criticism" at McMaster University in October 1983. These performances and photographic or film records of them, with the striking visual impact of the cow's mask worn by Pelletier, have caused the play to achieve enduring iconic and symbolic status for those who remain passionately engaged with radical feminist theatre. As Barbara Godard has discussed, the dramatic power of Marchessault's language and the capacity of the text to construct compelling myths is breathtaking. Its intense sensuality as performed by Pelletier, wherein mother cow and child calf together and with other cows in their journey to the Milky Way achieve simultaneous *jouissance* and spiritual union, can produce nothing short of ecstasy for spectators. The cows' subsequent communion with the flock of trickster crows gives an edge of heightened awareness and irony to the monologue.

Pelletier's character in *Joy* says that it was during rehearsal when she captured the performance magic in *Les Vaches* that her theories of acting became clear to her: "That day I fell into what I now call the true 'state of acting.' A very special physical and psychic state that has become the basis of my research" (20).

By 1980 there were frequent exchanges, collaborations and translations among anglophone and francophone theatre women. As Lynne Fernie has suggested in her message cited at the beginning of this essay, it was Rina Fraticelli, then Director of the Montréal Playwrights' Workshop, who took the initiative for the invitation to Pelletier to perform *Night Cows* in Toronto. The 1979–80 issue of *Fireweed* in which *Night Cows* first appeared also contained Nicole Brossard's "The Writer" from *A Clash of Symbols* and an excerpt from Alan Brown's still unpublished translation of *The Fairies Are Thirsty*. This first publication of *Night Cows*, along with the other challenging women's plays, was suggested by Barbara Godard, then member of the Editorial Committee responsible for French publications and cultural activities at *Fireweed*. My own experience and conversations with those who were there at the time have stressed the importance of Godard's passionate commitment to building bridges among francophone and anglophone feminist cultural activists. [13] Ann Saddlemyer, former Director for the University of Toronto's Centre for the Study of Drama and Master of Massey College, has reminded me of her practice in the 1980s of having students in Canadian theatre read *Night Cows* aloud in class. Several of those students, who have subsequently become specialists in theatre, have spoken of the electrifying effect of reading Marchessault's text and seeing Pelletier's performances.

Le Théâtre Expérimental des Femmes

Between 1975 and 1979, as Pelletier's skill as a feminist actor and theorist of women's acting matured and as her experiences with the systemically-grounded sexism in theatre practices and traditions grew increasingly troubling for her, she became convinced that she could not pursue her objectives for women's theatre while continuing to work with men. Despite the excitement of working with gifted and visionary people of theatre such as Ronfard, Pelletier became increasingly persuaded that the enormous work women have to do in order to uncover truths about their own experiences, desires and real physical strength from behind the multiple layers of stereotyped roles, convention-driven actions, and learned emotions, could not be done while working in mixed companies. Even unscripted improvisational work among creative people seemed to slip inexorably into patriarchal and heterosexual patterns, discourse and body movement when both sexes were involved. Despite the commitment to radical and untrammelled experimentation in the TEM's collective creations, Pelletier saw that the dynamics of gender relations were not ever set aside when women and men performed together on stage: "… in collective creation involving mixed groups, it was evident to me that the men led always, always, always. The women had few ideas, because they're not used to having them" (Gormley 89). Pelletier wrote in 1978 that the impact of social conditioning on gendered behaviour is so powerful that its effects are decisive, whether or not the performers are aware of this:

> *Mes conclusions sont claires: les femmes qui travaillent dans des groupes mixtes se font 'avaler' par l'idéologie mâle ambiente et elles se trouvent à servir des images qui ne viennent pas d'elles et qui souvent sont dégradantes pour les femmes. Je ne vois absolument pas comment un groupe d'hommes et de femmes peuvent s'entendre sur l'exploration d'un thème, quel qu'il soit.* ("*Histoire d'une féministe*" 110)

Realising that not even women are free of such unexamined assumptions and learned behaviours and that patriarchal ideology seriously inhibits women's spontaneity, creativity, and movement, Pelletier came to the belief that separatism was necessary, at least for a time. She felt the need to check out her own reactions and stage expressions working with women only in discussions, workshops and shows. She addressed this urgent feeling and the results of following through with it in a conversation with Tamara Bernstein in 1991 where she said that situating herself as a woman and exploring women with other women brought her to life, allowed her to "give birth to herself."

In a 1985 interview with Bañuta Rubess, Pelletier recalled the unnerving situation in which she and the women with whom she was working in 1979 found themselves when they decided to work with only women and thus were faced with the almost complete absence of models:

> [W]hen I decided to start from scratch, to work with women only, there were no models, nothing. I learned through the unknown. I started working with the unconscious, with fears, with dreams. I created new characters and other ways of expression. (180)

Despite the daunting challenges this situation presented, Beauchamp also saw Pelletier ready to give birth to the images that were lying in her woman's imagination, memory and body and struggling violently against obstacles that were in her space, sucking off her creative energy, so long as she was working in the service of the male imagination:

> She knows that there are images in her imagination, her memory, her body and her history. Images that ask to be born and to live. Images that shock her (how come? why are women ...? and why are men ...?) Images that inhabit her. Pol Pelletier is pregnant, full, huge. She firmly and even violently refuses to work with men.... She asks over and over again why actresses should serve only the imagination and creative energies of men.... She vehemently tries to get away from a mixed theatre collective in order to work with women ... without men. Women have to be able to work and to create with and for themselves. (60)

It was in these demanding circumstances that Pelletier separated from the TEM in 1979 and co-founded the Théâtre Expérimental des Femmes (TEF) with Louise Laprade and Nicole Lecavalier. The TEF and its house, La Maison de Beaujeu in old Montréal, immediately became for a large number of women an exciting space for productions and other events such as festivals, lectures and conferences, a gathering place for radical women working in a wide range of venues, a beehive of workshops, and a laboratory for queer and radical feminist theatre experimentation. Bennett has characterised the TEF as "an important model both within and outside [Québec]—an inspiration for women working in theatre elsewhere in Canada and also across the world" (viii).

The radical tone of the TEF was set in 1979 with the revival of *Les Vaches de nuit* and the TEF's first collective creation, *La Peur surtout*, an angry show on the subject of rape and other forms of violence against women. In the limited but flexible TEF space, Pelletier and the others decided to divide spectators' space, with women seated on one side of the playing area, men on the other. Although the decision was controversial, its impact was telling, since, at the same time that spectators were watching the action on stage, they were seeing the reactions of the other sex to performance events.

Gender-based differences in response to fear and violence were collectively high-lighted and intimately experienced.

The TEF continued to produce full-length productions, most created by its own company but some by invited companies. Early in its existence a transition occurred whereby there were fewer collective creations and more single-authored productions. Two productions of particular interest were done in 1981. The first was Pelletier's *La Lumière blanche* [*The White Light*], a feminist tragedy and the first play she wrote singly. The second was *La Terre est trop courte, Violette Leduc* by Jovette Marchessault, a particularly bold theatrical exploration of female sexualities, sensualities, and emotional sensibilities.

Pelletier's character in *Joy* describes *The White Light* as the story of three women who meet in the desert "determined to get to the bottom of the truth about the feminine condition" (*Joy* 33). They challenge themselves and each other aggressively throughout the play to move beyond social conditioning, hypocrisy, received truths, and self-delusion. In 1985 Amanda Hale described as follows the actions of these aggressive characters: "Three women [...] exchange information. They circle on hands and knees, sniffing each other out. Then they rise and commence a series of joyous and painful games in a process of unlaying the selves down to the core." The central character, Torregrossa, who is killed in the play, explains that she is a feminist "Out of a boundless need for beauty and grandeur and power" (*Joy* 33). The play is a richly layered and complex theatricalisation of women's search for their truths in patriarchal societies, including feminist activism. Torregrossa dies because these goals are still so far from sight, and indeed, because women themselves are unsure about the object of their search and the characteristics to esteem in other women. In a trough of discouragement, the character in *Joy* says regarding the challenge she felt at times about preserving the TEF's vitality and credibility: "In those days, working at the Women's Theatre was indeed like disappearing into the Desert at the Edge of the World" (34). In life, as in theatre, there is no way out of the desert at the edge of the world. Nevertheless, as Hale states, the play is a magnificent theatrical representation of the human condition as lived in the bodies, minds, experiences and dreams of women:

> *La Lumière blanche* is a powerfully transcendent human statement. It is built on a structure of brilliant images which mesh with the intellectual content to form a body of emotional sense. It is a journey through the desert of the soul, a purifying in the harsh light. And the performances of the three women meet the clarity and challenge of Pelletier's writing in creating a courageous and unrelentingly honest theatrical experience. (10)

In *La Terre est trop courte, Violette Leduc*, also produced at the TEF in 1981, Marchessault has created and Pelletier directed the most probing, bold, and far-reaching examination of women's alternative sensualities and sexualities that I know. The play dramatises the life of 20th century bisexual French author Violette Leduc, drawing extensive quotes from Leduc's own novels and so bringing her words alive on stage. Marchessault describes Leduc as follows, with honesty and no sentimentality, in the brief introductory text to the play, also reproduced in the program, "*La Passion de l'écriture et de l'impossible*":

> [...] *femme laide, bâtarde, obsédée sexuelle, voyeuse, sado-masochiste, paranoïaque, pleureuse chronique, assoiffée de luxe, voleuse à l'étalage, trafiquante durant l'occupation en France, vestale des homosexuels littéraires parisiens, putain, matricide, maquereau, délateur, ni ouvrière, ni bourgeoise, ni intellectuelle mais mendiante, humiliée, passionnée, démesurée [...].* (7)

In Marchessault's play we meet Violette Leduc at that point in her life when the influential publisher Gallimard has just censored the first 150 pages of her book *Ravages*, subsequently published separately under the title *Thérèse et Isabelle*. The censored pages tell the story of passionate love between two schoolgirls. The play brings to the stage Violette's relationship with Hermine, the woman whom she loved and who also loved her, but with whom she had a troubled relationship because of the relations she had with heterosexual men and several gay authors, along with her criminal activities. The play also brings male actors to the TEF stage for the first time. This is a complex, experimental play involving doubling of roles and layering of stage spaces in which Leduc's insatiable drive to write, accompanied by an almost equally insatiable sexual hunger, produces strong bonds with other writers, including Simone de Beauvoir, while also destroying all possibility for security, love and self-respect. The first production of *La Terre est trop courte* offered director Pelletier and actor Luce Guilbeault an extraordinary theatrical challenge and opportunity. Everyone with whom I have spoken recently about the performance, including translator Linda Gaboriau and myself, are able to recall this remarkable theatrical event as though it were yesterday (see Gaboriau, "Luminous" 95). Translated by Susanne de Lotbinière-Harwood as *The Edge of Earth Is too Near*, the play had a dramatic reading in New York through the collaboration of the Centre d'Essai des Auteurs dramatiques and the Ubu Repertory Company in October 1984 and in Toronto by Nightwood and Factory Theatres in April 1985. It had its first full production in English May 14–June 1, 1986 by Nightwood at the Theatre Centre, sponsored by the Gay Community Appeal. The production was directed by Cynthia Grant with Kim Renders as Violette Leduc and Martha Cronyn as Hermine. Sky Gilbert was nominated for a Dora award for his performance in the production.

In addition to regular performance seasons, lectures, and workshops, a particularly important event each year at the TEF, beginning June 1980, was the annual festival. Theme of the first year's festival was women's creativity. The idea for the festival was suggested by actor and translator Louise Ladouceur, who was Assistant Director to Pelletier for *La Terre est trop courte*. Laprade, Lecavalier and Pelletier enthusiastically supported the proposal for the festival, which proved to be seventeen days of non-stop artistic expression: theatre, performance, film, talks, poetry, photography, music, song, dance, mime, video, painting, installation, and workshops on all aspects of women's creativity, including technologies of doing theatre. This festival and the three which followed represent, all at the same time, a happening, a research laboratory, and a creative explosion. Women—francophones, anglophones and others—came from all over and stayed, attending and participating in all the events, talking, laughing, visioning and playing together. The photographs of the festival and Maureen Maxwell's drawings published in *Cahiers de théâtre. Jeu*'s 1980 special issue on "Théâtre-femmes" convey the extraordinary animation and joy released by these gatherings, the spirit of which was experimentation and celebration of women's bodies and spirits in uninhibited motion.

While the working language at the TEF was French, anglophones were occasionally invited to give lectures or workshops, participate in improvisation sessions, or give a performance. For example, actors and directors Roberta Sklar and Sondra Segal, co-founders of New York's Women's Experimental Theater gave a joint presentation at the TEF on February 8, 1982 in English on the subject of feminist acting theory. That same year in June the newly formed feminist theatre company Red Light Productions, co-founded by Joanne Gormley and Susan Poteet, presented a 10-minute play, *Bad Girls*. Red Light returned to the TEF in April 1983, with a full-length multi-media production, *Wild Gardens*, written and produced by Gormley and Poteet and workshopped in January 1983 at Playwrights' Workshop with the assistance of Rina Fraticelli. The press release for *Wild Gardens* describes it as "the story of one woman's and everywoman's madness, based on the premise that in our society all women at some time find themselves going crazy" (Gormley and Poteet). The play is both a parody of biblical texts, as far back as the Garden of Eden, and a humorous dramatisation of the distortions produced by existing myths and symbols in the theatricalisation of women's stories. Critic Michael Mirolla described the show as "an interesting blend of video and live action on a stage whose props are those a symbolic woman must deal with throughout life: a rolling pin, dough for bread, a bucket, a crib. These are mixed with the mythological trappings with which a woman has been encumbered: *the* apple, a picture Bible wherein is told the cautionary tale of Jezebel …" (C3).

Crossing Boundaries through Activism in Women's Experimental Theatre

In enthusiastic response to the TEF's annual festival programs, with Rina Fraticelli actively involved in bridging, the Women's Cultural Building Collective organised in Toronto in April 1983 "a sprawling, two-month multidisciplinary festival and celebration entitled *Building Women's Culture* which comprised discussions, films, performers, exhibitions and installations, and included collaborations with several organizations in dozens of locations" (Fraticelli 18). Pelletier participated in the Toronto festival, performing Marchessault's *Night Cows* and Helen Weinzweig's *My Mother's Luck* as part of Factory Theatre Lab's Brave New Works, produced at Theatre Passe Muraille.

During the winter of 1982–83, Pelletier, Fraticelli, and Helen Weinzweig had collaborated on this adaptation for theatre of Weinzweig's short story *My Mother's*

Luck. Pelletier also presented *My Mother's Luck*, along with *Night Cows* at the Great Canadian Theatre Company in Ottawa in September 1983, at the 3ʳᵈ TEF festival, at the "Theatre Works Festival" of the Playwrights' Workshop Montréal in November 1983, and at Toronto's Tarragon Theatre in January 1985. Pelletier directed the production and played the principal role. *My Mother's Luck* is a monologue delivered by a mother to a largely silent adolescent daughter on the verge of leaving home. The mother tells of the enormous hardships she has endured through her life. Lushington's description of the 1983 program in which Pelletier performed *Night Cows* and *My Mother's Luck* captures eloquently the powerful qualities of her acting: "In *Night Cows*, the playwright's individual brand of brainburst poetics sweeps the listener along on a night flight of fantastical imagery; lush, sensual, above all, playful, erupting with heady joy, impassioned in its anger, revelling in its hope" (62). Lushington's account provides a glimpse of the *mise en scène* created by Pelletier for the ostensibly realistic and historical *My Mother's Luck* story. Despite textual indications of many real props:

> There will be nothing but the two women, one wearing eighty pounds of sandbag weights around her wrists, her hips, her ankles …. The daughter … opens the show, tracing with painful deliberation a chalk circle on the floor around the chairs to delineate the space that encloses her …. (62–63)

For those familiar with Pelletier's performance practices and theories of acting, her material representation on stage of the isolation between the two women, using only a chalk circle drawn on the stage, and of the terrible psychological burden the mother bears as a result of her life of suffering, using eighty pounds of sandbag weights, is entirely consistent. Since 1975, she has not ever done realistic psychological theatre. As she said in response to a spectator's query about the unusual sight of a female character wearing weights instead of a costume: 'What was I going to do?'… I don't do realistic theatre!' In response to the audience's expectations of realism, historicism and psychological coherence, Pelletier played using corporeal and material means the full intensity of the experience itself, as Lushington's description shows: "As a woman, [Pelletier] has the warmth and impatient hunger of a crackling flame, as an actress the wingspan of a great eagle and the vocal strength of a bull moose, and as a director the sharp eye for detail of a hovering hawk" (63).

In addition to her more-than-fulltime activities at the TEF as actor, director and co-artistic director until 1985, Pelletier continued to work with anglophone and francophone friends, colleagues and associates in other theatres. In May 1985 *La Lumière blanche* was revived at the Théâtre d'Aujourd'hui in a co-production between the TEF and the Théâtre d'Aujourd'hui and then as an invited show in the Festival de Théâtre des Amériques/Theatre Festival of the Americas in May 1985. During the same bilingual Festival, she participated in a two-day conference, "The Next Stage: Women Transforming the Theatre." Participants included Cynthia Grant, Rina Fraticelli, Kate Lushington, Joanne Gormley and other women involved in every aspect of professional theatre activity.

Later in 1985, suffering from extreme burnout, Pelletier resigned from the Théâtre Expérimental des Femmes and left for purposes of spiritual and artistic renewal on travels that would last for five years.

Conclusion

Pelletier's career has been a challenging and uncompromising quest for forms of theatre in which actors and spectators dare to be entirely present, forms of theatre whose integrity and authenticity are so powerful that the shared experiential immediacy is irresistible. She has consistently refused the conventions of realism in theatre and, despite insistent and prestigious invitations, also refused to play roles from the theatrical repertory. Her artist's quest has been based on the belief that the actor's primary instrument is the body, which must be freed from the straitjacket of learned conventions and from the buzz of daily habits and routines, and which must also be trained to access the power within. This belief has had unique ramifications for women actors, directors, playwrights and technicians. For all these theatrical functions, sexism, compulsory heterosexuality and norms of gendered behaviour have worked to silence women and deny their experiences. Pelletier's passionately committed work has had a powerful impact in French and English Canada, and beyond, in challenging outworn traditions and in queering all forms of performance that have, up to now, been predetermined or restricted by tenacious beliefs regarding sexualities, sensualities and sensibilities. In doing this, she has made a remarkable contribution to experimental feminist theatre.

(2007)

Notes

[1] Because Canadian and Québec history since the 1950s remains to be written of female experimental theatre professionals, artists, writers, teachers, academics and translators positioning themselves as feminists, queer activists and cultural militants, I have complemented information available through primary documents and articles with conversations with several of those women who made wonderful encounters and conversations happen. Their personal anecdotes and archives, the warmth and enthusiasm of their accounts, along with the enduring friendships and collaborations among them, have been moving testimonials to the extraordinary excitement of the 1970s and 1980s. I extend my sincere thanks to them all for their generosity to me and, more than that, for the outstanding and determining contributions they made to cultural, artistic, literary, academic and theatrical scenes in francophone and anglophone Canada. Some of those who shared memories and personal archives with me and who made invaluable suggestions about what was happening in those turbulent times are Penny Farfan, Lynne Fernie, Rina Fraticelli,

Linda Gaboriau, Barbara Godard, Francess Halpenny, Dorothy Hénaut, Louise Ladouceur, Susanne de Lotbinière-Harwood, Ann Saddlemyer, Molly Thom, and Shelley Scott.

[2]   Lynne Fernie is a Toronto-based artist and filmmaker, particularly respected and admired for the 1992 film she co-directed with Aerlynn Weissman: *Forbidden Love. The Unashamed Stories of Lesbian Lives* (NFB, Studio D). The quotation is taken from an e-mail Fernie sent to Rina Fraticelli on September 25, 2006. It is reproduced with permission. Fernie and Fraticelli were early members of the *Fireweed: A Women's Literary and Cultural Journal* collective, founded in 1978.

[3]   Rina Fraticelli is a dramaturg and writer in theatre, writer, director and producer of films. As Director of Montréal's Playwrights' Workshop in the late 1970s and 1980s she played a central role in exchanges among francophone and anglophone women in theatre, thanks in particular to the felicitous fact that Playwrights' Workshop and the Théâtre Expérimental des Femmes shared space for about a year. Fraticelli created "Transmissions," a program to foster translations of Canadian plays. An outstanding initiative she took was the major report she released in 1982 on "The Status of Women in the Canadian Theatre" (extracts published in *Fuse*, 1982; Tr. in French, *Cahiers de théâtre. Jeu*, 1984.2). As Executive Producer of the National Film Board's Studio D, she oversaw productions of such films as "A Company of Strangers" and "Forbidden Love" and extended Studio D's mandate to ensure full participation of First Nations and visible minority women. She was formerly dramaturg at Factory Theatre Lab in Toronto. She received a Genie for producing "Fiction and Other Truths: a Film about Jane Rule." She is currently Executive Producer of the NFB's Pacific and Yukon Studio.

[4]   For further information on Pelletier's performance practices and theories on acting, see her articles in Works Cited, her autobiographical play *Joie*, as well as studies of her work by Féral, Forsyth, Moss and Robert.

[5]   *Bien à moi* was so far ahead of its time that it attracted almost no serious critical attention, was ignored by theatre historians, and was not published until ten years later.

[6]   Michel Tremblay is, by far, the most translated and performed Québec playwright. The translation of his *Les Belles-Soeurs* by Bill Glassco and John van Burek, first performed at the St. Lawrence Centre in 1973, was undoubtedly a major factor in alerting anglophone audiences to the exciting experimental theatre work being done in Québec. Much earlier, in 1968 when she was covering the cultural beat for the CBC program "Quebec Now," Linda Gaboriau translated an excerpt from *Les Belles-Soeurs* for her listeners because the play seemed to address so directly the question that preoccupied English Canada: "What does Québec want?." Gaboriau believes that Tremblay and Brassard were important in opening doors for women actors in Québec in the 1960s, 1970s, and 1980s: "They knew that there were a lot of very talented theatre women just waiting for challenging roles in new stories and they gave them these roles for the first time. It seemed that more women had

energy for innovation and experimentation than their male colleagues" (Gaboriau, Telephone). When Pelletier directed *La Terre est trop courte, Violette Leduc* at Le Théâtre Expérimental des femmes in 1981, she gave credit in the program to André Brassard as consultant on transvestites. Despite such evidence of sympathy from Tremblay and Brassard for experimental feminist theatre, Brassard told Savard in 1970 that he was incapable of directing the woman's masturbation scene in *Bien à moi*, an incapacity that forced Savard and Mousso to develop the *mise en scène* of the play on their own at home.

7   *La Nef des sorcières* was an early, but not the first, feminist show in Québec. For information, a chronology and photos of women's theatre during the period 1975–1985, see Camerlain, Demers and the special issue of *Cahiers de théâtre. Jeu* on "Théâtre-femmes." 16 (1980).

8   Robert Wallace expresses the universally shared view that Linda Gaboriau, who has translated about 70 Québec plays into English, "ranks as the pre-eminent translator of Québécois drama into English." (287) Winner of many awards for her translations and six-time nominee for the Governor General's Literary Award for Translation, she was the first translator to receive the GG for translating a dramatic work. She has played a role, impossible to overestimate, in encouraging theatre translation, intercultural and multidisciplinary exchange, collaborative productions, through Québec's Centre des auteurs dramatiques (CEAD), Inter-Act with Toronto's Factory Theatre, the Tadoussac residency program, and the PlayRites Colony at the Banff Centre for the Arts, which she currently directs. For a discussion of her career as a translator, see Robert Wallace's recent piece: "Linda Gaboriau. Playing with Performance."

8   Frances Halpenny and Molly Thom provided information on the Alumnae Theatre, founded in 1919 by a group of recent women graduates from U of T's University College who had been members of the Players Guild and who wished to continue to stay together. After World War II they were particularly interested in experimental theatre, wishing to bring theatre from other traditions to Toronto. The Alumnae Theatre did the first production of Beckett's *Waiting for Godot* in Canada, did the first production of a Québec woman's play outside Québec, Anne Hébert's *Le Temps sauvage*, recognised the power of *A Clash of Symbols* by commissioning Gaboriau's translation and mounting the production. Later, still under Thom's direction, it did a production of Caryl Churchill's *Top Girls*.

9   Anne Hébert's *Le Temps sauvage* was produced in 1966, directed by Albert Millaire.

10   Below are the original plays by feminist playwrights produced at the Théâtre du Nouveau Monde between 1976 and 1984. Jean-Louis Roux was Artistic Director of the TNM between1972 and1982. His support of these radical feminists in the face of ferocious opposition by the Church and financial risk following withdrawal of subsidies was strong. This chronology was taken from Belzil's and Lévesque 121–22. I have added information on *Célébrations*, which they do not include. The

production in 1983 of actor and playwright Maryse Pelletier's translation of Caryl Churchill's recent *Top Girls* deserves attention.

Year	Play	Playwright	Director
1976	*La Nef des sorcières*	Luce Guilbeault et al	Luce Guilbeault
1978	*Les Fées ont soif*	Denise Boucher	Jean-Luc Bastien
1979	*Célébrations (Les Vaches de nuit)*	Jovette Marchessault	Pol Pelletier
1980	*L'Hippocanthrope*	France Vézina	Jean-Pierre Ronfard
1981	*La Saga des poules mouillées*	Jovette Marchessault	Michelle Rossignol
1982	*Un Reel ben beau, ben triste*	Jeanne-Mance Delisle	Olivier Reichenbach
1983	*Cul-de-sac au 7e ciel*	Caryl Churchill (tr. Maryse Pelletier)	Olivier Reichenbach
1984	*La Passion de Juliette*	Michelle Allen	Yves Desgagnés

[11] A second production in English of *The Fairies Are Thirsty* in November 1984, at the time of Pope John Paul II's first visit to Montréal, with the participation of singer Pauline Julien, was sponsored by Concordia University, the Simone de Beauvoir Institute, and the Canadian Research Institute for the Advancement of Women. I am grateful to Penny Farfan for this information.

[12] Barbara Godard is one of Canada's leading feminist translators, literary scholars and theorists of literary translation. Her many translations of women's experimental writing, teaching, organisation of bilingual conferences, theoretical articles and books have changed the landscape of Canadian women's writing. They have been a major force in weaving links among radical women writing and teaching in Canada and around the world. She had early contact with *Room of One's Own*, specifically in translating several texts of *La Barre du jour*'s special feminist issue "Les corps, les mots, l'imaginaire," published in *Room of One's Own* (4.1-2 (1978)). She also co-created the Coach House Press Translation Series, which she co-directed with Frank Davey (1973–1985). These were among the first initiatives to disseminate experimental Québec writing to English-Canadian audiences. Brossard played a decisive role in the publication in 1979 by Coach House of Gaboriau's translation, *A Clash of Symbols*. For information on Barbara Godard as feminist translator and theorist see Mezei.

Works Cited

Beauchamp, Hélène. "Pol Pelletier: Artiste sur fond de scène urbaine. A Portrait, Dedicated to the Woman Artist Herself." *Women on the Canadian Stage. The Legacy of Hrotsvit.* Ed. Rita Much. Winnipeg: Blizzard, 1992. 56–68.

Bennett, Susan. Introduction. *Feminist Theatre and Performance.* Ed. Susan Bennett. Toronto: Playwrights Canada, 2006. vii–xvii.

Belzil, Patricia et Solange Lévesque. *L'Album du Théâtre du Nouveau Monde*. Montréal: Éditions Jeu, 1997.

Bernstein, Tamara. "Pol Pelletier: Giving Birth to Herself." *Canadian Theatre Review* 69 (Winter 1991): 44–49.

———. "Explorations into the Psyche." *The Globe and Mail* (February 9, 1991): C10.

Boucher, Denise. *The Fairies Are Thirsty*. Tr. Alan Brown. Vancouver: Talonbooks, 1982.

———. *Les Fées ont soif*. Montréal: Éditions Intermède, 1978.

Boyer, Ghislaine. "Théâtre des femmes au Québec, 1975–1985." *Canadian Literature* 118 (Autumn 1988): 61–80.

Camerlain, Lorraine. "En de multiples scènes." *Canadian Theatre Review* 43 (Summer 1985): 72–90.

Collective. *Trac Femmes. Cahier de théâtre expérimental*, Montréal (décembre 1978).

Demers, Dominique. "Le Théâtre Expérimental des Femmes. La Révolte sur scène." *Châtelaine* (octobre 1982): 192–200.

Conacher, Agnès. "Susanne de Lotbinière-Harwood: Totally Between." *Writing between the Lines. Portraits of Canadian Anglophone Translators*. Ed. Agnes Whitfield. Waterloo: Wilfrid Laurier UP, 2006. 245–66.

Féral, Josette. "Arrêter le mental. Entretien avec Pol Pelletier." *Cahiers de théâtre. Jeu* 65 (1992): 35–45.

———. "La place des femmes dans les théories actuelles du jeu théâtral: l'exemple de Pol Pelletier." *Nouveaux regards sur le théâtre québécois*. Dir. Betty Bednarski & Irene Oore. Montréal/ Halifax: XYZ Éditeur/ Dalhousie French Studies, 1997. 105–16.

———. "Pol Pelletier: le théâtre est le lieu de rencontre du visible et de l'invisible." *Mise en scène et jeu de l'acteur. Entretiens*. Tome 2: Le Corps en scène. Montréal/Carnières: Éditions Jeu/Éditions Lansman, 1998. 229–52.

Fernie, Lynne. Email to Rina Fraticelli, 25 September 2006.

Forsyth, Louise H. "A Clash of Symbols: When I Put on What I Want to Put On." *Canadian Theatre Review* 92 (Fall 1997): 27–33.

———."Jouer aux éclats: l'inscription spectaculaire des cultures de femmes dans le théâtre de Jovette Marchessault." *Voix et images*. 47 (hiver 1991): 230–43.

———."Self-Portrait of the Artist as Radical Feminist in Experimental Theatre: *Joie* by Pol Pelletier." *Theatre Research in Canada/ Recherches théâtrales au Canada*. 25. 1–2 (2004): 184–201.

————. "A Ship of Fools in the Feminine, Six Characters in Search of Self." *Theatre and AutoBiography. Writing and Performing Lives in Theory and Practice.* Ed. Sherrill Grace & Jerry Wasserman. Vancouver: Talonbooks, 2006. 167–82.

Fraticelli, Rina. "Any Black Crippled Woman Can! or A Feminist's Notes From Outside the Sheltered Workshop." *Room of One's Own* 8.2 (1983): 7–18.

Gaboriau, Linda. Telephone conversation with Louise H. Forsyth. 29 October 2006.

————. "A Luminous Wake in Space." *Canadian Theatre Review.* 43 (Summer 1985): 91–99.

Gagnon, Dominique, Louise Laprade, Nicole Lecavalier, Pol Pelletier. *À Ma Mère, à ma mère, à ma mère, à ma voisine.* Montréal: Éditions du Remue-Ménage, 1979.

Godard, Barbara. "Flying away with Language." "Introduction" to Jovette Marchessault, *Lesbian Triptych* 9–28.

Gormley, Joanne. "Talking to Pol Pelletier." *Fireweed* 7 (Summer 1980). 88–96.

Gormley, Linda and Susan Poteet. *Wild Gardens.* Press release. January 1983.

Guilbeault, Luce, et al. *La Nef des sorcières.* Montréal: Éditions Quinze, 1976.

————. *A Clash of* Symbols. Trans. Linda Gaboriau. Toronto: Coach House, 1979.

Hale, Amanda. "Enter, Stage Left." *Broadside.* 6.9 (July 1985): 10.

Lotbinière-Harwood, Susanne de. *Re-belle et infidèle. La Traduction comme pratique de réécriture au féminin. The Body Bilingual. Translation as a Rewriting in the Feminine.* Toronto/ Montréal:Women's Press/ Éditions du Remue-ménage, 1991.

Lushington, Kate. "The Possibility and the Habit." *Fuse* (Summer 1983): 62–63.

Marchessault, Jovette. *The Edge of Earth is Too Near, Violette Leduc.* Trans. Susanne de Lotbinière-Harwood. First performed at the TEF, Nov. 5, 1981.

————. *Night Cows.* Trans. Yvonne M. Klein. *Fireweed.* 5–6 (Winter-Spring 1979–80, bilingual publication) 168–79.

————. *Night Cows.* Trans. Yvonne M. Klein. *Lesbian Triptych.* Toronto: The Women's Press, 1985. 71–80.

————. *La Terre est trop courte, Violette Leduc.* Montréal: Éditions de la Pleine Lune, 1982.

————. *Les Vaches de nuit.* In *La Nouvelle Barre du Jour.* 75 (février 1979): 83–92.

Mezei, Kathy. "Transformations of Barbara Godard." *Writing between the Lines. Portraits of Canadian Anglophone Translators.* Ed. Agnes Whitfield. Waterloo: Wilfrid Laurier UP, 2006. 203–24.

Mirolla, Michael. "'Wild Gardens' Avoids Strident Attitude to Get Feminist Message Across." *The Gazette* (April 27, 1983): C3.

Moss,Jane. "The Body as Spectacle: Women's Theatre in Québec." *Women and Performance: A Journal of Feminist Theory* 3.1 (1986): 18–27.

Pellatt, Frances. "Wild Gardens – portrait of woman." *The Suburban* (April 27, 1983): B-5, B-13.

Pelletier, Francine. "3 femmes un théâtre." *Femme du Québec* 1.5 (novembre-décembre 1979): 5–6.

Pelletier, Pol. "Histoire d'une féministe." *Trac Femmes* (1978): 92–113.

———. "Petite Histoire du théâtre de femmes au Québec." *Possibles* 4.1 (automne 1979): 175–87.

———. "Jouer au féminin." *Pratiques Théâtrales* 16 (1982): 11–21.

———. "Myth and Women's Theatre." *In the Feminine. Women and Words/ Les Femmes et les mots.* Ed. Ann Dybikowski, Victoria Freeman, Daphne Marlatt, Barbara Pulling, Betsy Warland. Edmonton: Longspoon, 1985. 110–13.

———. *La Lumière blanche.* Montréal: Les Herbes Rouges, 1989.

———. *Joie.* Montréal: Éditions du Remue-ménage, 1995.

———. *The White Light.* Trans. Yvonne M. Klein. 1987 (manuscript available at CEAD). First performed in English in New York in dramatic reading in co-production by CEAD and Ubu Repertory Theater, November 1986.

Robert, Lucie. "Quelques réflexions sur trois lieux communs concernant les femmes et le théâtre. *Revue d'histoire littéraire du Québec et du Canada français* 5 (1985): 75–88.

———. "Changing the Subject: A Reading of Contemporary Québec Feminist Drama." *Women on the Canadian Stage: The Legacy of Hrotsvit.* Ed. Rita Much. Winnipeg: Blizzard, 1992. 43–55.

——— et Nathalie Piette. "Une carrière impossible: la dramaturgie au féminin." *Trajectoires au féminin.* Ed. Lucie Joubert. Québec: Nota bene, 2000. 141–56.

Roy, Hélène. "Une Nef … et ses sorcières." 53 min. Québec City: Vidéo femmes, 1977. Videocassette.

Rubess, Bañuta. "Interview with Pol Pelletier, March 1985." *Canadian Theatre Review* 43 (Summer 1985): 179–84.

Savard, Marie. *Bien à moi.* Montréal: Les Éditions de la Pleine Lune, 1979.

Wallace, Robert. "Linda Gaboriau. Playing with Performance. *Writing between the Lines. Portraits of Canadian Anglophone Translators.* Ed. Agnes Whitfield. Waterloo: Wilfrid Laurier UP, 2006. 287–308.

Weinzweig, Helen. *My Mother's Luck.* Toronto: Playwrights Canada, 1985.

Staging Lesbian Sex and the City

by Rosalind Kerr

When Canadian queer theorist Robert Wallace first began to identify a gay canon, he identified "the marginal positioning of theatre within Canadian culture"—which he compared to the marginal positioning of women and gay men inside the dominant culture of patriarchy—as something that could be "resisted and, eventually, overcome" (29). While Wallace's hopeful words were written with the knowledge that gay liberationist movements had improved the position of gay communities across Canada in the late 1960s and that these advances were reflected in the growing body of works by outstanding gay male playwrights, the same could not be said for lesbian theatre artists who had yet to claim an alternative space for themselves.[1] This extreme marginalization may also owe something to the subordinate role that nation-states have traditionally assigned to all women in the family-state hierarchy. Indeed, Patricia Smart queries whether or not feminism is compatible with nationalism, noting that: "[n]ations have without exception been the creation of fathers, wild spaces tamed and mapped and bordered by them, in order that they may then be passed on to sons … [n]ations … have used women as reproducers and educators and nurturers, all the while excluding them from power and from public space" (15). If feminist playwrights find themselves caught in an irresolvable paradox when they attempt to address issues of female subjectivity as it intersects with national identity, it should come as no surprise that lesbian feminist playwrights are even less likely to produce scripts with a universalist appeal. Since "a lesbian's *primary* erotic, psychological, emotional, and social interest is in members of her own sex" (Hart 281)[2] then, portraying lesbian experiences on stage usually has the effect, as Jill Dolan outlines it in *The Feminist Spectator as Critic,* of "denaturaliz[ing] dominant codes by signifying an existence that belies the entire structure of heterosexual culture and its representations (116).

Situated in the offstage space of "socio-sexual (in)difference," as Teresa de Lauretis defines it, the lesbian subject may be uniquely positioned to offer an *ironic* rewriting of the heterosexual contract and the male hierarchy it supports (161), but this critical perspective may also mean that lesbian theatre can never expect to appeal to the dominant masculinist culture. Even if we broaden out British playwright Nina Rapi's definition that proposes that lesbian theatre should ideally refer to "work by out lesbians which foregrounds the lesbian experience" (148) to include productions that implicitly or explicitly acknowledge that there are lesbians on either side of the footlights,[3] we must still recognize that lesbian theatre tends to attract only those audience members who care to read past the heterosexual imperative.[4]

Thus it is not surprising that lesbian playwrights have not found a way to speak nationally in the same way that their gay counterparts have. With the possible exceptions of Josette Marchessault in Quebec in the 1980s, and Ann-Marie MacDonald in Ontario in the 1990s, voices of lesbian Canadian playwrights have rarely achieved a national profile.[5] However, this is not to say that lesbian theatre does not exist, but that may be more productively read as an urban rather than a national phenomenon. Following after the gay theatre experience, English-speaking lesbian artists outside Quebec who are my concern here, emerged as a by-product of urban centres, primarily Toronto, where new alternative sexual and cultural communities were being formed. As Elizabeth Grosz lays it out,

> [t]he city is one of the crucial factors in the social production of (sexed) corporeality: the built environment provides the context and coordinates for contemporary forms of body. The city provides the order and organization that automatically links otherwise unrelated bodies: it is the condition and milieu in which corporeality is socially, sexually, and discursively produced. (104)

If we consider how our bodies are shaped by key structuring principles that inscribe and code our desires and discipline and train us to perform as social beings, then having a larger community to interact with outside the family unit opens up enormous potential for reinvention. Here Grosz elaborates,

> the city is also by now the site of the body's cultural saturation, its take over and transformation by images, representational systems, the mass media and the arts—the place where the body is representationally reexplored, transformed, contested, reinscribed. (108)

In the rest of this article I look at ways in which the lesbian bodies in several lesbian plays written between the late 1980s and today have been interactively produced by the urban landscapes reflected in their plays. Although my focus here is on the intersections of dramatic fictional worlds and their offstage references to real city locations, I acknowledge the need for an expanded project that addresses the actual theatre spaces that fostered the productions of these plays, most notably, Toronto's Nightwood Theatre, and to some extent, Buddies in Bad Times. The plays and performance pieces selected here all recently appeared in my anthology, *Lesbian Plays: Coming of Age in Canada*. They include: *Black Friday; Growing Up Suites I* and *II; Dykes and Dolls; Karla and Grif; A Fertile Imagination; Random Acts; Smudge;* and *Privilege.*[6] In each of these plays the urban landscape figures prominently, often with such specificity that entire neighborhoods and actual events are brought to life as they impact on the characters' lives. In addition to revealing some of the ways in which the cityscape acts as a locus for the production and circulation of power through the kinds of social marginality it dictates (Grosz 109), I intend to explore ways in which the lesbian subjects represented here manipulate realistic theatrical conventions to explore their non-heterocentric desires in their new-found communities outside the family sphere. While it is instructive to acknowledge that most of us have grown up accepting an oedipalized model which denies our desire for our own sex, I want to

read beyond reductive phallic models and track expressions of desire as positive productions using the Deleuzian model suggested by Grosz, where actions follow
unmapped, inventive and experimental trajectories (Grosz 180). While each play will
be read on its own terms, my goal is to look for ways to reconfigure lesbian desire as
it produces and is produced by the interactions of the lesbian subject in contact with
her environment.

Alec Butler's pioneering *Black Friday* (1989) had its first reading at Nightwood
Theatre's Groundswell Festival in 1988 and went on to a workshop-production as part
of the Four-Play Festival at Buddies in Bad Times Theatre at the Actor's Lab in
Toronto. Just as its production history indicates the growing presence of theatre communities interested in exploring feminist-lesbian experiences, the script itself references the presence of a radical lesbian community in Toronto by its inclusion of the
iconic Spike, a black butch biker dyke who accompanies Terry, the femme protagonist,
back to her home town in Sydney, Nova Scotia. Middle-class, defiantly and comfortably "out," Spike's leather-clad body bears the markers that Toronto has offered for a
productive re-exploration of the lesbian desire that Terry has not yet been able to
express to the mother and aunt/grandmother who raised her. As Spike replies when
asked if being lesbian is just about the sex,

> Naw, fucking is only part of it, Roddy. The idea of women having sex in
> a society that hates sex and women, not to mention lesbians, makes it
> dangerous. For me. For us. I hate the danger but I take it because I love
> women. That's why I'm a dyke! Does that answer your question? (33)

If Terry's six-year escape to Toronto has prepared her to risk coming out in
Sydney, Nova Scotia, Toronto also carries other less positive markers as the city where
her idolized father retreats after his betrayal of his fellow union members following
the events of Black Friday—an infamous day in Maritime history, October 13th, 1967,
when the steel mills were shut down. Despite the fact that she presents her fugitive
father as a broken-down barroom politician-poet who hangs out at the Brunswick
House—a well-known Toronto landmark—Terry is only disabused of her misplaced
admiration for him when she confronts the evidence on her visit home.

Deceptively naturalistic, the plot builds its arc around Terry's conflicting desires
to out herself to her strangely oblivious mother Effie and aunt/grandmother Rita by
parading her highly sexualized relationship with Spike before their eyes, at the same
time as she tries to force them to produce the evidence to clear her father's name.
When Terry's oedipally-driven worship of her father is exposed as undeserved, she is
finally able to recognize the centrality of her love for her mother/aunt/ grandmother
at the same time as they acknowledge that she is Spike's partner. In a further
significant development, her coming-out as a lesbian is paralleled by Effie and Rita's
admission that they are mother and daughter. By underscoring the connection
between the shame attached to admitting lesbian desire with the shame of admitting
to having an illegitimate daughter, *Black Friday* reworks the traditional oedipalization
process which forces the daughter to repudiate her desire for her mother and
overturns Terry's hyper-identification with her father.

Butler's choice of adding a question mark to her revised version *Black Friday?* speaks to his wish to leave spectators with hope that acknowledging Terry's desire for Spike will result in a productive future for all—whether in Toronto or Sydney. The metatheatricality of the final intense kiss between Terry and Spike leaves just such a message with audience members who are told that it is not for their benefit. As the lights go down, Butler reminds the Toronto audience that these pleasure-seeking lesbian bodies exist not only on stage but off.

Shawna Dempsey's and Lori Millan's parodic *Growing Up Suites I* and *II*, like *Black Friday* reference the precarious and persecuted existence of lesbians in Canada during the 1960s and 1970s. However, by the time the plays were produced, in 1994 and 1995 respectively, alternative theatre communities had emerged who were eager to hear their stories. *Growing Up Suite I* was performed, first in its original draft at the Le Lion d'Or with Choeur Maha in Montreal in 1994, and later in its final form at The Banff Centre, Alberta later in the same year, while *Growing Up Suite II* premiered at the Neutral Ground Artist run Centre, Regina in 1995. Both *Suites* address the kinds of experiences that Dempsey and Millan suffered from growing up lesbian in the bleak suburban mall landscapes of Scarborough and Etobicoke in the 1960s and 1970s when there were no available lesbian icons—except for the underwear section in the Eaton's catalogue. Fictionalized but intended as accurate reflections of racially and economically divided sleeper communities expanding on either sides of Toronto, the *Growing Up Suites* feature performances by Dempsey in which her body becomes a symbolic map where oppressive cultural messages are encoded and exploded.

In the first sequence in *Growing Up Suite I*, Dempsey appears dressed in a full corset with stockings and garters, looking larger than life, as if she had just stepped out of the Eaton's catalogue where her five-year-old self first glimpses her picture. Behind her on stage is a large chorus of middle-aged women dressed in conservative suits and hats in 1940s styles whose song swells up worshipfully as if they were embracing their undressed girdled selves in the form of Dempsey's stately icon. Already partially deconstructed by her incongruous buzz-cut, Dempsey's girdled body evokes the kind of slightly kinky erotic attraction that others might also have had to look for in the lingerie section of a catalogue at a time when any kind of sexualized images were regarded as sinful. Speaking retrospectively with occasional reminders that she is only an innocent five-year-old, Dempsey's sumptuous girdled body, utters her love for this image of "Winter, page 117" (49), turning herself into both her own object and subject of desire. What she maps is this little girl's dangerous refusal to give up the female/mother's body as her love object, an object she perceives to be "concealing body parts I knew I did not have/Body parts so powerful/ They needed hardware to keep them in place" (49). Reclaiming the phallic female/mother's body from its enlistment in the service of social modesty and restraint, Dempsey overwrites this image as her own personal lesbian pin-up who carries the promise of future sexual encounters when she comes of age. In drawing attention to the mail order consumerism of the 1960s suburbs where catalogue shopping at the one of the two biggest national department stores was still a popular way to shop, Dempsey puts her own material body into circulation for her spectators, suggesting to them new intensities of pleasure they might also experience.

For the rest of the *Growing Up Suites,* Dempsey continues to map out her desiring lesbian body as she grows from childhood to adolescence. Reflecting the violently homophobic cultural climate of Canada in the 1970s, where lesbian sexuality was still considered nonexistent by the school authorities, Dempsey's lesbian child now finds herself inscribing the hatred onto her own teenaged body when she accepts the interpellation of the schoolyard bully who yells, "Hey lezzie cunt-face, you gotta match? (54). However, *Growing Up Suite II* does not end here because Dempsey closes the piece with a more positive image. Bringing the prophecy made to Girdled Women in the Eaton's Catalogue to fruition, she finds the opportunity on a band trip to make sweet, if secret, love with a school mate she is boarding with.

Lisa Lowe's *Dykes and Dolls,* performed at another vitally important feminist-lesbian venue, Women in View Festival in Vancouver, in 1994, is another coming-out, coming-of-age solo performance that complements Dempsey and Millan's *Growing Up Suites.* While lacking a specific location, Lowe admits that she too was shaped by the bedroom communities of Toronto in the late 1960s and early 1970s. Making her stage space coincide with her bedroom as the only space in the world available for her to occupy Lowe addresses us in the persona of her own narrator as she invites us to hear about "the story of a lesbian, a genetic girl who seeks the love and gender she wants without any reckoning or remorse" (71). Through her embodiment of each of the characters from the scientist, the little girl in the pink tutu, to the adolescent in her boyish underwear and T-shirt, she requires us to participate in her revisionist encounters with a series of dolls that she is given to feminize her. The very intimacy of the bedroom site also implicates us in her outpouring of desire as she, in the persona of Girl, now forms an intense relationship as the butch to her femme Barbie doll. Entering fully into the playhouse fantasy of the affluent middle class way of life that Barbie sells to little girls with all her clothing, cars, and household goods, Girl rewrites the hetero-normative inscriptions by bringing Barbie to life and playing out different scenarios where she takes care of Barbie by driving her around, fixing her car and saving her from accidents. Since Lowe moves in and out of both roles, the burgeoning love affair that takes place between them reconfigures our similar girlhood desires to both have and be like Barbie. When Girl begins to tire of Barbie's attractions as "nothing more than a bad cliché" (75), she has thoroughly contested this cultural saturation and adapted it to suit her own libidinous impulses by having lots of exploratory sex with Barbie herself. To close the piece, Lowe regales us with Girl's continuing exotic and erotic adventures with another, but this time androgynous, doll of her dreams. Lowe's extended metaphor of dykes making physical contact with various plastic doll bodies pushes lesbian eros into unchartered territory and begins a lesbian reclaiming of consumerized cultural space.

Vivienne Laxdal's *Karla and Grif* had its premiere at the National Arts Centre English Theatre in 1991, followed by productions in Montreal 1992, San Francisco 1995, and Vancouver 1996. Not as closely related to autobiographical experiences as the plays discussed above, *Karla and Grif*, told from the perspective of the working-class lesbian stalker Karla, takes us to another Canadian city, in this case Ottawa in the 1970s and 1980s. Full of both fictitious and actual sites in and around Ottawa, Laxdal's play operates at the interfaces between Karla's outcast lesbian body and the city that produces it. The present-day action of the play, set in the corridor and interior of Grif's bachelor apartment, concerns Karla's surprise visit there on a night in October, 1991, three years after their sexual encounter on the last night of summer camp. While the middle class Grif now lives in a trendy part of the city overlooking The Market, which refers to Byward Market in Ottawa's historic merchant centre near the Parliament Buildings, Karla is indelibly marked by her rough and tumble working-class background exemplified by her trade as a chef, picked up at the local vocational school, Algonquin College. The only place where Karla and Grif have ever met on somewhat equal ground is, as might be expected, outside the city, at the fictional "Camp Cedar Rock" where underprivileged children like Karla are sent to mingle with the middle classes.

Told from Karla's limited awareness of her monstrous status as the unacceptable social partner for the closeted class conscious Grif, Laxdal's play succeeds because it focuses on the intense moments of contact between the two as Karla's desire for Grif leads her to contest her inferiorized status. The volatility which makes their relationship so riveting to watch stems from our knowledge of the unequal power dynamic that drives it. Thus Karla, stationed outside Grif's apartment, recalls a host of memories that bear witness to the intense bond that grew up between them over the many years that she did Grif's bidding as her devoted cabinmate. Grif, on the other hand, takes full advantage of her power over the hard drinking, knife-wielding Karla. Even so, their shared moments and fierce protection of each other reveal the potential for a profound if sexually and socially prohibited connection. Our discovery that this simmering desire resulted in a night of lovemaking on their last night of camp and that it is this unfinished business that has brought Karla to Grif's door three years later can be read as Laxdal opening up a space for us to share in Karla's fantasy that they could have a future to explore. This possibility may be shattered by the terrifying moments that bring the encounter to an end with Karla's ritualistic exorcising of her desire for Grif, but we are still left with the knowledge that Karla has in some sense taken possession of her city.

Susan G. Cole's *A Fertile Imagination* was produced by Nightwood Theatre at the Poor Alex in Toronto in 1991, and went on to have several other productions across Canada. It gives us a unique insight into the ways in which at least a certain segment of middle class lesbian professionals were contesting their exclusion from the hetero-normalizing organizations on which city life is premised. In writing a play that recreates in all its intimate domestic details the struggles of an ideal lesbian couple to reproduce without the benefit or sanction of the state, Cole carves out a theatrical counter-space in much the same way that the Lesbian Nation movement set out to do. [7]

Located in the late 1980s in the homey but modest downtown apartment of Rita and Del, the play contains many topical references to well-known Toronto landmarks and actual events that had happened to the characters. As well, its referencing of actual contemporary world media events of particular interest to the lesbian community expands the space well beyond Toronto. Peopling this lesbian cityscape are an elaborate network of like-minded friends and colleagues who are similarly engaged in fighting for greater equality, from Zee, their hip young black midwife; to the liberal feminist lawyer, Ms. Martel; and, at the furthest extreme, the separatist baby dyke Marge. At the height of the debate, Marge, who is working as their sperm courier, utters her utopic prediction of the ushering in of a "lesbian nation":

> Oh this is the way of the lesbian future. Revolutionary reproduction. Pretty soon there'll be enough dykes with tykes to fill a co-op. Then a city block. Then a whole city. There'll be no more violence against women. We'll have control over our lives, the streets, the schools. Amazon history will be mandatory. The local video stores will carry five copies of "Desert Hearts," a reel containing every single lesbian moment on "LA LAW" as well as the complete television catalogue of "Laverne and Shirley".... (183–84)

Del herself, as a radical feminist journalist, whose voice echoes her real life model Susan G. Cole, carries on a highly articulate debate drawn from her inflammatory daily columns which constantly reminds spectators that these events have an offstage reality that doubles their impact. Acted out onstage through the daily saga of Rita and Del's efforts to conceive, the issue of lesbian reproductive rights becomes embodied in Rita who has to undergo all the difficult physical steps to conceive. When the play ends with Rita's successful delivery of their baby, the play has achieved its purpose of carving out a lesbian domestic space. Del's final words suggest that a new order has begun:

> Our baby doesn't have a father, or even a father substitute. I'm not Daddy Del. I'm a woman and that's how I want it. I'm a woman who loves a woman and we're going to have a baby. I'm going to be a mother. (212)

Diane Flacks's *Random Acts* was first produced by Nightwood Theatre and Buddies in Bad Times at Buddies in 1997, and then toured to The High Performance Rodeo in Calgary, and Neptune Theatre in Halifax in 2000, and was also adapted as a TV special by CBC. By the time Flacks wrote *Random Acts* in the late 1990s, she was a well-known presence on the alternative theatre scene known for her cutting-edge, subversive solo performances. Although written before the events of 9/11, *Random Acts*, as its title implies, maps out the chaotic anxiety that characterizes life in a big North American city such as Toronto. Making Antonella Bergman, the Oprah-like feminist talk-show guru, the central body through whom all the other characters are filtered, Flacks invites us to share in her questioning of the ways in which the lives of women are being affected in a city that seem to have forgotten its underclasses. While the particular question that is posed to us is whether the now wheel-chair bound

Antonella will ever return to the Toronto-New York talk show circuit after her accident, the answers that the audience are asked to come up with implicate us all as city-dwellers participating in creating the inequities that self-help talk shows gloss over. By morphing into the disabled Antonella several times, Flacks underlines the precarious state of the urban female body, forcing us to witness the very real challenges that Antonella faces in getting through each day in her wheel-chair. With Antonella established as the host body, all of the large cast of characters that she also transforms herself into remain connected—so that we witness the interconnectedness of all the other even less advantaged female bodies that make up a big city.[8] Peripheral characters such as Sasha, the middle-class divorcée, Jen, the squeegee kid, and Gina, the trash-talking tow-truck operator, take on a living presence as they speak their rage.

While Flacks's monopolylogue[9] is intended to speak to the whole spectrum of female experience, one of them, the lesbian Lisa who is suffering from a breakup, is given a special voice. As the drunken distraught Lisa, Flacks claims a representational space for the desiring lesbian as someone who also needs to be heard. Lisa's anguish continues to move us because her increasingly out of control reactions to her break-up are shown as parallels to Antonella's similar journey through the stages of rage and disbelief in dealing with her disability. The frenzied build to the climactic finish requires that Brenda, as Antonella's mouthpiece, manage a multi-line telephone conversation with all the principal players in which Antonella is forced to accept the New York booking, and Lisa is told to "be proud and loud and here and queer and out and about and whatnot" (422)—directions that are meant to signal that a new queer millennium has arrived.

In *Random Acts,* Flacks shows us a Toronto being transformed by the information revolution typified by Antonella Bergman's talk show. Although in this particular staging, references to Toronto as an actual geographic space are present, Flacks's Toronto is rapidly become hyper-real and only accessible to us through Antonella's terminal screen. To reinforce this new cyberspace, Flacks's set featured a cyclorama throwing up an image of "*three, long, white towers of varying heights*" (404) on either sides of the triangular platform in which the office/home space of Antonella is glimpsed through a window frame. If we are left with a message of hope that wants us to embrace the interconnectedness of our queer bodies, Flacks has also confronted us with a new and potentially ominous virtual cityscape.

Alex Bulmer's *Smudge,* which was developed in collaboration with Kate Lynch, Diane Flacks and Alisa Palmer, had its first production by Nightwood Theatre at the Tarragon Extra Space in 2000, followed by another in London, UK. It charts the progressive loss of sight of the central character Freddie, who is based on Bulmer, mapping the parallel erasures of the familiar city landscape and her lesbian community and, in so doing, reveals the critical junctures between them. Thus, the use of a bare set demarcated by a scrim with a mirrored wall behind it creates a powerful visual image that Freddie's city has always been an illusory one, dependent on her own subjective reactions. Even from the opening lines her vulnerability both as a person with limited vision, and as a single lesbian woman trying to make it on her own operate together to intensify the precariousness of her state as she wanders the streets of her downtown Toronto neighborhood.

Because of her impaired vision, all of the locations she visits assume larger than life proportions which reinforce our general sense that the marginal lesbian presence in the city has to be constantly renegotiated. For Freddie this marginalization is even more pronounced as even the simplest of activities from walking about her College and Euclid Street neighborhood, crossing the street, taking a bus, to buying groceries become more difficult once she is "othered" even further by her white cane. Even her participation in the lesbian community is curtailed as she is no longer able to see the chicks at the local Dyke Club. But this is not to say that Freddie becomes immediately bereft, since Bulmer contrasts her growing isolation from the rest of the community with her burgeoning love relationship with Katherine, a partner who takes her at face value.

It is in the intense moments that they share concerning Freddie's growing inability to participate as an equal partner in their relationship that the demarcation between the sighted and the blind Freddie are most fully explored. At the same time each of these crucial events also alters Freddie's relationship with the city. Blown off as a joke, the incident when Freddie tries to buy Tampax in a gas station, signals that the city is no longer safe. In the climactic scene, their plans for a weekend escape fall apart, a tragic indicator that Freddie is not even able to escape from her defeat. As she tells it, the city streets have now been colonized by an evil urchin who stalks her as she tries to buy groceries for the occasion. Whether or not her alleged tormentor is real or only a figment of her paranoid mind, the chain of events whereby she drops the groceries and flees home believing that he is pursuing her, marks the end of her ability to continue her relationship with Katherine. When Freddie recounts beating the boy who she believes is following her, she is not only breaking up with Katherine, she is breaking up with Toronto. While Bulmer's play may map these two lost love affairs, it also shows that lesbians have claimed their space in this city.

The final play, Corrina Hodgson's *Privilege* was produced as *Unbecoming* at the SummerWorks Theatre Festival in the Backspace of Theatre Passe Muraille in 2004. Although a "coming-out story" like the first four pieces, it reflects a very different configuration of the interface between the lesbian body and the hostile city. Hodgson sets the play in a fictional large urban centre that resembles both Vancouver and Toronto in its references to certain addresses and neighborhoods but makes it deliberately anonymous to reinforce her point that Ginny has no place in which she can safely exist. It is her school uniform-clad "disturbed" adolescent body that is being mapped here as she finds herself forced to undergo psychological testing because she has been caught having sex with another girl in the washroom of their Catholic private school. Precociously intelligent and articulate beyond her years, Ginny, by refusing to accept any negative labeling of her act, turns the tables and instead interrogates all the heterocentric institutions that pathologize her actions. Filtered through her consciousness as she sits in her psychologist's office, she hallucinates a whole cast of characters who appear and disappear on cue as she engages in debate with them.

Thus her boozy career-driven mother, absent father, conventional girlfriend, opportunistic dyke lawyer, and unhelpful, possibly sexually unscrupulous doctor all seem to blend together as figments of a nightmare world she would like to overturn. Since she has discovered that no one wants to actually countenance the truth of her same-sex desire for Nat, she decides to interrogate the paradoxical opposite effect she has when she lies about the sexual advances of the Doctor. She then destabilizes the normative sexual identities of all the other characters by having them rapidly transit into each other as they find themselves caught in a series of bizarre scenarios that mark sexual rites of passage.

At some point Ginny's indictment of the socio-sexual conventions that are holding her prisoner runs its course—and she leaves the doctor's office to visit Nat's room again. This time—a re-enactment of their actual lovemaking before the play begins, happens all over again. Playfully mutual and tenderly experimental, Hodgson's slow description of their coming together makes a strong statement that lesbian/queer sex is part of her postmodern cityscape.

To conclude, these very diverse pieces representing close to twenty-years of urban lesbian experiences chart the ways in which the city continues to both constitute and be constituted by the bodies it produces. If there is any hope for a queer utopia where lesbian subjects can occupy not only urban but national political spaces, these plays have at least signposted the directions we need to take.

(2007)

Notes

[1] See L. Pauline Rankin, "Sexualities and National Identities." This important article charts the problematized relationship of lesbians within Canada over several decades. While it is not about theatrical representation it does make it possible to relate the various plays to the stages of the historical battles that lesbian have waged to promote equal rights.

[2] Hart is quoting from Martin and Lyon (1).

[3] Sisley offers a revised version of a description used to refer to gay theatre with "lesbian" substituted for "gay": "I define [lesbian] theatre as a production that implicitly or explicitly acknowledges that there are [lesbians] on both sides of the footlights" (53).

[4] Berlant and Freeman have some insights into this very complex issue when they comment that "lesbian theory has neglected to engage the political problem of

feminine spectacle in mass society. [...Theorists] do not imagine for *lesbians* points of access to social change in the public sphere specific to the positions that accrues to this particular subject identity" (219).

5   Louise H. Forsyth in her contribution to this volume labels Pelletier as queer; Marchessault no longer accepts that designation.

6   Some of the arguments presented here are taken from my introductions to the plays.

7   Ross traces various stages of lesbian activism.

8   McConachie describes the way in which the "dynamic oscillation between corporeality and signification in th[ese] embodied images," leads the audience to share in accepting the reality of their different lives (40).

9   "Monypolylogue" is Peterson's term(12).

Works Cited

Berlant, Lauren and Elizabeth Freeman. "Queer Nationality." *Fear of a Queer Planet.* Ed. Michael Warner. London and Minneapolis: U of Minnesota P, 1995. 193–229.

de Lauretis, Teresa. "Sexual Indifference and Lesbian Representation." *Theatre Journal* 40.2 (May 1988): 155–77.

Dolan, Jill. *The Feminist Spectator as Critic.* Ann Arbor: U of Michigan P, 1991.

Grosz, Elizabeth. *Space, Time and Perversion.* London: Routledge, 1995.

Hart, Linda. "Canonizing Lesbians?" *Modern American Drama: The Female Canon.* Ed. June Schlueter. London and Toronto: Associated UP, 1990.

Kerr, Rosalind, ed. *Lesbian Plays: Coming of Age in Canada.* Toronto: Playwrights Canada, 2006.

Martin, Del and Phyllis Lyon. *Lesbian/Woman.* New York: Bantam, 1972.

McConachie, Bruce. "Approaching the 'Structure of Feeling' in Grassroots Theatre." *Theatre Topics* 8.1 (March 1998): 33–53.

Peterson, Michael. *Straight White Male: Performance Art Monologues.* Jackson: U of Mississippi P, 1997.

Rankin, Pauline L. "Sexualities and National Identities: Re-imagining queer nationalism." *Journal of Canadian Studies* 35.2 (Summer 2000): 176–97.

Rapi, Nina. "Hide and Seek: the Search for a Lesbian Theatre Aesthetic." *New Theatre Quarterly* 9 (1993): 147–58.

Ross, Becki. "A Lesbian Politics of Erotic Decolonization." *Painting the Maple: Essays on Race, Gender, and the Construction of Canada*. Ed. Veronica Strong-Boag et al. Vancouver: UBC Press, 1998. 199–202.

Sisley, Emily L. "Notes on Lesbian Theatre." *A Sourcebook of Feminist Theatre*. Ed. Carol Martin. London: Routledge, 1996. 52–60.

Smart, Patricia. "The (In?) Compatibility of Gender and Nation in Canadian and Quebecois Feminist Writing." *Essays on Canadian Writing* 54 (Winter 1994): 12–19.

Wallace, Robert. *Producing Marginality*. Saskatoon: Sask: Fifth House, 1990.

Potluck Feminism—Where's the Meat?:
Sonja Mills's Comedy of Resistance

by Ann Holloway

Sonja Mills became high profile on the queer comedy scene in Toronto with the advent of Moynan King's Cheap Queers comedy event in 1996, staged initially at Buddies in Bad Times Theatre, in Tallulah's Cabaret. Cheap Queers (so named because the lucky audience got to see a lineup of great queer talent for only $3.99) came out of the spirit of Gay Pride. In an interview with Moynan in August 2006, she described her creative epiphany to me—she was walking by Ed's Warehouse, Toronto's pre-eminent bargain emporium, and the crazy, flashing lights made her think of a cabaret, at which point she envisioned a queer comedy night featuring five-minute pieces of the experimental, sexually provocative, and uncensored variety. She then solicited the help of Keith Cole in co-producing the show and they named themselves the Hardworkin' Homosexuals. As it turned out, Buddies had three nights open during Pride that year, so it became a three-night affair and, of course, caught on like wildfire. Moynan hand-picked her performers, including Sonja and myself; in fact, part of the reason I wanted to do an article on Sonja, aside from being a fan, is that we more or less started out together as comic performers. I was a professional actress dabbling in comedy writing, and Sonja was on her way to becoming an accomplished comedian, satirist, and playwright. Cheap Queers was the perfect environment for trying out new material on a real live audience. It was a way for the artist to hone the craft of comedy writing, and to establish a comic voice and persona. Ann-Marie MacDonald hosted the first line-up of 12–14 acts in 1996, and then Sonja took over as host. In the years following, until Moynan felt she needed a break in 2005, Cheap Queers hosted performers such as Keith Cole, David Bateman, David Roach, David Ramsden (who co-hosted several shows with Sonja), Toby Rodin, Kirsten Johnson, Peter Lynch, R.M. Vaughan, Alec Butler, Alex Bulmer, Dawn Whitwell, Mariko Tamaki, Elly Ray Hennessy, Jess Dobkin, the Delightful Divas, Sky Gilbert, and Gavin Crawford. Shawna Dempsey was the first performer flown in to host the event's "National Outreach Programme", as the Hardworkin' Homosexuals called it. Cheap Queers moved out of the ghetto in 2000 and went to Ted's Wrecking Yard and the Vatican; it was historically significant as being the only queer comedy event of its kind to mix both men and women—the mandate called for at least 50% women performers and 30% new talent, so there would always be brand new material, and new artists would have a chance to strut their stuff.

In 1995, Moynan King became the curator for an event called Strange Sisters at Buddies. Founded by Suzy Richter, Alec Butler, Marcy Rogers, and others, the mandate for Strange Sisters called for a strictly lesbian cabaret. The eight-minute pieces had to be initiated by a lesbian, the idea being that women artists would be hand-picked to perform their daring, burlesque-style, graphically sexual comedy in a highly-charged sexual atmosphere where taboos could be broken. It was thrilling to be in that theatre when it was packed to the rafters with girls having a blast and strutting their gear, often bare-breasted—as I recall, there was a communal boob flash at the end of the show in a display of exuberant bravado. One of the highlights of the festivities was the Boy Choir of Lesbos, founded by Moynan King, Ruthe Whiston, and Alex Bulmer, featuring lesbian girls in full boy choir regalia, exquisitely singing in a seriocomic style. Soon, everybody wanted to check out these strange sisters; the programming and audience had inevitably become more flexible than strictly lesbian. During the interview, as Moynan and I looked back on this time, it seemed to us that at Buddies, anyway, we were going less on the side of sexual practice—although that was always vitally important; the celebration of lezzie lust and girl love was always paramount—and moving more towards being defined by a sensibility better described as queer; it was a period of awareness where, in the spirit of inclusion and dissolving barriers, we were going past certain identifications to a place of shared attitudes. I will now turn to Sonja Mills and her very significant place on the Toronto queer comedy scene.

Sonja Mills hosted Cheap Queers for eight years, from 1997–2005, often in collaboration with David Ramsden; and it so happens her first comedy gig was in "Strange Sisters" in 1992, presented at Lee's Palace with Marcy Rogers as MC. Sonja had never performed on stage, let alone in a solo performance of her own original material, but she was determined to read her poem about fist-fucking to spite an ex-girlfriend who she knew would be in the audience. Mills's comedic observations about dyke sexuality come from her life and have a particular slant that is not just out, but way out. Put simply, Mills likes to shock and offend as well as delight; her humour is ribald, raunchy and irreverent. Sonja Mills's particular brand of stand-up tends to be more comic monologue than traditional stand-up with its male derived set-up to punch-line joke construction. Not that she isn't eminently capable of telling a joke, but she prefers to do it in the context of a thematized piece of theatre. Her work is more literary and character-driven than stand-up; says Mills—"It's really about the writing for me, as opposed to finding a vehicle to deliver a bunch of one-liners. My work is meant to be just as enjoyable for the reader as for the spectator" (Interview). This is why instead of reciting, Sonja reads her pieces for the audience; her particular mode of delivery is somewhat akin to a rant where the focus is on the rhythm and nuancing of the words and, yes, the humour. The material feels raw and off-the-cuff since Sonja often writes her material the day of the performance; the combination of freshness and comic technique creates a spontaneity that has become her signature. It is as if we are in her living room smoking and hanging out while she sends herself up, and wittily, incisively, critiques the feminist establishment and the social conflicts and obstacles that many lesbians face. It is in this spirit that Mills enacts "WUWU," a satirical piece that is nostalgic for me since it was the first time I saw Sonja perform her own material. Lisa Merrill's "Feminist Humour: Rebellious and Self Affirming,"

describes how feminists can make comedy "a powerful gesture of self-definition...
[b]y refusing to see the humour in one's own victimization as the 'butt of the joke' or
the 'object of ridicule', while seizing and redefining the apparatus of comic perspective
to include women's experience" (275). Whether one agrees with Sonja's method or
politics, and many don't, it is inspiring to see a woman dare to take a stand and
disrupt the status quo.

"WUWU" was written in 1995 for Fem-Cab, Nightwood Theatre's annual
feminist comedy cabaret. I saw it at Buddies, possibly at a "Free Jane," Sky Gilbert's
open mike comedy night which he hosted in drag as Jane. "WUWU," which stands for
Women United and Working for Understanding, parodies a conservative form of
feminism prevalent in the 1980s when certain sexual practices such as pornography,
S&M, and tribadism were deemed inappropriate for women since they were deemed
inherently male, penetrative, and therefore exploitative. The piece begins with Mills
stumbling out onto the stage, a discombobulated square feminist nerd in
Birkenstocks, baggy clothes, granny glasses and bad hair. She steps up to the podium
and reads what Mills says are verbatim quotes from women's group meetings she
attended at York University. In a drab, flat, enervated drone, Sonja enacts the meeting
as if she is chairperson, hosting World Wide Women's Day and welcoming "Women of
all colours of the rainbow, women of all races of the world, women of all sexual
orientations, disabled women, women of the First Nations, fat women, Jewish women,
women of all religions, immigrant women, and all women (except male-identified,
sado-masochistic women, and women who used to be men)" (1). This play on
diversity combined with the constant reiteration of catchphrases like "breaking the
silence of patriarchal oppression" subvert the idea of political correctness. Mills looks
back: "It was all about breaking the silence ad nauseum" (Interview). She was dating
someone in women's studies—the only reason she was at the meetings—and
"WUWU" lampoons the conservative feminist rhetoric contained therein. She says of
the 1980s—"it was a time when we still didn't have any actual power, just a lot of bad
ideas about how to get it" (Interview). The anti-porn debate was raging and one of the
bad ideas in Mills's opinion was getting rid of porn and fucking. Mills: "The idea was
that lesbians shouldn't fuck because penetration 'emulates the patriarchal power
dynamic'—how the hell was no porn and fucking without fucking supposed to
liberate us?" (Interview). Her character in "WUWU" is a take-off on what she calls the
"potluck feminists" of the time. Mills: "Invite 10 women to a potluck and for sure nine
of them will bring lentils. Now lesbians think it's perfectly O.K. to eat in restaurants,
but then it was all about the potluck and I couldn't see how that was liberating us"
(Interview). Mills says the biggest laughs came from women's studies feminists who
enjoyed seeing her poke fun at what she considered to be the overzealousness of the
earlier movement. This kind of critique would continue in Sonja's *Dyke City*.

Sonja received her first writer's OAC Recommender grant ($500 at that time—
1995) and her first writer's fee for *Dyke City* thanks to Sky Gilbert, then artistic
director of Buddies in Bad Times Theatre. Recommender grants (now called Theatre
Creator's Reserve grants) were development grants bestowed upon artists for new
works at the discretion of the theatre's artistic director. While somewhat intoxicated

at a party, Sonja had pitched her new play to Sky before she had started writing it. He later called her on it, so she had to come up with something. The episode I will be discussing is the second installment of the *Dyke City* series—*Dyke City Two: Secret of the Ooze*. It puts into practice the kind of laughter that Philip Auslander refers to in "'Brought to You by Fem-Rage': Stand-Up Comedy and the Politics of Gender," where he cites Cixous' "Castration or Decapitation?"—"Culturally speaking, women have wept a great deal, but once the tears are shed, there will be endless laughter instead. Laughter that breaks out, overflows, a humour no one would expect to find in women—which is nonetheless their greatest strength because it's a humour that sees man much farther away than he has ever been seen" (315). Suffice to say, there isn't a delicacy on *Dyke City*'s menu that a straight man would be able to consume—the swirl of seduction is an aphrodisiac custom-made for queer women.

The original *Dyke City*, workshopped in 1995, was performed in Tallulah's Cabaret on a relatively small stage with a suggestive and spare set representing the living room/kitchen of a modest downtown apartment. *Dyke City Two: The Secret of the Ooze*, produced in 1996, using the same set and performed in the same venue, was the second episode in what was to become a series of nine, at which point Sonja felt the series had run its course. The cast included Katherine Haggis as the central dyke character, Frances; Sarah Stanley as Jane—Frances's ex lover and current roommate; Caroline Azar as Leah—Jane's main squeeze; Ann Holloway as the homophobic Aunt Harriet—Frances's nemesis; and Peter Lynch as Uncle Phil—Harriet's deranged alcoholic husband.

Dyke City is structured as a sitcom, or dykecom, I think we would have to call it, involving a simple plot. I will recount the gist of it: Jane, Frances's sexually shy and reticent little buddy is smitten with Leah, an "out" new-age lesbian of the Birkenstock variety, who seems to be oblivious to Jane's passion for her. Although they have been seeing each other for ages, the subject of sex has not as yet been broached. This drives Frances, the arch-seductress, crazy, as does Jane and Leah's wholesome, vegetarian, crystal-gazing lifestyle. The inciting incident is the news that Frances has been asked to attend her sister's Catholic wedding, a heterosexual union that promises to be very dry in more ways than one. But it gets worse. Frances must not only attend the wedding, a ghastly enough prospect in itself, she has been asked to be Maid of Honour—a fate worse than death! As if matters are not dire enough, Frances encounters her crass Aunt Harriet at the wedding, who harasses her about her lack of a man. Harriet: "Don't give up hope so easily, honey! You're overweight and you're not very pretty, but don't give up hope! There's a man out there. Even for you!" (29). The irony is that Harriet's husband is both a hick and a sloppy drunk who can't stand the thought of touching her, evidenced by his show of revulsion whenever she comes near. Frances, undaunted by this tragic complication in her life, goes on to counsel Jane in the ways of seduction after inadvertently discovering how to push Leah's arousal button. Jane and Leah get it on, finally, and Leah is invited to shack up with the two buddies after some provisos are stipulated by Frances, the self appointed "king" of the castle. The ending subverts the traditional "boy gets girl" and "all's right with the world" comic ending. Instead, girl gets girl, and Jane, prompted by Frances, expounds the play's utopian message of hope—"…we're ALL in control of our own sexual destinies! All of us! You, me Leah, everybody!"(38)

Dyke City inverts the conventional sitcom, which has been known to describe the typical straight middle-class nuclear family, where Dad wears the pants and brings home the bacon, served up by Mom in a winsome frock. As audience, we can't help but make the critical jump between the traditional form and this dykecom's disruption of it. The only bacon in this family is the bacon that Frances wants to wolf down, much to the horror of her vegan roommate Janie. But *Dyke City* goes further than a sitcom can ever go, and this is because the more provocative style of stand-up comedy is implicitly contained within it. Frances keeps a running commentary going throughout the action—she has a metaphoric microphone in her hand when she satirizes feminist sexual politics that position the lesbian as deviant. Frances often seems to speak directly to us as she critiques the strange behaviour of lesbians who try too hard to be politically correct. Frances has no patience for those who do not own, embrace and celebrate their sexuality, evidenced by her disdain for the bicurious women who keep appearing when she is frantically trying to get a "date" on the sex hotline. To Jane, and her lover-to-be, Leah, who have been beating around the bush for a year instead of getting it on, Frances remarks wryly—"The two of you are going to sit around until you are ninety, talking about stewed eggplant and menstrual sponges, and waiting for the other one to make the first move"(5). When this subtle prodding fails to move Jane, Frances resorts to an approach better resembling a sledgehammer: "You've got to look her [Leah] straight in the eye and tell her you just want to ram your arm up her cunt"(5). This brash, in-your-face sensibility within the situation comedy format allows for a radical and resistant comedy. Philip Auslander, in his article on Roseanne Barr's HBO Special—"Brought to You by Fem-Rage," in which Barr explicitly blends sitcom with stand-up, cites David Marc's evaluation of situation comedy as an "'art of the middle' designed to appeal to the widest possible segment of the television audience [which] rarely reaches the psychological or political extremes that have been commonplace in stand-up comedy" (318). Mills pushes the "art of the middle" frame to its furthest limits and beyond by foregrounding Frances's transgressive wisecracks, which not only mock straightdom, but ridicule the very notion of behavioural codes around women's sexuality. What's more, she unabashedly expresses "want": something that is still taboo for a woman, gay, straight or otherwise. Frances is refreshingly lewd, lascivious, opinionated, loud and witty, but most significantly, she is a woman of appetite—appetite not only for meat, but for life and all it has to offer. Her contagious exuberance explains *Dyke City*'s comedic appeal. In a world that hates and fears eroticism, and especially the blatant flaunting of eroticism by queer women, it is refreshing to hear unabated desire proclaimed. In the face of a moral majority, what queers seek is an oral majority, and I mean that in both senses of the word "oral."

An alternative venue is crucial for experimental work in its developmental stages—a testing ground where artistic licence is assumed. Buddies' Tallulah's Cabaret was ideal for a queer sex-comedy of resistance like *Dyke City*. In the early 1990s, under the direction of Sky Gilbert, Buddies was a theatre committed to works that pushed sexual boundaries, reconfiguring desire in the process. This kind of theatrical space becomes a crucible of transformation, where repression can be turned back on itself with comic strategies like burlesque, irony, satire, parody and subversive wit. I mention parody because Frances is Mills's thinly veiled self-parody, and the play's effectiveness is partially derived from the fact that a large portion of the audience knows Sonja, if not personally, then certainly as an outrageous dyke comic. Frances, as Mills's not so alter-ego, became a known persona nurtured into existence by the creative environment; Frances's/Mills's emancipatory politics extend beyond the stage, opening out into authentic experience. Frances describes the lesbian dance that Jane drags her to as "the lamest, piece of shit, hole-in–the–wall, bad music, no smok-ing, no drinking, dance" (8). This hardly represents the hot, juicy, hedonistic flesh market of Fran's fantasy, where, as she later coaches Jane, the *modus operandi* is— "Pursue, pursue, pursue!"(13). But it is not only Frances's forthright position that makes her formidable; the character of Frances is non-recuperable as a model of fem-ininity. The image of Frances reluctantly standing up on a "soapbox", while Leah and Jane attempt to hem the pink frilly Maid of Honour frock she is being forced to wear, has the incongruous effect of a truck driver in a tutu. Braless, smoking, in her Greb Kodiaks, loudly lamenting the necessary addition of panty hose to the ensemble, she embodies a heady and rare presence—a sexually self-determined subject claiming her space in the world.

Now, as the year 2006 draws to a close, and *Dyke City* fades into memory, queer women continue to come out, speak out, and act out, no doubt inspired by artists like Sonja Mills, who have helped pave the way for the expression of radical sexual politics and resistance to heteronormativity. In "Hide and Seek: The Search For a Lesbian Theatre Aesthetic," Nina Rapi describes the lesbian subject: "A lesbian is … someone who out of necessity invents herself, fashioning a self in those in between spaces of the dominant order that have escaped categorization, continuously constructing and deconstructing boundaries in the process"(148). Whether Mills's comic vision inspires queer audiences, or ticks them off, we have an important model of a queer woman refusing to be "silenced, negated or misinterpreted" (Rapi 147).

(2007)

Works Cited

Auslander, Philip. "Brought to You by Fem-Rage: Stand-Up Comedy and the Politics of Gender." *Acting Out: Feminist Performances.* Ed. Lynda Hart and Peggy Phelan. Ann Arbor: U of Michigan P, 1993.

Merrill, Lisa. "Feminist Humour: Rebellious and Self Affirming." *Women's Studies* 15, (1988): 271–80.

Mills, Sonja. *Dyke City.* Unpublished. 1995.

———. *Dyke City Two: Secret of the Ooze.* Unpublished. 1996.

———. Personal Interview. Toronto. July, 2006.

———. "WUWU." Unpublished. 1995.

Rapi, Nina. "Hide and Seek: The Search For a Lesbian Theatre Aesthetic." *New Theatre Quarterly* 9 (May 1993): 147–58.

Queer and Now: The Queer Signifier
at Buddies in Bad Times Theatre

by J. Paul Halferty

In his 1995 essay, "Theorizing a Queer Theatre: Buddies in Bad Times," Robert Wallace suggests that Buddies in Bad Times Theatre is an "imaginative construction" whose "theatrical subjectivity," like its mandate, is not fixed, but has been constantly evolving since the company began to produce work in 1979 (137). Wallace argues that "Buddies" underwent a "literal and figurative reconstruction of [its] theatrical subjectivity" (138) when the company renovated and occupied its current home, at the 12 Alexander Street Theatre Project, [1] and changed its mandate to nominate itself a "queer theatre." [2] Using Wallace's essay as a point of departure, I examine the interim decade at Buddies to chart the shifting meaning of the term queer as it has been employed by the company to define its mandate from 1994 to the present. I organize the discussion of the queer signifier at Buddies in three sections. The first, called "Radically Queer," examines queer as it was defined and employed under the artistic directorship of Sky Gilbert from the late 1980s, when the company first started to employ the word queer in its "QueerCulture" festival, until 1997, when Gilbert resigned as artistic director. In "Radically Queer" I argue that queer was used to critique the stability of "gay," "lesbian," and "straight" identities, as well as the "professional theatre experience." In the second, called "Inclusively Queer," I examine what queer meant and how it functioned in the theatre's mandate from 1997 to 2004, under the artistic direction of Sarah Stanley and David Oiye, consecutively. [3] Here I argue that queer was de-radicalised, and used as a rubric to interpolate and represent stable constructions of gay and lesbian identity and community. In this section I examine the mandate and some marketing materials, and couch the discussion of Buddies' more amicable deployment of queer in terms of the financial pressures that attended occupying the 12 Alexander Street Theatre Project, and to the broader demise of queer politics in Canada generally. In the third and final section, called "Sexually/Aesthetically Queer," I explore the queer signifier in Buddies' new mandate, which changed in April 2004 under the continued artistic direction of David Oiye and Buddies Producer, Jim LeFrancois. In this section I argue that the current definition invokes aspects of each of the two previous mandates, using queer as a rhetorical and linguistic strategy for representing stable, but diverse, conceptions of lesbian, gay, bisexual, and transgendered (LGBT) identity—similar to the mandate from 1997 to 2004—and to articulate an anti-normative aesthetic for the company—a strategy akin to Gilbert's. I contend that Buddies' current, bifurcated definition of queer is of interest because it appeals to, and celebrates, stable conceptions of marginalized sexual identities, while it also de-sexualises queer to articulate it as an aesthetic that is "different, outside the mainstream, challenging in both content and form" (Buddies Mandate 2004). In this section I outline the 2004–2005 season, and briefly read three performances in relation to the new mandate: Daniel MacIvor's *Cul-de-sac*, Darren O'Donnell's *A Suicide-Site Guide to the City*, and Ann Holloway's *Kingstonia Dialect Perverso*.

My purpose in this essay is not to privilege one artistic director's tenure, approach, definition or deployment of queer over another. Rather, my aim is to contextualize, and then briefly examine, the changing signification and deployment of the queer signifier in this particular, theatrical context. Underpinning this discussion is a desire to demonstrate how queer's slippery signification continues to allow a wide range of meanings to be negotiated, making it politically and aesthetically valuable on the one hand, and potentially problematic on the other.

The current usage of the term queer emerged in the late 1980s through an imbrication of grassroots political activities, specifically those organized around HIV/AIDS, identity politics, gay liberation and lesbian feminism, and poststructural theoretical projects that critiqued essentialist conceptions of (sexual) subjectivity. Queer's lack of rigid definition has been its greatest strength, enabling "queers" to reject an exclusionary "ethnic model" [4] of political resistance for one that re-organizes resistance across commonly accepted conceptions of identity, such as sex, sexual orientation, gender, and race, to constitute a queer "positionality" that is defined against normative discourses. Ironically, queer's loose definitional value has also been its primary cause for scrutiny and critique. It has been deemed problematic and ineffective by activists and scholars who question the usefulness of a linguistic political strategy based on dissimilar constituencies whose goals can never be developed past an "anti-normative" rhetoric. For these reasons, queer political organizing lost much of its original momentum by the mid-1990s. The term's re-signification, however, continues to hold currency as a metonym for a diverse range of marginalized sexual identities, and as a fluid and oppositional identity for individual subjects. In practice, queer is often rife with contradiction and paradox as the term's greatest attribute—a definitional value that refuses to be fixed—is also (potentially) its greatest deficiency.

Radically Queer

In the Buddies context, queer was first actively used in 1989 when the name of the "Four-Play" festival, its yearly production of plays by two gay men and two lesbians, was changed to the "QueerCulture" festival (Gilbert, *Ejaculations* 148). This use of the term exemplifies the currency of queer's gender-neutral signifier before it was appropriated by academics to articulate a particular theory of postmodern sexual subjectivity. [5] Post-structuralist discourse and queer theory would, however, profoundly affect Buddies in the early 1990s, leading the company to position itself a "queer theatre."

By 1992, Gilbert began to employ queer as the primary linguistic signifier to describe the artists and work the company was presenting and producing.[6] In a letter to government funding organizations, Gilbert states: "For a long time I have been searching for a sense of QUEER [sic] Theatre which encompassed lesbian and gay issues as well as radical art. I think we are creating this art, and these artists, at Buddies (qtd. in Wallace, "Theorizing" 147). The progression away from "lesbian and gay" becomes still clearer in Gilbert's Artistic Director's message in the 1993 "QueerCulture Guide" in which he states:

> Let's talk about Queer, because it does *not always mean gay or lesbian*. It means sexual, radical, from another culture, non-linear, redefining form as well as content. […] If I were a nicer sweeter guy, I'd call Buddies in Bad Times a "lesbian and gay theatre for all people." But I'm not that nice. […] I feel compelled to call something queer what it is. (qtd. in Wallace. "Theorizing" 147, emphasis added).

For Gilbert, queer referred to much more than just the sexual fringes, it interpolated other marginalized subjects who, regardless of their sexual practices or orientation, were interested in the development of radical art. Gilbert used queer to define the company against mainstream culture, and to represent a "sexual," "radical," and clearly political aesthetic that did not always speak to issues of lesbian and gay identity.

Buddies' adoption of queer politics and its rejection of the assimilationist identity politics of gay and lesbian liberation and liberal feminism, which had taken root in the early 1980s, reflected similar stances by other activist groups like, for example, Queer Nation Toronto.[7] Similar to Queer Nation, Buddies enacted its own critique of essentialist understandings of sexuality and railed against the lesbian and gay politics that promoted tolerance and equality through the acquisition of civil rights and by fostering "gay and lesbian" community. As a queer theatre, Buddies was not interested in being a "nice," "gay and lesbian theatre"; rather it was interested in producing "radical, sexual work," regardless of the sexual orientation or gender identification of the people producing that work.

As president of Buddies' Board of Directors from 1986 until 1995, Sue Golding played an important role in the company's queer nomination and practice. Golding's politics were resolutely queer, and during her tenure she encouraged programming and events that were open, non-exclusive, and sexual.[8] In the summer of 1993, Golding, Gilbert, the Buddies' staff and Board of Directors gathered to plan for the move into the new space at 12 Alexander Street. At this meeting, Gilbert states that

> [Sue] made us redefine the mandate of the company. We wanted to make it perfectly clear – and Sue wanted to make sure that we didn't compromise – that [despite moving into the new space] we were still a queer, sexual place, a place where dykes and fags could work and party together. (2000: 232)

Golding wanted queer, not lesbian and gay, to be the central tenet of the new mandate, and wanted to ensure that the term was the principal signifier of the company's theatrical subjectivity. Under Golding and Gilbert, Buddies' mandate read:

> Buddies in Bad Times is an artist-run, non-profit, queer theatre company committed to the development of radical new Canadian work. As a pro-sexual company, we celebrate difference, and challenge the professional theatre experience by blurring and reinventing boundaries between: artistic disciplines, performer and audience, lesbian and gay, queer and straight, male and female, good and bad. We do this by: producing new work of artists and companies and providing them with tools, support and independence; producing the work of founding artistic director Sky Gilbert; providing a coherent developmental framework for artists and audiences to explore new work; advancing freedom of expression. (Mission Statement)

Under this mandate, Buddies' theatrical subjectivity was queer, and conspicuously *not* gay and lesbian. I would like to suggest that the company was queer not only because it called itself "queer," but because its mandate was principally focussed on what it *does*, not what it *is*, or *who* it serves. At this time, a queer theoretical/political critique focused on problems of "being," and simultaneously resisted and emphasised the "trouble" of being, to use Butlarian terminology, by constantly reinventing and re-positioning itself through discontinuous and subversive performative acts and utterances. In this mandate, queer was, as Chris Barry and Annamarie Jagose contend, "an ongoing and necessarily unfixed site of engagement and contestation" (qtd. in Sullivan 43).

Under Gilbert, Buddies nominated and performed "itself" as a queer theatre through a mandate focused on the constant reinvention of boundaries. It positioned itself against other professional theatre companies by asserting its desire to "challenge the professional theatre experience by blurring and reinventing boundaries." In this context, the professional theatre experience is, I would assume, the collective cultural production of professional theatres in Toronto, Ontario, and Canada—both commercial and not-for-profit—which, according to Buddies, wanted to keep the boundaries between "artistic disciplines, performer and audience ..." fixed. [9] In comparison, Buddies' queer theatrical subjectivity was continuously reinvented through the process of blurring boundaries, and through the "development of radical new Canadian work." In this mandate, Buddies defined itself in the same way that David Halperin defines queer: "oppositionally and relationally but not necessarily substantively, not as positivity but as a positionality, not as a thing, but as a resistance to the norm" (Halperin 66).

Upon moving into the 12 Alexander Street Theatre Project, Buddies, like Toronto's older alternative theatres, [10] was forced to move from a challenging, political, and radically queer paradigm, to one that amicably marketed itself with subscription seasons, and solicited private and corporate sponsorship. As the company chronology currently published on its website states: "The move to 12 Alexander was visionary and vision exacts a price. 1997 was the year designated to keeping the dream alive. Sarah Stanley was appointed as Sky Gilbert's successor in April, and Gwen Bartleman was appointed General Manager in July" ("About Us"). The life-and-death language used here is not without justification. In April 1995, after going over budget on costs for renovating 12 Alexander Street, and coming under budget on fundraising, the company began to run a deficit (Crew). In February 1997, the City of Toronto recognized the company's desperate financial position by converting a $90,000 loan into a grant. With this news, Gilbert felt comfortable enough with the theatre's financial situation to resign (Gilbert, *Ejaculations* 268–69). Buddies' finances, however, were still very unstable: the company was running a deficit and was teetering upon bankruptcy.

Queerly Inclusive

As the new artistic director, Sarah Stanley needed to make drastic changes to the company's personnel structure, development programs, and marketing strategies in order to, literally, "keep the dream alive." Stanley, with the help of Board president, Sonja Mills, and a general manager, Gwen Bartleman, put the company on the most logical path: cost-effective programming intended to appeal to and attract as wide a section of the lesbian, gay, and broader community as possible.

The mandate was changed under Stanley's artistic direction in 1997. When she resigned as artistic director, the mandate was not changed by the incoming artistic director, David Oiye, until April 2004. From 1997 to 2004, Buddies' mandate was as follows:

> Buddies in Bad Times Theatre is a Canadian, not-for-profit, professional queer theatre company dedicated to the promotion of lesbian and gay theatrical expression, and to creating an environment that supports the development of Queer Canadian Culture. As a company, we celebrate difference and question assumptions. Buddies in Bad Times Theatre is committed to theatrical excellence, which it strives for through its play development programmes, strong volunteer base, youth initiative, and ever increasing wealth of Canadian Queer Talent. (Mandate 2002–2003)

There are a number of important concepts about queer that can gleaned from this mandate. First, it is not used as a tool to critique essentialist conceptions of sexual subjectivity, but functions as an umbrella term employed to broadly embrace the gay and lesbian community. This mandate stands in stark juxtaposition to Buddies' mandate under Gilbert: instead of "challenge[ing] the professional theatre experience by blurring and reinventing boundaries," this mandate belies a desire to define concepts like "Canadian," "theatrical excellence," "professional theatre," "gay," "lesbian," and "queer," and to work profitably within these boundaries. Second, like queer, "Canadian" is called upon as another term of inclusion that defined the company. Under Gilbert, Canadian was only invoked in reference to the work being produced; within this mandate Canadian unites lesbians and gays in all areas of the country, and situates Buddies at the centre of this (theatrical) community. [11] In this mandate, queer continued to be one of the primary features of the company's theatrical subjectivity, but the ways in which the term was defined and deployed changed to become a symbol of inclusion, rather than a tool for critique.

In a 1997 interview Sarah Stanley stated, "What keeps me awake at night is money. We are looking for angels, for supporters who can come on board for the long term. And we want to open ourselves up to the community at large" (Bennett). These sentiments are evident in her two-season tenure, which is marked by fiscally conscious artistic decisions, and by open and inclusive language that courted the lesbian and gay community. In her first season, 1997–98, Stanley cut several productions, mounted a number of co-productions, and rented the theatre to a number of other companies in an obvious effort to cut costs, increase audiences numbers, and augment revenue. She opened her first season with Brad Fraser's *Martin Yesterday*, and followed this by presenting two plays: Diane Flacks's *Random Acts*, and *Baal*, by Rose Cullis. [12] By programming co-productions, presenting plays in association with other theatre companies, and renting the theatre, Stanley was able to share costs and capitalized on the theatre's space to earn much needed revenue. During her tenure she also remounted successful productions from the past, namely Robin Fulford's *Steel Kiss*, coupling it with the play's sequel, *Gulag*.

Stanley focused on opening the space to wider audiences, and to appealing to the gay and lesbian community. In her "Message from the Artistic Director" for the 1998–99 season, Stanley stated:

> Our community is celebrated for its cultural, political, social and athletic prowess. We are lauded for our ability to get things done. And, to top it all off, we are irrefutably tenacious! Buddies in Bad Times Theatre is no exception. We take enormous Lesbian and Gay Pride in celebrating our 20th birthday amid a large, dynamic and diverse community. This year we ask you to join us in strengthening our common and uncommon experience as a growing community. We beseech you to get involved in the discussion. We challenge you to help infuse our twenties with passion and promise.

In this message, Stanley does not invoke queer once; rather she situates and celebrates gay and lesbian identity as both stable and accomplished. The message then appeals to gays and lesbians to think of the theatre as an extension of the gay and lesbian community, and to think of their attendance at the theatre as a means of participation in the community: as an act of "Lesbian and Gay Pride." The only place in which the word queer is published in the 1998–99 Season Brochure is in the message from the Board of Director's president, Sonja Mills. In her message she "promises" to "conduct the affairs of this company in a responsible manner; [to] continue to search for new and better ways to support and serve artists, patrons, our staff and members of both the Queer and Theatre communities" (Message from the Board of Directors). In Mill's statement, queer is used as an inclusive term that, presumably, describes the gay and lesbian community. In no way could this employment of queer be read as radical or challenging; rather, in light of other appeals to the "Lesbian and Gay community" in this brochure, it functions metonymically for lesbians, gays and other sexual minorities.

David Oiye continued Stanley's wooing of the lesbian and gay community in order to increase patronage and stabilize the company's finances. Oiye welcomed "mainstream" work, and middle-class gays and lesbians (people Gilbert so deplored), [13] as well as fostering co-operation with other gay and lesbian organizations. In a 1999 interview with Kamal Al-Solaylee, Oiye stated:

> "Mainstream" has such negative connotations. Buddies recognizes that we need to reach out to a broader community base in order for us to survive financially. One of the elements of inviting so many high-profile rental companies was the ability to include them in our subscription series. It's an attempt to bring people into what can be considered a Buddies season. (Al-Solaylee)

Reading these statements, in which Oiye expresses his desire to produce "mainstream" work and to include "high-profile" rental companies in Buddies' subscription series, alongside a mandate that calls the company a "professional queer theatre company," demonstrates the extent to which the queer signifier had, relative to the previous mandate, been de-radicalised. Under Gilbert, the theatre had become alienated from a number of gay and lesbian community organizations; Oiye, and Stanley before him, worked to established strong ties with the lesbian and gay community, particularly *Xtra!*, "Toronto Lesbian and Gay bi-weekly," [14] and to forge new relationships within various queer and "straight" theatre companies, and professional artists in Toronto, Ontario, and Canada (see endnote 11).

During this period, queer is employed in tandem with a number of rhetorical constructions to create an inclusive environment at Buddies. For example, in the 2002–03 season brochure, which billed the company as a "Hotspot 4 [sic] queer urban culture," queer is employed alongside language like "a welcoming atmosphere" for "Buddies folk" where everyone is "at home." The look and language of this brochure is "youthful," "cool," and welcoming. On its second page there is a montage-style picture that depicts a group of young people talking and socializing with a caption that reads: "After a performance or during a festival, the Buddies experience differs from any other—people feel incredibly comfortable, and at home." While the gender-neutral and low definitional value of queer continued to be invoked by Buddies, the radical critique of lesbian, gay, and straight subjectivities, so important to its invocation under Gilbert, was abandoned.

Under the mandate from 1997 to 2004, queer was exploited as a linguistic strategy that positioned Buddies as an inclusive space "dedicated to the promotion of lesbian and gay theatrical expression." The de-radicalization of queer in this period, both at Buddies and elsewhere, needs to be understood within broader discursive, financial, and political contexts. For example, under the weighty complexities of negotiating the diverse militants who organized under Queer Nation's banner, nearly every chapter of the group had folded by the mid-1990s; while in academic circles, scholars like historian David Halperin were questioning if "queer politics may, by now, [1995] have outlived its political usefulness" (Halperin 112).

During the same period, Buddies' occupation of the 12 Alexander Street Theatre forced the company to market itself positively to the gay and lesbian community in order to attain/maintain solvency. The "mainstreaming" of queer at Buddies during this period, as well as the friendly way in which the company marketed itself, was an inevitable consequence of the financial pressures that attended the new space, and the deep cuts to arts funding during the 1990s. In this financial and political context, Buddies' efforts to graciously welcome its audience by being "mainstream" was not, in my opinion, a negative move, but a real financial necessity. It is, in fact, a credit to both Stanley and Oiye that they were able to keep the theatre open, increase audience numbers, procure corporate sponsorship, develop sponsorship and important relationships with gay and lesbian organizations, as well as introducing new pro-grams, like the "Ante Chamber Series," a development program where six playwrights work with company dramaturge Edward Roy, and "Queer Youth Programmes," which have provided a number of initiatives to engage and serve queer youth from across the province. Queer's changing signification, from an abstract positionality and form of critique, to a linguistic tool of inclusion was possible because of its low definitional value and its continued currency as a signifier for a wide range of sexual minorities. These changes in the meaning and deployment of queer at Buddies echo and corroborate a far-reaching re-signification and de-radicalisation of the queer signifier within North American culture.

Sexually/Aesthetically Queer

Marketed as the "Silver Anniversary Season," Buddies' 2003–2004 season marked the twenty-fifth anniversary of the theatre's founding. The season presented remounted shows by former artistic director Sky Gilbert, hired former associate artist—under Gilbert—Moynan King [15] to curate the "Hysteria Festival," [16] and Franco Boni—another artist with a long history at Buddies—to curate what was called "Retro-Rhubarb!." [17] During this season, Buddies also undertook the implementation of a Canada Council initiative called "Flying Squad," a program designed to assist theatre companies with strategic planning, capacity building, and to "further an organiza-tion's growth and development" ("Flying Squad"). Already in the mood to take stock, Buddies used this funding to hire theatre consultant Jane Marsland, who conducted meetings and interviews with the management, staff, Board of Directors, and Associate Artists to help the company chart a course for the future. According to Oiye, two dialectical questions were asked: the first was "are we a theatre company that does queer work, or are we a queer organization that does theatre?"; the second was, "how do we keep a queer company relevant in changing times, and to whom are we being relevant?" (Oiye). The answers to these questions, again according to Oiye, were as follows: Buddies is first and foremost a theatre that does queer work, and while Buddies is committed to the LGBT community, it also feels an obligation to develop and present "challenging" work that does more than just represent LGBT constituencies (Oiye). Based upon these two statements, Buddies rewrote its mandate with a renewed focus on how the company defines and employs the queer signifier.

The new mandate focuses on re-defining and re-deploying queer. It defines the term along two axes: the sexual, and the aesthetic. It uses queer's fluid definitional value in a bifurcating manner to signify the various sexual minorities the company seeks to represent, and to articulate an anti-normative aesthetic agenda that promotes theatrical performances that are "outside the norm." The current mandate reads:

> Buddies in Bad Time theatre is a not-for-profit, professional theatre company dedicated to the promotion of Queer Canadian Culture. We are dedicated to producing, developing, and presenting theatrical works that speak to one, or both, of the following criteria:
>
> 1. QUEER, referring to the Lesbian, Gay, Bisexual, and Transgendered identity encapsulates the core of our organization. Buddies is a queer-run organization committed to representing the LGBT community by supporting its artists, and by telling its stories.
>
> 2. QUEER, referring to anything different or outside of the norm, represents the nature of artistic work presented at 12 Alexander Street. Buddies is dedicated to work that is different, outside the mainstream, challenging in both content and form. (Mandate 2004)

In this mandate, queer's elastic signification is stretched far enough to describe both the company's commitment to a range of sexual minorities, and to the aesthetically challenging work it wants to develop. The mandate's openness is made explicit by the qualification that performances presented by the company need only address *one* of its definitions of queer, allowing Buddies to produce and present a wider range of work. Its opening statement, and its first definition of queer, repeat aspects of how queer was articulated in the 1997–2004 mandate, employing queer as a metonym for LGBT communities—although the addition of the "T" and "B" demonstrates the company's expanded commitment to sexual diversity. It does not reclaim queer to critique coherent conceptions of identity, but continues its use as a linguistic strategy to foster inclusivity and fluidity. The mandate's definition of queer is expanded by the second section, in which the term is pitted against anything that Buddies deems normative—an aesthetic understanding of queer akin to Gilbert's.[18]

The 2004–2005 season demonstrates the new mandate, in which queer denotes representations of LGBT communities and work that is "challenging in form as well as content." This season includes nine shows, as well as the "Rhubarb!" and "Hysteria" festivals. Its plays are almost equally split between those that speak to the mandate's first and second definitions of queer. The shows that in some way represent the first definition of queer are: *Snowman* by Greg MacArthur; *Cul-de-sac* by Daniel MacIvor; *Yapping out Loud* by Mirha-Soleil Ross; and *Rope Enough* by Sky Gilbert. The plays that fall under the second definition of queer are: *The Unnatural and Accidental*

Woman by Marie Clements; *Swimming in the Shallows* by Adam Bock; *A Suicide Site-Guide to the City* by Darren O'Donnell; *Kingstonia Dialect Perverso* by Ann Holloway; and *Hedda Gabler* by Henrik Ibsen, adapted by Judith Thompson. [19]

Daniel MacIvor's *Cul-de-Sac*[20] is an interesting example of Buddies' new mandate because it is both aesthetically innovative, which could, arguably, satisfy the mandate's second criteria, and represents issues specifically relevant to LGBT communities. The play, a one-person show acted by MacIvor, traces the life and death of "Leonard," a man whose quest for love is met with his violent murder at the hands of a young, drugged-up hustler called "Eric." In the play, Leonard retells his story through, and from the point of view of, each of his neighbours, all of whom live on the same suburban cul-de-sac. *Cul-de-sac* certainly qualifies as an example of the first definition of queer in Buddies mandate: MacIvor is an openly gay man, and the play represents LGBT community by telling one of its stories. The play's violent and, in my opinion, hopeful conclusion, where Leonard learns to say "yes" to his life instead of "no," is relevant to the queer communities who are subject to varying forms of violence, and who, by coming out, also publicly declare "yes" to their lives as gay, lesbian, bisexual, and transgendered individuals – much like Leonard learns to say "yes" in the public domain of the theatre, and before his community on the cul-de-sac.

A Suicide-Site Guide to the City,[21] written and performed by Darren O'Donnell, is also queer according to Buddies' second definition of the term: the play is "different" and "outside the mainstream, challenging in both content and form."[22] In terms of content, the play—which O'Donnell calls a "stand-up essay"—presents a series of musings on suicide, current political events, the erosion of civil liberties, and the need for urban "cultural workers" to effect a better, and more just world. The play's anti-capitalist sentiments reflect O'Donnell's own political activism (it is dedicated to the members of the Ontario Coalition Against Poverty), and aligns the plight and poverty of Toronto's chronically unemployed and working poor with the city's artists and cultural workers. It juxtaposes recent studies in urban political economy that cite a large population of cultural workers or "creative classes," as an essential element in a successful, post-industrial urban economy with the reality that many of the artists who O'Donnell knows are living on $19,000 a year. The play's politics are intended to implicate and politically motivate the audience of urban theatregoers, who O'Donnell self-consciously assumes are mostly artists and cultural workers, to effect political change. This sentiment is confirmed and developed by the "Talk Backs" that O'Donnell hosts after each performance to discuss with his audience the issues that emerge from the play.[23]

According to Buddies' second definition of queer, *A Suicide-Site Guide to the City* is "queer" because of its innovative form and its challenging content. The performance's *mise en scène* employs video, sound media, and it is self-reflexive about its own construction and presentation. It uses what could be described as Brechtian distancing devices, such as placing the sound designer/operator and lighting designer/operator onstage with O'Donnell, to similar political ends. It highlights the "performance" of the two onstage technicians by introducing them by name and keeping their actions – usually relegated to "backstage" spaces – within the audience's field of view. It also draws attention to the constructedness of O'Donnell's performance as "performance" (O'Donnell refers to his own theatrical performance as "pretending") by detailing the date, time, and place when each section of text he recites was originally written. The play makes light of the complexities of subjectivity, identity and performance by asking if the "Darren" currently speaking the text is the same "Darren" who wrote it two years earlier. According to Buddies mandate, *A Suicide-Site Guide to the City* qualifies as a queer text because its form is innovative and its content is challenging to both the "capitalist establishment," and to the demographic that O'Donnell assumes attend small theatre: leftist, urban, cultural workers.

Kingstonia Dialect Perverso, a one-person show written and performed by Ann Holloway, does not represent the LGBT community, nor does Ann Holloway identify as bisexual or lesbian;[24] for these reasons the work is not queer according to Buddies' first definition of the term. The play's content, however, is graphically sexual. It presents a woman who speaks powerfully and openly about sex in a manner that patrons, who are unaccustomed to blatant "dirty talk," may find surprising and even offensive. The play begins as a pseudo-scientific lecture given by "Ann Semblance," a professor of Linguistics whose area of expertise is the dialect of Kingston, Ontario. In this talk she examines the syntax and cadence of the dialect, as well as revealing some personal experiences gained while conducting research in Kingston. The lecture and the character slowly break down, leading to two other characters: an English domestic, and a contemporary woman. These two characters continue the action by telling the stories of their lives cast against the backdrop of Kingston in the 1960s and '70s, and then Toronto in the 1980s and '90s.

According to Buddies' mandate, the play's form is somewhat queer: it incorporates a number of genres of performance (an academic lecture, mimetic dramatic action, stand-up comedy, and "slam poetry"); however, it is the play's content that pushes the limits of "decency" by verbally conjuring graphically grotesque images of bodies, bodily fluids, and, of course, sex, which is the "queerest" element of this play. When queer is defined along these aesthetic lines, *Kingstonia* fulfills Buddies' mandate by producing a play whose blatantly sexual content is definitely "outside the mainstream" and would, in my opinion, prohibit its production at any other theatre in Toronto.

The queer signifier, as it was defined and functioned under Gilbert, was particular to its time. The tenacity of its critique, and its undefinability, made it contextually important and useful for opening up new spaces for a variety of marginalized sexualities. Politically, as demonstrated by the short life of groups like Queer Nation, queer lacks the ability to unite individuals for sustained and specified political action. Its currency at Buddies as a method for describing lesbian and gay identities in the 1997 to 2004 mandate, shows the extent to which its low definitional value remained effective, even when its critique of identity had waned. The current re-invocation of queer in Buddies' mandate exploits the term's malleable properties of signification, and enables the company to extend its programming by defining the term according to its own aesthetic, sexual, and political ends.

On the one hand, I am happy to see the theatre moving in a direction that entails more risk, one that expresses a commitment to both LGBT communities and to innovative, potentially radical Canadian theatre. On the other, I am troubled by an invocation of queer that is so open that the term is almost meaningless. I think the previous mandate's commitment to the "promotion of lesbian and gay theatrical expression" was problematic because it limited the work the company could undertake. With this in mind, I understand and support Buddies' current redefinition of queer as it allows the company to situate itself on the fringes, and to occupy multiple, and (potentially) shifting sites of resistance to an array of heteronormative, and normative discourses. I think that queer, when invoked in this way, is always moving, and always critical. But, despite my sympathy for this utopian vision of a fluid queer signifier, I wonder what pitfalls are possible when just about anyone or anything can be queer.

Queer's lack of a rigid definition makes the term effective, by creating room for multiple oppositional voices, and problematic, by potentially negating the need to specifically address the LGBT identities as the primary sites of heterosexist violence. Although queer's power as a critique of coherent sexual subjectivity has waned, its currency as a term defined in opposition to the "norm," as exemplified in Buddies' new mandate, is still productive and holds currency. As the term's mutable qualities are the object of constant change and re-signification, the future of queer remains murky; yet, Buddies' redefinition of queer in order to reinvigorate the company's aesthetics, while remaining committed to its LGBT constituencies and politics, is a promising definitively queer step into the future.

(2007)

Notes

¹ Buddies is the resident company of the Alexander Street Theatre Project, a building, owned by the City of Toronto, with a separate board of directors. Through a lengthy application process, Buddies won a forty-year lease of this building from the city.

² Wallace's essay explicates and contextualizes Buddies' "theatrical subjectivity" beginning in 1979, its "coming out" as a "gay," and then "gay and lesbian," theatre in the mid-1980s, and its subsequent self-nomination as a "queer theatre."

³ The artistic directorship of Stanley and Oiye are obviously not synonymous; however, when Oiye took the helm at Buddies in 1999, he did not change the company's mandate, but continued to work under the tenets articulated during Stanley's tenure. Because this essay focuses on the definition and deployment of

"queer," I chart this history via changes to the company's mandate, and specifically its use of the queer signifier.

4 Taking the American Black Civil Rights Movement as its example, the "ethnic model" denotes some (but certainly not all) of the strategies of the lesbian and gay liberation movement. The lesbian and gay liberation movement is based upon a stable conception of a homosexual subject, constituted through same-sex sexual orientation, to form a community. Over about the last twenty years the movement has focused on procuring anti-discrimination legislation and civil rights. For a history of this movement in Canada see Warner.

5 Teresa de Lauretis is credited with coining the phrase "queer theory" in 1991, and attaching to it a specific post-structural critique. In "Queer Theory: Lesbian and Gay Sexualities," de Lauretis articulates "queer" as a way to emphasise the differences implicit in the phrase "lesbian and gay." In a rather deconstructive move, she argues that contained within the phrase "lesbian and gay" are "ideological assumptions, exclusions, and silences." "Queer theory," de Lauretis suggests, "conveys a double emphasis – on the conceptual and speculative work involved in discourse production, and on the necessary critical work of deconstructing our own discourses and their constructed silences"(iv). De Lauretis does not define queer in relation to a particular gender, sexual object choice, or sexual practice; for her, queer theory articulated a means through which to expose the "exclusions and silences" implicit in a unified conception of "gay" and "lesbian" identity.

6 Buddies, both under Gilbert and currently, *produces* and *presents* in association with other theatre companies. It is important to differentiate what producing and presenting means, especially in relation to discussion of theatrical mandate. Work that Buddies *produces* means the play was developed by the theatre through one of its development programmes. An example of a play from its 2004–2005 season that Buddies produced is Ann Holloways's *Kingstonia Dialect Perverso*. Work that Buddies *presents* means that the play is developed by another theatre company, and Buddies has negotiated an agreement to *present* the play as part of its season. An example of a play that Buddies presented in 2004–2005 season is da da kamera's *Cul-de-sac*. The complexities of how Buddies' mandate as the presenter relates to da da kamera's mandate as the production company, is beyond the focus and scope of this paper. When examining plays that have been presented by Buddies as part of one of its seasons, I will be reading them within the Buddies context, and in relation to the Buddies mandate; however, I will draw attention to and differentiate between Buddies productions, and plays which Buddies presents.

7 Modeled after the group founded in New York 1990, Queer Nation Toronto was a confrontational group of "Queer Nationals" who organized a number of kiss-ins, rallies, and poster campaigns, with slogans like "Queers are Here, get used to it" and "Gays bash back." For an account of Queer Nation chapters in Canada, as well as queer challenges to identity see Warner.

[8]   The most famous and interesting of these may be fundraisers called "Dungeon Parties." The parties had the usual drinking, music, and dancing, but also provided consensual space for various forms of sexual expression and practice. They were attended by gays, straights, lesbians, members of the S/M community, anyone and everyone who were respectful of people's (sexual) boundaries and wanted to party and have a good time. In his memoirs, Gilbert states: "Sue [Golding] was adamant about it. We were a sex-positive theatre and should do nothing to stop sex at the parties. [...] I cannot stress enough how important these Dungeon parties were for queer politics in the city. Nowhere else were dykes and fags partying and having sex in the same space" (*Ejaculations* 193). See also 190–95.

[9]   It is important to note that, at this time, Buddies also worked in association with, and presented the work of, other Canadian theatre companies; however, these companies were usually part of what could be safely called the avant guard or the "fringes" of Toronto theatre in the 1980s and 1990s. For example, the companies Buddies collaborated with for its 1995–96 season were: da da kamera, Tothin Theatre, VaVa Venus, Sto Union, Video Cabaret, East City Productions, Dancing Faggot Division, Modern Times Stage Company, DNA Theatre, and fFIDA (Fringe Festival of Independent Dance Artists). During this season, the company also collaborated with artists Ken Brand, Sonja Mills, Margaret Hollingsworth, and Nadia Ross.

[10] Becoming less radical as a result of acquiring property is not unprecedented in the history of Canadian, and specifically Toronto theatre. In the late 1970s and early 1980s, the Toronto Free, Factory, Passe Muraille and Tarragon theatres each underwent a similar transformation. On this topic, Robert Wallace states that the acquisition of property "introduced a new era in the history of these theatres in which they underwent a shift in their priorities: once governed by primarily political (read: nationalistic) and aesthetic concerns, these theatres now became equally, if not more, preoccupied with financial survival" (*Producing* 102–03).

[11] The extent to which Buddies sought to represent gays and lesbians across Canada is exemplified by the programming of the 2000–2001 season, the focus of which was the promotion of "queer culture across Canada." The company website states: "Over the 2000–2001 season [Buddies] explored the notion of a national queer repertoire by programming Vancouver-based artist Dorothy Dittrich's award-winning musical *When We Were Singing*; Winnipeg playwright Ken Brand's comedy *Burying Michael*; and *PileDriver!* from Edmonton-based companies Guys in Disguise; and Three Dead Trolls in a Baggie" ("About Us").

[12] *Random Acts* was produced by Mything Productions, Nightwood Theatre and Buddies in Bad Times; *Baal* was presented by "Inanna Productions in association with Buddies in Bad Times" (1997–1998 Season Brochure).

[13] Gilbert has been quoted in many papers decrying the problems with middle-class, assimilationist, gay men – who he calls "sweater-fags." See Gilbert's "This Panther's."

14 For an obviously biased, but nonetheless interesting and illuminating account of Buddies relationship with *Xtra!* and other gay and lesbian organizations during Gilbert's tenure, see Gilbert, *Ejaculations* 208–11.

15 Moynan King and Kirsten Johnson were Associate Artists at Buddies under Gilbert. Their contracts were not renewed when Sarah Stanley became Artistic Director.

16 "Hysteria: A Festival of Women" began in association with Nightwood Theatre during the 2003–2004 season. The festival features wide rage of performances by women, as well as art exhibitions, and music.

17 "Rhubarb!" is a yearly festival of new work that began with the theatre's inception in 1979, then called "New Faces of '79," and renamed "Rhubarb!" the following year. For an overview of "Rhubarb!", see Boni.

18 Defining queer as an aesthetic to represent "work that is different, outside the mainstream, challenging in both content and form" directly echoes Gilbert's sentiment in the 1993 "QueerCulture Guide," quoted in Wallace and cited above, where he stated that queer art is "from another culture, non-linear, redefining form as well as content."

19 Buddies produced Greg MacArthur's *Snowman*; Mirha-Soleil Ross' *Yapping Out Loud*; and Ann Holloway's *Kingstonia Dialect Perverso*. The company presented Daniel MacIvor's, *Cul-de-sac*, which was billed "a da da kamera production"; Marie Clements' *The Unnatural and Accidental Woman* in association with Native Earth Performing Arts; Adam Bock's *Swimming in the Shallows* in association with Theatrefront; Darren O'Donnell's *Suicide-site Guide to the City* in association with Mammalian Diving Reflex; Sky Gilbert's *Rope Enough* in association with Cabaret Company; and an adaptation by Judith Thompson of Henrik Ibsen's *Hedda Gabbler* in association with Volcano.

20 *Cul-de-sac* was presented by Buddies, but produced by da da kamera, an independent production company with its own particular mandate. The artistic director of da da kamera is Daniel MacIvor, and its producer is Sherrie Johnson. For da da kamera's mandate, as well as a complete list of *Cul-de-sac*'s development partners, and presenters, see the da da kamera website: www.dadakamera.com.

21 *A Suicide-Site Guide to the City* was presented by Buddies, but produced by Mammalian Diving Reflex, an independent production company with its own particular mandate. The artistic director of Mammalian Diving Reflex is Darren O'Donnell, and its producer is Naomi Campbell. For Mammalian Diving Reflex's mandate and a complete list of *A Suicide-Site Guide to the City*'s co-producers and presenters, see the Mammalian Diving Reflex website: http://mammalian.ca

22 In the performance O'Donnell says that while he identifies as straight, he has had some satisfying sexual experiences with men, and is open to more. As part of the performance he also asks a random audience member, male or female, to come on stage and make-out with him. At the performance I attended, the person who accepted his invitation was a man.

[23] At the Talk Back that I attended, O'Donnell asked the audience to indicate by a show of hands who considered themselves to be "cultural workers"—nearly the entire Sunday afternoon "pay-what-you-can" audience raised their hands.

[24] Although Holloway has sex with men, she does not identify as strictly heterosexual. She does identify as "a queer freak Kingstonian pervert (prevert)." "My whole approach to sex" says Holloway, "has more of a queer, or an outsider sensibility. What this means is I do the choosing, I engineer the dynamics, and I own my own pleasure and my desire. It does not fit into a neat package. I refuse to be represented in terms of heterosexuality, because it always recalls the heterosexual binary" (Holloway).

Works Cited

"About Us: Company History". *Buddies in Bad Time Theatre Website.* 13 November 2006. http://www.buddiesinbadtimestheatre.com/about/index.cfm.

Al-Solaylee, Kamal. "Bad boys no more: David Oiye heads makeover at Buddies in Bad Times." *eye magazine* (30 September 1999): 46.

"Baal-busting rockers" *eye magazine,* Toronto: http://www.eye.net/eye/issue/issue_01.08.98/theatre/baal.php.

Bennett, Julia. "Stanley Looks for Buddies in Bad Times." *The Globe and Mail* 25 March 1997. C: 1.

Boni, Franco. *Rhubarb-O-Rama! Plays and Playwrights from the Rhubarb! Festival.* Winnipeg: Blizzard, 1998.

Crew, Robert. "Buddies, Can You Spare 600,000 Dimes?" *Toronto Star* April 18 1995, sec. C: 4.

de Lauretis, Teresa. "Queer Theory: Lesbian and Gay Sexualities." *differences* 3.2 Summer (1991): iii-xviii.

Gilbert, Sky. *Ejaculations from the Charm Factory: A Memoir.* Toronto: ECW Press, 2000.

———. "This Panther's last hurrah," *eye magazine.* 3 December 2006. http://www.eye.net/eye/issue/issue_03.13.03/city/pink.html.

"Flying Squad." *Canada Council For the Arts website.* 31 March 2005. http://www.canadacouncil.ca/grants/theatre/wx127252257531406250.htm

Halperin, David M. *Saint Foucault: Towards a Gay Hagiography.* New York: Oxford UP, 1995.

Holloway, Ann. Personal Interview. Toronto: 17 November 2006.

Isaacs, Paul. "Killer Guide." *eye magazine* (10 March 2005): 86.

"Mandate 2002–2003" in "Section E: Profile" Application to Toronto Arts Council, March 1, 2001. Toronto: Buddies in Bad Times Theatre.

"Mandate 2004" in *2004–2005 Subscription Season Program*. Toronto: Buddies in Bad Times Theatre.

"Message from the Artistic Director." *1998–99 Season Brochure*. Toronto: Buddies in Bad Times Theatre.

"Message from the Board of Directors, A." *1998–99 Season Brochure*. Toronto: Buddies in Bad Times Theatre.

"Mission Statement." *1995–96 Season Brochure*. Toronto: Buddies in Bad Times Theatre.

Oiye, David. Personal Interview. Toronto, 28 March 2005.

Sullivan, Nikki. *A Critical Introduction to Queer Theory*. New York: New York UP, 2003.

Todd, Rebecca. "Baal-busting Rockers." *eye magazine*. 3 December 3, 2006. http://www.eye.net/eye/issue/issue_01.08.98/theatre/baal.php

2002–3 Season Brochure. Buddies in Bad Times Theatre.

Wallace, Robert. *Producing Marginality: Theatre and Criticism in Canada*. Saskatoon: Fifth House, 1990.

———. "Theorizing a Queer Theatre: Buddies in Bad Times." *Contemporary Issues in Canadian Drama*. Ed. Per Brask. Winnipeg: Blizzard, 1995. 136–59.

Warner, Tom. *Never Going Back: A History of Queer Activism in Canada*. Toronto: U of Toronto P, 2002.

Writing Gay: Is it Still Possible? [1]

by Sky Gilbert

I've been an activist in the gay community for many years, and in 1979 I founded Buddies in Bad Times Theatre—Canada's largest professional gay and lesbian theatre. I have written many, many gay plays, and published gay novels, and published two poetry collections on gay themes. I'm known as an outspoken drag queen, AIDS radical and sex positive, promiscuous homo. Recently my partner and I rented a DVD movie called "Gay Sex in the '70s"—a low budget one-hour American documentary released by Lovett Productions in 2005. It was, to say the least, a disappointment. I had imagined there would be candid documentary footage of out queers of the period—and maybe even frank discussions by some quirky personalities. (It's my experience that talking-head documentaries are much more interesting when the heads are entertaining). To our chagrin, the flick turned out to be a bunch of interviews with boring gay seniors, nostalgic for the good old days of rampaging promiscuity, inter-cut with '70s porno footage. I object to the film mainly because movies like these simply serve to propagate the myth that gay sex was so very different in the '70s than it is now.

Yes, of course, there was less concern over safe sex in the '70s, and—because the gay liberation '60s was so close at hand—everyone was a little less hypocritical about their sexual habits. But otherwise, when it comes to sex, things were pretty much the same as they are now. "Gee," groaned these wizened geezers "Whatever happened to the days when you could just cruise down the streets in your cutest outfit and end up in an alley getting sucked off? And oh – the orgies!" Unfortunately, it isn't so much that times have changed; but that these men certainly have. If you're young and cute you can still easily get a good blow job in an alley anywhere, and orgies today are rampant—they just don't tend to take place in gay bars anymore. Instead they usually happen in the recently renovated homes of well-to-do middle-class gay professionals living in any gentrified downtown core. Sure, today, men pick each other up on the net more than they do in bars. But the bathhouses, toilets and parks (to pick a few places at random) are still filled to bursting with horny faggots. Just because the guys in this video are unattractive in a conventional way, and much more impor-tantly—because they have obviously decided not to be interested in sex—they are unlikely to get any. After all, horny old leather daddies who still consider themselves worthy of sex seem to have no trouble finding it. So it's only old guys like the ones in this video who are complaining that the party is over.

Because it is most *defiantly* not over.

I mention this because I have set out to write about contemporary queer theatre in Canada, and I wouldn't want to sound like an old coot, bitter because the good days have left him behind. Though I'm nearly fifty-five years old, I want to make it clear that I'm not angry for the obvious reasons. I'm not angry because none of the nearly forty gay plays I've written has had a professional production in Canada since their premieres. That merely makes me sad, and believe it or not, I have come to terms with that sadness. What I AM bitter about, is the extent to which gay attitudes to queer culture have changed since I came out in Toronto.

Let me give you an idea of what the political climate was like for queers in Toronto during the early '80s. Significantly, the clone look was in vogue—inspired by Tom of Finland (Touko Laaksonen) an iconic twentieth-century Finnish artist who created pornographic drawings of masculine gay men in various forms of macho drag—cowboys, sailors, construction workers, s/m daddies and military men. Butch gay guys (or gay guys who wished they were butch) donned work boots, handlebar mustaches and plaid shirts in adoring imitation. And the lesbians who had been wearing plaid shirts and Birkenstocks in the early '70s—while labeling all penetrative sex rape—were changing their attitudes too. The lipstick lesbian was being born, if not quite in public, in the minds of writers like Susie Bright, for instance. Susie Bright (also known as Suzie Sexpert) was one of the first American writer/activists to declare herself a sex positive feminist (she founded the first women's sex magazine, *On Our Backs*, in 1984). In other words, the disco '70s had been our chance to revel in gay liberation, sex in public, party drugs, as well as in a kind of naive gender essentialism. Gay men had been seen as, well, typical gay men (effeminate, but sexually aggressive in a nancy way) and lesbians were assumed to be feminists (politically aware, worshipping the Goddess). But towards the end of the seventies our comfortably alternative gender categories were beginning to get fucked. Could gay men be slutty and masculine, instead of just slutty and girly? Could lesbians be penetrated during sex, or even go back to the old fifties butch/femme stereotypes, and still retain their self-respect? As celebratory and revolutionary as these changes were, there was a fly in the ointment—Anita Bryant. A huge backlash against gay liberation and women's liberation) was flourishing. It was spearheaded by the Christian Right. So when the police raided Toronto's gay bathhouses in 1981, it was the perfect time for queers to take to the streets. We still carried with us the potent memory of gay liberation and sexual liberation to give us the courage of our sexual convictions. Yes, maybe we all were a bunch of whores—but possibly that was okay—maybe even something to be proud of. There was still a heady whiff of anti-establishment politics in the air, and that inspired us to take our stand. We were mad as hell, and radical '60s politics made us feel justified in proclaiming that we weren't going to take it anymore.

I started producing my own gay plays in 1979. They were biographies of iconic queer writers and artists: Constantine Cavafy (*Cavafy or the Veils of Desire*, 1981); Pier Paolo Pasolini (*Pasolini/Pelosi*, 1983); David Hockney (*Life Without Muscles*, 1982); Frank O'Hara (*Lana Turner Has Collapsed!*, 1980); and Patti Smith (*Art/Rat*, 1980). It seemed like an important and revolutionary thing to do. There were no gay TV shows and very few gay movies. There were no out gay theatre artists that I had heard of—

except of course for John Herbert. His groundbreaking and heartbreaking gay play, *Fortune and Men's Eyes*, predated *The Boys in the Band* and gay liberation itself. But Herbert wasn't produced professionally anymore when I first came on the scene in the early '80s. Toronto gay playwrights Larry Fineberg and John Palmer wrote plays that were as much about straight people as gay ones. Transplanted Brit, Paul Bettis's radical improvised experiments seemed gay, but were also very formally confusing (they lacked narrative) for the few people who managed to venture up the stairs to Toronto's Theatre Second Floor (an experimental theatre opened by Bettis in Toronto in 1975). I was literally the only game in town when it came to writing commitedly about gay life, gay subject matter, in a frank and political way. I'm not bragging here. I think—for some gay men today—what I did back then might seem to them NOT something to be particularly proud of. That's how much times have changed.

But I'm getting ahead of myself. I quickly found that I had exhausted my own (and my audience's) affinity for gay theatrical biography. So I decided to write some drag plays. The decision was a conscious one. I had John Waters (who had not yet broken through to the mainstream) at the back of my mind—as well as Stefan Brecht's analysis of The Ridiculous Theatre in *Queer Theatre*, published by Suhrkamp in 1978. I very deliberately arrived at the decision that it was time to bring '70s transgressive drag to downtown Toronto, and hopefully rock the worlds of the complacent masses (straight and queer). That's what I did—with *Drag Queens on Trial*, *Drag Queens in Outer Space*, and *Lola Starr Builds Her Dream Home*—all written in the late '80s. With my drag musical, *Suzie Goo: Private Secretary*, in 1990, I reached the pinnacle of my popularity. All my drag queens were very popular—all these shows were sold-out and well-reviewed in the mainstream press. But some fags were conflicted about them. (For instance, during the late '80s drag queens were barred from some gay bars.) But looking back, it was the last time I really felt at home in my own community. Ever since then, as a playwright, I have felt at odds with Toronto's gay theatregoing public—not only perilously behind the times, but despised by many as a relic and a malignant force.

How did this happen? Well, I don't take it personally. It has nothing at all to do with me. Times have changed. And in this case I'm actually the opposite of those guys in the "Gay Sex in the '70s" DVD. The guys on that DVD have gotten older and more conservative in their sexual habits, while sex has stayed raunchy. Heterosexual and homosexual prostitutes still ply their wares, swingers and s/m clubs abound for straights, and bathhouses are still full for queers. But a lot of gay men have become hypocrites about their sex lives. I haven't changed my radical views, but gay culture around me has grown very, very conservative.

The culprit? AIDS. The heady radicalism and proud gender exploration that typified the late '70s was to make way for much more careful times. At first there was nothing to do but bury the dead, and perhaps even more importantly, to stave off the prophecies of doom which seemed to be coming to fruition. Was Anita Bryant right? Were our sinful lives to be rewarded with this punishment? Though gay men pretended that such paranoid thoughts were beneath them, most of us couldn't help wondering if maybe she was right and we were paying for our fun with our lives. The result was an enormous cultural shift. Gay men could not stop having sex (no one who likes sex can stop having sex unless they get ill or die) but they could PRETEND that they weren't having sex. Wouldn't that solve the problem? And hey, why not go further. To escape the querulous finger of an avenging God, wouldn't it be best to not just pretend that we were not having sex, but also to do our best to APPEAR to be better people, in fact THE BEST people? If we were really good, then maybe God wouldn't strike us down anymore, and maybe normal people would start to like us.

For me, watching this shift in our public presentation of ourselves has been scary. It's been scary watching gay men turn from raging limp-wristed iconoclasts into straight-acting, church-going, ever-so-good citizens.

It didn't take long for queers to change their focus from marching in the streets for bathhouses, to marching in the streets for better medical care, the right to marry, and the right to adopt. And since these were our new values, wouldn't it be better to march in nicer, more acceptable, clothing? Let's try and keep the drag queens and the dykes on bikes a little bit less visible in the parades. After all the Christian Right is always using them against us, and it might suit our agenda better to do so.

I'm sorry but I don't agree.

But things have only gotten worse. As we fags began to act nicer and dress more conservatively, and claimed that we weren't all that sexual, and that all we really wanted was to get married (in a church preferably) and have kids like anyone else— we began to be a little more accepted by the mainstream. After all, AIDS—as much as it has been an opportunity for vituperation from conservatives—had been a big guilt trip for liberal straights. Liberals feel bad for us, just like they feel bad for People of Colour. And AIDS just makes us more sympathetic. Sure. There were, and are, a lot of straight people on our side; that is, as long as we're good little fags and dykes. So, sure enough, we began to get representation in the mainstream media. Gay movies, appeared—and unlike movies of the '60s and '70s we weren't a problem. There were a couple of drag queen movies in the '90s—significantly, "The Adventures of Priscilla Queen of the Desert" (a 1994 Australian Academy Award winner); "To Wong Foo Thanks for Everything, Julie Newmar" (an American 1995 hit starring Wesley Snipes, Patrick Swayze and John Leguizamo). Straight guys, more often than not, played the drag queens, and the storylines were pretty similar—the queens weren't so much looking to get laid as they were hoping to be loved by the local rural townsfolk. And amazingly—they were! Uncles and aunts in South Dakota were embracing the sanitized drag queens in these flicks. After all, the drag queens didn't talk dirty and acted campy in only the most acceptable way—they were basically acting funny in a straight way, in dresses. It was all a fantasy, but the liberal straights liked it.

And, by golly, we liked it too.

Not to be outdone, the theatre offered us drag queens in more thought-provoking vehicles. The genre of AIDS play which had developed (and somewhat taken over) gay theatre in New York in the late '80s, came to full flower with *Angels in*

America (first produced by San Francisco's Eureka Theater in 1991), which also offered America a very sanitized version of the gay experience. Yes, the leading character was a drag queen, but he was, conveniently, dying—not cruising (too late for cruising now!) and consumed with regret. One gay character in *Angels in America* has sex in the bushes—but is almost immediately very ashamed. (In fact, in a climactic scene, he wails in deep regret for his evil deeds.) And there are lots of straight characters for heterosexual liberal audience members to identify with. And, most significantly, *Angels in America* was advertised as—not a play about homosexuality (too narrow a topic to spark enough interest for a Broadway hit)—but instead as a play about a much more 'universal' issue: America. So the liberals flocked to see it, and cried. Oh, how they cried. Am I being fair? After all, admittedly, there is one very queeny, foul-mouthed character in the play—a character who actually sounds like a real-life campy faggot. But he was black. Like the effeminate character—Jack—on that popular TV show "Will and Grace," he was not the main character, not the hero, and not dying. After all, being a funny sidekick is almost the same, iconically, as being black. Real gay characters, campy and sexual, were most easily tolerated by the liberals when marginalized, dramaturgically, not when portrayed front and centre of the play as real, sympathetic people.

And here we are in the new millennium. Ellen Degeneres, whose TV sitcom was cancelled in the late '90s because she admitted that she was a lesbian (on the show and off), has subsequently been forgiven and embraced by Americans. Not only does she have her own new talk show—it's a huge hit! There's only one problem: she is not allowed to talk about being a lesbian on the show (or discuss queer issues with her guests) and she must support the War in Iraq, and act like what pretty well every sensible middle class American person understands to be A Very Nice Person. There are lots of effeminate gay men on television, which makes most gay men happy, right? The only problem is that almost all of them are decorating your house, and get a lot of unsympathetic laughs for being snippy, bitchy, testy and easily irritated stereotypes. But politics isn't important anymore, and neither is presenting the real details of our lives. Those things are old-fashioned, and will only lead to trouble. What's important is that straight white liberals accept us, and invite us to their dinner parties. And they do. And maybe said straight white liberals will talk all those rural Christians into loving us, and then the Right-wingers will stop beating us and leaving us tied to fence posts to die.

Praise the Lord.

As you can imagine, this is a very different atmosphere in which to produce gay theatre than the one that existed when I came out of the closet twenty-five years ago. There was once a necessity for us to make everyone understand our significant differences from the mainstream. There is now a necessity for us to erase our differences and to make everyone understand how much we are the same. The result? A backlash against gay culture, from within the gay community. Writers like Bert Archer write books like *The End of Gay*, and, in interviews, muse on whether we really need gay bookstores anymore. It is significant, I think, in this context, that

Toronto's gay and lesbian bookstore (Glad Day) is presently in deep financial trouble, and the Oscar Wilde Memorial Bookshop in New York City recently closed. In the late '90s, Daniel Harris published a book called *The Decline and Fall of Gay Culture*, and at the same time Michaelangelo Signorile wrote books (including *Life Outside: The Signorile Report on Gay men: sex, drugs, muscles and the passages of life*) about how gay men are moving to the country and leading much more conservative lives. Andrew Sullivan, a gay conservative, writes quite often about how important it is to remember that queers can be good citizens. In the meantime, as might be expected, these good citizens are spending less time visibly cruising bars (they're using the internet now). So gay streets are beginning to close down. Castro Street in San Francisco, Christopher Street in New York City, and Church Street in Toronto are all on the wane. In their place, there are lots of gayish shops opening up. After all, shopping is normal.

No one's ashamed to go shopping.

Interestingly, now that queers have abandoned the notion of being outsiders and different, the trans movement has taken over that particular paradigm. Trans people don't talk about how they are like everyone else, they make a big deal about how much they are not like them, how their difference causes hardship because of the prejudices against them. They even go so far as to suggest that straight people (and conservative queers) could learn something from their explorations of gender and sexuality. As might be expected, old-style ('70s) gays and lesbians are a little insecure about all these somewhat outrageous and riotous trans people. They kinda wish they wouldn't rock the boat.

I certainly wish we would.

What is the aesthetic result of all this wishy-washiness? Well, you don't see a lot of queer art anymore. There are not as many queer novels and poetry collections being published, partially because there are not as many bookstores to sell them. But more importantly, there just doesn't seem to be any point. Why write a gay novel or produce a gay play when most queers don't like being called queers anymore? So you have so-called lesbian plays like Susan Cole's *A Fertile Imagination*, about dykes trying to have a baby. And you have Diane Flack's recent memoir (*Bear With Me: What They Don't Tell You About Pregnancy and New Motherhood*) about what it's like to be a lesbian mother. These are SORT OF queer (the authors are somewhat out, anyway), but are mainly concerned with so-called universal issues like raising a family. The fags, always more mainstream than the dykes, have just skipped writing about gay subjects altogether. A perfect example: Daniel MacIvor's witty, poetic, brilliant productions (which were stupendously directed and dramaturged by Daniel Brooks). But MacIvor's most famous play, *Here Lies Henry* (first produced by Buddies in Bad Times Theatre in 1995 and revived in 2006 to critical acclaim), is about a man who MIGHT be gay. And, of course, he might not. (I now teach theatre at the University of Guelph. I put *Here Lies Henry* on a gay reading list at Guelph and someone challenged me—is it a gay play?) Michael MacLennan, a gay Vancouver native who now divides his time between Toronto, Vancouver and L.A., and has been nominated for two Governor General's Awards, writes gay plays, some of which have somewhat challenging, political content. But he is spending more and more time these days writing for television—where he seems to be quite at home. John Cameron Mitchell—an American film director famous for his hit Broadway play, *Hedwig and the Angry Inch* (1998), makes gay movies (his most recent was "Shortbus") using Canadian actors and featuring explicit sex, but will anyone come and see them? Probably not—so he will get eliminated by the only judge and jury most people trust these days—the marketplace. I don't know many Canadian playwrights or novelists who like to identify as queer—it is generally considered limiting and ghettoizing, and ultimately, irrelevant. After all, being straight is just like being gay or lesbian, in the ideal world that we, at the very least, are certainly IMAGINING that we live in. We imagine that we have been accepted, and the Christian right is mainly located in small towns anyway, so there's no need for us to PUSH our sexuality, as artists. We'll just write about straight people, and not make an issue of being queer. Why bother?

Of course there is a good reason to bother—it's terribly important to raise our voices, if only to keep our own sanity—but it's very discouraging when the rewards are so few, and no one seems to be listening.

I recently tried to get my queer theory thesis published at an American publisher. Now leaving aside the notion that these publishers may simply have not liked my book (which is quite possible) one of them mentioned that academic presses just aren't publishing queer theory that much anymore. Queer theory is 'out'—even in the world of academic publishing. What is 'in'? The bottom line: making money, staying alive, justifying their existence as academic publishers in a mega-world, a world that finds it increasingly impossible to understand the purpose of any brand of writing which is not mass communication.

But, sadly, I still continue to write gay plays, gay poetry, and gay novels. The audience for them is diminishing, and most of the gay community looks upon them with disdain (why is Sky still doing THAT?). But you know what? I don't mind. As long as I can get some funding from somewhere to put on my little plays and write my little books for my little audiences I will continue to do so. And when the public funding runs dry, I will photocopy my books and put on my plays in people's basements. It's important to keep being little, doing little things, valuing the opinion of a few who don't fit in, of tiny communities. The mega-corporatized global world we live in is the ultimate triumph of capitalism. And, after all, it is not only queers that are being forgotten, cast aside. It is any individual identity, any attempt at difference, and any expression of a sensibility which is not mass marketable.

Of course the western world—married to its basically fundamentalist notions of God, family and capitalism—is now coming up against a Third World which has its own, quite different fundamentalist views of the same things. There are those of us who would rather not get involved in that discussion, who would rather not choose between two fundamentalisms—between the globalized corporate modern western fundamentalism, and the more feudal Third World fundamentalism—but would rather try and make people understand that nurturing our little differences is what makes us valuable and human. Because I think understanding difference is the most important thing of all. But those of us who aren't willing to take sides in the battle of the mass fundamentalisms will probably get trampled in the dust by those who want to make money, be Just Like Everyone Else, fit in, and BELIEVE.

Because that's what it's all about, isn't it?

I predict that gay and lesbian plays will be a thing of the past in Canada in a few years. I predict that transgendered theatre may have its day, but it too will pass—in the modern western world every artistic movement is eventually co-opted. Mainstream culture consumes the alternative, and normalizes it with lightning rapidity. And since queers are the only ones who really cared about queer culture in the first place—when they stop caring, it will disappear. I don't like this; I think that young queers need to hear and speak about their difference. I passionately pray that all the queers will continue to write gay, about their experience—frankly and proudly and with bold iconoclasm. But regrettably, I don't think that is the way it is going to be. I hope all the optimistic, respectable lesbians and gays—and their friends, the liberal hetero-sexuals—are right, and we have moved into a world where celebrating difference is not what is important, because deep down we are all the same, and everyone every-where knows it.

I wish and hope we are living in that world already. But you know what? We're not.

(2007)

Note

¹ This piece is an informal, personal rant with an historical bent. I have supplied a list of books mentioned in the Works Cited so readers will be able to locate them with ease.

Works Cited

Archer, Bert. *The End of Gay*. Toronto: Doubleday, 1999.

Brecht, Stefan. *The Original Theatre of the City of New York: From the Mid-Sixties to the Mid-Seventies.* Frankfurt am Main, Suhrkamp, 1978.

Cole, Susan. *A Fertile Imagination. Lesbian Plays: Coming of Age in Canada.* Ed. Rosalind Kerr. Toronto: Playwrights Canada, 2006. 168–212.

Crowley, Mart. *The Boys in the Band.* New York: Samuel French, 1993.

Flacks, Diane. *Bear With Me*. Toronto: McClelland and Stewart, 2005.

Gilbert, Sky. *Art/Rat*. Unpublished.

———. *Cavafy or the Veils of Desire*. Unpublished.

———. *Drag Queens In Outer Space*. Toronto: Playwrights Canada, 1997.

———. *Drag Queens On Trial*. Toronto: Playwrights Canada, 1997.

———. *Lana Turner Has Collapsed*. Unpublished.

———. *Life Without Muscles*. Unpublished.

———. *Lola Starr Builds her Dream Home. The CTR Anthology: Fifteen plays from Canadian Theatre Review*. Ed. Alan Filewod. Toronto: U of Toronto P, 1991.

———. *Pasolini/Pelosi*. Unpublished.

———. *Suzie Goo: Private Secretary*. Toronto: Playwrights Canada, 1997.

Harris, Daniel. *The Decline and Fall of Gay Culture*. New York: Hyperion, 1997.

Herbert, John. *Fortune and Men's Eyes*. New York: Grove Press, 1967.

Kushner, Tony. *Angels in America, Part One: millennium Approaches*. New York: Theatre Communications Group, 2003.

MacIvor, Daniel. *Here Lies Henry*. Toronto: Playwright's Canada, 1997.

MacLennan, Michael Lewis. *The Shooting Stage*. Toronto: Playwright's Canada, 2002.

Signorile, Michael. *Life Outside*. New York: Harper Collins, 1997.

Sullivan, Andrew. *Virtually Normal*. New York: Vintage. 1996.

Cultivating Queer: The Invisibility
of the Canadian Gay Play

by David Allan King

In a 1976 issue of *Canadian Theatre Review* on the theme "Homosexuality and the Theatre," guest editor David Watmough remarked, "the personal declaration of homosexuality in our Canadian theatre can easily lead to unemployment" (6). Watmough, along with contributors like Eric Bentley, Robert Wallace, Graham Jackson and Eric Nichol, began to examine the history behind the "homosexual play," navigating towards its angry existence just prior to the HIV/AIDS epidemic and the emergence of Toronto's Buddies In Bad Times Theatre.

Thirty years later, there is some hesitation in declaring times have changed since Watmough's remarks, including his other chief observation: "There is no such thing as a gay play; no more than there is such a thing as a straight play. There are good plays and bad plays, and they are written by either homosexuals or heterosexuals" (7). To varying degrees, the identity of GLBT artists within the workplace, the self-identification of our authors and the very existence of a "gay play" remain subject to speculation and even heated debate.

One obvious, fundamental development in the "homosexual theatre" of the 1970s is perhaps reflected in the scrutiny of "queer" and "culture" that have since taken place. In 1989, Robert Wallace returned to *Canadian Theatre Review*'s 1976 edition on "homosexual theatre" as a source for his own guest editorial devoted to "Gender, Sexuality and Theatre." What Watmough once described as the "homosexual" theatre of the 1970s evolved into what Wallace observed as the emergence of Canadian "gay theatre," one lifted from its "homosexual" confines of sexuality into a social identity whose "subversive" existence of experimentation and risk could actually set an example for the Canadian stage, in a broader, I daresay, *queerer* context of "discursive practice" ("Theorizing" 136).

Clearly in the 1970s and 1980s, it was never a secret that GLBT artists played a role in the history and growth of Canadian theatre. This was no perhaps better demonstrated than the 1979 creation of the theatre that we now know as Buddies In Bad Times,[1] which developed into North America's largest home for gay and lesbian material and has inspired, on several levels, hundreds of Canadian theatre companies and artists to risk exploring GLBT (or queer) content and/or characters on the Canuck stage. Across the country, artists such as Michel Marc Bouchard, David Demchuk, Brad Fraser, Sky Gilbert, John Herbert, Daniel MacIvor, John Palmer, Kent Stetson and Michel Tremblay all carved out a platform for gay male material that has since affirmed the significance of GLBT culture inside and outside Canadian stage doors, as well as its preservation through publication.The lesbian play, whether supported from this gay-male presence or not, subsequently emerged thanks to the courageousness of writers such as Alec Butler, Marie-Claire Blais, Moynan King, Jovette Marchessault, Shawna Dempsey, Lorri Millan and Ann-Marie MacDonald—only recently celebrating its Canadian success in play anthology form. (see Kerr).

Since the earliest creative offsprings of these writers were presented to the Canadian public, issues of outed authorship grew for some to be contentious and for most secondary to their creations. Instead, time, funding and audiences for the gay play have served as the greatest signifiers of its development. In the 1970s, Ed Jackson speculated on whether or not funding was even possible for the gay play, noting, "I think you would have to try twice as hard" (qtd. Freed 12). Buddies emerged shortly thereafter, and for nearly three decades has forged ahead to great risk and enormous sacrifice to assure resources were in place to shelter GLBT/queer performing arts, at least on the Toronto landscape.

In that institutional context, similar 'Buddies' have not emerged in Canada's other vast regions, whose lack of queer performing arts homes remains a reflection of either public priority, reduced funding in the Canadian arts, struggles with a visible GLBT presence, or all three. As potential purveyors of these types of performing arts institutions (particularly in other major urban centres outside of Toronto), and in a country considered progressive around the world on GLBT equality, it may now be important to consider that others' past reticence in opening 'pink' stage doors may not be as relevant to development in intercultural matters as Watmough's original posit on the importance of "good plays," queer or straight. In this sense, rose-coloured glasses may have obstructed our earliest vision of the gay play.

Reference to "intercultural" is both relevant and problematic, particularly when it comes to the gay play today. Educators and sociologists, encouraging a more diverse, interactive interrogation of cultural and educational practices than those implied by "multicultural," have more recently adopted the term. Without neglecting the values of tolerance and respect for racial and ethnic differences multiculturalism has advanced, the intercultural attempts to extend, as author Kenneth Cushner describes, "comparisons, exchanges, cooperation, and confrontation between groups" (4). This interaction incorporates other aspects of identity (i.e. gender, sexual orientation, class and disability) into its exchange, to not only understand and value "tolerance," but, as Cushner mentions, "diversity of thought, expression, belief, and practice of those who are different from themselves" (4).

Under any mandate specialized in an aspect of multiculturalism or inter-culturalism, theatre that defines itself as such slides into the discursive" (Butler 122), immediately creating its own existential hurdle: that of surpassing ghettoization. Gay, lesbian, bi or trans theatre is certainly no exception. As celebrated writer Michel Tremblay observes, "A ghetto, for me, is a way of thinking. A danger surfaces when one decides that there is nothing but that ghetto that is any good" (qtd. Ruel 15). Any intercultural material, in order to invite Canadians' participation in understanding our diversity, requires some levy of universal appeal to attract a broader-based (one might suggest, conventional) audience. As Cushner assures, "a pluralistic society can be an opportunity for majority and minority groups to learn from and with one another" (4). Today, with GLBT content available to the stages of everything from community theatres to the most commercial of venues, to what degree its content remains compromised, antiscepticized, repressed or even censored in reaching Cushner's "majority" can only be measured by the creator(s) at-hand, the framework established for the creation process, and the willingness of its audience to devote itself to some degree of risk.

In the absence of performing arts institutions specialized in the gay play outside of Toronto, it remains in project form across our country, paving the way for extraordinary challenges in exposure, funding and networking. While other Canadian theatres adapt to their own potential risk-taking associated with "producing marginality,"[2] various project-based companies specializing in GLBT theatre have emerged in almost every Canadian region, and have come and gone like the winds of August. In 1999, Montreal's OUT Productions began a website devoted to reducing this regional invisibility by creating the Pink Network (Reséau rose),[3] Canada's first network of GLBT performing arts groups and a sister organization to the much larger U.S. Purple Circuit.[4] To date, members of the network have held one meeting to assess its potential for growth in touring, advocacy, and resource sharing. While it is unsure if the Pink Network will be better equipped to assist with future networking, over a dozen companies like Vancouver's Raving Theatre, Calgary's Teatro Berdache, Edmonton's Guys In Disguise and Toronto's Buddies have thus far demonstrated their presence, interest, and support for increased outreach.

In order for many of these companies to seduce a broader-based audience outside of the GLBT community, inclusion in Canada's intercultural policy and programming is significant. Despite its place amidst the intercultural, the gay play has so far received an arm-length distance from still uneven multicultural and intercultural policy and practice. Funding agency programs are an example of this imbalance. Depending on the level of government, some are geared towards multiculturalism support for projects reflecting our Canadian "visible" minorities. Other arts programs, aimed at interculturalism, still exclude GLBT projects from their roster for support. In this example, the "INvisible" minority that creates the gay play appears to remain invisible, still working "twice as hard," as Jackson once predicted, to raise funds for their projects (qtd. Freed 12).

Another contemporary shift that has occurred in the mandates of these companies has been incorporating the gay play into "queer" programming. Not unlike the term "intercultural," the theoretical understanding of "queer" has varied amongst theatre practitioners in its discourse. The term has, like "gay," eliminated the clinical sexuality associated with the term "homosexual," not only expanding in areas of social identity, but challenging "dominant labeling philosophies" and gender categorization embedded in the potentially divisive terms "gay and lesbian," (Meyer 2). In an even broader context, however, "queer" art today has often come to signify the subversive, experimental and risk-taking potential of art itself, as well as the inclusion of other artistic disciplines. In 1994, at Buddies, Artistic Director Sky Gilbert launched its new home at 12 Alexander Street in Toronto as a theatre for new Canadian work which is "experimental and innovative," and " [which] questions the bounds of theatre and dance, or theatre and performance art" (Letter). Over a decade later Buddies' mandate dedicates itself to "the promotion of gay, lesbian and queer theatrical expression," [5] a suggestion of the importance in establishing a "queer" framework for itself while simultaneously safeguarding its foundations as a home for gay and lesbian creation.

The inclusion of "gay and lesbian" in Buddies' mandate is a significant one facing companies and artists exploring "queer" as it relates to "the gay play" today. As Canada's gay theatre claims its place in the growth of both "intercultural" and "queer" art, the very identity of "the gay play" finds not only new opportunity and possibility for support, but potential risk of further invisibility in that inclusion. While the need to celebrate its sameness is crucial in reaching our Canadian audiences, gay theatre's historic ability to challenge convention and reflect Canada's gay and lesbian culture remain equally pertinent to its existence. Vancouver playwright C.E. Gatchalian, an example of today's emerging out, non-white writers, provides a reminder of this historic distinction:

> In Judeo-Christian society, gays have repressed who they are, what they really think, what they really want to say, for the sake of polite society. The counter-world of art has historically been able to escape polite society, despite all the efforts to censor it... from Marlowe, to Shakespeare, to Wilde, Williams and Albee, one can detect a distinct gay sensibility, a ruthless, subversive insight into the way human relation-ships operate and are constructed. Gay sensibility is subversive. Good theatre is subversive. It brings up all the (sometimes painful) truths of life, of society, that we lose track of in the hustle and bustle of the quotidian, that we bury under the carpet of polite society. (21)

Amidst plays by and about women, rooted in the black diaspora, spoken in Yiddish or exploring the Italian-Canadian experience for example, gay Canadian theatre is—in all its maturity—rarely as angry, directed to its own audience, or considered to be the strange "other" it once was. Instead, armed with a greater canon of plays, gay theatre now holds in its hands the possibility for celebrating its cultural significance in Canada, an earned heritage that must provide not only a sense of its particular relatedness to all our lives, but the preservation and celebration of its cultural differences. However invisible it was and remains, its contributions are in plain view; the key to its preservation may well rest in balancing the strengths of its historic invisibility with its commitment to maintaining visibility.

(2007)

Notes

1 Several sources exist on the history of Buddies, including those by Wallace as well Sky Gilbert's more recent "memoir," *Ejaculations from the Charm Factory.*

2 I use the term in reference to Robert Wallace's *Producing Marginality,* which refers to Canadian cultural differences in theatre as well as social marginalization.

3 See OUT's website at http://www.out.ca.

4 See the Purple Circuit website at http://www.buddybuddy.com.

5 See Buddies' website at http://www.buddiesinbadtimestheatre.com.

Works Cited

Butler, Judith. "Gender Is Burning: Questions of Appropriation and Subversion." *Bodies That Matter: On the Discursive Limits of Sex.* New York: Routledge 1993. 121–42.

Cushner, Kenneth, ed. *International Perspectives on Intercultural Education.* Mahwah, New Jersey, London: Lawrence Erlbaum Assoc., 1998. 4–13.

Freed, Forster. "A Local View." *Canadian Theatre Review* 12 (1976): 8–14.

Gatchalian, C.E. Interview with *Xtra! West Magazine.* Vancouver: Pink Triangle. Vol. 253, 1 May, 2003. 19–21.

Gilbert, Sky. "Artistic Director's Letter 1994." Letter to the Theatre Advisory Committee of the Ontario Arts Council, 1 March 1994. Toronto: Archives of Buddies in Bad Times Theatre. 1–13.

———. *Ejaculations from the Charm Factory: A Memoir.* Toronto: ECW, 2000.

Kerr, Rosalind, ed. *Lesbian Plays: Coming of Age in Canada.* Playwrights Canada, 2006.

Meyer, Moe, ed. "Introduction: Reclaiming the Discourse of Camp." *The Politics and Poetics of Camp.* New York: Routledge, 1994. 1–22.

Tremblay, Michel. Interview with Stéphane Ruel. *"L'Homosexualité au théâtre"* [translation]. *Magazine l'Intégral.* Centre des gais et lesbiennes de Montréal pub. Vol. 5, 1, Fall 1997. 14–15.

Wallace, Robert. "To Become: The Ideological Function of Gay Theatre." *Canadian Theatre Review* 59 (Summer 1989): 5–10.

———. *Producing Marginality: Theatre and Criticism in Canada.* Saskatoon, Sask.: Fifth House, 1990.

————. "Theorizing a Queer Theatre: Buddies in Bad Times." *Contemporary Issues in Canadian Drama.* Ed. Per Brask. Winnipeg: Blizzard, 1995. 136–59.

Watmough, David, ed. "Setting the Stage." *Canadian Theatre Review* 12 (1976): 6–7.

Cheap Queers

by Mariko Tamaki

How to explain Cheap Queers? In the simplest of terms, Cheap Queers, organized by the Hardworkin' Homosexuals,[1] is an annual cabaret series falling and the last week of June, on the cusp of Toronto's Pride Season. With a ticket price hovering around a mere $5, it is the cheapest entertainment in town (especially in relation to other Pride events). It is for queer and queer friendly audiences and artists. It is a city staple of bizarreness and fun, a three-cabaret-circus hosted by a variety of venues throughout Toronto's downtown core.

That, in a nutshell, is Cheap Queers.

As a local artist, queer and writer, and as someone privileged to have performed on Cheap Queers' stage, I love Cheap Queers. It is a truly unique artistic experience.

What makes it so unique, you ask?

Its performers.

Imagine, if you will, the parade represented by this sampling of Cheap Queers' gems: Keith Cole in a '80s style at-the-beach-bikini T-shirt and blonde wig spinning in circles to Cher; Shane MacKinnon in a banana skirt tribute to Josephine Baker tossing his costume at the screaming crowd; David Tomlinson as Tori Amos' brother Cori Amos giving the audience a look of artistic disdain; Abi Slone doing a dramatic reading of Prince; Shoshanna Sperling stomping on stage as Saucy Gaucho; radical performance/poet/artist, Pretty Porky and Pissed Off in white cafeteria outfits starting a maple cookie brawl; Euro-rock divas 'Ina unt Ina' glamming it up with their disco beats; Jess Dobkin blowing bubblegum bubbles out her bum; and Elly Ray Hennesey Snow squatting over an empty martini glass, her fantastically expensive dress hiked up over her knees, the audience screaming ... .

All of this for the price of a Happy Meal™. And as a performer, thankfully, I've never had to pay for this festival of delights. I have, however, had to sing for my supper, in my own various states of undress.

I've evolved as a Cheap Queers performer since I first performed for their cabaret in June 2001. That first year at Cheap Queers I brought a poem, I think, from *True Lies: The Book of Bad Advice*, which I was then in the process of editing. I remember sitting in the audience that evening watching the other queers up on stage, and feeling worried. Scared is probably a better assessment of my mood at that moment, *stiff*. The thing is this. Toronto is pretty saturated with queer cabarets. If you are gay, especially if you are a woman and you are gay, there are lots of places where you can get up in front of an audience of your peers and perform. Torontonians are lucky, lucky, people in this way, and we don't appreciate it as much as we should (ask anyone from Calgary, we're totally spoiled by our plethora of venues). I matured as a writer because of these opportunities to get on stage, at cabarets including Toronto's Clit Lit, [2] a monthly reading series at The Red Spot, organized by Elizabeth Ruth (1998–2002); Girl Spit (1995–1997) at various venues in Montreal, organized by Zoe Whittall; and Strange Sisters (1989–present) with various curators, which is part of Buddies in Bad Times Theatre's seasonal programming. By the time I got the phone call to appear at Cheap Queers (in the beginning it was a phone call, which always made me feel a little like a superhero), I considered myself to be something of a seasoned performer. Cheap Queers, however, is a different beast from these events. Clit Lit especially, was a place where, typically, female artists could go and read knowing that the audience would give them their utmost attention. Clit Lit and Girl Spit were warm and supportive environments where novelists and poets could share their work. It was, let's say, very quiet at Clit Lit, thoughtful maybe, especially when people were reading. The only real break in the silence was the odd ring of the cash register as people bought drinks.

Cheap Queers, by contrast, is a hockey arena for homosexuals (and friends). Cheap Queers is a party and it is LOUD, super loud, the kind of loud that's made up of too many things to count loud, although you can usually pick out a little bit of background music, the bark of the inappropriately-dressed queers, the cash register skittering and ringing non-stop. This noise, I noticed that first night, does not necessarily stop when the show starts. It drops in volume but tends to hang in the air like cigarette smoke (back when you could smoke in bars, something you can no longer do anywhere in Canada). Sometimes the performers have to cajole the audience a little, sometimes a lot, to get a little space. I remember looking at my little piece of paper with my little poem, that first night, feeling like a small woodland creature about to jump on the highway.

The three nights of performances that make up every Cheap Queers all have different, relatively obscure, titles that act like some sort of strange cipher for incoming (untutored) audiences: *Carpe Diem, Doris* (2002), *No Thin Towels in Da Haus* (2004), and *Where Am I Going and Why Am I In This Hand Basket?* (2003), to name a few. Each night has a different line-up and, as the themes suggest, performers are not grouped together, in any way that I have ever seen, with any kind of common pursuit in mind. Poets, dancers, opera singers, writers and actors are mixed together and the host, the Cheap MC, conducts the whole mishmash. Like the circus they preside over, the Cheap MC's are not your typical MC's, dulcet-toned and orderly; Cheap Queers' hosts have a tendency to appear in various states of undress, in various states of inebriation (not all of them are undressed and tipsy but the memorable ones tend to be). They saunter on stage and yell at the audience to get them beers, they bark at the first row and make fun of their outfits. At my humble lesbian readings the introduction was "This is Mariko Tamaki, please give her your utmost attention and consideration" at Cheap Queers, that first night in 2001, it was more like "YOU'RE UP SISTER!"

The stage that year, at Ted's Wrecking Yard on College Street in the heart of Little Italy, was a small black square about a foot off the ground, covered with a thin layer of grey carpet. I had to shimmy around Cheap MC Keith Cole, who towered over me, dressed in a miniskirt and sweating under his giant wig. I remember feeling a bit on the edge of a cliff-ish, adjusting the microphone a previous performer had licked as part of a performance.

I read a story about why people who practice sado-masochism can't be trusted. It was a risk, I knew, given the fact that at least a percentage of the audience was into leather. The risk paid off. The audience loved it. It was one of the best performances I've ever done.

Why? Clearly, while other events had given me a safe space to perform, Cheap Queers, a carnival of chaos, had given me a challenge. The result was the difference between getting applause, which means only, really, that you've finished reading, and getting a loud, rip-roaring Cheap Queers' audience bellow of appreciation, which means you've succeeded, which means you've survived, are appreciated, and are embraced into the fold.

And here's another thing: watching the riotous applause that was earned by my fellow performers, who took to the stage and let loose a variety of queer apparitions, like the ones mentioned at the beginning of this paper, had two effects on me. They made me want to push the bar, to experiment, to get loud and bizarre in a way that seemed appropriate in that space. They made me feel free to do so.

In a recent article in *Bitch Magazine*, queer activist Matt Bernstein-Sycamore, a.k.a. Mattilda, was asked what the word "queer" meant to him. Mattilda replied, "To me, 'queer' is the radical potential to choose one's gender and one's sexual and social identities, to embrace a radical outsider's perspective, to create culture on our terms, and to challenge everything that's sickening about the dominant culture around us" (qtd. in Rasmussen 57). I like this definition because of the element of choice, of tactical force, it suggests. Queer is not just queer because it is, what it *happens* to be, but queer is queer because of what it *makes itself* to be, what it chooses from the spectrum to accomplish this task, and what it rejects.

Cheap Queers is a space where the (self-and Cheap Queers'-chosen) Queers are able to make queer, can pick and chose from their experiences and references to create queer in whatever shape they desire, with relative impunity. And this is reflected in the statement that went with my first offer to perform at Cheap Queers, literally, from the lips of founder Moynan King, "Do whatever you want."

The last Cheap Queers performance I did was Cheap Queers show at Buddies in Bad Times Theatre this past summer, 2006. It involved painting myself blue, as part of a BLUE MO' GROUP performance with Lindy Zucker. It seemed appropriate, to myself and Lindy, to take Toronto's then newest, most high-tech and commercial art and drag it down to Cheap Queers' level. I had never painted myself before, but decided that IF I was to paint myself, to run around the stage slamming on a toilet seat with a bowling pin, that the only place to do that would be Cheap Queers.

It was awesome.

(2007)

Notes

¹ Founded in 1996 by Moynan King, the Hardworkin' Homosexuals collective, which currently also includes Keith Cole, Jonathan Da Silva and Shelley Brazier, was created in order to produce the Cheap Queers' cabaret.

² For more information on Clit Lit see Ruth.

Works Cited

Ruth, Elizabeth, ed. *Bent on Writing.* Toronto: Women's Press, 2002.

Rasmussen, Debbie. "Running From the Altar." *Bitch Magazine.*Truth Issue. 29. 2005: 52–57.

Tamaki, Mariko. *True Lies: The Book of Bad Advice.* Toronto: Women's Press, 2002.

Suggested Further Reading

Queer Play Anthologies

Armstrong, Gordon et al. *Plague of the Gorgeous & Other Tales.* Winnipeg: Scirocco Drama. 1996.

Boni, Franco, ed. *Rhubarb-O-Rama: Plays and Playwrights from the Rhubarb Festival.* Winnipeg: Blizzard P, 1997.

Gilbert, Sky, ed. *Perfectly Abnormal. Seven Gay Plays.* Toronto: Playwrights Canada, 2006.

Kerr, Rosalind, ed. *Lesbian Plays: Coming of Age in Canada.* Toronto: Playwrights Canada, 2006.

Wallace, Robert, ed. *Making, Out: Plays by Gay Men.* Toronto: Coach House Press, 1992.

Books

Boone, Joseph A., et al, ed. *Queer Frontiers: Millenial Geographies, Genders and Generations.*Madison, Wisconsin: U of Wisconsin P, 2000.

Dickinson, Peter. *Here is Queer: Nationalisms and Sexualities and the Literatures of Canada.* Toronto: U of Toronto P, 1999.

Dolan, Jill. *Utopia in Performance: Finding Hope at the Theater.* Ann Arbor: U of Michigan P, 2005.

Gilbert, Sky. *Ejaculations from the Charm Factory: A Memoir.* Toronto: ECW P, 2000.

Goldie, Terry, ed. *In a Queer Country: Gay and Lesbian Studies in the Canadian Context.* Vancouver: Arsenal Pulp, 2001.

Heinze, Michael. *Love, Identity, Sexuality. The Gay Experience in Contemporary Canadian Drama.* Trier: WVT, 2007 (forthcoming).

Román, David. *Acts of Intervention: Performance, Gay Culture and AIDS.* Bloomington: Indiana U P, 1998.

Savran, David. *A Queer Sort of Materialism: Recontextualizing American Theater.* Ann Arbor: U of Michigan P, 2003.

Solomon, Alisa & Framji Minwalla. *The Queerest Art: Essays on Lesbian and Gay Theater.* New York: New York UP, 2002.

Spence, Alex, ed. *Homosexuality in Canada: a Bibliography.* Toronto: Pink Triangle, 1979.

Spence, Alex. *Gay Canada: a bibliography and videography, 1984–2000 including many added citations from 2001 and early 2002.* Toronto: Canadian Scholars', 2002.

Troka, Donna, et al, ed. *The Drag King Anthology.* New York: Harrington Park, 2002.

Wallace, Robert. *Producing Marginality. Theatre and Criticism in Canada.* Saskatoon: Fifth House, 1990.

Usmiani, Renate. *Michel Tremblay.* Vancouver: Douglas and McIntyre, 1982.

———. *Second Stage: The Alternative Theatre Movement in Canada.* Vancouver: U of British Columbia P, 1983.

Articles

Armstrong, Gordon. "Top Boys: Canadian Gay Plays – Getting It On." *Theatrum: The Theatre Magazine* 31 (November 1992–January 1993): 16–21.

Bateman, David. "Canadiana or the Quintessence of Queer." *Canadian Theatre Review* 124 (2005): 51–55.

Bennett, Susan. "Radical (Self-)Direction and the Body: Shawna Dempsey and Lorri Millan's Performance Art." *Canadian Theatre Review* 76 (1993): 37–41.

Downton, Dawn Rae. "Angels, AIDS, and Kent Stetson." *Canadian Theatre Review* 57 (1988): 54–57.

Fortier, Mark. "Shakespeare with a Difference: Genderbending and genrebending in *Goodnight Desdemona, Good Morning, Juliet.*" *Canadian Theatre Review* 59 (1989): 47–51.

Gilbert, Reid. "(Re)visioned, Invisible, and Mute: Male Bodies in Rumble Productions' *Strains.*" *Modern Drama* 39 (1996): 160–76.

Gilbert, Sky. "Closet Plays: An Exclusive Dramaturgy at Work." *Canadian Theatre Review* 59 (1989): 27–28.

———. "Drag and Popular Culture." *Canadian Theatre Review* 58 (1989): 42–44.

———. "Dramaturgy for Radical Theatre." *Canadian Theatre Review* 87 (1996): 25–27.

———. "Inside the Rhubarb! Festival." *Canadian Theatre Review.* 49 (1986): 40–43.

———. "Political Theatre: Because We Must." *Canadian Theatre Review* 117 (2004): 25–28.

————. "Steal Well: Racial and Ethnic Diversity in the Club Queen World." *Canadian Theatre Review* 103 (2000): 28–31.

Giles, Jim. "The Other Side of Alternative Theatre: An Interview with Sky Gilbert." *How Theatre Educates: Convergences and Counterpoints with Artists, Scholars, and Advocates.* Ed. Kathleen Gallagher and David Booth. Toronto: U of Toronto P, 2003. 182–88.

Gobert, Darren R. "The Antitheatrical Paradox in Michel Marc Bouchard's *Les Feluettes, ou La Répétition d'un drame romantique.*" *Canadian Literature* 188 (2006): 47–61.

Goldie, Terry. "Queer Nation." http://www.robarts.yorku.ca/pdf/rl_goldie.pdf.

Graefe, Sarah. "Reviving and Revising the Past: The Search for Present Meaning – Michel Marc Bouchard's *Lilies, or the Revival of a Romantic Drama.*" *Theatre Research in Canada* 14.2 (1993): 165–77.

Grant, Cynthia. "Nightwood Theatre, Toronto: Notes from the Front Line." *Canadian Theatre Review* 43 (Summer 1985): 44–51.

Grignard, Christopher. "Monstrous Ejaculations: Sky Gilbert's *Ejaculations from the Charm Factory: A Memoir.*" *Canadian Theatre Review* 120 (2004): 50–56.

Heinze, Michael. "Culture Transfer – Brad Fraser's *Cold Meat Party* at the Royal Exchange Theatre in Manchester, England." *Canadian, Literary and Didactic Mosaic. Essays in Honour of Albert-Reiner Glaap on the Occasion of his 75th Birthday.* Ed. Michael Heinze and Elke Muller-Schneck. Trier: WVT Wissenschaftlicher Verlag Trier, 2004. 47–59.

Kerr, Rosalind. "Once Were Lesbians…: Re/Negotiating Re/Presentations in *The Catherine Wheel* and *Difference in Latitude. Modern Drama* 39.1 (1996): 177–89.

Loiselle, André. "The Corpse Lies in *Lilies:* The Stage, the Screen, and the Dead Body." *Essays on Canadian Writing.* 76 (2002): 117–38.

Moss, Jane. "Dramatizing Sexual Difference: Gay and Lesbian Theater in Quebec." *American Review of Canadian Studies* 22.4 (1992): 489–98.

————. "Sexual Games: Hypertheatricality and Homosexuality in Recent Quebec Plays." *American Review of Canadian Studies* 17.3 (1987): 287–96.

Nicholls, Liz. "World on a String." *Canadian Theatre Review* 95 (Summer 1998): 31–37.

Noble, Bobby. "Is Trans the New Butch? A Half-Lesbian Explores Non-Phallic Manhood." http://www.fabmagazine.com/features/butch/index.html.

O'Connor, Christy. "Is Lesbianism Dead?" *Fab: The Gay Scene Magazine.* 6 April 2006: 28–31.

Rocheleau, Alain-Michel. "Gay Theater in Quebec: The Search for an Identity." Trans. Luke Sandford. *Yale French Studies* 90 (1996): 115–36.

Schwartzwald, Robert. "From Authenticity to Ambivalence: Michel Tremblay's *Hosanna*." *American Review of Canadian Studies* 22.4 (1992): 499–510.

———. "Fear of Federasty: Quebec's Inverted Fictions." *Comparative American Identities: Race, Sex and Nationality in the Modern Text*. Ed. Hortense J. Spiller. London and New York: Routledge, 1991. 175–95.

Smith, Jane Orion. "Feminist Lesbian Aesthetic in Scenography." *Canadian Theatre Review* 70 (1992): 23–26.

Wallace, Robert. "Performance Anxiety: 'Identity,' 'Community,' and Tim Miller's *My Queer Body*." *Modern Drama* 39.1 (1996): 97–116.

———. "Signifying 'Lesbian'/Strategizing Error." *Resources for Feminist Research* 25 (3/4) (1997): 82–91.

———. "Theorizing a Queer Theatre: Buddies in Bad Times." *Contemporary Issues in Canadian Drama*. Ed. Per Brask. Winnipeg: Blizzard, 1995. 135–59.

———. "To Become: The Ideological Function of Gay Theatre." *Canadian Theatre Review* 59 (1989): 5–10.

———. "Technologies of the Monstrous: Notes on the Daniels's *Monster* Trilogy." *Canadian Theatre Review* 120 (2004): 12–18.

———. "What's eating Sky Gilbert? Gay theatre has finally moved into the mainstream but the man who helped make it possible is not impressed." *Toronto Life* March 1997: 45–6, 48.

Watmough, David. "Homosexuality and the Theatre: Setting the Stage." *Canadian Theatre Review* 12 (1976): 6.

Wilson, Ann. "Laughter in the Theatre of Mourning: The Politics of Ken Garnhum's *Beuys Buoys Boys*." *Canadian Theatre Review* 77 (1993): 13–20.

Wray, B.J. "Imagining Lesbian Citizenship: A Kiss & Tell Affair." *torquere* 1 (1999): 25–46.

Special Issues of Canadian Theatre Journals

Canadian Theatre Review 59 (1989): "Sexuality, Gender and Theatre"

Canadian Theatre Review 12 (1976): "Homosexuality and the Theatre"

Canadian Theatre Review 24 (1979): "Michel Tremblay Casebook"

Jeu 54 (1990): "Théâtre et homosexualité"

Notes on Contributors

Judith R. Anderson is currently enrolled in the PhD program at the University of Alberta. In addition to queer and performance theory, her research interests include Canadian and medieval drama. She has also worked for the Manitoba Theatre Centre.

David Bateman received his PhD in English Literature/Creative Writing from the University of Calgary in 2001. He has taught at various institutions across the country including Emily Carr Institute for Art and Design (Vancouver), Trent University (Peterborough), Thompson Rivers University (Kamloops), and the University of Calgary. He is also a writer and performance artist whose shows have been seen in a variety of venues nationwide. His most recent work (*Lotus Blossom Special; Metamorphosis and Misidentification in Madama Butterfly*) was presented at Western Front (Vancouver) in 2005 and has been produced in Kamloops, Calgary, and Peterborough. His first book of performance poetry (*Invisible Foreground*) was published by Frontenac House Press (Calgary) in 2004 and a second collection (*Impersonating Flowers*) will be published in 2007.

Susan Bennett is University Professor in the Department of English at the University of Calgary. She is widely published on a variety of theatre and performance topics and is editor of the Playwrights Canada Press volume on *Feminist Theatre and Performance*. Her most recent research looks at theatre and tourism.

Susan Billingham teaches Canadian literature at the University of Nottingham in England. Her interests include women's writing, First Nations writers, language-focused and experimental texts, and feminist, postcolonial and queer theories. She has published articles on Lola Lemire Tostevin, Shani Mootoo, Timothy Findley, Daphne Marlatt and Betsy Warland, as well as a book on bp Nichol's *The Martyrology*. She is currently working on a monograph exploring lesbian, gay and queer agency in Canadian writing in English.

Neil Carson retired in 1996 from the University of Guelph where he had been Professor of English with a particular interest in theatre. His writings include works on Canadian drama (*Harlequin in Hogtown: George Luscombe and Toronto Workshop Productions*, University of Toronto Press, 1995), Elizabethan drama (*A Companion to Henslowe's Diary*, Cambridge University Press, 1988 and 2005), and American drama (*Arthur Miller*, Macmillan, 1982). He is currently revising his work on Arthur Miller for a second edition.

Marcia Blumberg teaches Theatre and Humanities courses at York University in Toronto. She received her PhD in English from York University and completed a post-doctoral fellowship at the Open University (United Kingdom) working on theatre, activism, and representations of HIV/AIDS. Specializing in contemporary theatre, she has presented numerous international conference papers, published many articles on theatre, and co-edited a book with Dr. Dennis Walder, *South African Theatre As/And Intervention*.

Peter Dickinson teaches in the Department of English at Simon Fraser University. He is the author of *Here is Queer: Nationalisms, Sexualities, and the Literatures of Canada* (U of Toronto Press, 1999), *Screening Gender, Framing Genre: Canadian Literature into Film* (U of Toronto Press, 2006), and co-editor, with Richard Cavell, of *Sexing the Maple: A Canadian Sourcebook* (Broadview Press, 2006).

Louise H. Forsyth, Professor emerita (University of Saskatchewan), specializes in Quebec women playwrights and poets and feminist theories of theatricality. Her three-volume anthology of plays by francophone women in English translation will soon appear. She is a founding and honorary lifetime member of ACTR/ARTC; was Chair, French (UWO); Dean, Graduate Studies and Research (U of S); President, HSSFC. She is on the editorial board of *TRIC* and Advisory Committee "Equity in Canadian Theatre: The Women's Initiative."

Reid Gilbert is a college professor at Capilano College in Vancouver. He is a co-editor of *Canadian Theatre Review* and a member of the Editorial Advisory Board of *Theatre Research in Canada*. He has written a play, and is widely published in Canadian and international journals and collections on drama. He has co-written (with Sylvan Barnet) *A Short Guide to Writing about Literature*, now in a second Canadian edition.

Sky Gilbert is a writer, director and drag queen extraordinaire. He was the artistic director of Buddies in Bad Times Theatre from 1979–1997. His many award winning, published and anthologized plays (including *Drag Queens On Trial, Suzie Goo Private Secretary* and, more recently, *Bad Acting Teachers*) have been performed across Canada and internationally. In April of 2007 ECW Press published his fifth novel, *Brother Dumb*. He received The ReLit Award for his fourth novel, *An English Gentleman*, in 2005, and the Margo Bindhardt Award from the Toronto Arts Council in 2004. Sky is University Research Chair in Creative Writing and Theatre Studies at the University of Guelph.

Darrin Hagen, "radical gender warrior and drag artiste," is a playwright and television personality. He has written fourteen plays, the first of which, *The Edmonton Queen*, is about to hit the shelves in a 10th Anniversary edition. He was named one of the 100 Edmontonians of the Century. To the best of his knowledge, he's the only Drag Queen on that list. Other plays are *Tornado Magnet, BitchSlap!, PileDriver!*, and *The Neo-Nancies: Hitler's Kickline*.

J. Paul Halferty is a PhD candidate at the University of Toronto's Graduate Centre for Study of Drama, where he is undertaking a dissertation that focuses on gay male playwrights in Canada from the late 1960s to the late 1990s.

Ann Holloway is a professional Canadian actor, playwright and comedian. Her most recent performances are her own comic monologue *Kingstonia Dialect Perverso*, R.M. Vaughan's *Monster Trilogy*, both directed by Moynan King and produced by Buddies in Bad Times Theatre, and a staged reading of her new play *Mummy* in Groundswell 2006, as part of Nightwood Theatre's Playwright Residency program. Ann is currently writing her doctoral dissertation on comedy of resistance in modern Canadian women's drama at the University of Toronto.

Rosalind Kerr is Associate Professor of Dramatic Theory in the Department of Drama at the University of Alberta. She publishes on early modern Italian actresses and contemporary Canadian theatre. Other Playwrights Canada publications are *Staging Alternative Albertas: Experimental Theatre in Edmonton* (2002) and *Lesbian Plays: Coming of Age in Canada* (2006).

David Allan King received his MFA in Directing from the University of Alberta and his BFA in Theatre Performance from Concordia University. A writer and director, David is the co-founding and current Artistic Director of Montreal's project-based OUT Productions (out.ca), as well as educator and freelance writer in travel, arts, and culture. His produced plays include *Crystals, Karaoke and Cross-Border Shopping; This Generation Next; The Critics' Circle*; and the web-based, theatrical monologues *Ma sortie dans ma province*.

Frances J. Latchford is an Assistant Professor in the Atkinson School of Women's Studies and Arts and Letters at York University in Toronto. She is a feminist philosopher who teaches courses on love, gender, and sexuality. Her research focuses on sexuality studies and adoption studies. She is particularly interested in questions concerning subjectivity with respect to sexuality and the family. She is currently writing a book that investigates the relationship between adoptee subjectivity and modern political, biological, psychological, and sexual discourses.

J. Bobby Noble (PhD, York University) is an FtM transsexual man, and an Assistant Professor of sexuality, gender and masculinity studies in the Sexuality Studies Program, housed in School of Women's Studies at York University (Toronto). Bobby's book publications include: the newly-published *Sons of the Movement: FtM's Risking Incoherence in a Post-Queer Cultural Landscape* (Women's Press, 2006); an earlier monograph: *Masculinities Without Men?* (University of British Columbia Press, Winter 2004) listed as a Choice Outstanding Title, 2004; and the co-edited collection, *The Drag King Anthology* (Harrington Press 2003), a 2004 Lambda Literary Finalist.

Elaine Pigeon received her PhD in English Studies from the Université de Montréal in 2003. Her dissertation *Queer Impressions: Henry James's Art of Fiction* was published by Routledge in November 2005. She is currently editing a collection entitled *Henry James's Bostonians: The People, the Place and the Novel* (Edwin Mellen Press forthcoming). She teaches twentieth-century literature and composition part-time in the English Department of Concordia University and courses on language and culture at the Université de Montréal.

Mariko Tamaki is a Toronto writer, performer and PhD student in Linguistic Anthropology at the University of Toronto. In the past, Mariko has performed with Pretty, Porky and Pissed Off and is currently working as part of the dynamic duo TOA (with Lindy Zucker). Mariko's published works include *Cover Me, True Lies: The Book of Bad Advice,* and *Fake ID.* Mariko's most recent project, *Skim,* a graphic novel collaboration with cousin Jillian Tamaki, will be released by Groundwood Books in Spring 2008.

Robert Wallace is Professor Emeritus of English and Drama Studies at Glendon College, York University. His books include *Theatre and Transformation in Contemporary Canada* (1999), *Producing Marginality: Theatre and Criticism in Canada* (1990), and *The Work: Conversations with English-Canadian Playwrights* (1982, co-written with Cynthia Zimmerman). His play, *No Deposit, No Return,* was one of the earliest gay productions in New York City (1975). He has lectured about Canadian theatre and cultural policy in the United States, Mexico, the Czech Republic and the United Kingdom where, in London (2002), he delivered the annual Canada House Lecture, published as *Staging a Nation: Evolutions in Contemporary Canadian Theatre* (2003). He has written and produced 10 features for CBC radio, edited more than 20 volumes of Canadian plays including *Quebec Voices* (1986), and *Making, Out: Plays by Gay Men* (1992), and published dozens of articles about Canadian theatre and queer performance.

B.J. Wray has published numerous articles on Canadian queer performance. B.J. holds a PhD from the University of Calgary and completed a post-doctoral fellowship in performance studies at the University of California, Berkeley. B.J. is currently finishing law school at the University of Toronto and will be articling with the Department of Justice in Vancouver. Current publications include, "Balancing Conflicting Rights," written for the Ontario Human Rights Commission on the topic of how to assess competing human rights claims such as freedom of religion and sexuality equality.